the small garden

ENCYCLOPEDIA

the small garden ENCYCLOPEDIA

GREENWICH
EDITIONS

This edition published in 2004 by
Greenwich Editions
The Chrysalis Building
Bramley Road, London W10 6SP

An imprint of Chrysalis Books Group plc

ISBN 0 86288 651 1

Printed in China

Credits
Edited, designed & typeset: Ideas into Print
Photographs: Neil Sutherland
Garden designs and illustrations: Ian Smith and Debbie Roberts of Acres Wild, Billingshurst, West Sussex, UK
Decorative borders: Ian Mitchell
For Quadrillion: Graeme Proctor, Neil Randles

The publishers would like to thank Robinsons Greenhouses of Southampton, UK, for supplying a greenhouse for photographic purposes.

Compiler
Sue Phillips is a popular TV and radio gardener, and writes regularly for a wide range of newspapers and magazines. A keen gardener since the age of four, she is a qualified horticulturalist who trained at Hadlow College in Kent. She has since run her own nursery and been Gardening Advisor for a leading garden products company. Sue has been a full-time gardening writer for 15 years and has written over 20 books and contributed to many more.

Contributors
Peter Blackburne-Maze, John Feltwell, Carol Gubler, Nicholas Hall, Jenny Hendy, Ann James, Mike Lawrence, Sue Phillips, Yvonne Rees, Wilma Rittershausen, Rosemary Titterington

Photographer
Neil Sutherland has more than 30 years' experience in a wide range of photographic fields, including still-life, portraiture, reportage, natural history, cookery, landscape, and travel. His work has been published in countless books and magazines throughout the world.

Half-title page: Dwarf sunflowers barely 30cm(12in) tall bring color to the small garden.

Title page: Flowering shrubs, elegant grasses, and varied perennials overflow a gravel path and surround a garden seat in a quiet corner.

Copyright page: Stunning lily flowers and *Zea* 'Harlequin' form part of a dazzling plant group.

INTRODUCTION

The Compact Garden

To some people a small garden is a positive benefit, as you need less time and effort to keep it well-stocked and tidy. But to frustrated large-scale gardeners a small garden is a problem of logistics – how can you possibly fit in all your favourite plants and express your creativity? In both cases, the solution starts with good design. Small gardens are not just large gardens in miniature. They need very different ingredients and a major shift in emphasis. Attention to detail is the key. When it comes to planting, every available space counts, so plants must be perfect – in quality, behaviour and the contribution they make to the garden. You might prefer to use a few larger plants strategically or many more small plants for a more varied effect. And to pack in the maximum interest you will need to make use of vertical space, as well as the ground floor of the garden. Certain techniques are particularly valuable in a small space. For example, there are intensive and decorative ways to grow vegetables, fruit and herbs so that you no longer want to hide them away at the end of the garden. This book shows you how to plan and create the small garden of your dreams so that it looks the way you like, is simple to manage, environmentally friendly and gives lasting enjoyment all year round.

Sue Phillips

CONTENTS

An arch of *Hedera colchica* frames a view of warm-toned kniphofias.

PART ONE

PLANNING A SMALL GARDEN

Putting a garden together means combining design flair and practical considerations. Whether you are adapting an existing garden or starting from scratch, remember that a proper plan is an invaluable guide that steers the garden towards the desired end.

FIRST THOUGHTS

Small gardens have a great many advantages over large ones. Since there is only a limited space to fill, you can afford to spend more per unit of area than the owner of a huge plot. Consequently, the space can be developed to the full, to create a really inspired result. And unlike a big garden, where large plants, mass plantings and large-scale features are needed to make an impression, in a small garden you can use lots of different plants and interesting architectural detail to create a more intimate effect. Often, you can use original ideas and novel, or even recycled, materials for little expense. It is also feasible to make frequent minor changes, so that the garden alters subtly over the years – or to change it completely if you fancy a change of scenery without the bother of moving house. It takes little more effort or expense to redesign and replant a small garden than to redecorate the living room. However, the one thing a small garden needs to make it stand out is style. Try to have some idea of the type of garden you want to create, even if you do not prepare a formal plan. This way, each time you visit a nursery you will come back with plants, furniture or containers that contribute to your goal, instead of making impulse purchases that you do not know where to put when you get them home. Distinctive styles of garden have 'ingredients' that set the mood. You can adapt ideas from home interior magazines to develop your own style.

Lawns

Left: A circular lawn immediately softens the hard-edged boundaries of a square plot and creates a more informal feel to the garden. It is also an easy shape to mow; just start at the edge and work round in circles.

Left: Instead of positioning a square lawn in the centre of a square site, try placing it on the diagonal, which produces a far more interesting effect. Or use two overlapping square lawns of different sizes.

Patios

Above: Sometimes it is better to site the patio at the far end of the garden, if this is where it will receive most sunshine. Make sure there is hard path connecting it to the rear of the house.

Above: Introducing a curve and a slight change of level is instantly softer and changes the whole look of the garden. Visit other gardens and look at magazines for ideas at the early planning stages.

Paths

Below: A less formal route can make the same size and shape plot look completely different. This path cleverly distracts the eye away from the true, straight garden boundaries.

Beds and borders

Left: Disguise the boundaries of a regular plot with informal plant borders. Make them unequal in size and length for a natural effect. Use some groups of taller plants so that you cannot see through to the boundary.

Left: Patio beds in interlocking shapes can be much more interesting than squares and rectangles. It is much easier to look after plants in beds such as these than to grow them in containers.

Trellis

Right: By breaking up the plot into individual sections, you make it more interesting, limiting both what can be seen and the pace and route you use to walk around it. Even a small garden might benefit from being divided into a series of garden rooms in order to add an air of secrecy and surprise to the general scheme.

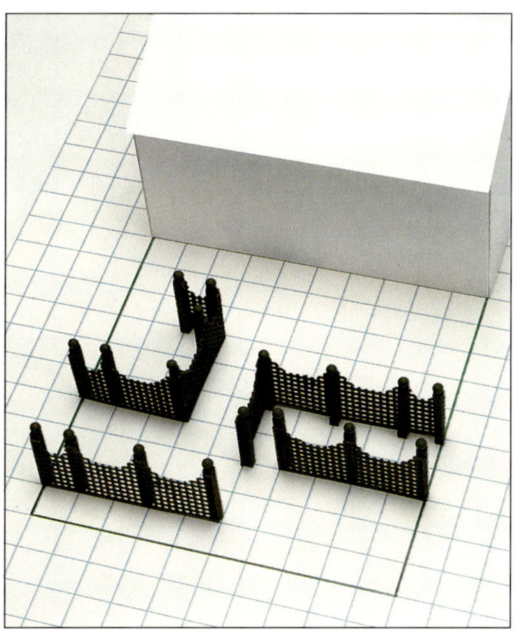

Getting an idea of how it will look

Plants can take several years to reach their full size and appearance, so it can be difficult to tell how they are going to look together. Try a few simple techniques, such as cutting pictures from plant catalogues and making simple models, to guide your buying decisions.

***Right:** Cut out photos of plants, entire small features such as ponds, patios or borders, and hardware such as paving and trellis, and file them away until you are ready to start planning all or part of the garden. They are a great source of inspiration.*

***Left:** Although your collection of pictures will not all be on the same scale, laying them out together is a good way to get a feel for how different plants and features will look. It also lets you compare several alternative schemes.*

***Below:** To help you visualise how a bed or border will look - here an island bed - try making a simple model with pieces that represent the colour and size of the plants.*

STARTING FROM SCRATCH

Taking over a vacant plot or a brand new house looks like the easiest option when it comes to garden planning, as there are no existing features to be considered. However, the lack of features means you need to use more imagination. It can be challenging to divide up a totally empty oblong plot into interesting shapes, with no obvious starting point. Many people take the easy option, which is to grass over the whole area and cut beds later. This is quite a good idea, as a brand new garden – even a small one – needs time and money to develop, and when you first move into a new house there is plenty to do indoors. Laying grass does at least give you a clean, tidy, easily maintained outdoor surface to use in the meantime. Turf is quick and cost-effective in a small garden, but in autumn a lawn sown from seed costs less and will be ready to use by the spring. Do take time to prepare the ground well first. The gardens of new homes, often have badly compacted soil due to heavy construction vehicles, and may contain builder's rubble. Both will make gardening less successful unless dealt with. Once this is done, you can take time preparing a garden plan. There is no need to create the whole garden at once. You can stagger both the work and expense over several years if necessary. In a small garden the top priorities are often an area of paving that can be developed into a fully equipped patio over the years, plus the basic framework planting of compact trees and shrubs. Even a very basic garden can be given a look of maturity by using tubs of summer flowers around doorways and on paving. Use containers when you first move in to provide instant colour, making you feel at home right from the start.

Lack of paving
If you go straight in from the garden through the patio doors, you walk a lot of dirt indoors. One of the first jobs in a brand-new garden should be to lay a hard path or, better still, a patio outside back doors and patio doors.

Subsoil brought to the surface
Bulldozers, etc., are often used to level sites roughly before building, and digging trenches for drains or foundations can also bring subsoil to the surface. Look out for piles of soil that look blue or yellow and are sticky in texture, indicating heavy clay subsoil. Alternatively, the subsoil may be a light sand or chalky colour, with a coarser, stonier texture while the surrounding topsoil is darker brown. Subsoil is very infertile, so is best removed. Do not mix it with the remaining topsoil or you will have trouble getting anything to grow. If necessary, buy a lorry load of good-quality topsoil.

Builder's rubble
This looks worse than it is and does not take long to clear away. Hire a skip or share one with your neighbours to get the job done quickly. Carefully clear away any spilt bags of cement or piles of builder's sand, as both are very alkaline and may affect plants grown in the area later. Save any useful timber, bricks or paving to recycle into the garden later.

Tackling the basic problems

When you move into a new house, there are usually many things that need doing indoors, and the garden does not take top priority. In this case, dig, improve and level the whole garden then grass it over. This makes it tidy and keeps it quick and easy to look after. You can think about designing beds and borders and leave planting them until later.

Tackling perennial weeds

Use an old watering can fitted with a rose to water in a glyphosate-based weedkiller. This is taken in through the leaves and kills the roots. Several applications are often needed for problem weeds or old-established clumps, so wait to see if they regrow and then retreat them while the new growth is young. Spring is the most effective time to start treatment, but whenever the weeds are growing actively and the soil is moist you should get good results from this strategy.

Improving chain link fencing

You can replace chain link with more attractive types of fencing, (but remember that the best side of any new fence should face your neighbour's garden, leaving you the sides with the posts). Otherwise, simply plant climbers or shrubs suitable for wall training, especially evergreens such as pyracantha, or Lonicera japonica *cultivars, and use the fence to support them as they grow.*

Disguising a manhole cover

Where a manhole cover is to be surrounded by paving, you can buy a special tray that fits into the top in place of the usual lid. You can then set bricks, paving or gravel into the tray to match the rest of a patio. Where the manhole cover is in the lawn, you can often stand a large plant container on top (trailing plants, such as nasturtiums, or a small weeping tree, such as Rosa *'Nozomi' on a short stem, are ideal), or plant a spreading conifer such as* Juniperus x pfitzeriana *'Old Gold' to one side so that the branches hide the cover. Alternatively, you can incorporate the cover in a border where it can be surrounded by shrubs that screen it from the house. Do not plant anything with water-seeking roots, such as hydrangea, nearby.*

Preparing the soil

To improve the soil structure and its water-holding capacity, spread and dig in well-rotted organic matter. Digging is traditionally done in autumn. If done in spring, add only very well-decomposed organic matter.

1 Spread a layer of well-rotted organic matter over the soil. It could be garden compost or, as here, manure. It should be at least 2.5-5cm(1-2in) deep.

2 Dig the ground over to the full depth of the spade, turning the soil over so that the organic matter is buried beneath the surface. Rake and level.

MAKING OVER AN EXISTING GARDEN

You are very lucky if you can take over an existing garden that is exactly how you want it. 'Secondhand' gardens usually need adapting to suit a new owner. Start by taking stock of what is already there. Draw a plan of the garden and mark in key features you want to keep, such as good trees and shrubs, or features that it is not practical to change, such as an existing outbuilding or brick walls. Then make a new plan showing how the garden could be altered, given new plantings and features around the existing framework. While this is happening, begin clearing up. The garden may have been neglected by the previous owners or the property may have been left empty for a while. Investigate overgrown beds to discover any good plants hiding amongst the weeds. If you do not intend keeping a bed or if it is too overgrown to salvage, dig out any plants worth saving or take cuttings from them. Then treat the area with a glyphosate-based weedkiller. This kills everything, including roots, and is a good way to clean up beds ready for a new start. (You can plant or sow six weeks later, as soon as the weeds are dead.) Grass over unwanted beds; the new grass is much brighter green but soon blends in with the surrounding turf. Add new features in easy stages to stagger the work and expense. New beds are easy to cut from the existing grass and can be planted as they are ready. Where possible, alter old features instead of replacing them. Improve poor lawns by feeding and killing weeds, transform old paving by paving over the top, reshape overgrown hedges and renovate shrubs.

Identifying what you inherit

If the previous gardener is a keen gardener, get them to walk round the garden with you, if possible, before they move out, identifying the plants and alerting you of any areas of bulbs or choice plants that you may not be able to see at the time. Put in plant labels as you go or mark the items on a garden plan. Neighbours may know the names of shrubs and other plants that are not in flower at the time. If it seems likely that there may be hidden treasures – and you can wait to find out what they are – spend a year observing the garden to see what comes up each season. Local gardeners or nurseries may be able to identify a plant if you take them a flowering sprig.

Perennials in overgrown bed
While plants are in flower, push a long label into any clumps that you want to retain. Even if you do not know their name, it will remind you to keep them. Dig up or spray with weedkiller any unwanted plants and the weeds around them, but avoid any plants you want to keep. If the bed is to be completely cleared, cut perennials close to the ground and move them. You can do this at any time, so long as you replant them (even temporarily) straight away, so that the roots do not dry out. Then keep them well watered.

Conifers
Check to see whether conifers have turned brown at the base and treat accordingly.

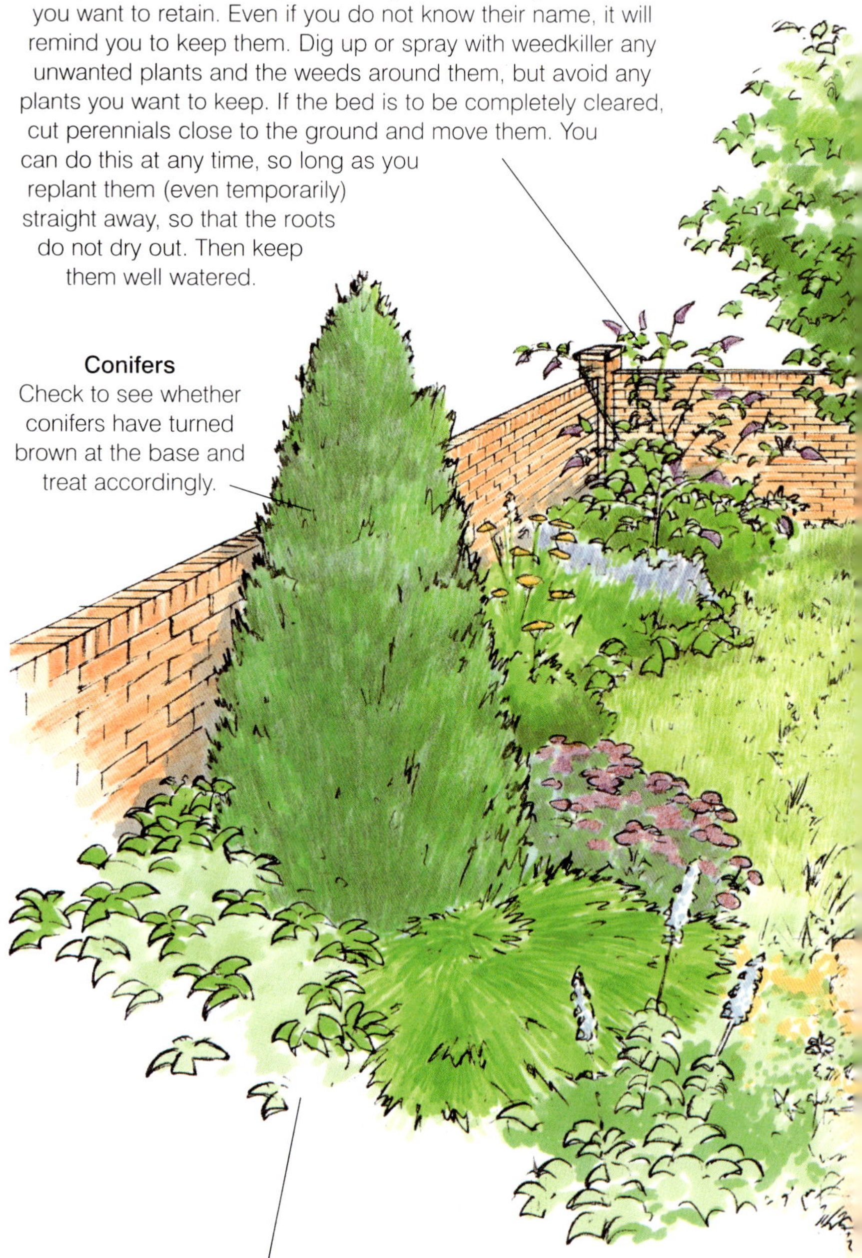

Shrubs to keep
Clear weeds from around shrubs as soon as possible and start pruning to restore the shape. Spring is the best time for major pruning, but you can shorten branches and lightly thin overcrowded shoots at any time. Remove all-green shoots from variegated plants. If shrubs need to be moved, do this in early spring. Move evergreens and conifers in early autumn or late spring.

Tree to keep
Cut off any lower branches to tidy the shape and lift the crown of the tree. This increases clearance under the canopy. If it is a large tree, ask a tree surgeon to thin the crown, which reduces the amount of shade it casts. Also use a tree surgeon to remove dead or dangerous branches, reduce the size or improve the shape generally.

Fences
Repair any broken sections or replace badly damaged panels. After the garden has been cleared, but before replanting (while access is easy) treat the whole fence with a suitable wood preservative.

Paving
Clean up very dirty paving with a pressure washer. Alternatively, scrub it with a stiff broom and patio cleaning product. Water on path weedkiller to kill any weeds growing in the cracks between paving slabs. Pull out large weeds by hand.

Ivy on fence
Clear ivy carefully from fencing panels. The stems grow between the slats and if you tear them out in handfuls you may rip the wood. The best method is to cut through the ivy stems at ground level, then leave them to die off. When the leaves are brown and the stems are brittle, they are much easier to remove without causing damage.

The most important jobs to do first

Even a garden that has been well tended is likely to have been left to fend for itself before you move in. Even the keenest gardener will have been looking forward to their own new garden rather than taking care of the old one. At the very least, anticipate overgrown grass and weedy borders. If the garden has been left for a long time, it could be worse.

Clearing piles of rubbish
Make clearing away piles of rubble or garden rubbish a priority. Snails and vermin quickly inhabit them and can prove difficult to eradicate later on. Dig piles of decayed grass clippings or similar material into the soil as a soil improver.

Trimming long grass
To tidy up an overgrown lawn, start by using a rotary line trimmer to take the grass back to a mowable height. Be sure to rake off the long cut grass. Keep topping it regularly with a rotary or hover mower and it will soon begin to resemble a lawn again. This treatment will kill most of the upright weeds within a few cuts; any rosette weeds, such as dandelions, can be killed by watering them with a liquid lawn weedkiller the following spring.

Above: *To rejuvenate a neglected buddleja, use a pruning saw to cut all the old woody stems down to about 60cm(2ft) from ground level in mid-spring.*

Above: *Remove entire brown branches from conifers, cutting back to a junction with a healthy green stem.You may need to replace the plant in the long term.*

Cutting back brambles
Using secateurs, cut back bramble stems close to ground level. When strong new shoots appear, spray them with a brushwood killer to destroy the roots. Several treatments may be needed if brambles are old and well established, as fresh shoots may keep appearing for a time.

Tackling overgrown beds
Kill off unwanted plants and weeds by spraying these areas with a glyphosate-based weedkiller. For best results in a long-neglected garden where the growth is very woody, cut down everything with a rotary line trimmer and wait for strong young shoots to grow before applying the weedkiller.

Preparing fences for climbers
If you intend growing climbers on fences, treat the timber and then hang trellis on hooks fixed to the fence. You can grow clematis on this. The trellis can be lifted down to clear stems growing between slats, and also to permit future timber treatment of the fence.

PROBLEM SPACES

Not all gardens are the perfect rectangle shape that makes for easy design. Houses at each end of a row on a modern estate often have a wedge-shaped site; old cottages may have L-shaped gardens, where a previous owner has bought additional ground from a neighbour, and town houses often have long, narrow gardens. But, awkward though they may look initially, odd-shaped plots can become most attractive gardens. Their unusual shapes often suggest a suitable layout. For example, a wedge-shaped site outside a modern house lends itself perfectly to a 'designer' garden based round a geometric lawn or gravelled area. This could be an offset diamond shape, a circle or perhaps two overlapping half-circular shapes of different sizes. The remaining shapes round the edge make interesting 'pockets' for planting. An L-shaped plot is ideal for dividing up into 'garden rooms', each with a character of its own. This works in a small garden, using low features that do not block the view, such as dwarf walls and lavender hedges. Do not make the mistake of laying a straight path down a long narrow garden. Instead, break it up into a series of individual areas using trellis or banks of shrubs to stop you seeing right to the end, and use mirrors, a water feature or fountain to reflect light if the garden is kept shady by high walls or overhanging trees. Connect the various features by a path that winds from side to side across the garden, as this makes a narrow area look wider. And alternate areas of grass with gravel or paving, as this also acts as a visual 'full stop'.

Protecting the mirror

To protect the mirror acrylic from damp, paint the back surface with the compound sold for undersealing car bodies. It is sticky stuff, so stir it well before use and apply it carefully with a clean brush. You may wish to wear gloves to protect your skin while you use this material. Depending on the conditions, the coating may take a few hours to dry thoroughly, but it will form a weathertight seal on the back of the mirror panel.

Making a garden mirror from acrylic

Left: This is the acrylic sheeting that you can use to make garden mirrors. Peel back the transparent covering on the front and you will see that it is highly reflective. It has the advantages of being lightweight, relatively easy to cut to size and safe to use in the garden. Its major drawback it that it is flexible and can cause a distorted reflection if not fixed firmly to a trellis panel or similar support structure, as shown here.

1 Mark out the shape of the final mirror by holding the trellis panel against the back of the acrylic. The paper surface on the back of the acrylic makes it easy to mark the lines with a pencil.

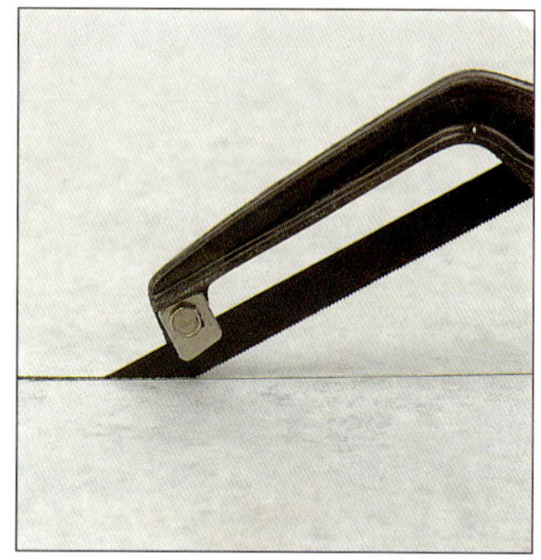

2 Cut the acrylic sheet with a hacksaw or padsaw fitted with a fine blade suitable for cutting plastic materials. Do it slowly and support the sheet close to the cutting line to prevent splitting.

3 You can drill through the acrylic with a normal power drill. Do it carefully and make sure it is supported with a wooden spacer as shown here. These holes will take nuts and bolts.

4 Fix the mirror to a trellis panel with bolts passed through the trellis and into the acrylic sheet. Attach nuts on the back of the mirror but do not tighten them too much in case the plastic cracks.

Left: The furthest brick arch has a mirror behind the statue that creates the impression that the garden continues into another area. It also makes the 'real' garden appear much brighter and lighter, which is a useful bonus in a small garden enclosed by high walls or fences.

Below: Perspective trellis placed over a mirror on a wall makes even more of an illusion, as it suggests a definite 'depth' to a recess. Surrounding a mirror with plants like the campanula seen here makes them appear twice as abundant due to their reflections.

Using plants as garden features

In a plantlover's garden where space is very short, you can use suitable plants to provide effects that, in other gardens, are often created using hard surfaces. Let plants act as garden dividers, boundaries, floor covering and architectural features. Trimmed evergreens or topiary shapes formed from evergreen plants make good 'green' statuary in the garden, while dwarf box or lavender hedges create alternative 'walls'. Use post-and-wire fences with espalier or fan-trained trees for space-saving garden dividers.

Right: *To stop your view extending straight down to the end, divide up a long narrow space visually by using larger 'feature' plants. Avoid making a path run parallel with the boundaries - in a formal garden, make a few L-bends.*

Below: *In a very tiny plantlover's garden, there is no need to occupy space with anything but wall-to-wall plants, leaving a single path to take you where you need to go. By planting this densely, plants act as their own ground cover.*

PROBLEM SPACES – A WEDGE-SHAPED GARDEN

Above: An octagonal model is a very attractive space-saving style of greenhouse. The door occupies one side and the other seven sides are entirely filled with benching. You can add shelving above them to double the display.

This is a more common 'problem shape' than you might think. It is most often found on modern housing estates, where high-density housing has been crammed into a site that was probably itself an irregular shape in the first place. The result is some very oddly shaped gardens. However, what at first looks like a problem can in fact be an opportunity to create some very interesting, asymmetrical designs that would never look at home in a more conventionally shaped plot. The very oddest corners can always be put to good use by screening them off to hide utilities, such as a shed, storage area, oil tanks, dustbins or compost heaps, which often pose a problem in a normal garden as there is nowhere convenient to put them. As well as the problem of the shape, do not forget to take into account the soil and aspect of the garden, and the way you want to use it. This garden, for instance, gets plenty of sun and the owners want to make the most of it, with plenty of paving for sitting out. They also want to reduce routine garden maintenance and are keen to take full advantage of every labour-saving opportunity, without totally excluding the sort of plants that bring a bit of seasonal variety into the planting scheme. A design revolving around a circular gravel garden is the perfect solution. It also removes one of the most potentially time-consuming garden features, namely the lawn. In a hot, dry garden this would need both mowing and watering to keep it in good condition during the summer months.

Right: Gravel gardens not only make striking design features in a small garden, but are also very low-maintenance areas. This is particularly the case if you first cover the soil with landscape fabric and plant Mediterranean subjects and drought-tolerant rock plants through it, before covering the whole area with gravel.

A wedge shaped garden plan

Storage area
Few gardens make space for vital but potentially unsightly working or storage spaces, where you can put a garden store chest (a compact alternative to a shed) and stack flowerpots, plant stakes, or keep compost bins. An awkward-shaped area at the end of an odd-shaped garden makes the perfect place to hide these away.

Trellis panels
Panels supported by a fence post at either end make instant inexpensive screens; cover them with climbers or wall shrubs to complete the effect.

Greenhouse
A circular or octagonal greenhouse makes the best use of space in a tiny garden, as there is only enough room for you to stand just inside the door; the rest of the interior is filled with staging for plants. The shape ties in well with the circular theme incorporated in the design of this garden.

Gravel garden
In a hot, dry, sunny garden, a striking and ultra low-maintenance feature like this can replace a lawn. In an area with wet or clay soil, you could still make a gravel garden. Simply dig plenty of gravel into the ground and make a raised edge of bricks to retain a deep gravel mulch. Use it to grow sunloving plants or to avoid mowing a lawn or weeding a normal border.

Millstone and cobbles
A water feature looks best positioned where you can see it all the time, both from inside the house and when you are relaxing on the patio in summer. This millstone feature does not have any standing water, so it is quite safe, and since there are no plants or fish, it is almost maintenance free. You could use an algicide in the water to stop the cobbles turning green.

Planting into gravel
As an alternative to using containers to decorate the patio, plant architectural evergreens, such as phormium and yucca, through a deep layer of gravel in spaces between paved areas. By using shapely, hardy shrubs like these you gain year-round effect without the need to keep replanting or watering containers and deadheading bedding plants.

Mixed planting
Narrow borders of shrubs and flowers around the edge of the garden add seasonal variations of colour and shape, but since they occupy only a small area in total they are very quick and easy to maintain.

Pergola
A pergola is a good way to create a shady area in an otherwise hot, sunny garden. At the same time, it provides somewhere to grow climbers, which are often absent in a small garden that is not surrounded by high walls or fences. Climbers growing up pergola poles are much less work to look after than masses of flowers in tubs.

Circular shapes

The circular shapes repeated throughout the design make it hang together attractively and distract attention from the unusual shape of the garden. If anything, they turn it into an advantage.

PROBLEM SPACES – A LONG THIN GARDEN

Long narrow gardens are a common feature of older terraced town houses. It is almost as if the original builder tried to compensate for the narrow frontage by extending the garden a long way out at the back. A typical feature is often a long, narrow, concrete path running straight down to outbuildings. This only accentuates the long narrow shape of the plot and is best removed entirely. Once this has been done, the plot offers plenty of scope for developing into a whole series of mini gardens. The object is to stop you seeing straight to the end of your land from the house. Instead, it should unfold gradually around you as you walk further into it. A long, lean garden is probably the only small garden shape that lends itself to developing into several very distinct areas. You can use trellis and mirrors, arches and arbours, screens and climbers and all sorts of similar structures to restrict the view between adjacent areas, so that the garden alternately narrows and widens out, revealing new aspects. Since you cannot see them all at once, you can use features with widely different styles that you would not normally mix together in the same small garden. You can walk from a very formal area into a very informal one, or lead from a modern, paved seating area into a natural woodland garden. It also makes it very easy to include features such as a potager, hobby garden, or other specialist feature that would normally be difficult to incorporate into a more traditional plot where everything is seen at once. The opportunities are endless.

Shrubs underplanted with bulbs

Use wild-style but decorative shrubs, such as *Viburnum lantana* or *V. opulus,* corylus and *Prunus subhirtella* 'Autumnalis Rosea', underplanted with carpets of spring bulbs, to give the sensation of a woodland clearing in your garden. For the most natural effect, choose *Anemone blanda* (as shown here), *A. nemerosa,* snowdrops, hardy cyclamen, scilla and dwarf narcissi. Alternatively, use several different types, each in separate drifts.

Lawn and shrub area
The circular lawn and surrounding shrub borders make a neutral foreground for the wild garden, but also create a complete change of scene from the 'busy activities' garden close to the house.

Fruit cage
You need not settle for the utility look of a commercial fruit cage kit. An attractively styled fruit cage can be a very ornamental addition to a small garden. Be inventive: use wooden finials and arched supports for a gothic effect or use coloured wood stains for uprights and add trellis sections for a stylish modern look.

Terrace
The brick terrace overlooks a small gravel garden planted with herbs. These supply year-round interest, fragrance and culinary supplies - all of which are very useful situated so close to the house and outdoor dining area.

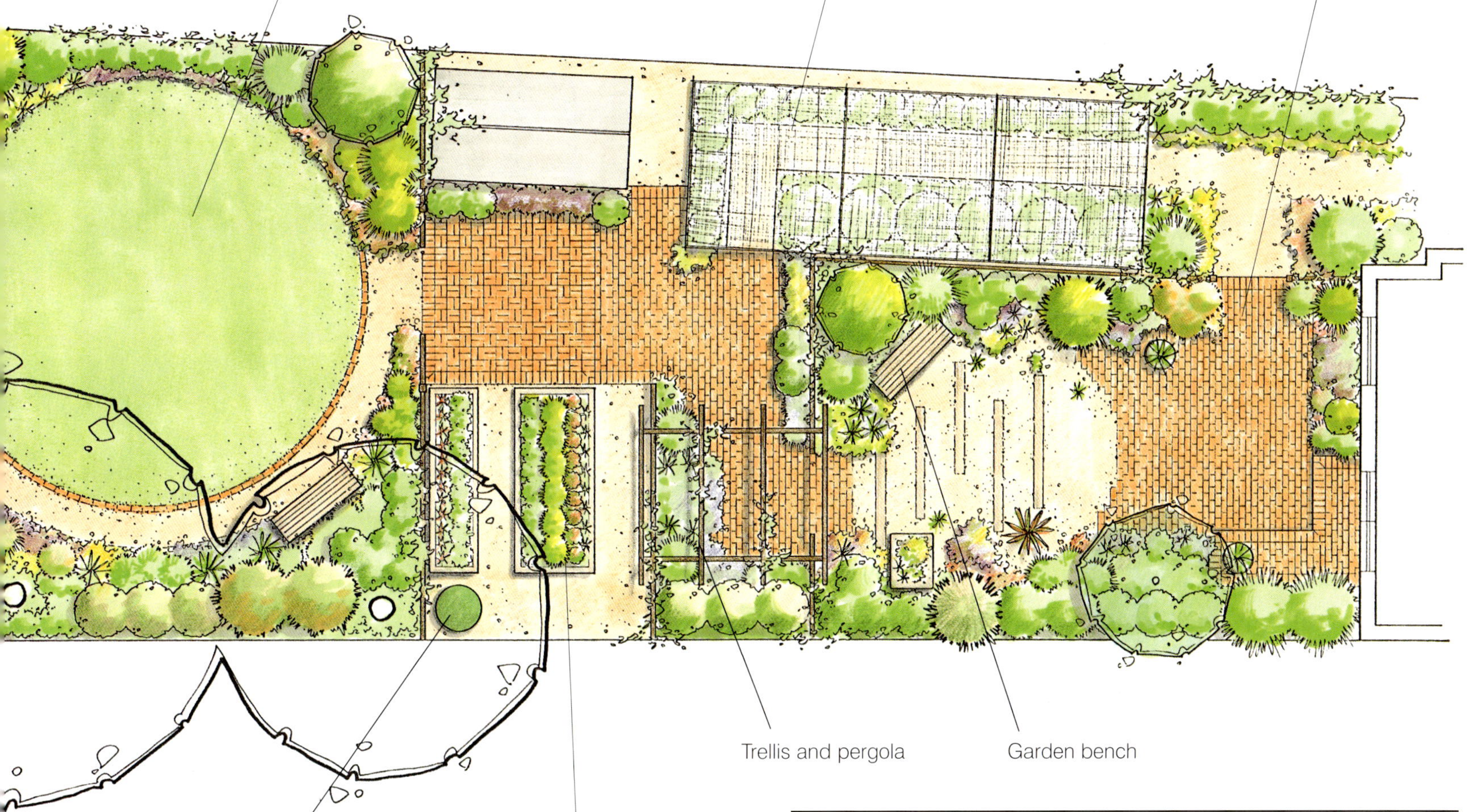

Compost tumbler
A compost tumbler is a very efficient alternative to two normal compost bins, allowing you to make compost from start to finish in six weeks in summer.

Vegetable beds
A couple of deep, intensively cultivated vegetable beds should provide a good selection of fresh salads and the more choice and unusual vegetables. By selecting naturally decorative varieties, they also make an attractive feature of the garden.

A wild garden water feature

In a sunny spot dig a shallow bowl-shaped depression 45-60cm(18-24in) deep in the centre and line it with a butyl pond liner. Stand baskets of water plants on the bottom, ensuring that the marginal plants are at the right depth. Use spreading marginals or bog plants around the sides to hide the liner edge. The gently shelving edges allow birds and animals to get in and out safely to drink or bathe.

PROBLEM SPACES – AN L-SHAPED GARDEN

L-shaped gardens are often found wrapped around the sides of relatively modern homes at the end of roads in housing estates and at the top of cul-de-sacs. These are probably the best sort of L-shaped garden to deal with, since the whole garden can be seen from the house, though not all at once. This gives you a unique opportunity to create a different view from each room. Plan the garden with this in mind, using each window as a frame for a different focal point. Of all problem plots, this one lets you harmonise the house and garden most of all, so allow the theme of the room and the garden to blend, especially if the house has large windows. Vary the type of paving underfoot and the planting in beds and borders to create different looks when seen from indoors. But remember that they also need a unifying theme, since you will see the different ingredients one after another when you are outdoors walking round the garden. A modern theme like the one shown here is ideal.

The other type of L-shaped plot is a long garden with the foot of the L out of sight around the corner. The great temptation here is to use the hidden portion for the less attractive features, such as a traditional vegetable plot, fruit garden, outbuildings and compost heaps. However, in a small garden you need to make the most of all the ground available, so regard it as a variation on a long thin garden and develop it as several separate themed areas.

Above: In a children's play area a surface of bark chippings is kinder to small knees than gravel or paving. If the bark is spread over firmed soil or perforated black plastic, it will be possible to plant through it at a later date.

Left: Circular lawns look at home in virtually any style of garden, from formal to informal designs. Their character depends on the style of the hard surfaces and planting around them in the garden.

Existing trees
Existing tall trees at the end of the garden have been retained to provide privacy and shelter. Replacing them with new ones would have been expensive and they would take several years to fill the space.

Pergola
A short pergola set at an angle to the boundaries of the garden avoids the angular appearance this shape of garden can easily present. It is also a valuable way of introducing height to a level garden, and an opportunity to grow climbers. But the basic pergola frame is incredibly versatile. You could use it as the basis of a fruit cage or as a garden swing. By placing a seat underneath, it converts into an arbour.

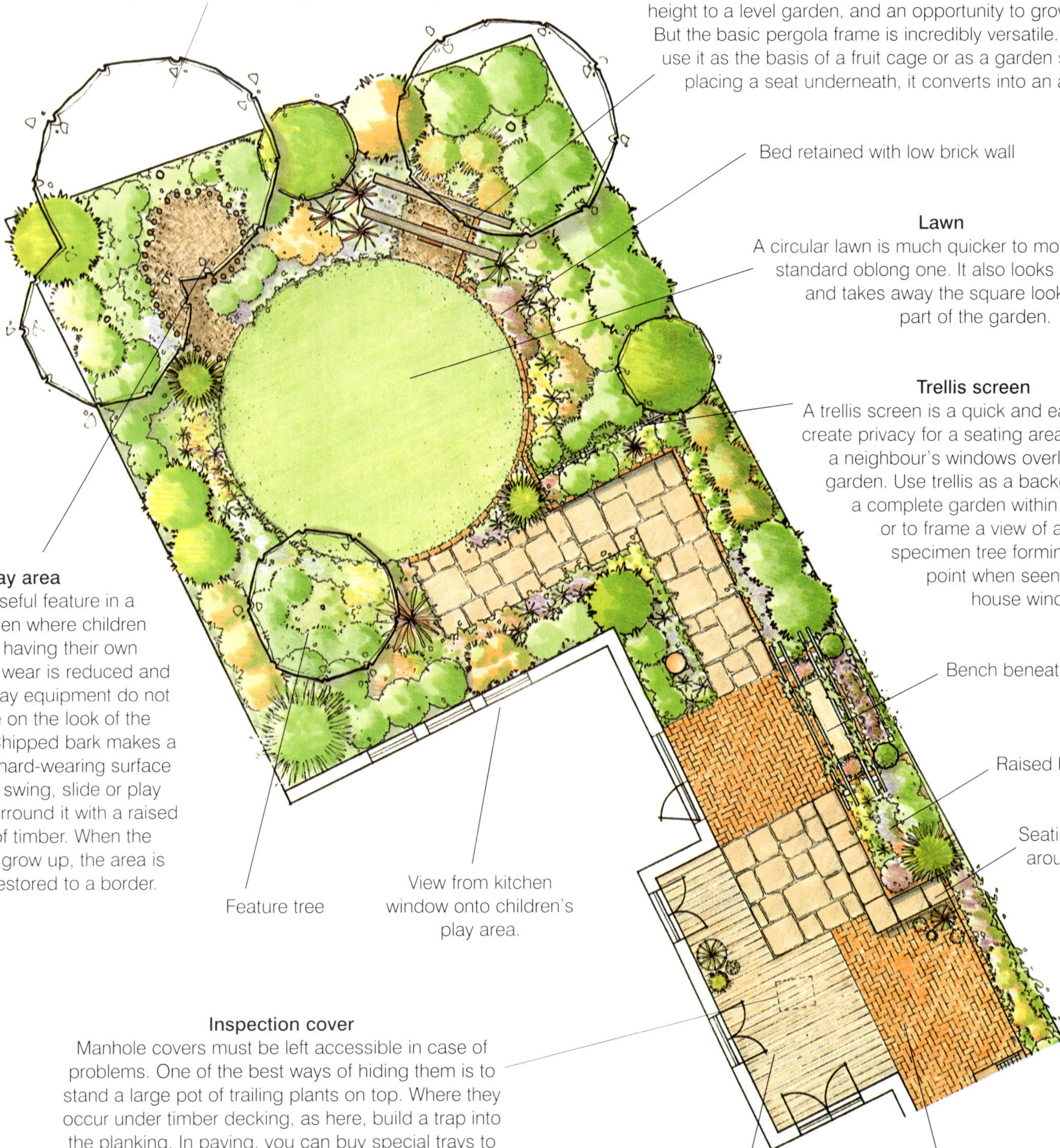

Bed retained with low brick wall

Lawn
A circular lawn is much quicker to mow than a standard oblong one. It also looks modern and takes away the square look of this part of the garden.

Trellis screen
A trellis screen is a quick and easy way to create privacy for a seating area, or where a neighbour's windows overlook the garden. Use trellis as a background for a complete garden within a garden or to frame a view of an urn or specimen tree forming a focal point when seen from a house window.

Play area
This is a useful feature in a small garden where children play. By having their own area, lawn wear is reduced and toys or play equipment do not intrude on the look of the garden. Chipped bark makes a resilient, hard-wearing surface under a swing, slide or play house. Surround it with a raised edge of timber. When the children grow up, the area is easily restored to a border.

Bench beneath arbour

Raised herb bed

Seating/plinth around bed

Feature tree

View from kitchen window onto children's play area.

Inspection cover
Manhole covers must be left accessible in case of problems. One of the best ways of hiding them is to stand a large pot of trailing plants on top. Where they occur under timber decking, as here, build a trap into the planking. In paving, you can buy special trays to replace the inspection cover. This allows you to fit paving slabs into the top so that the hard surface appears to be seamless.

Timber deck

Brick patio

DESIGN OPTIONS FOR THE SAME SPACE

When designing your own garden, go about it in the same way as a professional designer. Start by 'interviewing yourself'. How do you want to use the garden? As a low-upkeep, outdoor leisure room or a plantlover's paradise? Write down the features you regard as essential – perhaps a pond or greenhouse – the kinds of plants you like and any 'must-have' favourites. Even if you think you already know the answers, this helps to concentrate the mind when you start to prepare a design. But unlike the professional, who would probably only show you one finished idea, you can afford to spend time considering your options. So make at least three completely different plans for the same space. Be creative; see how many different ideas you can devise for the space that meet the same specification. You do not have to come up with them all at once. In fact, it is a good idea to think about just one style of garden in a day and develop the idea to the full, as if each one was the actual garden you were going to make. Leave time for your mind to clear before going back to them. Then compare all the designs critically, just as if you were your own 'customer'. Choose the design you like best, the one you think meets your needs and gives you what you want from the garden. One of your originals may turn out to be perfect, but more likely you will see good and bad ideas in all of them. In that case you can try another alternative which combines the best of the earlier tries. After a few alterations, you will get closer to your ideal. Allow yourself enough time and do the design work in winter when you are not pressured to get on with the preparation and planting.

Right: A geometric design, in which straight-edged features such as paths and formal water features are set at an angle to the house, disguises the shape of a traditional rectangular plot, and turns it into a very modern abstract-looking garden.

Below: Formal gardens look symmetrical. The area is often divided into halves or quarters by paths that meet at a central feature, such as a statue. A formal design could occupy an entire garden, or be a 'garden room' within a larger plot.

Above: Informal gardens can be quite adventurous. You can used coloured tiles and unusual surfaces to make a garden in which the plants are used more like decorations to the various 'designer' touches dotted around.

Above: Informal gardens have a more relaxed look and, instead of straight lines, use curving paths and lawn edges. Borders are undulating, with trees and shrubs grouped together and plants used in a much more natural-looking way. Even the pond looks like a fairly natural feature of the land.

Right: If you have a particular interest, say in water gardening, the whole design can be based around this. Even in a small space, with permanent paving and plumbing, there is still scope for seasonal effects in the border around the edge, so the garden need not look the same all year.

DESIGN OPTIONS – A FORMAL GARDEN

Although formal gardens are normally associated with grand old houses, many of the features that epitomise them adapt well to small-scale use. A formal garden is a surprisingly practical, low-maintenance way of using a small rectangular plot. Formal gardens make good outdoor 'rooms', with hard surfaces underfoot and interesting geometric features (such as the lily pond in the design shown here), where you would normally expect to find a lawn. Since they invariably use a lot of paving, walling, ornaments and upmarket containers and structures, they are relatively expensive to create. (But at least you only have a small area to fill.) However, once everything is in place, they are probably cheaper to keep up than an informal garden, and you certainly do not need much equipment to look after them. This means that you do not need to provide anywhere to keep a mower, or store garden furniture in winter. It is easy to create a formal garden that does not have a lawn.

Plan of the formal garden design

The thing that sets a formal design apart from any other is the use of straight lines and symmetry to create a classic feel. You could almost design the garden with a geometry set or squared paper. But this style of garden does not suit every house. You can introduce the odd formal feature within an informal garden, but in general, only a formal type of house looks right with a totally formal garden.

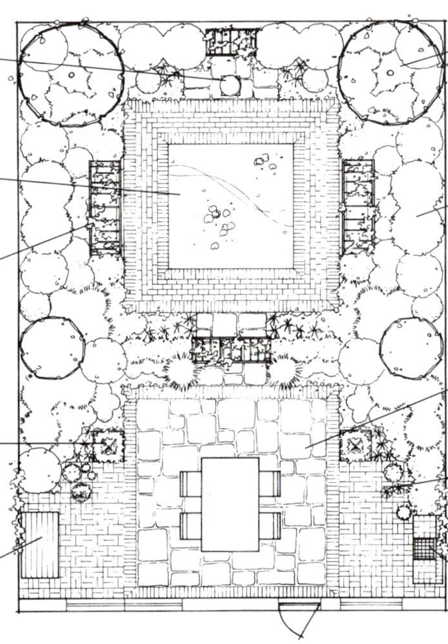

The benefits of a formal garden design

If you use stone benches or classical hardwood seats and tables, they form part of the architecture of the garden and can be left out all year round. To keep the cost of statues, large terracotta urns, etc., to a minimum, grow your own topiary and use plenty of hedging and trained, block-shaped evergreens as living walls and sculpture. A formal garden provides plenty of opportunities for growing plants that are often difficult to fit into a modern or informal setting due to their very symmetrical shapes (such as tulips). Walls or evergreen hedges provide a wonderful backdrop against which to appreciate the shapes of plants such as standard trained wisteria.

Below: Typical ingredients of a formal garden include paving, arches, containers, geometric-shaped beds and ponds, plus raised plinths for statues and containers or as decorative features on their own. Keep the layout symmetrical.

Bench beneath rose arbour
Plant scented roses for ambience, or a nearly thornless variety such as 'Zéphirine Drouhin' for comfort. Combine roses with the classic purple-leaved grape vine *(Vitis vinifera* 'Purpurea'). Its foliage sets off the rose flowers well.

Focal point
A formal garden needs something to draw the eye to the end of a view. This is called the focal point, and in a small space a striking urn set back into a niche carved from an evergreen hedge serves the purpose without taking up too much room.

Specimen trees
For the end of the garden, choose a pair of matching specimen trees with a striking shape, such as the weeping form of the Persian ironwood *(Parrotia persica* 'Pendula'), weeping cherries or classic topiary-trained yews or hollies.

Lily pond
Choose a geometric shape for a formal pool; round or square are the most popular kinds, but make it echo the shapes used elsewhere in the garden. Do not try to plant it in a natural way.

Classic border planting
Use evergreen hedging or shrubs at the back of the borders for year-round interest and to outline the structure of the garden. Fill in foreground detail with the smarter spring bulbs, such as lily-flowered tulips and stately herbaceous plants, including acanthus, delphiniums and lilies.

Versailles planters
Use these containers for topiary shapes or an obelisk planted with clematis.

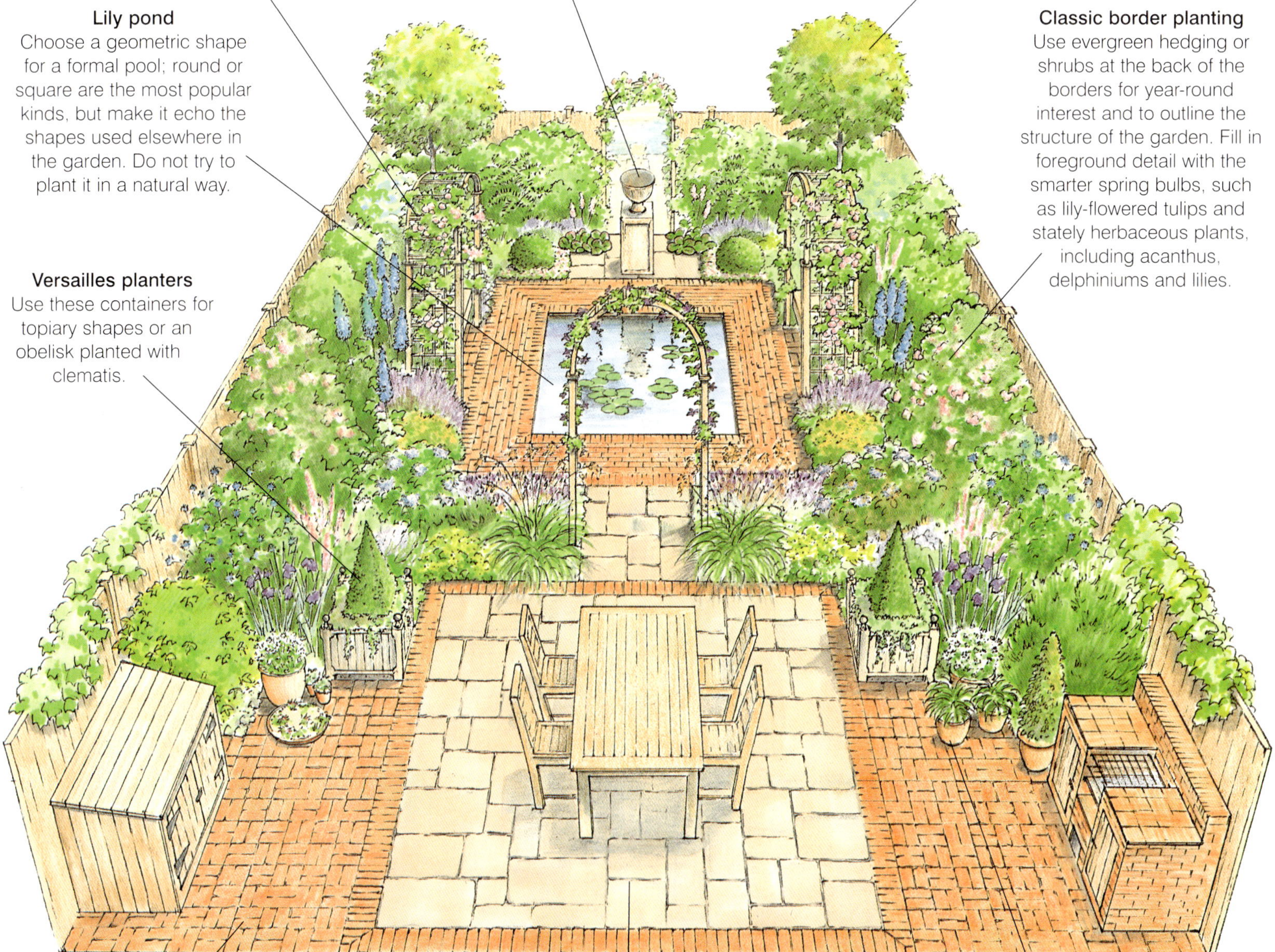

Paving
Bricks laid in stretcher bond have been used around the pool, and in basketweave bond on either side of the paving outside the patio doors.

Terrace
The terrace is the classical equivalent of the modern patio. You can still have garden furniture and use the area for outdoor entertaining, but keep to classical styles in order not to ruin the effect of the rest of the garden.

Containers on the terrace
Avoid garish modern displays in favour of understated, classical simplicity. Use terracotta or reconstituted stone urns, amphorae or pots with a raised motif.

DESIGN OPTIONS – A GEOMETRIC GARDEN

A modern design for a very regular, rectangular plot does everything in its power to take away the squareness of the shape. The aim is to distract attention from the parallel sides by confusing the eye with powerful diagonals or bold offset patterns. These can divide the garden into geometric shapes that have much in common with classic formal designs, but with a very different perspective. The end result can be peculiarly striking. However, gardens like this are much harder to design than a formal garden, since there is no readily apparent starting point. The best way to go about the task is to gather up ideas from similar gardens you have visited (take photos to act as reminders later on) or seen in magazines and start trying to put them together to suit your requirements. After a few attempts, you will find it all starts to fall into place. However, this is not the sort of garden you could create without a plan, unlike some types of informal gardens that you can literally leave to grow up around you. And while the shapes seen on a plan of the garden may be easily recognisable as geometric, they do not appear so when planted up, since the planting style is very informal. You need a distinct range of ingredients from which to select. Include one or two bizarrely shaped architectural plants that make living focal points, and carpets of mixed plants to set them off. Use the same formula in reverse, using carpets of architectural features such as cobbles with a group of containers or a piece of abstract sculpture. And use plenty of lines: linear, horizontal features such as railway sleepers set in gravel, and straight- sided raised beds with upright features such as pergola-arches and plants such as bamboo. These gardens are great fun to plan.

Right: Sleepers add a variety of form and texture to an area of gravel, without the inconvenience of tending plants growing in it.

Plan of the geometric garden design

A modern geometric design should stop you looking straight down to the end of the garden, while teasing you with a focal point that your brain tells you to look at. However, to get there, the eye has to zigzag backwards and forwards between parallel lines like a pinball machine.

Arbour

Do not suddenly introduce a curvy rustic arbour or shaped seat. Keep all the edges straight, in order to retain the effect of this distinctive design style. Soften the shape with climbers. Choose something evergreen if possible for year-round effect.

Specimen tree

This specimen tree dominates a complete corner of the design, so make it a good one. Choose a striking, preferably evergreen tree, but one with a non-traditional appearance, such as *Genista aetnensis*. Try a craggy pine, fig tree or perhaps a cryptomeria. Alternatively, train a large shrub into a tree by growing it on a single stem. *Crinodendron hookerianum* or *Clerodendrum trichotomum* var. *fargesii* are both possible candidates.

Sleeper wall

Constructing a wall from old railway sleepers is very easy. If they are to stand on soil, simply lay them edgeways onto a bed of dry mortar mix. The cement takes up moisture from the ground and sets slowly. On paving, stand them onto a wet mix. As they are heavy enough to leave just standing in place, you also have the freedom to redesign the space easily later on.

Sleepers in gravel

Sink sleepers to their tops in gravel, making sure they are perfectly parallel. They are easier to walk on than the gravel and act as stepping stones leading you across this abstract version of a gravel garden.

Concrete slabs on the patio

Square, textured concrete slabs complete the modern geometric look, and team up beautifully with the gravel and sleepers. Choose striking, well-designed, modern patio furniture in complementary colours to go with them.

Barbecue

A modern design like this is going to appeal to younger gardeners who will almost certainly want to enjoy high-tech outdoor living. A built-in barbecue with all the trappings is an essential. Include a cupboard in the wall below the cooking surface where barbecue fittings can be kept when not in use.

DESIGN OPTIONS – AN INFORMAL GARDEN

When you mention informal gardens, most people think of rambling cottage gardens or wild gardens. Both are very informal in style, but informal gardens can also be modern in outlook. The same basic principles apply to all: no straight lines, use of natural materials and plenty of contrasting plant shapes, leaf sizes and textures with harmonious colours. But by using fashionable plants such as grasses or new varieties of perennials, plus stylish furniture and props, you can create a whole new look. To give it a designer edge, base the garden on a series of coordinating shapes instead of letting paths ramble aimlessly, and plant in distinct groups with, perhaps, groups of pebbles in between instead of letting plants merge randomly together cottage-style. Use a wide mixture of plants so that the garden changes as much as possible throughout the seasons and always provides something fresh to enjoy. Vital ingredients should include at least one good small tree, a mixture of flowering shrubs with as much good foliage as possible, perennials, plenty of grasses and scented plants. There is no need to restrict yourself to wild-style flowers or old-fashioned plants; create a modern look using architectural shrubs and perennials with striking shapes: spiky sea hollies, pokerlike kniphofia, upright *Sisyrinchium striatum* and flat heads of *Sedum spectabile*. Look for inspired plant associations, such as the flat-topped *Solidago* 'Crown of Rays' with the tiered creamy flowers of *Phygelius* 'Moonraker'. Add enough hardware to balance the planting. Natural materials, such as planed wood and rough timber, cobbles and paving look good in an informal garden. An informal water feature adds the finishing touch.

Right: Perennials are excellent for an informal design. Make the most of those with strong shapes and appealing colours, such as lupins.

Plan of the informal garden design

Curving lines, unfussy plant groupings and a few simple features are the essence of an informal garden. Aim to make a garden that looks as if it just happened naturally; if it runs wild when you are away on holiday, far from looking unkempt on your return, it just looks like romantic disarray.

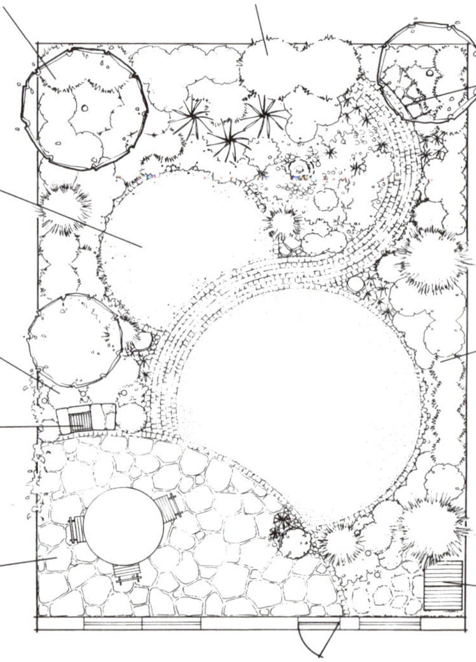

Weeping birch
A weeping birch provides fresh foliage in spring, early summer catkins, yellow autumn foliage and a shining white trunk that stands out well in winter.

Bamboos
Evergreen bamboos make a good screen. Unlike hedges, they stop growing once they reach maximum height, which in many popular varieties is about 1.8m(6ft). Provide plenty of organic matter so that the soil does not dry out badly in summer.

Water jet
The water from this fountain bubbles over cobblestones and drains back into an underground reservoir, where it is recycled by a submersible pump. It is a safe feature for a garden where small children play.

A bench under a tree
A bench under a tree makes a good focal point from the house, yet when you are sitting on it, you get a completely different view of the garden.

Chamomile lawn
Although a chamomile lawn does not take the hard regular wear of grass, it does make a decorative, fragrant feature with stepping stones or a brick surround to walk on.

Concrete sett path
Concrete setts make a textured path reminiscent of cobblestones, but because each sett is flat-topped it is easier to walk on.

Flowering shrubs with timber posts
Do not look straight into the back of a border when working at your barbecue. Instead, place three smooth, timber poles among some low flowering shrubs.

Grasses and perennials
Choose a mixture of flowering grasses and hot red, orange and yellow perennials for the latest look in informal style planting.

Random stone paving and concrete sett edging
Use the same type of concrete setts as used for the path to surround other features, such as the patio and chamomile lawn, to add a feeling of continuity.

Three timber posts
This trio of timber posts acts as a visual balance for the three on the left of the garden, and partly screens the garden store.

Garden cupboard
Use a garden 'cupboard' to store essential garden tools, a tiny hover mower for the grass, and barbecue gear when not in use, so there is no need to find room for a walk-in shed.

Red peonies, clipped box trees, an olive tree and a painted wall panel recreate a Mediterranean-style courtyard garden.

PART TWO

GARDEN STYLES

The smaller the garden, the more it needs a theme to define its personality. The best way to stamp a style on a small garden is to decide from the start what you want and to make sure that every major purchase really says what you mean.

WHAT STYLE OF GARDEN?

When space is short, a garden needs a linking theme, so that instead of planting and furnishing it with a random mixture of ideas, it pays to have a particular style in mind. That way, everything you do has a focus: the plants you buy, the pots, seating and paving all give out the same message. The result not only looks unified, but can also save you a great deal of money in plants and accessories that quickly lose their appeal when they do not look as good as you hoped once installed. A garden does not have to be fashionable to be stylish. What is fashionable may not look right for your home or neighbourhood, or suit the way you want to use your surroundings. An ultramodern, minimalist garden, for instance, would never look right around an old-fashioned cottage. But with thoughtful planning and good design you can often adapt unlikely styles to suit a range of different surroundings. For example, you could have a wild garden in the middle of town or a Japanese garden outside an American or European city basement. And if you are worried that you might get bored with one distinctive style of garden all the time, you can always divide up the space into smaller 'cameo' areas, each with its own identity. Alternatively, you could change part of the design or planting scheme every few years to give the garden a regular face-lift. Or even change the style completely, leaving only hard surfaces and other permanent features as the common factor. It is only practical to consider making such sweeping changes to a small garden, where plenty of style can be achieved with relatively few 'props'; in a large one, the disruption would be enormous and the cost prohibitive.

Below: Create a Mediterranean-style garden in a warm sunny, sheltered spot and grow sunloving, drought-tolerant succulents and plants with grey or furry foliage.

Right: Alpine plants are the perfect way to fill a small garden with detail. Sink gardens are ideal for choice 'treasures' ; larger plants look more natural in raised beds.

Right: Turn a cool shady corner into a lush foliage garden using strong shapes such as tree ferns and a mixture of hardy ferns.

Left: An enthusiast's garden is often designed to house a particular interest; in this case a collection of bonsai plants. The gravel surface and generally minimalist style add an oriental atmosphere, but this is not intended to duplicate a real Japanese garden.

Above: An oriental-style garden uses open spaces as part of its design, so let the plants and other ingredients make bold shapes against uncluttered backgrounds. Irises, plenty of raked sand, large smooth stones and bamboo screens set the scene.

Right: Recreate the atmosphere of a country garden with a series of 'still-lifes', using strategically placed groups of artefacts from the attic. Tuck them into odd corners where there is nothing much happening.

Below: In a cottage garden, all the space is traditionally used to grow flowers. To emphasise the cottage character, keep paths and paving simple and use rustic fencing with clay pots as ornaments.

Above: In a garden with plenty of trees, you have the basis of a good woodland garden. Fallen logs, a mulch of fallen leaves or bark chippings, and mossy tree stumps create atmosphere; add shade-loving or woodland plants and carpets of spring bulbs for colour.

A FAMILY GARDEN

This style of garden has to be immensely versatile to cater for the changing needs of a growing family. It must be inexpensive to create, quick and easy to look after, safe and tough enough to withstand family fun, yet it also needs to look attractive all the year round and cater for outdoor entertaining. The most essential ingredients of a family garden are a patio with built-in barbecue area and space for a table and seats, a rough lawn capable of standing up to ball games and pets, and 'indestructible' shrubs that either bend or recover quickly from damage. Good examples include shrubby willows, such as *Salix alba* varieties, *Cornus alba*, *Ribes sanguineum*, philadelphus, buddleja, weigela and hebe; planted round the edge of a garden, they provide shelter and privacy, as well as acting as a good barrier. For trees, choose apple or pear trees, crab apples or amelanchier. Avoid potentially poisonous plants (garden centres identify these on the labels), prickly plants such as berberis, or those with sharp-edged leaves, including bamboo and many grasses. And avoid water features such as ponds; fountains are safest while children are young. Optional extra features might include a play area for swings and a slide, surfaced with bark chippings (which are easier on young knees than gravel, but cleaner and harder wearing than grass), a nature garden to encourage wildlife, and a small area where children can enjoy tending their own plants. If very young children use the garden, make sure that the garden is secure.

Shrubs
A stout framework of shrubs makes a safe boundary for a garden. Choose non-prickly and non-poisonous species that are resilient enough to recover quickly from damage resulting from boisterous games. This is *Cornus alba* 'Elegantissima'.

Sorbus racemosa 'Sutherlandii' (shrub)

Annuals
Use cheap and cheerful hardy annuals such as this nasturtium, which seed themselves and recover fairly well in case of accidents. Nasturtiums are edible, although they do not taste very pleasant. This is *Nasturtium* 'Gleam'.

Water features

For safety's sake, while children are small, avoid ponds and instead choose a type of water feature that does not have any standing water. Barrel ponds, pebble fountains or a lion's mask fitted to a wall are all ideal.

Barbecues

These are a popular feature of family gardens. Do not site built-in barbecues too close to plants, to the house wall or to fences due to the risk of heat damage and fire. However, you can grow containers of herbs such as rosemary so that they are handy for the barbecue, as the twigs release a pleasant fragrance when thrown onto the hot coals. Do not leave a portable barbecue such as this outside when not in use, as it rusts after the heat has removed the protective layer of paint. If you want to use the barbecue on the lawn, stand it on a large paving slab to avoid the heat scorching the grass.

Garden lighting

A good way to keep your barbecue party going after dark is to install some form of garden lighting.There are a number of options, ranging from these miniature 'oil' lanterns and garden candles on spikes to electric garden lights that you can leave permanently in place; use these to floodlight the garden or just provide gentle illumination. Solar-powered lights are ideal where wiring would be difficult; they recharge themselves as natural light falls on them during the day.

Safety first

Poisonous plants: You can tell which these are by looking at the labels on plants in garden centres, which nowadays give this information voluntarily. There are also books on poisonous plants in the library. Teach children not to put berries, leaves, etc., that they find in the garden into their mouths, and make sure that you keep garden products, especially slug pellets and pesticides, in a locked cupboard.

Garden products: Keep children and pets indoors until weedkillers have dried after application. Keep grazing pets, such as rabbits and guinea pigs, in runs on a patch of grass that is not treated with weedkillers or similar products. The debris and bedding removed when hutches are cleaned out makes a good activator for a compost heap.

A YEAR-ROUND GARDEN

The basis of a truly all-year-round garden is evergreen plants. But the great benefits of a garden like this demand hard work at the design stage. Without careful planning, it is all to easy for a largely evergreen garden to look very green, and remain exactly the same all year round. Begin with the framework planting. Use evergreen hedges and screens to outline the shape of the garden, and select compact evergreen shrubs and ground cover plants to form the foundation of colourful borders. To keep this foundation planting as varied as possible, make use of the full spectrum of foliage colours, shapes and textures; some evergreens have bright gold foliage, and conifers supply good red and blue shades. Incorporate species that also offer good flowers, fruits or berries, such as escallonia, arbutus and pyracantha. Look out for variegated evergreens, such as elaeagnus, pittosporum and unusual forms of ivy, and strong shapes, such as bamboo. You can also find a few evergreens with brilliant autumn colour, such as *Nandina domestica* 'Fire Power', and good evergreen perennials, such as *Liriope muscari* and ophiopogon. Add at least 10-20% of deciduous shrubs, variegated foliage, flowering perennials, bulbs and grasses to bring seasonal highlights to the garden. This also makes it easier to compose a varied and interesting scheme. For fine detail, team evergreens with hard architectural features, such as a statue swathed in evergreen climbers, a trimmed holly tree, an empty terracotta jar laying on its side in a carpet of pink-tinged variegated ivies, or creeping thymes growing in the cracks between paving.

Plant associations

Team pink/orange-tinged birch trunks *(Betula albo-sinensis* and *B. utilis*) with pieris or rhododendron. Craggy pine trunks team well with golden bushy conifers. Acer trunks with red dogwood stems stand out brilliantly in front of blue conifers in winter. Conifers and heathers are a classic combination.

Coloured evergreens
The *Choisya ternata* 'Sundance' shown here and other coloured foliage evergreens are specially valuable for adding variety to what could easily become a sea of very similar-looking shades of green.

Variegated evergreens
Make the most of variegated evergreens such as euonymus and hebe to 'lift' a collection of evergreen shrubs. There are plants with shades of cream, gold, silver, lime and lemon in their leaves, and a wide range of markings, including speckles, dapples, blotches, splashes and neat edgings to the leaves. This is *Hebe* x *franciscana* 'Variegata'.

Carex conica 'Hime-kan-suge' ('Snowline')

Bricks and statues
In a small garden, it is specially important that all the 'hard' ingredients have something in common to avoid a bitty effect. Here, both the bricks and the statue are terracotta, a colour that makes a particularly good contrast with deep green foliage.

Hedera helix (ivy)

Ajuga reptans 'Braunherz'

Architectural plants
Bold, architecturally-shaped plants, such as this *Mahonia* x *media* 'Buckland', provide the structure of the garden. Do not overdo them; each one needs to stand alone so that you can see its shape, striking foliage or other distinctive feature. Leave them standing in their own space or surround them with shorter 'filler' plants. These are the plants to team with hard features, such as an urn or statue, for the greatest effect.

Santolina chamaecyparissus nana

Hedera helix (ivy)

Euonymus fortunei 'Emerald Gaiety'

Seasonal effect

The non-evergreens in a garden like this need to work hard, without making hard work. Choose bulbs of the type that can be left permanently naturalised between shrubs, including a mixture of dwarf spring bulbs (which do not have obtrusive foliage that makes the garden look untidy for weeks after the flowers are over), summer bulbs such as lilies, and autumn bulbs such as colchicum. Also add some perennials that look good over a long season but will not need dividing frequently, such as hostas, euphorbia, hardy ferns, *Alchemilla mollis* and perennial grasses. Where possible, also use compact or ground-covering evergreens that also provide seasonal colour and interest, such as heathers and *Gaultheria procumbens*.

A MEDITERRANEAN GARDEN

A totally paved garden is ideal for a hot or dry climate where grass does not thrive, but also makes an attractive low-maintenance garden that maximises a small space. It could form a complete garden, or be one feature of several within a small garden. The essence of this style of small garden is wall space and containers. Climbers are best grown up a pergola, trellis or netting; wall-trained shrubs can be tied up to horizontal wires secured to special wall nails. Either way, it is a good idea to use plant supports that hold stems well away from the wall to allow for good air circulation. Wall plants are best grown in narrow beds left at the foot of walls when laying paving, but thorough soil preparation is essential, since soil in this situation is naturally very dry and impoverished. Containers, including hanging baskets, wall planters and tubs and troughs, are the popular way of adding seasonal colour and changing interest to a garden of this type. However, they need regular watering, feeding and deadheading to keep plants flowering well, and this can be a problem for people who are out all day. Containers can be fitted with an automatic watering system. As an alternative, consider growing drought-tolerant plants, such as acaena (New Zealand bur), spreading junipers, whipcord hebe or parahebe, in cracks between paving or where paving slabs have been removed to make a small bed. Unless the slabs were originally laid over well-improved soil with this idea in mind, remove the slabs, plus foundations and subsoil, to a depth of at least 60cm(24in) and replace with new topsoil, otherwise even drought-proof plants will not grow well.

Scented herbs

These play a great part in creating a Mediterranean-style ambience. Drought-proof evergreen thyme, rosemary and ornamental sages are both decorative and also useful in the kitchen. To make the most of aromatic herbs, plant creeping thymes in cracks in the paving on a patio where they will occasionally be walked on. Plant sages, rosemary and strong-flavoured Greek oregano in terracotta pots or a multi-storey herb planter close to the back door. To repel flies, grow pots of mint or bush basil. And make up a hanging basket planted with trailing herbs and suspend it near the back door; it will make an unusual novelty for a Mediterranean-style theme.

Zinnias
These half-hardy annuals need a warm, sunny summer to produce a good crop of flowers; they are excellent for cutting, which acts like deadheading, and ensures that the plants produce a continuous crop of new buds all summer long. This is *Zinnia* 'Hobgoblin'.

Compact plants
Good, compact shrubs for a Mediterranean-style border in a small garden include potentilla, cistus and hebe. More unusual dwarf shrubs, such as *Lotus hirsutus* and *Convolvulus cneorum* (shown here), were once grown on large rock gardens, but are now used as novelty container plants.

Anisodontea capensis 'Sapphire' (half-hardy perennial)

Hebe 'Sapphire' (shrub)

Suitable plants
Drought-tolerant, sunloving plants are the most practical kind to grow in containers in a warm sunny spot. Pelargoniums, anisodontea and portulaca all make a good show, and have the typical, brightly coloured flowers of Mediterranean-style plants. Daisy flowers, such as osteospermum, gazania and mesembryanthemum, are also firm container favourites. Many flowers in this group only open properly in sunshine. This is *Pelargonium* 'Pak Cherry' (half-hardy perennial)

Lotus hirsutus (shrubby perennial)

Portulaca 'Sundial Mixed' (half-hardy annual)

Gazania 'Daybreak' (half-hardy perennial)

Salvia officinalis 'Purpurea' (hardy perennial herb)

Permanent plants

Other good permanent plants for a Mediterranean-style garden include: *Olearia* species (daisy bush), pittosporum, agapanthus (good for pots), *Cytisus battandieri* (pineapple broom) and *Fremontodendron californicum* (both good for wall training). Ceanothus, *Romneya coulteri*, callistemon (bottlebrush), *Carpenteria californica*, *Vitis vinifera* 'Purpurea' ornamental grape vine (climber) Fruiting grape vines (outdoors)

Terracotta and natural wood
Terracotta pots and natural, untreated wooden boxes complete the Mediterranean style; all team up well with plain stone or concrete paving slabs or gravel, and patio or courtyard walls. Pale terracotta washes produce a warm tone and make a superb background colour for the silver, blue or green foliage and brightly coloured flowers that are typical of Mediterranean-style gardens.

A COUNTRY GARDEN

Country gardens are full of flower, but look much more sophisticated than cottage gardens. They are closer in character to the gardens of grand country houses or small stately homes, though on a smaller scale. Their borders are filled with elegant perennials such as delphiniums, and their roses are long-flowering hybrid teas and floribundas. Flowering shrubs, particularly perfumed kinds such as philadelphus and lilacs, fill the back of mixed borders. The design is likely to feature quite a lot of hard architecture, such as a terrace, pergola and gazebo, plus formal features, such as fountains, yew hedges, rose beds, topiary and herbaceous borders. Even in a small garden, the area is traditionally divided up into several smaller 'garden rooms', often characterised by distinctive paving, ornate seats, statuary and decorative containers. Modern updates of the traditional country garden style often include themed 'garden rooms', such as scented gardens, colour-coordinated areas (perhaps a white border), butterfly borders and wildflower patches. Lawns are a major feature of country gardens and are traditionally well kept, closely mowed and cut with a cylinder mower with a roller on the back to produce the desirable striped finish. Enthusiasts also find country-style gardens a convenient way of displaying particular families of plants that interest them. For instance, clematis lovers will often grow different varieties of these climbers up through shrubs and small trees, on trellis over walls and outbuildings, and up pillars and obelisks in borders – a great way to make the most of a limited space.

Perennial plants
A herbaceous border was a traditional feature of a country garden; classic plants, such as acanthus, lilies, alstroemeria, lupins (here 'Lulu Mixed') and delphiniums, were an essential part of the recipe.

An echo of the past
Antique tools, such as scythes and ditching tools, brass plant sprayers, or even an old lawnmower, make fascinating decorations inside a shed. Galvanised buckets and tin baths can be painted or left natural and recycled as plant containers. Nowadays, you can buy copper plant labels, 'turned' wooden pressers for flattening potting mix in pots and trays before sowing seeds, and trowels with wooden handles.

Country character

Traditional features that evoke the atmosphere of a country garden include yew hedges; topiary; staddle stones; stone statues and urns in focal points (often formed by making a niche in an evergreen hedge); formal gardens within gardens; large lush lawns, including croquet lawns. All can be recreated on a small scale

Alstroemeria 'Orange Gem'

Herbaceous borders and island beds
Perennials were usually seen against the background of a yew hedge or perhaps an old, red brick wall. Since the original plants were mainly quite tall, a true country border would have needed a lot of staking and tying up during the growing season. It was also difficult to get at the hedge to cut it, unless the garden was large enough to allow a path to be left along the back for access. Today, compact varieties of all the old favourites are available that need little or no staking, and easy-to-cultivate island beds have taken over from the old style of borders. This is the compact *Delphinium elatum* 'King Arthur'.

Lilium 'Talent'

Antique furniture

Antique garden furniture includes items such as Victorian wrought-iron benches and Edwardian wire seats. Today, modern reproductions are made of all the old garden furniture designs, such as Lutyens seats, cast aluminium Victorian-style tables and chairs, and new wire seats. Unlike plastic-framed, upholstered furniture, all of these can be left outdoors all year round, so you do not need storage space for them in winter. In a traditional country garden, arches and other garden structures were generally smarter and more elegant than those in a cottage garden.

Traditional tools
A regular feature of genuine country gardens surrounding large country houses was the sight of gardeners at work in the grounds. You can recreate this feeling of activity by placing old garden tools and equipment around the garden; a wooden wheelbarrow or weathered gardening tools are ideal. An ancient spade pushed into a border makes a good plant support. Bear in mind that old gardening tools are often very heavy, with rough wooden handles, so they are better left for decoration; keep your light stainless spades and hoes for real use.

A COTTAGE GARDEN

A cottage garden is deliberately intended to look very natural, almost as if the flowers had appeared randomly all by themselves, without having been planted. This effect is partly achieved by growing plants that look 'in keeping', and partly by the way they are grown. Typical cottage garden plants include hardy annuals (violas, calendula and cornflowers), wild-looking perennials, such as hardy cranesbills, and cultivated forms of wildflowers, such as coloured primroses and violets. Equally authentic are culinary, decorative and medicinal herbs, shrub roses, flowering fruit trees, old-fashioned shrubs, such as myrtle and flowering quince, spring and summer bulbs, such as daffodils and lilies, and chrysanthemums and dahlias – originally grown for sale as cut flowers at the garden gate. In old, original cottage gardens, plants were put in wherever there was a gap, with no thought for design or correct spacing. Spreading and self-seeding plants were allowed to ramble around at will, smothering out weeds and any plant unable to stand its ground, all of which contributed to the romantically disordered muddle. Today, many enthusiasts find a cottage garden is the ideal way to house a collection of choice 'treasures', which may be rare, old, named varieties of traditional plants, new perennials or even rock plants and miniature shrubs. These must be kept separate from the more invasive colonisers that would soon smother them; they are best grown in containers, raised beds or a special area of their own. And although plants are grown closely spaced, plan the planting to appear random.

Hardy fuchsias
Most real old cottage garden plants were hardy, since cottagers were farm workers on low incomes and with no facilities such as greenhouses in which to keep tender plants through the winter. Hardy fuchsias were popular for their long flowering season and bright colourful flowers with dancing 'ballet skirts'. In winter, hardy fuchsias, such as this 'Mrs Popple', die back to ground level in cold areas. Leave the dead stems and mulch heavily for winter protection, then prune the dead stems off at ground level in spring.

Tender perennials
Nowadays, a much larger range of tender plants have joined the ranks of cottage-style plants. Those with daisy flowers, such as argyranthemums and this *Dendranthema* 'White Gloss', look particularly suitable, but the rich variety of a cottage garden makes this an ideal garden style for the plant collector who wants to grow a bit of everything.

Old roof tiles
Salvaged building materials make authentic cottage garden props. Roof tiles can be recycled as edgings to paths, while bricks and stone flooring slabs make good paths and paving. Simply lay them over prepared soil and plant creeping thymes and similar aromatic plants in the cracks to add to the cottage garden atmosphere.

Pinks
Old varieties are valued as collector's plants. Their perfume is stronger than modern varieties, although the flowering period is shorter.

Lavender

Aromatic plants are a vital ingredient in the cottage garden mix, and lavender is an old favourite. It was once cultivated for the flowers which were dried and made into lavender bags, then kept in drawers of clothes to perfume them. It is one of many classic cottage garden plants that attracts butterflies and bees in huge numbers. Other good traditional aromatic plants include thyme, marjoram, honeysuckle, roses and sweet peas. Plant aromatics along the side of a path, around the door, or over an arbour for a traditional effect in a cottage garden. This is *Lavandula angustifolia* 'Munstead'.

Annuals

Hardy annuals such as pansies were old cottage favourites, as they did not need any heat to raise, and many self seeded naturally, so did not make any work. However, some half-hardy annuals have also become cottage favourites, notably scented tobacco plants - the *Nicotiana* species shown here. In bygone times, cottagers cultivated the tall 'smoking' species, which they used to make their own tobacco.

Natural materials

Anything made of natural materials adds to the rustic character of a cottage garden. A wooden trug is ideal for gathering flowers or vegetables, or just for carrying light garden equipment, such as gloves, a trowel, secateurs and string. Look out, too, for willow or hazel plant supports of various types. Use rustic poles to make fencing, garden furniture or pillars and pergolas.

Antirrhinum 'Liberty Cherry'

Pansy

Antique watering can

This and other old items of gardening equipment make authentic 'stage setting' decorations for a cottage garden. Arrange them so that they look as if they were abandoned years ago, and the garden has grown up around them. Weathered old garden seats, chimney pots, wooden wheelbarrows and plant boxes all look the part. They can often be found at antique fairs and junk shops.

A WOODLAND GARDEN

A garden that has a thriving population of trees can be developed – without any major clearing and replanting – as an attractive woodland-style garden. This is true regardless of whether the trees concerned are wild native species or ornamental garden varieties. In fact, this theme is a good way of restyling a small garden that has previously been rather overplanted with trees. There is no reason why the foundation of your woodland should not be, for example, flowering cherries. Natural woodland normally needs clearing of brambles, unwanted saplings of weed species such as sycamore, and similar scrub before you can start planting. Old woodland also has its own build-up of rich, fertile leafmould that needs little improvement. Elsewhere, prepare the soil well by digging in large quantities of well-rotted organic matter, since the sort of plants that thrive in woodland like humus-rich soil and usually prefer lime-free conditions. Plant 'drifts' of choice woodland plants, carpets of early spring bulbs that flower before the trees come into leaf, or shade-loving wildflowers. Add camellias, azaleas and dwarf rhododendrons for a spring spectacle, and Japanese maples with colourful leaves for foliage detail. You can also plant shade-tolerant garden species, such as *Anemone blanda*, hostas and *Cornus controversa* 'Variegata' for a less wild and more decorative effect. Avoid ground under very large old trees, as it is full of roots and growing conditions are poor; overhanging branches deflect rainwater, while tree roots take up all the available soil moisture and nutrients. Use this space for a seat or tree root sculpture.

Grasslike plants
The variegated woodrush *(Luzula sylvatica* 'Aureomarginata') is a good plant for growing in dry shade under trees, where few other plants are happy. After planting, keep new plants watered for their first summer but once established, they spread slowly and form strong resilient clumps

Ground cover
For mass ground cover in a woodland garden, choose decorative, low-growing, but tough, spreading plants. *Rubus calycoides* 'Betty Ashburner' and the variegated ground elder *(Aegopodium podagraria* 'Variegatum'), shown here, are ideal. Variegated ground elder tolerates poor growing conditions and is perfect for brightening up shady places. It is much less invasive than the plain green version, which is a common weed.

Athyrium filix-femina (lady fern)

Blechnum spicant

Woodland garden surfaces
Grass does not grow happily in the shade of a woodland garden; instead, use a surface of bark chippings or make a path between carpets of woodland-style ground-covering plants using tree trunk slices, or old railway sleepers or large treated planks sunk into the ground. Even in a very small garden, you could blend wooden decking or decking tiles with a small tree and a group of suitable plants to create the authentic woodland feeling.

Leafmould

This accumulates under trees in wild woodland, forming a deep, rich, naturally lime-free soil. At home, collect dead leaves and rot them down in a leafmould cage to enrich the soil and topdress woodland plants. Use products such as sulphur chips to acidify neutral soil, making it suitable for lime-hating plants including rhododendrons.

Rubus calycoides 'Betty Ashburner'

Cornus controversa **'Variegata'**
The wedding cake tree makes a tiered shape, with branches forming distinct layers outlined in cream-and-green foliage. This striking small tree or large shrub only thrives where it is sheltered by surrounding trees, and is seen at its best in light woodland.

Choice woodland plants
Moist, fertile, leafmould-rich soil and light shade provide superb growing conditions for a great many choicer woodland plants, such as *Corydalis flexuosa, shown here.* Violets, hardy cyclamen, hellebores, lily-of-the-valley and epimediums all enjoy the same conditions, and many can be quite difficult to grow elsewhere.

Hardy ferns
Hardy ferns are known for their delicate lacy foliage and fondness for shady woodland conditions. Most, such as the lady fern *(Athyrium filix-femina),* thrive best in moist shade. However, the soft shield fern *(Polystichum setiferum* 'Congestum'), shown here, likes fertile, humus-rich but well-drained soil that is not too wet in winter. A few, including *Blechnum spicant,* thrive in dry shade; they are useful for growing under large trees, whose roots take up a lot of the moisture.

A WILD GARDEN

A wild garden is not simply a normal one that has been left to run wild. It is a slice of the countryside recreated specially, using native trees shrubs and flowers planted in a very naturalistic style. Since there are no rules for wild gardening, you can also decorate the garden with cultivated flowers, though for authenticity it looks best to use those that are close cousins of wild plants. 'Accessories' such as fallen logs and tree stumps, rocks, pebbles, bark chippings and a shallow pool can all be used to colour the scene, depending on the local landscape. For instance, on a heavily wooded site, a woodland-style garden will look most at home. You could create a small clearing and have a tree surgeon thin a dense canopy of branches to allow more light in so that a greater range of plants will grow. On a hot dry sunny site, a wild style that uses rocks and drought-tolerant plants will look most natural. In a damp garden, a pond flanked by moisture-loving plants with hazels and willows looks the part. And in a more normal garden, you could create a meadow-style garden with mixed hedgerows, a shallow pond or even a running stream with pebbled banks and drifts of shrubs and flowers. It is also possible to create a more normal-looking garden with informal beds and borders planted with native species and wilder-looking cultivated flowers. A natural garden attracts wildlife, as it supplies plenty of food, plus drinking and bathing facilities. And it is likely to be quicker to keep up than a traditional flower garden.

Wildflowers

Include groups of wildflowers among shrubs. Choose those that suit the soil and situation. Low-growing wildflowers, such as cowslips or primroses, violets and trefoils, look good grown in grass; mow short paths for access through longer grass that is only cut twice a year, in early spring and autumn.

Feeding the birds

Birds need most feeding from autumn to late spring, but if you feed throughout the summer, avoid putting out peanuts or anything with large particles during the nesting season, as inexperienced parents may try to feed these items to small chicks.

Small trees and shrubs with fruit or berries provide a good source of food for birds in autumn and winter; holly, cotoneaster, sorbus, *Viburnum opulus* (shown here), vaccinium and many rubus species, such as Japanese wineberry, are all useful.

Rhus typhina 'Dissecta'

Birdfeeders
Place a bird table within easy reach of trees and shrubs to which birds can quickly escape if a predator threatens. Feed peanuts in hanging net containers; use squirrel-proof containers if these or other rodents are a problem. Feed a mixture of bird seeds of various sizes so that there is something for a wide variety of different birds. And smear fat onto tree bark, as some species appreciate this.

Nestboxes
To attract birds to nest in the garden, put up nestboxes; different sized openings are available to suit various birds. Place the boxes above head height, in a sheltered place safe from cats and other predators; under the eaves of a shed or on a tree trunk facing away from the prevailing wind. Some birds will also nest in containers lodged firmly on their sides amongst tight-knit branches in a hedge.

Ilex aquifolium 'Alaska'

Ground cover plants such as this *Rubus* 'Betty Ashburner' encourage insects that are food for birds.

A LOW-MAINTENANCE GARDEN

Some styles of garden need plenty of regular attention to keep them looking good, but if quick and easy maintenance is your goal then make use of low-labour features and gardening aids. Paving or decking plus shrubs (especially evergreens) and ground cover plants form the basis of good easy-care designs. Architectural features, such as topiary, sculpture and ornate but unplanted containers, add interest without making work. For extra variety, blend a mixture of surfaces underfoot, such as stone slabs, cobbles and old brick, to create contrasts with surrounding plants. You can cut down chores such as weeding by covering border soil with a deep mulch of bark chippings, compost or gravel to prevent annual weeds. But if starting from scratch, then the best plan is to lay perforated plastic sheeting or woven anti-weed fabric over the ground and plant through it, for permanent weed prevention. Containers or flower beds are most easily watered by installing a drip irrigation system. The most routine jobs in a low-labour garden are topping up mulches (which tend to move with time), cleaning paving and raking gravel. (If you decide to retain lawns and hedges, cutting them is a chore that can be subcontracted, while a power washer makes it quick to clean paving.) However, it usually takes quite a bit of time and effort to convert an existing garden to a low-maintenance format. Some people like to do the work in small stages over several years, while others call in builders to do the construction work all at once, leaving them free to enjoy their spare time on the more creative aspects of gardening.

Irrigation systems
Save hours of watering in summer by putting in a watering system. Various types are available. Perforated pipes leak water continuously along their length and are ideal for watering newly planted shrubs, rows of vegetables or flower beds. The sort with individual nozzles are best for watering containers, windowboxes and hanging baskets on a patio, or for use in the greenhouse. For the greatest time-saving, connect irrigation up to the tap via a timer mechanism that turns the water on and off at preset times, enabling the watering to be done while you are away from home – even during holidays.

Hydrangea macrophylla

Santolina chamaecyparissus

Pachysandra terminalis

Leaky hose keeps border watered

Gaultheria procumbens

Weed prevention
You can avoid weeding entirely. When making a new bed, prepare the soil specially well, then cover it with a layer of perforated black plastic or special woven plastic mulching sheet. Plant shrubs and perennials through this, cutting crosses where they are to go, then tucking the flaps back closely around the stems. Cover the sheeting with a decorative mulch of bark chippings or gravel to hide it afterwards.

Container plants
You can save time planting and replanting containers with new seasonal displays several times a year. Instead, plant slow-growing perennials or compact shrubs that can be left in the same container for several years without repotting. Evergreen types, such as those shown here, are best, as they provide year-round interest. Permanently planted containers need protection from freezing solid in a cold winter. Plunge them to their rims in a garden bed, lag them with bubble wrap plastic or move them under cover temporarily.

Time-saving

Keep track of latest product innovations, as many are aimed specifically at people who want to garden well, but quickly. Slow-release fertilisers and feed sticks for containers, water-retaining gel crystals for hanging baskets and potting mixtures that last for a whole season.

Leucothoe walteri 'Rainbow'

Gaultheria mucronata

Rhododendron 'Salmon's Leap'

Calluna vulgaris 'Marleen'

Choisya ternata 'Sundance'

Gravel and paving
Although more expensive to lay than grass, gravel and paving need considerably less upkeep than a lawn. An occasional rake-over or wash down, and perhaps an application of path weedkiller in spring is all that it takes. In a small garden without much space for paving, the cost need not be excessive, especially when you consider that you do not need to pay for a mower and its servicing, or give up space to a shed in which to store it.

A PLANTLOVER'S GARDEN

People whose main interest is growing and collecting plants usually prefer to concentrate their resources on the green parts of the garden. For them, 'hard' features are often seen as a waste of money and space that could more profitably be spent on plants. However, a garden made of nothing but plants can easily end up looking like a botanical collection - especially if plant labels are also very conspicuous. Good planting helps. Group plants together to make coordinated plant associations, and use suitable plants as architecturally as possible so they form a contrasting backdrop for others. One of the best ways to accommodate quantities of plants attractively without a lot of 'frills' is to make a formal garden surrounded by a wall or hedge, with a path through the middle and wide borders each side. Or instead you could create a series of beds in a conventional style garden, each providing a set of growing conditions that suit particular plants. However, a small amount of 'hard' landscaping makes the job of designing a plantlover's garden much easier. A little architecture can also contribute to their well-being by improving the growing environment - for instance, raised beds topped with shingle and decorated with a few rocks improve drainage for growing choice alpines, while drought tolerant sunlovers enjoy patio surroundings

Spiky shapes
Grasses, irises and similar strong horizontal shapes grouped together make a bold modern look, or you can create a softer effect by blending them with other more rounded plants.

Coloured foliage
Red or silver foliage contrasts well with green leaves and colourful flowers. Used throughout a planting scheme, they help to relieve a crowded border by breaking it up into smaller visual 'bites'. This is *Leucothoe* Scarletta

Molinia caerulea 'Moorhexe'

Carex buchananii

Stachys 'Primrose Heron'

Festuca glauca Blue Fox

Sisyrinchium striatum

General design

Avoid the temptation to overcrowd the garden, which is always a problem when space is short. It is far better to redesign a small part of the garden every year and use the opportunity to change the planting, than to keep cramming in new plants until nothing looks good.

Striking shapes
Good forms of unusual plants, such as this *Robinia pseudoacacia* 'Lace Lady', are specially sought after by keen plantspeople. When space is short, there is no point in wasting it on inferior plants.

Collectables

When plants suddenly become fashionable, as happened with grasses, a huge range of previously almost unobtainable varieties 'explodes' onto the market. The result can often mean overkill for a keen plant collector, who wants to grow them all at once. To avoid a new passion swamping a garden, choose only your top favourites and blend them carefully into the existing garden, rather than 'dumping' them in the first available space, where they will never look their best. And do not be afraid to stand the new purchases, in their pots, in several different places all round the garden to gauge the effect before deciding where to plant them.

Borders
To make the best use of the space, plan borders carefully, so that the plants are tiered. Plant shrubs under trees, perennials under shrubs, and bulbs under perennials. But to avoid the garden looking cluttered, leave an occasional open area with just a specimen plant or well-chosen plant group for contrast.

A SUBTROPICAL GARDEN

A subtropical garden is a good way to fill a small plot with big style. Here, instead of choosing plants in scale with their surroundings you do the exact opposite, and go for jungle giants instead. But there is no need to risk real tropical plants outdoors. There are plenty of large exotic-style shrubs and perennials that look the part and yet are perfectly hardy. Foliage is going to play a big part in a garden like this. Pick plants with large leaves, tall stems and bold architectural shapes. Bamboo, phormium, *Fatsia japonica*, large hardy ferns, *Trachycarpus fortunei*, *Arundo donax*, *Yucca fortunei*, cordyline palms and colletia make a suitably jungly background. Plant these in dense drifts round the edges of the garden. For really huge leaves, grow paulownia, *Catalpa bignonioides* 'Aurea' or *Ailanthus altissima* and cut them down close to ground level in spring every one to three years. Add perennials such as *Darmera peltata*, lysichiton, and zantedeschia for their striking flowers and foliage. Add big terracotta pots of tender plants such as agave, bottlebrush (callistemon) or abutilon for summer highlights. For seasonal flower, bed out tender plants with tropical looks: castor oil plant (ricinus), tithonia, cannas or any of the giant tobacco plants (*Nicotiana tabacum*, *N. sylvestris* or *N. knightiana*). Choose suitably tropical-inspired garden furniture – bamboo seats (though they need putting away when not in use), or slatted wooden painted 'campaign' style tables and chairs. Add bamboo screens or a planter's cabin instead of a summerhouse or gazebo, and vigorous climbers like *Campsis radicans* in a sheltered sunny spot.

Summer bulbs
Cannas have some of the most exotic-looking flowers you can get, yet are tough enough to grow outside for the summer. Grow the fat tubers in large pots and start them into growth in a heated propagator or greenhouse. Move them outside a few weeks after the last frost. Most varieties grow 90cm-150cm (3-5ft) tall. After flowering, reduce watering and let the foliage die back naturally. Then let the tubers overwinter in their pots in dryish compost in a frost-free greenhouse or conservatory. Other good, exotic-looking summer bulbs with similar growing habits include eucomis (pineapple flower, 45cm/18in) and tigridia (peacock flower, 30cm/12in).

Climbers
Choose climbers with spectacular flowers that are perfectly hardy despite their tropical appearance, such as this *Solanum crispum* 'Glasnevin' or *Passiflora caerulea*. In a cold location, all sorts of slightly tender shrubs can be trained out flat over trellis covering a sheltered sunny wall; phygelius also looks very tropical.

Evergreen shrubs
Use evergreen shrubs, such as New Zealand flax (phormium, here *Phormium tenax* 'Pink Panther') and purple-leaved cordyline palm *(Cordyline australis* 'Atropurpurea') to create a year-round backdrop; the foliage is dramatic and exotic, but hardier than it looks. Other good evergreen foliage plants include pittosporum, Chusan palm *(Trachycarpus fortunei)* and hardy yucca *(Yucca gloriosa)*. In a cold situation or harsh winter, move cordyline, trachycarpus and pittosporum under cover.

Props

Choose folding seats and tin tables on a decking-style verandah to suggest a planter's bungalow in Malaya. Enthusiasts use tropical houseplants and jungle-theme recordings indoors, and plenty of bamboo and large-leaved foliage plants around the garden to complete the illusion.

Tender shrubs

Use tender shrubs, such as *Acacia dealbata,* abutilon and bottlebrush (callistemon), outdoors in pots on the patio in summer. There they provide a dramatic foliage backdrop to tropical-looking summer flowers, even when not in bloom themselves (although both abutilon and bottlebrush flower in summer). Before the first frost threatens, move them into a cool conservatory or heated greenhouse for the winter. This is *Callistemon citrinus* 'Splendens'.

AN ALPINE GARDEN

Keen plant enthusiasts, limited to a small garden, can often make better use of the space than the person with a large garden but only limited funds to develop it. One way of making the most of a tiny area is to grow naturally small plants, and to choose a style of garden that allows all the available space to be used for beds instead of being taken up by lawns. An alpine garden is a good example. Here, everything is on a small scale. The garden consists of wall-to-wall plant beds, filled with a huge variety of rock plants, dwarf bulbs and miniature shrubs, decorated with chunks of rock and topdressed with fine gravel. This makes a good background to the plants, as well as providing well-drained growing conditions. Narrow stone-flagged or gravel paths wind between rocky outcrops to provide access for enjoyment and essential jobs such as weeding and watering. A seating area outside the patio doors can continue the alpine theme, with stone slabs and sink gardens planted with more rock plants. Hardwood benches or stone seats and tables look the part and can be left out all year round. Enthusiasts may also like to have a cold frame or small unheated greenhouse to protect delicate plants or for propagation. These can be landscaped attractively into the scheme, perhaps half-hidden behind a screen clad with climbers, which provide light shade in summer. While this type of garden is not suitable for a family with young children or dogs, it can prove very practical for anyone who does not want the bother of maintaining a lawn, or who lacks storage facilities for mowers and garden furniture.

Summer-flowering species
The vast majority of rock plants flower in spring, so to keep the rockery looking colourful, choose plenty of plants with summer flowers and long flowering seasons. Good ones include *Campanula cochleariifolia* (shown here), helianthemum, *Parahebe catarractae, Campanula carpatica* 'Blue Clips' and *Gypsophila repens* 'Rosea'.

Drought-resistant sunlovers
Silver foliage plants, such as this *Artemisia schmidtiana* 'Nana', and those with succulent leaves, such as *Sedum spathulifolium* 'Cape Blanco' and *Sempervivum* 'Commander Hay', are naturally drought-resistant, ideal for the most sun-baked situations where many other rock plants fail.

Dwarf trees
Mini trees, such as this woolly willow *(Salix lanata),* look naturally stunted and add an authentic air to a rock garden. It grows to a maximum of 90cm(36in) high, and has fat yellowish-grey catkins in spring and felty-textured, grey, disc-shaped leaves. These are shed in winter, leaving a craggy branching shape. Other good deciduous mini trees and shrubs for a rock garden include *Forsythia viridissima* 'Bronxensis', *Salix* 'Boydii', *Betula nana* and *Ulmus parvifolia* 'Frosty'.

Parahebe catarractae

Sedum spathulifolium 'Cape Blanco'

Campanula carpatica 'Blue Clips'

Low spreading plants

Many rock plants are clump-forming, so include a few low spreading kinds that wander about the garden without becoming a nuisance. They provide a visual link between islands of plants that would otherwise look adrift in a sea of gravel. *Pratia pedunculata* (shown here) is ideal. It grows just 3cm(1.2in) high and has pale blue flowers for much of the summer. Another good linking plant is *Campanula* 'Elizabeth Oliver', which has tiny, double blue flowers that look like tiny powder puffs.

Helianthemum 'Rose of Leeswood'

Variegated leaves

Plants that flower early and then have good variegated foliage for the rest of the season are well worth their place in a rock garden; *Arabis ferdinandi-coburgi* 'Variegata' can be found in most good garden centres. It has short white spikes of flowers in spring.

Rock pinks

These have silvery-blue foliage with mini carnation-like flowers. In a well-drained sunny situation, they form neat mounds that never outgrow their welcome. These are *Dianthus* 'Spring Star'.

Lewisias

These have colourful long-lasting flowers. The plants like a hot sunny spot with very well-drained gritty soil. As they are unusually susceptible to rotting off at the neck, plant them in a rock crevice, with the rosettes of foliage facing sideways instead of upright. these are *Lewisia* 'Ashwood Mixed'

Rocks

To create the most natural rock feature without using rock taken from the wild, choose old local stone recycled from another rockery where possible. Alternatively, use reconstituted stone or make your own fake rocks from hypertufa, the same material used to clad sink gardens. Avoid using rocks altogether, by making rock features such as screes or sink gardens, which look more at home in a small garden.

Grit

To mulch a rock feature, use fine gravel or grit to a depth of 2.5-5cm (1-2in). Tuck this under plants to improve surface drainage and prevent collar rot. Top up by sprinkling more grit between plants after tidying the rock garden in autumn. Choose grit of a suitable colour to match any stones used in the rock feature.

Arabis fernandi-coburgi 'Variegata'

Gypsophila repens 'Rosea'

A WET GARDEN

There are several ways to improve a permanently wet garden, such as making raised beds, digging in plenty of grit to improve the drainage or laying land drains emptying into a soakaway. The easy way is simply to grow plants that enjoy the conditions. Quite a number of border plants need soil that never dries out, and bog garden plants are happy in squelchy conditions. Some pond margin plants are also happy in boggy soil and will not mind ground that is subject to flooding. By mapping the degree of wetness all round the garden, you can plan the right plants for the worst problem spots. However, there are a few things to take into account when dealing with a wet garden. The first is that moisture-loving plants only thrive where the soil never dries out. If yours tends to do so in summer, then excavate the area where the true bog plants are to go, line it with perforated black plastic and backfill with a mixture of garden soil and well-rotted organic matter. This will help to keep it wet all year round. Otherwise, mulch the area heavily in spring and be prepared to water if the soil gets dry later. The other problem is that many popular moisture-loving plants are too big for most conventionally planted small gardens. Gunnera, rodgersia, eupatorium and ligularia grow tall and spread wide, while many shorter plants, such as darmera, moisture-loving iris species and lythrum can also spread quite rapidly. If you grow these in a normal border, either use them sparingly as specimen plants to contrast with smaller species, or restrict them by growing them in a big pot sunk into the ground. And make the most of more modest plants, such as *Lobelia nummularia* 'Aurea', *Iris sibirica*, hostas and astilbes contrasted with reedy shapes like zebra rush. If the ground is too wet for grass, a normal garden will be very difficult to maintain. An alternative would be a wilder, walk-through garden, with large spreading moisture lovers planted in drifts, and winding paths of bark chippings or cobblestones rambling amongst them. Use architectural features, such as an occasional giant plant, a clump of red-stemmed cornus for winter interest, plus a knotty tree stump, rustic seat, willow structure or natural driftwood sculpture.

Schoenoplectus 'Zebrinus' (zebra rush)

Marginal and bog garden plants
Plants that like to grow in boggy soil or even in very shallow water around the edge of a pond are ideal for wet gardens. Choose a mixture of upright, linear, reed shapes, such as zebra rush (*Schoenoplectus* 'Zebrinus'), plus plants with colourful foliage and flowers, such as *Lobelia cardinalis* 'Queen Victoria', shown here, and *Mimulus luteus* for a compact wet garden plant grouping that works. Read labels carefully before buying, since many moisture-loving plants become very large.

Gunnera manicata
This spectacular bog plant has huge dramatic, prickly-backed leaves and thick prickly stems. Being herbaceous, it dies down for the winter and needs protecting from hard frost. Cut off the dead leaves and fold them over the crown like a tent. Do not be in a hurry to remove the dead leaves in spring, as the new growth is susceptible to late frosts. Despite its size, a single specimen placed in a striking situation in a small garden can look superb. It can also be grown in a large container to restrict its size, but provide suitable winter protection.

Making a pond in a wet garden

It may be possible to create a natural pond, if the soil is the type of clay that 'puddles' and makes a (free!) watertight lining when trodden down hard inside the dug-out pond shape. However, this only works on some kinds of clay; elsewhere, such ponds always leak. A pond liner is not an option on ground with a high water table, since rising water levels can cause the liner to 'balloon' up, which pushes out plants, etc. However, you can create above-ground water features, such as fountains or pebble pools, which in any case take up less room in a small garden.

Mimulus luteus

Moisture-loving plants
Hosta and astilbe (shown here), grow well in a bog garden or damp border. As long as the soil stays moist enough, they are both happy grown in sun.

Hostas
Protect hostas from slugs and snails, which can reduce them to ribbons in no time. Snails are less of a problem on acid soil, as they need limestone to form their shells. As an alternative to slug pellets, sprinkle a circle of sharp gritty sand or prickly holly leaves around hostas and other severely affected plants. Alternatively, spray plants with yucca extract, which is now sold as a 'green' remedy. Encourage natural predators, such as frogs and toads, which are commonly found in wet gardens. This is *Hosta fortunei* var. *aureomarginata*.

Props/Accessories
Choose suitably themed accessories to set off plants with waterside associations. Large smooth stones, pebbles and rounded gravel suggest shelving stream banks and pondsides, while wooden duck-boards create good paths or 'bridges' through boggy areas.

A potted pond
You could use a 'potted pond' to provide some genuine water in a tiny wet garden, where there is not room for a proper pond. Potted ponds are also less work.

AN ORIENTAL GARDEN

An oriental-style garden contains characteristic ingredients: raked gravel, smooth stones and oriental-style ornaments, such as a bamboo deer scarer, a stone bridge over a dry 'river' of pebbles or a stone lantern. Added to these are a few typically architectural plants, such as bamboos, grasses, flowering cherry, craggy conifers, Japanese maples and irises. You might also add shelves of small potted bonsai-style conifers, half hidden behind a bamboo screen. Oriental themes are ideal for low-labour small gardens because, lacking grass and traditional flower beds, they require very little maintenance. True oriental gardens are full of symbolism, and each individual rock is placed with great care and much thought, but the idea can be adapted to create various minimalistic gardens, including those known as 'stone gardens' (see page 66). Oriental gardens contain more rocks and gravel than plants, although most Westerners would probably prefer a few more plants than you find in an authentic example. However, to keep in with the theme, choose plants that have a striking character of their own, that suit the soil and growing conditions, and that look good when viewed against a background of stones. Use several different sizes of gravel and cobblestones in broad curving sweeps to resemble the patterns left by waves on the seashore. Keep them 'clean' by regularly raking them into a wavy pattern. Oriental gardeners consider this a highly therapeutic occupation; it is certainly far more relaxing than the Western equivalent – mowing the lawn – and needs doing less often. Quiet contemplation is the name of the game.

Deer scarer
This is a traditional water feature intended to frighten away bad spirits, rather than deer. Each time the swinging bamboo tube fills with water dripping from the narrow pipe, it tumbles, striking the rock and making a dull hollow thump. Being very regular, this is surprisingly relaxing. The tube swings back into place ready to be refilled.

Japanese umbrella pine
This *Sciadopitys verticillata* is a very slow-growing conifer that makes a striking shape and contrasts well with the other ingredients of an oriental garden. (It does not tolerate lime, so do not risk it on chalky gardens). Since many typically oriental plants are evergreen, the overall shape of the garden remains all the year round.

Craggy pines
The naturally craggy character of this blue pine, *Pinus leucodermis* 'Blue Giant', is ideal for an oriental garden. It is a blue form of the Bosnian pine, an excellent species for a dry or chalky garden. Its drought-tolerant nature makes it suitable for growing in a container, which would also restrict its size.

Other suitable conifers

Many other striking conifers complement the oriental style; look for low, dome-shaped pines such as *Pinus mugo* 'Gnom'; pines with very long, blue needles, such as *Pinus griffithii*; ground-hugging junipers and *Cryptomeria japonica* cultivars for their bronze-red winter colouring. Also choose conifers that look like natural bonsais and duplicate the shape of old gnarled or weathered trees.

Open space

Oriental gardens are minimalist, so you need fewer ingredients than for a normal western-style garden. It is important that everything in the garden is perfectly placed and empty space is just as much a part of the design as the objects that frame it.

Plants with distinctive shapes

These are a feature of an oriental-style garden. Dwarf trees, especially those that can be trained and shaped and have an oriental connection, are particularly suitable. The small trees commonly used in bonsai look the part, such as this Japanese maple *(Acer palmatum* Dissectum Viride Group).

Bamboo

This is typically oriental-looking, but many kinds grow too big for a small garden. However, this *Arundinaria auricoma* stays compact enough to grow in containers or in the ground; use it to make small screens or a circular clump surrounded by small stones or gravel. The upright stems of bamboo contrast well with the shapes of pines and other conifers and maples; the three plant types make a natural plant association that always works well.

Raked sand

Fine gravel or gritty granite sand is raked into elaborate wavy patterns that are intended to represent the patterns left by waves on a seashore. Since the patterns are disturbed by birds or anyone walking over the garden, the sand needs raking regularly to keep the patterns intact. However, this job is considered an aid to meditation in a real oriental garden, where it is done with a special bamboo rake. A wooden hay rake makes a good substitute, producing wider teeth marks than a normal rake. To save work, you could include a small patch of rake-patterned gravel amongst paving.

A STONE GARDEN

As a complete contrast to traditional plant-packed gardens, a stone garden is distinctly minimalist. Its inspiration is oriental, and its main interest lies in the clever use of different hard surfaces - usually a mixture of cobbles, gravels of various sizes and colours, and craggy rocks. These are spread out to create swirling patterns rather like those made by waves on a seashore, which are decorated in a small way with plants. Only the most striking, architectural plants are used. Bamboo, craggy conifers such as pines, and birches with coloured bark are favourites. You can also use dramatic conifers like *Cedrus atlantica* 'Glauca Pendula', *Sciadopitys verticillata* or *Cryptomeria japonica* 'Spiralis', which all contrast well with stone. For small scale detail, opt for perennials like the corkscrew rush *Juncus effusus* 'Spiralis' planted in a big clump or mounds of dome shaped santolina or dwarf conifers. A stone garden is a very practical way of designing a small front garden as the hard surfaces provide extra parking places when required. Plants can be placed so they do not obstruct this purpose, leaving the garden looking perfectly decorative the rest of the time. A stone garden also makes a good mini-feature in a back garden, perhaps adjacent to a modern rock plant feature like a raised bed, or a pond or other water feature - especially one with a striking abstract style. You could also use the idea teamed with low spreading plants as the basis of a stylish designer herb garden. It has lots of applications. When designing the feature, begin by taking a good look at the various types and grades of gravels and pebbles available, and plan the hard layout first, leaving plants till last.

Perennials

Balance a big group of conifers with lower clumps of evergreen, drought-tolerant perennials, such as the *Verbascum* 'Jackie' shown here, to make a spiky-shaped plant associations. Evergreen grasses always look good in this setting, due to their rather modern, high-tech style.

Stones

Many larger garden centres now supply bags of smooth stones and stone chippings of various sizes and colours, but for the biggest selection try to find a specialist stone merchant; the garden centre may be able to suggest one. For the best effect, keep to stones of one colour – say warm honey tones or blue-grey granites – and provide the interest by varying the size and texture throughout the garden. Use chippings to create a 'stream' running through banks of cobbles, with larger rocks grouped in outcrops.

Conifers

Striking shapes are what is wanted in this type of garden. Combine conifers with naturally arching, ground-hugging and upright shapes into a grouping, but use at least one really outrageous type as a specimen plant for a focal point. Weeping conifers, such as *Cedrus atlantica* 'Glauca Pendula' and *Sequoiadendron giganteum* 'Pendulum', are superb for this purpose. (Despite being a form of giant redwood, the sequoiadendron is a small tree suitable for a small garden!). On a smaller scale, go for a novelty, such as *Cryptomeria japonica* 'Spiralis', which has leaves like ringlets.

Juniperus squamata 'Blue Alps'

Juniperus communis 'Depressa Aurea'

Leucanthemum hosmariense

Dianthus 'Spring Star'

Suitable trees

Where space permits, a suitable tree completes this type of garden. Again, it needs to be a striking architectural type, and capable of withstanding hot dry conditions at times. Some of the more dramatic and unusual birches, such as *Betula albosinensis* (pink and orange bark) or *Betula jacquemontii* (dazzling silver-white bark) are ideal. They have brightly coloured trunks and a good shape that provide winter interest, and a light canopy of leaves that does not create deep shade or a serious leaf problem in autumn. (A deep layer of wet and slimy leaves would be difficult to clear from a stone garden.)

Stately blooms of *Papaver orientale* 'Patty's Plum' catch the morning light.

PART THREE

CHOOSING PLANTS

Depending on the design style you choose, you could fill a small garden with many small plants or a few larger ones. But to make the most of the space, choose plants that offer you more than just one reason for buying them.

PLANTS FOR SMALL GARDENS

An enormous number of plants are suitable for small gardens. Since so many houses nowadays have small – even tiny – plots, garden centres cater much more for this group of gardeners than for the owners of huge gardens, so it is not difficult to find a good range of appropriately sized subjects. Even so, it is possible to make mistakes. Before buying, look at the plant care label or information boards alongside plant displays and check the plant's height and spread. With trees or shrubs, also look for the size after ten years. These figures are not totally reliable, since the growth of individual plants will vary according to the climate and conditions where they are planted, but it is a good general guide and gives a useful indication of likely growth rate and how far apart to plant. But do not feel that because the garden is small you must restrict yourself only to miniature plants – far from it. The effect you want, the time you are prepared to spend looking after the garden and the style of planting you prefer all help to determine the kinds of plants you choose.

Above: Annuals provide instant colour over a long flowering season, but because you replace when they come to an end, you can easily change your colour scheme or planting style as often as you like. Use them in containers around the garden.

Below: Japanese maples look ornamental all year round and stay compact. Varieties have purple-red leaves, finely divided leaves or green leaves with autumn colours.

Below: Alpines are naturally compact and charming and also make good container plants. The most compact forms can be left for five years or more before you need to replant a sink garden such as this one.

Left: Save space by growing climbers up through shrubs. Naturally compact *Clematis texensis* makes the perfect climbing partner for teaming with bush roses (here 'Blushing Lucy'). Both need hard annual pruning at the same time.

Below: Breeders are constantly bringing out new and dwarf forms of traditional old favourites. These sunflowers only grow about 30cm(12in) tall, but are perfect replicas of their tall cousins. They make wonderful plants for tubs or windowboxes.

Right: As the demand for compact plants increases, plants that were once very unusual become widely available. Diascia is one of the most successful 'new' introductions. They are slightly tender, sometimes shortlived perennials ideal for containers or well-drained beds.

Plants that can regularly be cut hard back

Many shrubs grown for their foliage can be cut hard back. This makes them produce larger foliage than before and stops them flowering, thus emphasising their dramatic shapes and striking foliage

Ailanthus altissima *(tree of heaven). A real giant; cut back to 30cm(12in) each spring to keep it compact and encourage the 90cm(3ft)-long leaves.*

Catalpa bignonioides *(Indian bean tree) and* Paulownia tomentosa *are fast-growing large trees with huge leaves. Young trees can be cut down to a few feet (60-90cm/2-3ft) above ground level every two to three years to keep them compact and encourage enormous foliage.*

Cercis siliquastrum *(Judas tree). One of the few good, compact trees for a small garden. It will regenerate if cut back hard occasionally. The foliage will be good but it will not flower well.*

Cornus alba *'Elegantissima' and 'Spaethii'. Cut older stems down close to the ground in early spring to encourage bigger foliage and strong red stems that show up well in winter*

Ornamental elders. Cut back to 90cm(3ft) above ground every two to three years to keep them shrubby instead of treelike, and to encourage better foliage without flowers or fruit.

Eucalyptus. Most species can be cut back to within 15-30cm (6-12in) of ground level every few years. This makes them grow bushy instead of treelike, and makes them produce the more attractive juvenile foliage (which is circular in some species) instead of the long narrow leaves of the adult plant.

Spiraea japonica *var.* fortunei *'Goldflame'. Cut back to 15cm (6in) above ground in spring to encourage stronger shoots and larger leaves, and discourage flowering (the pink flowers clash with the gold-orange leaves).*

Treat Philadelphus coronarius *'Aureus' the same way to produce better foliage.*

Keep *Acer negundo* 'Flamingo' compact by cutting it down close to the ground every few years in spring.

CHOOSING A GOOD PLANT

When choosing garden plants, most people buy on impulse, picking whatever takes their fancy from the plants in flower. (Buying a plant in flower means that you can be sure that it is the correct variety.) But some plants need particular conditions and it is all too easy to get them home, only to find that you have nowhere suitable to put them. Worse still, you plant them in the wrong spot and they do not grow. Plants need matching to the situations where they are to grow. This is why it is essential to know your garden, the soil type and whether it is acid, alkaline or neutral, and which areas are in full sun, partial or total shade at given times of the day. Then by planting the right plants in the right places, they will be able to do their best. Nowadays, most garden centres and nurseries provide full information about the individual preferences of each plant they sell. Most popular plants will grow in any reasonable garden soil, but some are useful for particular 'problem' places. Always start by choosing the best-quality plants you can find. They will perform well from the start; much better than waiting for second best plants to catch up.

Take your plants home carefully. Carry them upright and protect them from damage. Do not leave plants in a hot, airless vehicle and do not let them protrude from a sunroof or window as you drive home; ask the garden centre to deliver tall plants. Once home, take plants outside and water them thoroughly before planting as soon as possible.

Choosing a good climber

Small size is no reason to reject a plant, but here the sparseness of the leaves suggests that the plant is potbound.

Flowers at the top and few leaves indicate that it has been in the pot too long.

Right: Select climbers, here clematis, with bright green, unblemished foliage. Pallid, yellowing leaves may indicate that the plant has been in the pot too long and is lacking both nutrients and water.

This plant is full of flower but the stems have not been tied in, which is evidence of neglect.

Choosing a good fuchsia

There are signs of rust on the leaves. This problem spreads quickly and could affect your other fuchsias.

This plant has been stopped once and is becoming straggly. It may have had too little light and has also become potbound.

This plant has been pinched out too far up the stem and is a poor shape. It would be difficult to do anything constructive with such a plant.

A generally neglected plant with signs of rust. A hard pinch back will improve the shape, but it may be best to avoid buying it at all.

A fine bushy, healthy plant immediately catches the eye. A nursery selling plants like this is worth a visit.

Right: Always examine plants for signs of disease or insect infestation. Look at the stem and underneath the leaves as well as on top. If the base is a shiny brown, it could be that the plant has had problems with grey mould (botrytis) at some stage.

Low-growing herbs

Avoid plants that are limp or drooping, with few sparse stems and pale leaves, and pots with a mass of root protruding from the base. Make sure that the soil has not dried out and shrunk away from the sides of the pot.

Buying perennials

Because true perennials die down in winter, the best time to buy them is in spring, when a few shoots have appeared. Choose healthy-looking plants with rich green leaves or plump growth buds. Avoid any with pale or sickly foliage, or those that have been shredded by pests.

Shrubs and trees

SUITABLE TREES

Trees are a useful feature in a small garden. Not only do they provide height, which can often be lacking from a miniaturised landscape, but because they grow on a single stem or trunk they do not occupy as much floor space as bulkier shrubs, thus leaving room for other plants to be grown underneath them. Trees are a good way of adding an extra tier of plant material to a small garden, and they provide a natural framework for climbers to grow on, which again enables several plants to be grown in the space normally occupied by one. However, it pays to choose with care. Many of the trees described as 'small' in nursery catalogues are only small in comparison with large trees. Plenty of flowering cherries, rowans and weeping pears will reach 6m(20ft) or more within 10-15 years, which makes them far too big for many small gardens. Of the larger small trees, amelanchier, *Crataegus laevigata* 'Paul's Scarlet', crab apples, such as *Malus hupehensis* 'John Downie', flowering cherry *Prunus pendula* 'Pendula Rosea', mulberry, and edible quince (*Cydonia oblonga*) are all good choices, as they provide seasonal attractions at several different times of year and only reach about 4.5m(15ft) high.

Where a treelike shape is needed but space limits the choice to something much smaller, there are still plenty of options. Choose plants that are basically treelike shrubs, such as tree hibiscus *(Hibiscus syriacus)*, tree peony or Japanese maple (*Acer palmatum* cultivars). Or go for shrubs that have been grafted onto an upright stem to make a small weeping or standard tree: the Kilmarnock willow (*Salix caprea* 'Kilmarnock'), the pink-green-and-cream variegated *Salix integra* 'Albomaculata', and shrub roses, such as 'Canary Bird', all make good small trees. When grown on a short trunk, the stems of *Pyrus salicifolia* 'Pendula' (the weeping pear) can arch right down to the ground.

Training a shrub as a standard

Some shrubs can be trained into standard shapes to make mini trees, and this is increasingly being done to cater for small gardens. Flowering currant *(Ribes sanguineum), Buddleja globosa, Hibiscus syriacus,* weigela and *Clerodendrum trichotomum* are easily trained as standards at home in much the same way as you would grow a standard fuchsia from a cutting. You can also convert an older plant with at least one good straight upright stem by removing the lower branches.

Unusual species

Azara microphylla
Chordospartium stevensonii
Koelreuteria paniculata
Liquidambar styraciflua 'Parasol'
Sophora microphylla

Shrubs to train as small trees

Acer palmatum cultivars
Arbutus unedo
Buddleja globosa
Clerodendrum trichotomum
Hibiscus syriacus
Populus alba 'Richardii'
Ribes sanguineum
Weigela

Small flowering trees

Amelanchier lamarckii (also good autumn colour)
Caragana arborescens
Cercis siliquastrum (judas tree)
Crataegus 'Paul's Scarlet'
Prunus 'Amanogawa'
Prunus cerasifera 'Pissardii'
Prunus incisa
Prunus subhirtella 'Pendula Rosea'

Below: *Pyrus salicifolia* 'Pendula' makes a small to medium-sized tree. Use it as a focal point in a lawn or at the back of a border.

Decorative fruiting small trees

Cydonia oblonga (fruiting quince)
Malus 'Dartmouth'
Malus 'John Downie'
Malus 'Golden Hornet'
Malus 'Red Jade'
Morus alba (white mulberry)
Morus nigra (black mulberry)

Small trees for striking foliage

Acer japonicum 'Aureum'
Acer negundo 'Flamingo' (pink /green variegated leaves)
Acer palmatum cultivars
Acer pseudoplatanus 'Brilliantissimum' (20cm/10in coppery pink young foliage)
Gleditsia triacanthos 'Ruby Lace'
Gleditsia triacanthos 'Sunburst'
Pyrus salicifolia 'Pendula'
Robinia pseudoacacia 'Frisia'
Salix caprea 'Kilmarnock'
Sorbus aria x *hostii*

For colourful/peeling bark

Acer griseum
Betula albosinensis
Betula papyrifera
Betula pendula 'Youngii'
Betula utilis jacquemontii

Keeping trees artificially compact

Crab apple varieties are now available grafted onto dwarfing rootstocks, making previously medium or large kinds suitable for planting in a small garden.

Trees can be coppiced (cut down almost to ground level each spring) to keep them smaller but with bigger leaves. These include *Ailanthus altissima, Catalpa bignonioides* 'Aurea', eucalyptus and *Paulownia tomentosa. Cercis siliquastrum* also regenerates if cut down hard.

Trees that are regularly trimmed and trained remain compact compared with unrestricted plants of the same species. Hence espalier, wall or wall-trained shrubs can easily be kept to the required size, as can standard bays, topiary evergreens or cloud-trimmed conifers.

Trees in pots stay compact since the roots are restricted; the bigger the pot, the bigger the tree can grow. Use pots to keep large woodland trees, fruit trees or decorative garden trees a suitable size for a small garden.

A more extreme form of pot growing is bonsai, where very tiny containers are used. Root and shoot pruning is more drastic, and branches are forced into gnarled craggy shapes using copper wire.

Above: Unlike many gold-leaved trees, *Robinia pseudoacacia* 'Frisia' keeps its bright colour all season. Even in winter, when it loses its leaves, the tree makes a nice shape. It slowly grows to 7.75m(25ft).

Above: Grafted onto a tall stem and grown as a standard, the dwarf pink-green-and-cream variegated *Salix integra* 'Hakuro-nishiki' makes a wonderful small tree.

Salix caprea 'Kilmarnock' grows no taller than the height of the stem it is grafted onto.

Acer palmatum cultivars are sometimes grafted onto short stems to make them into small standards.

EVERGREENS

Evergreens are the backbone of any garden where all-year-round interest, privacy and shelter are important. In this case, plant the garden with a mixture of two-thirds evergreens for year-round effect and one-third flowering shrubs, plus bulbs, perennials and ground cover plants to provide seasonal highlights. Even in 'normal' gardens, a small percentage of evergreens are useful as background foliage, and many traditional hedging plants, such as privet, box, holly, laurel and yew, are evergreen and act as a permanent framework to the garden. Potentially large foliage evergreens withstand clipping well, so their size can be easily restricted. Where they are grown as specimen plants (variegated forms of holly and privet are often used in this way) they can be pruned to size. In a very small space, ivy can be incredibly effective. For example, a tiny, dark, sunken courtyard planted entirely with drifts of different varieties of ivy, in a huge range of leaf shapes, variegations, and textures, plus only a few large stones for contrast, can look outstanding despite the difficult situation. You can also use 'ropes' of ivy very effectively to outline paths, steps or beds to add winter detail to a tiny town garden.

Above: Ivies are endlessly versatile in a small garden. Use them in containers, especially year-round ones, and winter hanging baskets. Let them self cling to unattractive walls or form them into ropes to outline beds or paths. Choose small-leaved ivies, as the plants remain more compact.

Left: Evergreens form a big part of the year-round framework of a garden, and in a small space it is a good idea to choose kinds that offer not only striking shapes but also a second benefit, such as flowers or coloured or variegated foliage, as shown here. All of these remain very compact.

Versatile evergreens

For general use in beds and borders, there are many naturally compact or slow-growing evergreens that provide flower and berries plus great foliage or architectural shapes without outgrowing their welcome.

Arbutus unedo (strawberry tree)
Brachyglottis (Dunedin Group) 'Sunshine' (formerly *Senecio greyi*)
Ceanothus thyrsiflorus var. *repens*
Choisya ternata 'Sundance'
Danae racemosa (Alexandrian laurel)
Daphne odora
Euonymus fortunei var. *radicans*
Genista lydia
Hebe
Helianthemum
Lavender
Myrtus communis tarentina
Olearia haastii (daisy bush)
Phlomis fruticosa (Jerusalem sage)
Rosemary
Santolina
Viburnum davidii
Vinca (periwinkle)

On acid soil:
Gaultheria mucronata
Heathers
Kalmia angustifolia
Pachysandra terminalis
Dwarf rhododendrons
Skimmia

Coping with large evergreens

Large evergreens, such as bamboos, fatsia, camellia and pittosporum, can also be kept compact by growing them in containers, which restricts the roots and produces a natural dwarfing effect. Some large evergreens, such as pyracantha, fremontodendron and evergreen ceanothus, can be comfortably accommodated by training them flat against a wall.

Above: Helianthemums are ultra-compact shrubs 20-60cm (8-24in) tall, depending on the variety. They have masses of fragile-looking papery flowers in bright hot colours, from late spring to midsummer. Trim lightly after flowering to keep a good shape.

Below: Hebes must be the ultimate, compact, small-garden evergreen. They are available in a range of sizes and a wide variety of flower colours. All have a long flowering season. Grow them in beds or tubs. Large-leaved hebes grow tallest and are less hardy.

Right: Although you might not think so from the size some species reach, many bamboos make extremely good evergreen plants for containers. They look particularly striking in decorated ceramic pots, such as this one housing *Bambusa* 'Aurea'. To keep them growing well, repot bamboos into fresh soil-based potting mix in spring every 2-3 years.

ARCHITECTURAL PLANTS

A garden consisting entirely of short plants would look very dull; even a small garden needs some height to contrast with low, ground-hugging shapes. A few large, striking specimen shrubs are the answer. Hamamelis (witch hazel) or *Mahonia* x *media* 'Charity' team well with more compact shrubs to form a group, or to add height at the back of a border. Plants with particularly good architectural shapes, such as *Yucca filamentosa* or *Aralia elata* 'Variegata', make stunning specimen features used on their own in a paved courtyard or patio, perhaps surrounded by a circle of cobblestones, or in minimalistic gardens of gravel and stones. *Cornus controversa* 'Variegata' makes a spectacular specimen, with its tiered layers of branches. You can cut off the lower branches to make an unusual flat-topped small tree. Specimen shrubs with a more conventional shape but a striking appearance include *Magnolia stellata*. In a sheltered, slightly shaded spot or in a more traditional-style small garden it can be grown in the lawn. Surround it with a circle of bare soil to avoid grass competing for nutrients and water and to prevent the base of the stems being damaged by the lawnmower or rotary cord trimmer.

Below: Cordyline palms *(Cordyline australis)* are fairly hardy, but in cold or wet areas grow them in containers and move them under cover in winter to protect them from the worst weather.

Spiky shapes
Cordyline australis
Phormiums
Yucca gloriosa

Prickly/spiky foliage
Acanthus spinosus (a perennial)
Colletia armata
Colletia cruciana
Mahonia sp.
Paliurus spina-christi
Poncirus trifoliata (Japanese bitter orange)

Finely cut foliage
Acer palmatum dissectum
Caragana arborescens 'Lorbergii'
Rhamnus frangula 'Aspleniifolia'
Rhus glabra 'Laciniata'
Salix babylonica 'Crispa' (leaves curled in tight rings)
Sambucus nigra 'Linearis'
Sambucus racemosa 'Plumosa Aurea'
Sambucus racemosa 'Tenuifolia'
Sorbus 'Chinese Lace'
Syringa x *laciniata*

Reed-shaped stems
Arundo donax
Bamboos (any)
Miscanthus sp.

Contorted stems
Chaenomeles speciosa 'Tortuosa'
Corylus avellana 'Contorta'
Robinia pseudoacacia 'Lace Lady'
Tilia platyphyllos 'Tortuosa'

Peeling/colourful/patterned bark
Acer capillipes (snake bark maple)
Acer griseum
Arbutus menziesii
Betula albosinensis
Betula utilis jacquemontii
Broussonetia papyrifera (paper mulberry)

Large/striking leaves
Coppiced ailanthus, catalpa, eucalyptus and paulownia (see page 71)
Fatsia japonica
Ficus carica (fig)
Trachycarpus fortunei

Dramatic flowers and foliage
Carpenteria californica
Dendromecon rigida
Fremontodendron californicum
Romneya coulteri
Sophora microphylla
Tree peony (any)
Trochodendron aralioides

Narrowish upright shapes
Ballerina apple trees and 'Maypole' crab apple
Ginkgo biloba 'Fastigiata'
Malus 'Golden Hornet'

Weeping shapes
Betula pendula 'Youngii'
Caragana arborescens 'Pendula'
Malus 'Red Jade'
Prunus subhirtella 'Pendula Rosea'
Pyrus salicifolia 'Pendula'
Salix caprea 'Kilmarnock'
Salix integra 'Hakuro-nishiki'

Striking shapes
Aralia elata 'Variegata'
Corokia cotoneaster (wire netting bush)
Genista aetnensis
Melianthus major
Musa basjoo
Pseudopanax crassifolia (New Zealand lancewood)

Above: The hardy banana *(Musa basjoo)* is a real stunner if you want lush, exotic, tropical-looking foliage. It is only truly hardy in milder areas and even here may die down to ground level in winter. If grown in a pot, it can be moved under cover.

Right: *Aralia elata* 'Variegata' makes a wonderful shape with 'layers' of tiered foliage, but loses its leaves in winter. It is perfect for a small garden, reaching 3m(10ft) in time. Trim off the lower branches if you want to turn it into a tree.

Making the most of a specimen plant

Unless you are in a hurry to see the final effect, there is no need to pay extra for a large plant; small specimens establish themselves better than large ones and quickly catch up in good conditions. Plant them a suitable distance from other plants in the garden to avoid over-crowding, shading or the risk of smothering smaller species. Select a site where the full beauty of the plant can be appreciated from various parts of the garden. Place it so that it becomes part of several different views when seen from different directions.

Since a small garden only has room to house a very few of the larger shrubs, be sure to choose only the most striking examples. Plants that provide the right effect for the style of garden and that suit the site and growing conditions are the best value for money. Choose only top-quality plants, well-furnished with evenly spaced stems and healthy foliage. Species that provide interest in more than one season are specially valuable; witch hazel, for example, has autumn foliage tints and flowers in winter and early spring.

Below: *Mahonia* 'Charity' has neat rows of prickly evergreen foliage that looks good all year round. Even the flowers are architectural, appearing in cartwheel shapes all over the top of the plant in winter. They are beautifully scented, rather like lily-of-the-valley.

CLIMBERS AND WALL PLANTS

Climbers and wall plants are a good way of fitting potentially large plants into a small garden. By growing tall climbing roses, honeysuckle and clematis over arches, it is possible to coil long stems around the uprights and 'concertina' them into a smaller space. This technique also makes them flower better, since more of the stems are close to the horizontal, and thus form more flower buds. And training large shrubs, such as pyracantha, *Fremontodendron californicum* or evergreen ceanothus, flat against a wall is often the only way to accommodate them when space is short. They are also much easier to manage. However, in general, the more naturally compact types of climber, and those that can be successfully pruned, are the easiest to cope with in small gardens. Passionflower (*Passiflora caerulea*) is a good choice as it can be hard pruned each spring without sacrificing summer flowers. Check the ultimate size on plant care labels or in catalogues or a book before buying. This is vital with climbing or rambler roses, as some grow huge.

Annual climbers

If space is very short, then annual climbers are the best choice. They give almost instant colour, yet are conveniently cleared at the end of the season, letting you start afresh each year.

Cobaea (cup-and-saucer vine)
Eccremocarpus
Ipomoea (morning glory)
Lathyrus odoratus (sweet pea)
Maurandella (formerly *Asarina*) *antirrhiniflora* (climbing snapdragon)
Rhodochiton atrosanguineus
Thunbergia (black-eyed Susan)

Below: Climbing roses and clematis make a perfect plant association that always works well. By growing two or even three plants over the same bit of wall, you double or treble the interest from the same space. But consider potential pruning problems when deciding on varieties.

Clematis for the small garden

Choose clematis varieties that flower on the current year's growth (these are the ones that flower from midsummer onwards, including the late-flowering viticella kinds). All of these are cut back to 15cm(6in) above the ground in spring. Or choose naturally compact 'no-prune' varieties. Avoid species clematis such as montana, orientalis and tangutica, as they grow much bigger than hybrids and are best left unpruned.

Naturally compact clematis that need no pruning:

Clematis alpina species
Clematis florida species
'Alice Fisk' (red/grey)
'John Warren' (blue)
'Lady Northcliffe' (lavender-blue)
'Louise Rowe' (pale mauve)
'Miss Bateman' (white)
'Snow Queen' (white)
'Violet Charm' (blue-violet)

Prune hard in early spring:

Clematis x *durandii*
'Allanah' (red)
'Elsa Spath' (violet)
'Hagley Hybrid' (shell pink)
'Madame Edouard André' (claret)
'Margot Koster' (pale mauve)
'Pink Fantasy' (pale pink)
'Prince Charles' (mauvish blue)
'Rouge Cardinal' (burgundy)

Climbing and rambling roses

Naturally compact varieties include:
'Aloha' (deep pink)
'Bantry Bay' (medium pink)
'Compassion' (pale apricot pink)
'Masquerade' (tricoloured: red orange and yellow)
'New Dawn' (pale blush pink)
'Schoolgirl' (orange)
'Swan Lake' (white),
'White Cockade' (white)
'Zéphirine Drouhin' (pink, thornless)

Compact climbers

Solanum jasminoides 'Variegata'. Lemon/lime variegated leaves and white potato flowers in summer.

Vitis vinifera 'Purpurea'. The red leaves turn purple in the autumn as bunches of small, sweet, edible purple grapes appear among them.

Lonicera x *italica* Harlequin ('Sherlite'). Variegated leaves and three-tone flowers of pink, apricot and gold flowers in early to midsummer.

Jasminum officinale Fiona Sunrise ('Frojas'). Gold foliage and white scented flowers in summer and autumn.

Above: By choosing naturally compact varieties of climbing or rambling rose, you can virtually eliminate pruning; deadheading is all you normally need to do.

Right: Passionflower *(Passiflora caerulea)* flowers all summer and can reach a good size. Control it by hard pruning every spring.

Wisteria for the small garden

Wisteria are so big that they are difficult to accommodate in confined spaces (although they can be trained around the edge of a car port, gazebo or similar structure). A much better way to grow them is trained as standard plants, when they remain very compact and also flower much sooner than wall-trained plants, which can take seven years or more to bloom.

COMPACT SHRUBS

Some widely available shrubs, such as hebe, helianthemum, potentilla and *Genista lydia*, are naturally compact. You can also get compact varieties of shrubs that normally take up quite a bit of room – some berberis, for instance. These are all ideal for creating the effect of a normal shrubbery on a small scale. Their big advantage is that they never outgrow their welcome, so you do not need to keep cutting them back hard to fit. This means that, unlike bigger shrubs when treated this way, you never risk missing out on a season's flowering while they recover. Using compact shrubs also allows you to fit more of them into the space and thus create a varied tapestry of colour over several seasons. Planting one normal-sized shrub in the same space would provide only one set of flowers and foliage. Compact shrubs have other uses, too. Many of the drought-resistant kinds, such as hebes, make ideal subjects for planting permanently in pots or windowboxes, so you do not need to keep replanting these containers with new bedding. Those with long flowering seasons or good foliage are ideal here. But there are some situations where even the most compact of the normal garden centre range of shrubs are too big.

Above: Pocket shrubs with more than one attraction are especially valuable for a small garden. *Weigela* 'Florida Variegata' has good cream-green variegated leaves that complement its own flowers in midsummer, and those of its neighbours for the rest of the season.

Shrubs/trees that are miniature versions of full-sized plants. Suitable for rock features - very slow growing.

Betula nana, fragile-looking mini tree 30-45cm(12-18in) high.
Forsythia viridissima 'Bronxensis', covered in yellow flowers in spring. 30cm(1ft).
Jasminum parkeri, low mound with yellow unscented flowers in spring. 20cm(8in).
Rhododendron 'Chiff-Chaff', yellow flowers in spring. 38cm(15in). (Other similarly sized varieties are available from rock plant specialists.)
Salix 'Boydii', gnarled stems with grey felty leaves. 30cm(1ft).
Salix lanata, a compact, characterful mini tree with woolly catkins in spring and crinkly grey leaves.120 x 90cm(4 x 3ft).
Sorbus reducta, suckers to form a clump, good autumn colour and red berries. 30cm(1ft).
Ulmus parvifolia, miniature Chinese elm, 45cm(18in) high.

Miniature gardens

Sometimes you need plants that are true scaled-down versions of larger species. An enthusiast's rock garden, for instance, in which the whole garden is given over to rock plants and gravel screes, would need authentic-looking shrubs on a similar scale. (Some compact conifers can be useful here, too.) And if you had a very specialised feature in the garden, such as a model village or a miniature railway, then you would need plants that were on a similar scale to the buildings to create a realistic effect. Such plants do exist and while they are fun to seek out, you will not find them at your usual sources. The best places to find the unusual varieties involved are specialist alpine plant nurseries; use mail order to buy from distant suppliers.

Shrubs that are compact versions of normally large plants

Berberis thunbergii 'Bagatelle', globular reddish-purple foliage. Height and spread: 30 x 30cm (1 x 1ft).
Berberis thunbergii 'Bonanza Gold', golden foliage. 45 x 30cm (18in x 1ft).
Berberis thunbergii 'Helmond Pillar', narrow upright plant with reddish-purple foliage. 120 x 30cm(4 x 1ft).
Berberis thunbergii 'Aurea', globular plant with yellow foliage, turning green in summer. 90 x 90cm(3 x 3ft).
Berberis thunbergii 'Atropurpurea Nana', globular plant with glowing red-purple foliage. 60 x 60cm(2 x 2ft.)
Ceanothus 'Blue Mound', hardy evergreen variety with deep blue flowers. 90 x 90cm(3 x 3ft).
Cytisus kewensis, compact mound- shaped broom with cream flowers in spring. 40 x 40cm(16 x 16in).
Ilex crenata 'Golden Gem', gold and green foliage, clip or grow as bush. 60 x 60cm(2 x 2ft).
Philadelphus 'Erectus', a compact variety with upright stems and scented flowers. 150 x 90cm(5 x 3ft)
Philadelphus 'Manteau D'Hermine', a compact variety with white scented flowers in early summer.120 x 90cm(4 x 3ft).
Spiraea betulifolia aemiliana, hummock-shaped shrub with stunning autumn foliage colours. 60 x 60cm(2 x 2ft)

Other naturally compact shrubs

Ceratostigma willmottianum
Cistus
Daphne burkwoodii
Daphne mezereum
Erica
Hebe
Helianthemum
Lavender
Potentilla
Rosemary
Sarcococca humilis
Weigela florida 'Foliis Purpureis'
Weigela 'Florida Variegata'

Compact berberis varieties

Left: Most berberis make quite large spreading shrubs, but several compact varieties are also available. Those shown here include columnar, globular and compact shrubby shapes in a variety of foliage colours. All are easy to grow and trouble-free.

COMPACT CONIFERS

Compact conifers encompass a fascinating selection of evergreen shapes, foliage textures and colours, providing a year-round framework that really brings a collection of rock plants, heathers or dwarf perennials and grasses to life. You can get completely prostrate mat-forming plants, neat dome-shapes, eccentric craggy shapes or almost geometrically precise spires and cones. And you can have any of those shapes in dark turquoise or powder blue, bronze-tinged, yellow or old gold, and several shades of green, with long needles, short bristlelike leaves or lacy-looking foliage. Some species are better for some jobs than others. Pines and junipers are the most drought-tolerant types, best for growing in rock features, such as screes or gravel gardens, and between paving. These are also the best kinds for containers, as they are likely to dry out occasionally in this situation. (Bonsai conifers in tiny pots need watering twice a day in summer to stop them drying right out and shedding their needles.) Some specially striking small conifers make compact specimen plants due to their striking shapes: *Abies koreana*, which has bright violet cones even on small plants, is a modest, rather than dwarf conifer, and *Chamaecyparis pisifera* 'Filifera Aurea' has golden threadlike foliage that resembles a loose haystack.

Compact conifers for alpine troughs and sinks

Chamaecyparis lawsoniana 'Gnome'
C. l. 'Green Globe'
C. l. 'Minima Aurea'
Chamaecyparis obtusa 'Kosteri'
C. o. 'Pygmaea'
Cryptomeria japonica 'Nana'
Cryptomeria 'Vilmoriniana'
Cryptomeria 'Vilmoriniana Compacta')
Juniperus communis 'Compressa'
Picea glauca var. *albertiana* 'Alberta Globe'
Thuja occidentalis 'Tiny Tim'
Tsuga canadensis 'Jeddeloh'

Compact conifers for a small rock feature, gravel or stone garden

Juniperus communis 'Compressa'
Juniperus horizontalis 'Montana'
Picea abies 'Gregoryana'
Picea mariana 'Nana'
Picea glauca var. *albertiana* 'Conica'
Pinus densiflora 'Umbraculifera'
Pinus strobus 'Nana'

Small 'character' conifers for use as evergreen shrubs

Abies koreana
Chamaecyparis lawsoniana 'Ellwood's Gold'
Chamaecyparis obtusa 'Tetragona Aurea'
Chamaecyparis pisifera 'Boulevard'
Chamaecyparis pisifera 'Filifera Aurea'
Cryptomeria japonica 'Spiralis'
Picea orientalis 'Aurea'
Taxus baccata 'Standishii'
Thuja occidentalis 'Rheingold'
Thuja orientalis 'Aurea Nana'

Below: When grown in a sunny spot, *Thuja occidentalis* 'Rheingold' develops lovely foxy-auburn tints. It makes a bushy shape about 107cm(42in) tall, ideal for a small specimen shrub.

Chamaecyparis lawsoniana 'Minima Aurea'. This is slow growing, with tightly packed, rather curly gold foliage that contrasts well with the deep green centre of the bush.

Juniperus communis 'Compressa'. This is one of the most tolerant and popular garden conifers, rarely reaching 90cm(3ft) high, even when it is quite elderly. It forms a neat upright cone with very dense tidy foliage.

What does 'compact conifer' mean?

The term 'compact conifers' is a rather imprecise one. Take it to mean 'very slow-growing conifers that stay small for a long time'. Given long enough in good growing conditions, many can eventually achieve quite a respectable size. So if you are shopping for plants for a rock feature or for general small garden use, the thing to look for is the size after ten years. This is usually given on the label along with the plant's other statistics. A plant that grows 5-15cm (2-6in) a year (height at 10 years 1.5m/5ft or less) could be considered small enough for a rock feature, where the poor dry growing conditions would also help ensure that it remains compact. A conifer with a growth rate of up to 20cm(12in) a year (height at 10 years 3m/10ft) is small enough to use as an evergreen shrub or hedge in a small garden, but would soon outgrow a rockery.

Above: Junipers are the more rugged of the conifers.Their spiky 'metallic' foliage looks good set off against smooth pebbles.

Picea glauca var. *albertiana* 'Conica'. This cultivar develops into a neat, densely packed pyramid with bright green new growth in spring. Young plants reach 90cm(3ft) high in ten years.

Picea mariana 'Nana'. This very dwarf form has blue summer foliage and is perfect for rock gardens. It reaches 40cm(16in) high and less than 30cm(12in) across in ten years.

Picea glauca var. *albertiana* 'Alberta Globe'. This is a rounded form with bright green spring foliage. It reaches 60cm(2ft) high in ten years.

Above: Many small, slow-growing conifers have irregular or even craggy shapes that make good accents in an evergreen garden.

COMPACT AND MINIATURE ROSES

If you like the look of roses but do not have room for a conventional rose bed, you can achieve a similar effect in a small space by using naturally compact patio roses, miniature roses or ground cover roses. However, these pint-sized variations also have other uses for which full-sized roses would not be suitable and this makes them much more versatile. For example, patio roses can be grown in beds on their own, as an edging around a border or in containers. Use miniature roses in raised beds, on top of hollow-topped walls around a patio and similar positions. Ground cover roses planted around patio roses make a contemporary version of a traditional rose garden on a small scale, while prostrate and ground-hugging types are brilliant for covering a bank or trailing over a low wall. 'Nozomi' is particularly sensational when grafted onto a short upright stem; its naturally arching habit produces a delightful small weeping tree that looks like a waterfall of blossom when in flower, ideal for a patio container or small border. Small arching varieties that repeat-flower all summer, such as Magic Carpet, also make good plants for hanging baskets.

Miniature roses
Miniature roses usually grow about 30-45cm(12-18in) high and have clusters of delightful, delicate, scaled-down flowers. They need better growing conditions than normal roses and appreciate well-drained soil and a sheltered spot. The stems are often affected by late frosts. The plants are easily rooted from cuttings and grow well on their own roots, often becoming less vigorous than the same varieties when grafted onto rootstocks. They need no pruning except the removal of frost-damaged stems in late spring. Suitable ones include:

Angela Rippon
Bush Baby
'Little Flirt'
Pandora
Rise 'n' Shine
'Stacey Sue'
'Stars 'n' Stripes'

Patio roses
Patio roses are basically dwarf floribundas. They grow bushy, up to about 45cm(18in) tall and have clusters of flowers at the tips of the shoots. Popular examples include:

Duchess of York
Gentle Touch
Gingernut
Perestroika
Sweet Dream
Top Marks

Right: Choose the right rose for the job. Although there is very little difference in height between the various types, some have a neat upright habit, while others are positively wide-ranging. Allow sufficient space for them all to develop if you plan to grow them in the same bed.

Above: One of the most popular patio roses ever is Sweet Dream. It grows into a neat shape, the flowers are a good long-lasting colour and they stand up well to rain. If you want an unusual low-flowering hedge, try a row of Sweet Dream roses.

Ground cover roses

Ground cover roses include those that spread, arch or are totally prostrate. Take care when choosing ground cover roses for small gardens as not all types are small; some, such as *Rosa wichurana,* can spread almost 6m(20ft), although its variegated form is a very much smaller plant. Like patios roses, ground cover roses need only light pruning to retain their shape. Most named varieties are good, compact kinds. They include:

Avon
Essex
Ferdy
Flower Carpet
Grouse
Magic Carpet
'Nozomi'
R. x *jacksonii* 'Max Graf'
Partridge
Suffolk
Sussex

Above: Ground cover roses have a dwarf spreading habit and long flowering season. Give them a sunny spot with rich soil. They only need light pruning. Ideally, plant them through perforated plastic sheet covered with bark chippings, since the prickly stems are difficult to weed between once they cover the ground.

Right: Standard roses are a good way of adding height to a border, and in a really tiny garden could substitute for a small tree. Prune the top just like a normal rose bush, cutting the bushy stems back to about 15cm(6in) from the top of the trunk in late spring. Remove shoots growing from the sides and base of the trunk.

ANNUALS AND BEDDING PLANTS

Despite all the work needed to grow, plant and look after bedding plants, they are more popular than ever, especially for growing in containers and hanging baskets on the patio. Bedding plants are ideal for instant colour, as they are generally planted out just as they are starting to bloom. They also have a long flowering season and prolific blooming potential, so they can be relied on to keep a small area ablaze with colour for months on end, unlike other kinds of plants that come and go during the summer, leaving large expanses of green. Nowadays, the trend in bedding plants is away from traditional delicate pastels and old formal favourites, such as *Begonia semperflorens* and ageratum, towards stronger, bolder colours, such as reds and orange. Subtropical-looking tender perennial plants, such as datura, canna and hedychium (ginger lily), are particularly popular. Named varieties of gazania and compact 'patio' dahlias are very much in demand, while species fuchsias and shrubby salvias (which look nothing like the bedding varieties) in bright reds and blues are also becoming very sought-after. Exotic-looking annual climbers, such as mutisia, *Mina lobata* and *Lablab purpureus* (hyacinth bean) are perfect for covering arches or trellis quickly and a decorative way of screening sheds or walls.

The best plants for a continuous display of flowers in containers and hanging baskets

Argyranthemum
Brachyscome
Fuchsia (bush and trailing)
Lobelia
Petunia
Swiss balcon pelargoniums (a specially free-flowering ivy leaf type with plenty of small flowers)
Zonal pelargoniums

Scented annuals and bedding plants

Lathyrus odoratus (sweet pea; knee-high varieties are suitable for containers)
Malcomia maritima (Virginian stock)
Matthiola bicornis (night-scented stock)
Matthiola incana (stock)
Nicotiana 'Fragrant Cloud'
Zaluzianskya capensis (night stock)

Left: Annual flowers create an instant riot of colour, perfect for filling a new garden or bed for the summer while you decide on a more permanent planting scheme.

Above: Create an impression of rapid maturity by using a mixture of tall climbing and trailing bedding plants so they all run into each other. The effect looks very natural.

Trendsetting plants

If you want to stay ahead of trends, look out for unusual half-hardy perennials with striking flowers, such as *Leonotis leonurus*, which has tiers of pomponlike orange flowers, and *Sutherlandia frutescens*, which has silvery foliage and scarlet pea flowers followed by big inflated green pods. Many of these plants can be spotted in the 'new varieties' pages of the mail order seed catalogues, making it relatively inexpensive to raise your own plants from seed or plantlets. If you want to be first with the latest in new plants, it is worth cultivating the specialist nurseries known for their new introductions. Find them at plant shows and put your name on their mailing lists.

Right: Pelargoniums are fairly drought-tolerant and keep flowering throughout the summer as long as they are regularly dead-headed. Do not overfeed; they will grow leafy instead of flowering well.

Below: *Sutherlandia frutescens* is easily raised from seed, although plants are sometimes available from nurseries specialising in tender perennials. It has curious inflated seed pods after the flowers are over.

Above: Gazanias love a hot sunny spot and are fairly drought-tolerant. Raise plants from seed every year or take cuttings of your favourites and keep them through the winter.

Below: Between them, a mass of informally planted calendula, impatiens, begonia and bedding dahlias make a colourful, summer-long, cottage-style display.

Keeping tender perennials

While seed-raised bedding plants can be replaced every season, it becomes expensive to treat choice tender (half-hardy) perennials in this way. If you want to maintain a sizeable collection of these plants, a frost-free greenhouse is a very useful facility. Take cuttings of half-hardy perennials in late summer, root them in small pots and keep them in a light frost-free place for the winter.

PERENNIALS

Perennials fill out the lower tiers of the garden. Since the individual plants are smaller than trees or shrubs, these are the plants that provide the most opportunities for decorating the garden in seasonal colours. A well-planned garden should include a changing selection of perennials for spring, early summer, midsummer, late summer and autumn interest. Those that have very long flowering seasons are useful for providing continuity, but do not overlook plants with shorter display seasons, especially if they provide valuable seasonal markers that you grow to look forward to the appearance of every year. Plants like omphalodes for spring, peony for early summer, pinks for midsummer, rudbeckia for late summer, and *Sedum spectabile* and *Liriope muscari* for autumn, followed by schizostylis for late autumn. Although most popular perennials are grown for their flowers, plants like hostas and hardy ferns are in great demand as foliage plants, for creating backgrounds to flowers, or for filling difficult shady places where there is little choice. The sort of plants that thrive in shade are generally those with more subtle flower colours, like Solomon's seal *(Polygonatum multiflorum)*, kirengeshoma and tricyrtis. The vast majority of popular, brightly coloured border perennials thrive best given full sun for half the day or more, and for the rest of the time are happy in the light dappled shade cast by surrounding plants. However, for problem hot, dry, sunny spots, or specialist habitats like gravel gardens, then look out for perennials with natural drought resistance. Those with thick succulent leaves and stems, like *Sedum spectabile*, or thick linear almost leathery leaves like bearded iris are ideal for this situation. Conversely, perennials needing moist conditions often have large or thin leaves - the hardy ferns and hostas again. There is some natural overlap between plants that live in borders that stay damp all year round, bog gardens and plants that grow in shallow water round the margins of ponds. But by choosing the right perennial for the spot, you can keep the garden full of colour and variety, and also complement a year-round framework of woody plants.

Hemerocallis 'Frans Hals', a normal full-sized cultivar that grows 90cm(36in) high.

Hemerocallis 'Stella de Oro', a compact cultivar 30cm(12in) high with grasslike leaves.

Classic perennials
Achillea
Astilbe
Bearded iris
Crocosmia
Delphinium
Kniphofia
Lilies
Lupin
Oriental poppy
Peony
Phlox
Scabiosa
Solidago

Compact slow-spreading perennials
Adiantum pedatum 'Pumilum' (dwarf maidenhair fern)
Astrantia
Corydalis flexuosa
Dianthus
Euphorbia amygdaloides 'Rubra'
Geranium cinereum 'Apple Blossom'
Geranium traversii elegans
Heuchera
Heucherella
Hosta
Kirengeshoma palmata
Omphalodes cappadocica
Platycodon grandiflorus 'Mariesii'
Polemonium 'Brise d'Anjou'
Primula
Ranunculus ficaria 'Brazen Hussy'
Salvia x *sylvestris* 'Mainacht'
Schizostylis coccinea
Sisyrinchium striatum
Solidago 'Golden Thumb'
Trillium grandiflorum
Uvularia grandiflora
Veronica gentianoides

Corydalis flexuosa

Left: *Primula japonica* is one of the candelabra primulas, so-called because of the way its flowers grow in tiers. It does well in moist soil in sun. It looks specially good grown with astilbes or hostas, both of which are happy in sun if the soil is moist enough.

Matching perennials and places

However tempting it is to go for the latest, newly fashionable varieties, choose perennials that will suit the growing conditions in your garden. Always pick the plant for the spot to avoid problems. There are real sunlovers that revel in well-drained or even 'problem' dry conditions, and bog plants that need permanent moisture and do not even mind if their crowns are under water; some are also happy on the marginal shelves of a pond. Others are definite shade-lovers, while many more grow happily in the light shade under shrubs, as well as in a more open situation. Using lightly shaded areas is a specially valuable strategy for perennials, because in a small garden this enables you to tier the planting – virtually using several different plants in the same spot – to keep the space colourful and varied throughout several seasons.

Left: *Astrantia major* is a useful and attractive self-seeding perennial that finds its way all round the garden. The papery flowers last well in the garden and flower again later if they are cut back when they go over.

Left: Bearded irises have spectacular flowers, but only for a short time. Plant them with the top half of the tuber above ground and where the plants receive sun all day and are not shaded by other plants

Right: *Sisyrinchium striatum* looks like a miniature iris but flowers earlier, with very different flowers. The plant self-seeds readily into dry crevices, providing plenty of strong, self-sufficient seedlings

Left: *Euphorbia griffithi* 'Fireglow' is a superb example of a dual-purpose perennial, having 'glowing ember' flowers in early summer and good foliage that provides season-long background colour in a border with dappled shade.

Fashionable flowers

Fashions change, and gardening is no exception. Each year, nurseries bring out new varieties or make scarce old plants widely available by mass propagation techniques, so there is always something coming along to tempt buyers. Find out what is new by visiting flower shows (where you can often buy plants to bring home with you), reading gardening magazines and watching TV gardening programmes. Currently, the main fashion trend is for perennials, with some kinds particularly becoming popular. These include diascia, euphorbia, grasses, hardy ferns, hellebores, hemerocallis, hosta, penstemon and phygelius, plus almost anything new and unusual. All are very versatile and fit happily into most types of garden, either in garden beds or containers. Expect new or fashionable plants to cost slightly more than the old favourites, especially if they are in short supply, slow-growing or difficult to propagate. The price usually drops as the plants become more widely available.

Naturally compact varieties of perennial plants

Delphinium 'Magic Fountains' 90cm x 45cm(36 x 18in) in height and spread

Lupinus 'Gallery Pink' 60cm x 45cm (24 x 18in)

Gaillardia 'Goblin' 35cm x 35cm(14 x 14in)

Alstroemeria 'Little Princess' 30x 30cm(12in x 12in)

Geranium sanguineum 'Shepherd's Warning' 20 x 30cm(8 x 12in)

Above: *Alchemilla mollis* is a useful 'go anywhere' plant that flourishes in sun or shade and self-seeds where it is happy. Cut it back hard after flowering to produce a flush of fresh foliage.

Cottage garden plants

Cottage gardens traditionally had small flower gardens based on low-growing perennials, with biennials and hardy annuals.

Creating an easy-care cottage garden bed
Traditional cottage garden perennials were aggressive spreaders. These were allowed to spread and self-seed, rambling around the garden at will to give an informal, slightly haphazard effect that needed little upkeep. For an easy-care cottage garden bed, choose vigorous spreaders such as curled tansy (an ancient herb, *Tanacetum vulgare*, with big heads of yellow flowers whose leaves were once used to protect meat from flies), gardener's garters (a striped grass, *Phalaris arundinacea* 'Picta') and bachelor's buttons (a double buttercup, *Ranunculus acris* 'Flore Pleno') and mix these with some self-seeding annuals and biennials.

Cottage garden treasures
Nowadays, cottage gardens are likely to house fascinating old-fashioned flowers and other 'treasures'. This is a far more labour-intensive garden, since choice little plants need a lot of attention and regular weeding. Keep small treasures, such as old pinks, separate from vigorous spreading plants that would soon smother them. Many treasures need particular growing conditions in order to thrive. Old pinks need well-drained soil in a very sunny spot, and little or no organic matter. Many old-fashioned perennials are shortlived and must be propagated regularly so that old plants can be replaced every three years. Divide old primroses after flowering to rejuvenate them.

Compact rock garden perennials

In a very tiny border, you can grow perennials of the type listed here that are normally recommended for rock gardens, as long as the soil is adequately drained. The following tips will help you succeed with them.

Topdress rock garden perennials with gravel to assist surface drainage. This also provides an ideal medium for the plants to self-seed into. If possible, leave self-sown seedlings where they appear, as they are more drought-tolerant than transplants. Weed out any that come up where you do not want them to grow.

Aquilegia alpina
Aquilegia flabellata
Campanula carpatica
Crepis incana
Delphinium 'Little Butterfly'
Diascia rigescens
Fragaria 'Red Ruby'
Iberis sempervirens
Myosotis scorpioides Maytime
Origanum rotundifolium
Tiarella cordifolia
Veronica prostrata
Viola sp.

Rock plants are often shorter-lived than conventional perennials, so take cuttings in late spring or early summer every two to three years (ideally just after flowering). Use these to replace old plants. Spreading plants tend to die out in the middle.

Rock garden aquilegias hybridise as readily as normal garden species and the two cross with each other, so if tall aquilegias are in the area, expect self-sown seedlings to grow much bigger than your original plants.

Do not risk growing choice or scarce rock plants, or those that need specially good drainage, in a level border unless the ground is naturally gravelly or stony and exceptionally fast draining. Save those for a raised bed or rockery.

Left: Iberis sempervirens *is a miniature evergreen plant that spreads wider than its height and in spring and early summer is covered in white 'candytuft' flowers. Trim after flowering.*

Below: *Golden marjoram and a compact campanula growing together provide a contrasting display in a rock garden.*

GRASSES

Grasses are the most fashionable of perennial plants. Huge lists of hitherto never seen varieties are now appearing in nursery catalogues and on plant stands at gardening shows. The description 'grasses' covers a huge range of plant species, many of which may seem difficult to get to know at first as they do not have common names. To complicate things further, 'grass' is also loosely applied to any grassy-looking plants, such as sedges and bamboos. But bear with them. What they all have in common is linear leaves, and in the garden, long narrow leaves make wonderful contrasts with other, more rounded shapes of foliage and flowers. This makes grasses indispensable 'go anywhere' plants. You can sprinkle a selection of medium-sized flowering and foliage grasses throughout a perennial border to improve it in an instant. Use taller grasses, such as miscanthus and bamboos, amongst shrubs to add a variety of plant shapes and forms. Grasses are particularly valuable in a heather and conifer garden or one composed mainly of evergreens, where they add movement, seasonal variation and sounds; rustling foliage is a great feature of grasses. And shorter, more drought-tolerant species, such as festuca and many of the sedges, are outstanding for rockeries and containers. You can even get grassy plants that grow in bog gardens and pond margins. So despite the difficulty with their names, grasses are well worth using all round the garden. If you like the look of it, try growing it.

Grasses for wet soil and bog gardens

Carex elata 'Aurea' (Bowles' golden sedge)
Carex grayi (mace sedge)
Carex pendula
Juncus effusus 'Spiralis' (corkscrew rush)
Schoenoplectus 'Zebrinus' (zebra rush)

Larger grasses to go with shrubs, heathers, conifers, etc.

Miscanthus sinensis 'Morning Light'
Miscanthus sinensis 'Zebrinus'
Pleioblastus auricomus
Pleiobastus variegatus

Colour and shape

Grasses make wonderful tall, vertical shapes, splayed fountain shapes, short tussocks or even hairy mats with serrated edges. They can be very colourful, too; there are grasses in various shades of blue, green, bronze, purple and red, or greens with cream, white or gold variegations.

Below: This group of compact, slow-growing grassy plants features a bamboo, a sedge, a grass and a member of the lily family (*Ophiopogon*), which is often regarded as an honorary grass because of its linear leaves.

Left: *Carex elata* 'Aurea' is actually a sedge, but is usually included along with grasses as it looks like one. This species thrives in sun or light shade and needs damp soil.

Decorative grasses for borders
Bouteloua gracilis (mosquito grass)
Hakonechloa macra 'Alboaurea'
Imperata cylindrica (Japanese blood grass)
Milium effusum 'Aureum' (Bowles' golden grass)
Stipa gigantea (ornamental oats)
Stipa tenuifolia

Good grasses for rock features and containers
Acorus gramineus 'Ogon'
Carex comans
Carex 'Evergold'
Carex hachijoensis
Festuca glauca cultivars, such as Blue Fox and 'Golden Toupee'

Grasses for a hot, dry, sunny border or gravel area
Festuca glauca cultivars
Elymus arenarius
Helictotrichon sempervirens
Pennisetum alopecuroides
Stipa gigantea

Grasses for small gardens

Medium-sized grasses, such as pennisetum and decorative miscanthus, look attractive in borders with other perennials. Or make a bed entirely from a mixture of tall and medium-sized decorative grasses. Although grassy plants are grown mainly for their foliage, many kinds also have superb flowers and seedheads. You can find feathery plumes, arching tassels, 'foxtails' and millet-like sprays, as well as ornamental oats, quaking grasses and fluffy caterpillar-like heads. Leave the dead heads on the plants throughout winter; they look brilliant rimmed with frost, and birds will feed on the seeds.

Festuca
These dwarf evergreen grasses need sun and well-drained soil.

Pennisetum
These have spectacular plumelike seedheads. Provide winter protection in cold regions.

Bamboo
Bamboos look good grown in a row as a screen, but since many popular species can become invasive, grow them in large tubs or pots in a small garden, which keeps them naturally compact. Choose compact, slow-growing varieties for planting in borders in small gardens.

Miscanthus
These are mostly tall cane-stemmed plants that tolerate wet and clay soils. Some very decorative new compact varieties are now also available.

Below: These compact grasses and sedges are particularly showy and make superb contrasts with plants with rounded leaves such as hostas, bergenia and *Alchemilla mollis*. The molinia is suitable for dry shade, but the others all need a reasonably sunny situation.

Above: *Festuca glauca* is a slow-growing, drought-proof dwarf grass, ideal for a gravel garden, rockery or scree. Plants form a neat hummock shape, with blue feathery flowerheads.

A container of *Hedera helix* 'Duckfoot' provides the focal point of this tiny patio.

PART FOUR

SMALL-SCALE GARDENING

A small garden is not just a miniature version of a big one. It takes a very different set of ingredients to create the desired effect. Here, the emphasis is on creating fine detail to make the garden look intimate and inviting, not just cluttered.

BOUNDARIES

The type of boundary you choose does a lot to establish the style of the garden. However, in a small garden there is also the question of space to consider. Hedges often take up a great deal of room, so avoid traditional beech, hornbeam or privet that need planting in staggered rows for stability and can be 90cm(3ft) wide at the base. Yew can be planted in a single row and clipped to make a hedge as little as 30-45cm (12-18in) wide. You can also achieve a hedge-like effect by growing climbers on chain link fencing. (This is also a good way to disguise the fencing and cheaper than replacing it with something more attractive.) You could plant climbers on a structure of posts and wire netting to make a fast-growing screen for 'instant' privacy and shelter or to hide a local eyesore. This has the advantage of stopping at the required height and needing little trimming. Of the non-living boundaries, walls are virtually maintenance- and problem-free and ideal for growing self-clinging climbers, such as ivy and parthenocissus. You can put in wall nails to support horizontal wires for espalier or fan-trained trees or wall shrubs. Fences do require periodic maintenance, so put up netting or trellis (held 10cm/4in away to permit air circulation) on which to grow climbers such as clematis or passionflower. These supports can be lifted down and laid flat on the ground when the fence needs attention.

Above: Privacy and shelter are two vital ingredients for a patio, and where there is no existing wall or hedge to do the job, a trellis screen is the quickest and most decorative way of providing both.

Right: In a wilder style of garden you can make a form of very open weave 'trellis', using rustic sticks woven between stronger stakes driven into the ground.

Right: If you want a conifer hedge that is easy to keep at 90-120cm (3-4ft) tall and does not need endless clipping, then thujas are the best choice. Cheaper hedging thujas are available, but if you only need a few, opt for a named variety so that you can choose the colour or plant shape you prefer.

Above: Although this is a clinging ivy, it has been wired onto the fence rail to prevent it becoming top heavy and being blown off in the wind. It requires clipping only three times each year.

Below: The variegated ivy *Hedera helix* 'Chrysophylla', here bound and clipped on a section of post-and-rail fence, turns a brilliant shade of yellow in spring when covered in young growth.

Below: Colour makes a stunning background to a busy border. A large range of water-based timber treatment stains is available to restyle old fences. Blue is effective teamed with orange and purple.

Natural boundaries

Natural materials are fast becoming favourites for informal fencing panels, as an alternative to traditional woven timber strips. Natural panels last from five to ten years; less in a very windy site, but longer if the panels are firmly fixed and treated with a suitable preservative. Panels can be used permanently or temporarily to protect new shrubs or while a hedge grows. Many different types are available or you can make a very rustic-looking kind yourself from hazel twigs, bamboo canes or peasticks.

Left: *Long strands of dried heather stapled together make attractive and long-lasting russet-toned panels. Though more expensive than many forms of fencing panel, these are very robust and make a superb background to plants. Ideal for a natural-look garden or rustic situation.*

Right: *Bamboo canes or a mixture of canes and straight, slender willow wands, as here, make a striking and unusual fence panel. Sticks can be left natural or treated with water-based stains to colour them. For a novel effect, group canes of different colours together in the same row.*

Left: *Traditional sheep hurdles are made from thick hazel wands bent round stronger stakes. They are available as ready-made panels to fix to stakes hammered into the ground. But you can make your own in situ by bending birch or other flexible twigs around a row of poles 30cm(12in) apart.*

HARD SURFACES

Paths and paving have a huge effect on the garden – not only on its appearance, but also on its day-to-day use. Choose hard surfaces that reflect the style of the garden. For instance, in a cottage garden, gravel paths and cobblestones look the part, while a country garden usually has stone slabs or granite setts, and contemporary gardens may have a wild 'designer' arrangement of coloured tiles set amongst paving. Paths must be practical, taking people where they need to go as quickly as possible – hence the popularity of straight paths from the garden gate to the front door. You can introduce gentle curves to soften the effect in an informal garden, but people will still take a straight route along them. If they are too curved they will lose their purpose and people will take 'shortcuts' across the lawn or through flowerbeds. Some paths are not designed to get somewhere fast; informal paths encourage you to roam around the garden enjoying the flowers. Here, curves help to slow you down and do just that. This type of path can be narrower than 'serious' ones, and need not have proper foundations as it will not get heavy use. Paving or gravel could be laid loosely over beaten earth, allowing plants to be grown in the path for extra interest. Stepping stones set into a regularly used route over a lawn make an informal 'path' that prevents the grass wearing out into a muddy track. Seating areas need not be immediately behind the house; instead choose a spot that gets evening sun, even if it is at the end of the garden. But put paving outside entrance doors, as this helps keep dirt from treading indoors.

Right: To avoid wearing out the grass, sink 'stepping stones' to make an informal path over a route you cross regularly – perhaps to the back gate, garage or washing line. As well as keeping the lawn in better condition, they can also form an integral part of the garden design.

Above: Combining different surface textures is an interesting way to create variety on a patio, and also 'tells' people where to walk. Pebbles feel knobbly underfoot, so you stay on the paving which feels more secure. This way you avoid treading on plants grown in crevices.

Right: Good-quality decking makes a superb background for architectural plants in striking containers. The timber surface contrasts well with the more traditional-looking grassy lawn and rose beds beyond, creating two separate garden areas that blend nicely together.

Right: A steep sloping path is safest converted to steps; build these properly using bricks that stay non-slip in winter. Brick steps look good with any type of hard path – paving, gravel or brick; make them more ornamental by standing pots at the sides.

Below: Gravel is the modern equivalent of an ash path, made at old cottage gardens by using clinkers swept from the fireplace to fill muddy puddles. Here the gravel is laid directly over firmed soil; paths should be narrow and wandering for an authentic look.

Above: Bricks can also be laid straight over firmed soil. This does mean you can move the path later, but it will not take heavy regular use without becoming uneven. In this case, lay the bricks using mortar onto a 10-15cm(4-6in)-thick layer of hardcore.

Path edging

Old roof tiles can be reused as capping for walls or an edging for beds and paths in a cottage garden. Using a masonry cutting disc on an electric drill you can cut them easily without the risk of damage.

1 Cut each pantile in half and bed the pieces into the soil, so that they overlap and the curves fit into each other, leaning slightly outwards.

2 Leave 7.5cm (3in) of the tile edges standing above soil level. Support them evenly on both sides and tread down gently to secure them.

3 When the entire surface of the path is firmed down, spread a layer of shingle, rake it lightly and tread it up against the tile faces.

Coping with a gradient

Right: *Use rows of brick pavers, railway sleepers or stone setts partly sunk into the ground to convert a slightly sloping path into a series of long shallow steps. They also prevent rain washing the gravel downhill. Make sure the bricks are firmly fixed.*

1 Excavate the area over which you want to lay the gravel until you reach solid subsoil. Set out preservative-treated boards around the perimeter of the excavated area and drive in stout corner pegs.

2 Secure the boards to the pegs with galvanised nails. Add more pegs at roughly 1m(39in) intervals along the boards all round the area to prevent the boards from bowing outwards later on.

LAYING DOWN GRAVEL

A path or other gravel area can be an attractive feature in any garden, especially when used to provide contrast alongside flat paving materials and low-growing plants. Areas of gravel are also a particularly popular feature of oriental-style gardens. True gravel is available in a range of mixed natural-earth shades that look particularly good when wet, while crushed stone, which is rough-edged rather than smooth, is sold in a range of colours from white through reds and greens to grey and black. Although both are attractive and are relatively inexpensive to lay, they do have several practical drawbacks. They need some form of edge restraint to prevent the stones straying onto lawns or into flower beds. They need regular raking and weeding to keep them looking good. They can attract dogs and cats, who find them ideal as an earth closet. And lastly, pushing a laden wheelbarrow along a gravel path is very hard work! However, if you do choose gravel, work out carefully how much material to order. Decorative aggregates are sold in small carry-home bags, weighing from 25 to 50kg(55 to 110lbs), and by volume in large canvas slings or in loose loads that are delivered to your door. You will need a bulk delivery for all but the smallest areas. Bear in mind that a cubic metre of gravel weighs about 1.7 tonnes and will cover an area of just over 13sq m to a depth of 75mm(3in).

3 The best way of discouraging weeds from growing up through a gravel path is to put down a porous membrane (landscape fabric) over the subsoil.

4 To form a firm base for the gravel, cover the membrane with a layer of crushed rock or fine hardcore. You will need at least 50mm(2in) of rock on firm subsoil, and more if it is soft.

5 Compact the base layer by running a heavy garden roller over it. Fill in any hollows and roll it again until you no longer leave any footprints in the surface. Thorough preparation prevents sinking in the future.

6 Without disturbing the base layer, spread out the gravel or decorative stone. Fill the area up to the level of the perimeter boards.

7 Level the gravel. Draw a wooden straightedge along the tops of the boards to identify high spots or hollows. Rake again.

Left: In an oriental-style garden that relies on architectural detail as much as plants for its interest, you can make a plain gravel path into a much more unusual feature by bedding in irregularly shaped stepping stones at intervals. As well as looking attractive, they are comfortable to walk on.

A gravel walkway with brick patterns

You can mix gravel with smooth slabs or block pavers to create attractive patterns and contrasts. The blocks also help to keep gravel off lawns and beds. This simple path is cheap and easy to make. Rake the ground to remove any debris, level it and tread it down. Cover the compacted earth with a good layer of moistened sand and flatten it.

1 Lay a line of bricks from side to side, level with the straight edges – here, pavers set on edge. Make these firm and level.

2 Fill the triangular spaces with shingle and tread it down gently. Do not to push the bricks out of line before it has settled.

3 Edge this simple but effective formal path with suitable plants. The path is cheap and easy to make and you only need to cut a few bricks. Gravel is an ideal alternative to grass for narrow paths such as this.

SOFT SURFACES

Grass is the surface most people automatically choose to cover those parts of the garden where they do not intend to grow flowers and shrubs. It acts rather like a self-regenerating carpet, and makes a natural green backdrop that sets off trees and flowers perfectly. However, to keep grass looking good it needs regular mowing and if it gets heavy wear – for instance from children and dogs playing on it – then feeding and occasional repairs will also be needed. Grass is not always the easy option it is often believed to be. You can make lawn care easier by using paving or gravel in places that get heavy wear, such as the sitting-out area, and by laying hard paths along routes where you frequently walk, say from the back door to the shed or washing line. But in some situations, other forms of soft surface may be more suitable than grass. For instance, under trees, where grass does not thrive due to heavy shade or dry soil, a surface of bark chippings looks pleasing and natural but needs no work to maintain. On a slope that is difficult to mow, ground cover plants grown close together make a dense layer that smothers out weeds, looks good all year round and flowers seasonally. In a hot, dry, sunny spot where grass needs frequent watering, a thyme lawn made of spreading varieties grown through gravel creates a low leafy effect, yet needs no mowing or irrigation; it is also delightfully scented.

Above: A thyme lawn makes a very pretty feature in a decorative 'edible garden'. Plant a mixture of creeping varieties in a random pattern. Well-drained soil and a sunny spot are essential. Dig in plenty of gravel for good drainage.

Right: Bark chippings are the ideal mulch around ground cover plants. Cover the soil immediately after planting to a depth of 5cm(2in). Small chippings are a more effective mulch than large ones and last three years or more.

Above: A living carpet of ajuga with contrasting groups of hosta is a decorative way to clad moist ground in a slightly shady area. Since you cannot walk over the plants, add wooden stepping stones or an informal path of bark chippings.

The design value of lawns

You can use the lawn to link larger features, or to influence the visual impact of your garden as a whole. Its length, width, shape and position can make the plot appear wider, larger or just more interesting than it actually is. Remember to plan an area of grass from a practical point of view, so that it is relatively easy to maintain. All parts must be accessible to your mower, with no areas narrower than the width of the machine. When experimenting with shapes, bear in mind that curves and circles create a softer, informal look, while harder, geometric figures, such as squares and rectangles, appear more formal. Try positioning your shapes on the diagonal or slightly at an angle for more interesting and less predictable effects.

Below: A good way to make the most of a sloping site is to divide it into two small lawns linked by steps. By making the near lawn short but wide and the top one long and narrower, the garden appears bigger than it really is.

Hard-wearing lawns

Hard wear areas and gardens used by children and pets need a grass seed mixture with a high proportion of ryegrass, plus drought-resistant varieties, such as crested dog's tail, that will produce a good-quality, resilient turf that recovers quickly. Specialist suppliers can also make you up a mix that contains clover in as high a percentage as you like. Although clover is unacceptable in a smart sward, it is hard-wearing, stays green during drought and can be mown in the same way as a lawn if you do not like the flowers.

Above: A meandering lawn breaks up the straight edges of a regular plot, creating a charmingly informal effect. By making the lawn disappear round a border with tall plants you create the impression that the garden is larger than it is.

Soleirolia amongst pebbles

Grass will not grow in a very shady area, but helxine or ivy will thrive. Combine a cobblestone surface with these low creeping plants to make an attractive feature. Use this idea between paving stones, as an edging to a path or as unusual ground cover in a problem area.

1 Prepare the soil well, adding plenty of organic matter. Put in the plants 23-30cm(9-12in) apart. Helxine can become invasive close to lawns or flower beds.

2 Select smooth, evenly-sized, coloured cobblestones. Press them into place between the plants. Group them in clusters if you do not want a solid surface.

3 Tuck more cobbles around the plants and bed them down firmly. Move any that create large areas of one colour; aim for a mix of speckles and colours.

4 Water the whole area to get the plants off to a good start and to firm the stones into place. This is particularly important if you are going to walk on them.

5 The end result is a very self-sufficient feature. The cobbles act like a mulch, preventing weed seeds from germinating and keeping the plant roots cool and moist. In a sunny spot, sink cobbles into gravel and plant creeping thymes instead.

DECORATIVE LAWNS

Comparatively speaking, small lawns get much heavier wear than large ones. In a tiny garden you have no choice but to use the same route across the lawn to the washing line or shed. And there is probably only one convenient, sunny spot to put garden seats on a nice day when you want to sit outside. So you use the same patch of grass all the time. No wonder it soon starts to look patchy and worn out. In winter, worn areas of grass become slippery with liverwort or algae, or just turn to mud which gets trodden indoors. In summer, heavily used grass cannot grow fast enough to replace itself, and thin patches let in moss and weeds which makes the lawn look scruffy and ill-kempt. And if you keep walking over the same route, you eventually wear a track across the lawn where the water collects after rain and the grass never grows. The best way to keep a small lawn looking perfect all the time is to stay off it. For a real enthusiast with a fine lawn and no family this is a feasible option. Some people get round the problem by replacing a small lawn with a hard surface such as paving or gravel, to create a courtyard style garden. But if you want a small lawn that stays well groomed and lush despite normal family use, the solution is to give it more concentrated care than a large lawn. The first step is to solve any existing problems and make repairs. Once this is done a good programme of spring and autumn lawn care will keep grass strong, green and healthy and always looking its best.

Laying stepping stones in a lawn

1 Instead of wearing a track through a small lawn, sink a few 'stepping stones' to walk on. Rest the slabs on the grass; cut round them with the back of a spade.

2 Remove the slab and lift the turf. (If you can leave the slab standing for several days, the grass under it turns yellow and leaves a shape for cutting round.)

4 Offer up the slab. If it is proud of the surrounding turf, make the hole deeper. If too deep, add a layer of gravel. The mower needs to pass straight over the slab.

5 Press the slab down well so that it sits securely. The snug fit and vertical sides of the hole help to hold it in place; it pays to ensure the best fit in the first place.

Edging a lawn

A well-kept lawn makes the perfect backdrop to the whole garden and small details, such as well-made lawn edges, make all the difference, both to the appearance and to the time needed to keep it looking its best.

1 To keep the lawn edge looking tidy, use a half-moon edger to slice away a vertical strip about 7.5cm(3in) deep all round the perimeter of the lawn.

2 Push the edging tool into the ground and remove the thin sliver of cut turf, leaving a shallow 'gulley'. Work all round any flower beds and trees planted in the lawn.

Lawn edges need redefining each spring as the soil gradually spills back.

3 Once a firm horizontal edge has been made, it does not take long to trim the lawn edges after mowing the grass. This adds the finishing touch to the lawn.

3 Remove all the turf, leaving clean vertical edges to the shape. Make sure the soil is firm and perfectly level; the hole should be very slightly deeper than the slab, and the same uniform depth all over. Make sure there are no stones, and firm the soil well down.

6 Fill narrow gaps with fine dry soil or potting mix tipped onto the slab and brushed into the cracks. For wider gaps, mix grass seed with the soil and water well.

7 Set an irregular row of slabs into the lawn, a comfortable walking pace apart. The path will be firm and dry underfoot and the lawn remains in good condition.

Below: Stripes add the traditional finishing touch to the perfect lawn. Using a cylinder mower and a grass box, mow from one end to the other, working at right angles to the house. Avoid turning circles at the ends of the rows.

Alternative lawn edgings

There are other ways of improving lawn edges. Where the lawn flanks a gravel path, prevent stones spilling onto the grass by putting in a row of rope-edged tiles. A cheaper alternative is to sink a row of bricks in at an angle.

Left: *Make a narrow trench with a spade and sink in rope-edged tiles so that only the rope edge remains visible above the grass. You can now edge the lawn quickly using a nylon line trimmer instead of shears.*

Right: *An attractive, old-fashioned, jagged brick edge looks good in a cottage garden or vegetable plot. You can use new or secondhand bricks; although it does not give the same straight surface as tiles, you can still use a nylon line trimmer for edging.*

Above: *Where the lawn runs up to a bed, put in a mowing strip – a narrow row of paving slabs onto which flowers can spill. This way, you avoid mowing your flowers and getting yellow scallop shapes all round the edge of the lawn. The mower edges the lawn as it cuts the grass.*

Aerating the soil

If the surface of a lawn is hard, rain cannot soak in and all the air spaces in the soil disappear, making it difficult for the grass to grow. If you want a perfect lawn, the answer is to aerate the ground every few years

Right: A lawn aerator makes a series of holes 5cm(2in)deep that alleviate soil compaction. A hand version is quite adequate for a small lawn, but motorised versions can be bought or hired in.

1 Press the prongs into the lawn, down to their full depth. Lift out the aerator and move it 5cm(2in) away and repeat the process. Work in this way all over the lawn.

2 As the lawn will now be able to make better use of it, apply a lawn fertiliser. You could also apply a top dressing, brushing it around so that some goes into the holes.

Rescuing a damaged area of lawn

Thin, yellow or balding patches are often a sign of a lawn that needs a good care programme, but for speed, restore the worst areas individually using this technique. Spring or autumn are the best times to do the work.

1 When the soil is moist, loosen compacted soil with the points of a garden fork or aerator. Push in the tines horizontally to a depth of about 5cm(2in) using your foot.

2 Rock the handle gently backwards and forwards so that the tines make a short arc in the soil. Repeat this every 5cm(2in) across the patch to be treated.

LAWN CARE

To keep it in perfect condition, a small lawn takes about as much work as you would give to a flower bed, so do not think of it as an easy option. The lawn care season starts in spring, about six weeks after grass begins growing. Apply a slow-release lawn feed. Although it is more expensive than normal spring and summer lawn feed, it keeps the lawn fed little and often for the rest of the season – the best option for a small lawn that gets a lot of use. If there are weeds or moss in the grass, use a product that also contains a suitable treatment. Some kinds of weeds with small leaves need a special product as they are not easy to eradicate. Begin mowing regularly every time the grass needs it. It grows faster in cool damp weather and slower in very hot, dry or cold conditions. If you cut it to about 3.75cm(1.5in) high, you will find the grass stays green in dry weather and is much harder-wearing and easier to look after than a lawn that is cut very short. What is more, you need not alter the height of the blades (as is often recommended), as grass can be cut at this height all year round, regardless of growing conditions. In autumn, give the lawn a special treat. After cutting it as usual, rake and aerate it (power equipment is available to make the job easier), then feed it with a special autumn feed. This will not make the grass grow faster or greener; the aim is to build up the roots so that the grass grows more thickly, moss, weeds and liverwort cannot get in, and the lawn is toughened up for the winter.

3 Evenly sprinkle a top dressing of, say, a litre of potting mix to a handful of grass seed over the area. This improves the soil and gets new grass growing fast. This is essential to keep out weeds.

4 Use a spring-tined lawn rake to work the mixture into the surface of the lawn. Some will go into the holes left by the fork. Water the treated patches well, and protect them with canes.

Weeds in the lawn

Above: Treat dandelions and other broad-leaved weeds with selective lawn weedkillers.

Above: Clover helps to feed the lawn, as it fixes nitrogen from the air in its root nodules.

Above: Plantains leave bare patches where they have been killed. Loosen soil; reseed gaps.

Above: Use a selective lawn weedkiller on daisies. It takes a few weeks to work; be patient.

Left: Some lawn weedkillers are sold ready mixed in disposable sprayer packs. Do not reuse the pack to spray anything else once it has been used up.

5 Apply liquid lawn weedkillers with a watering can fitted with a dribble bar. Keep one can specially for weedkiller, as even the tiniest trace is enough to harm plants. Washing the can out well is not enough.

Reinforcing a heavily used lawn

Small lawns get a lot of wear, especially if the grass is used as a playground for children and dogs. However, you can reinforce the surface to help it withstand this sort of use. If you are laying a new lawn, choose a seed mix or turf designed to stand up to rough treatment.

1 Weeds colonise the exposed soil where the grass has failed. Spike, feed and topdress in autumn. While this treatment starts to work, reinforce the grass with strong plastic mesh.

2 Choose mesh with small holes. Ask for one that is recommended for this purpose. Unroll the mesh over the lawn surface shortly after cutting the grass so that it lies flat.

3 Use special pegs with flat-topped heads to hold the mesh securely in place. When hammered in, they lie flush with the surface so that you can mow over the top. Keep the mesh taut.

4 Treat patches or reinforce a whole lawn. Once in place, grass grows through the mesh and hides it, but you can still feed and spike the lawn. The mesh protects the ground right from the start.

5 Once the mesh has been down for a few weeks it is virtually undetectable, but lasts for very many years.

FRAMEWORK PLANTING

Trees, shrubs and evergreens form the backbone of most gardens, creating a bold, year-round structural shape. These are the first plants to put into both a design and the actual garden; once they are placed, you can judge the overall effect and see what space is left for smaller details. Use trees and large evergreens to screen a poor view or create privacy – perhaps masking nearby buildings or power lines. Similarly, use them to frame a good view – perhaps adjacent countryside – to give a casual onlooker the impression that the whole property is surrounded by similarly favourable aspects, if only the plants were not in the way. Use a framework of plants to divide a garden into smaller garden rooms, each with its own character. This idea works even in small gardens, but use dwarf hedges of santolina or lavender, or upright features, such as a pergola or arch, to separate different areas without taking up valuable space. In winter the outline of the garden is clearly visible, even though most plants are dormant or lacking leaves. Use a character tree, shrub or evergreen as a centrepiece in a lawn or small paved garden, where it can cast its unique personality over an entire area. Magnolia or flowering cherries are often used in this way, although in a small space, contorted hazel, Japanese maple or a close-trimmed upright yew – or even a piece of topiary – can create a similar effect.

Right: The graceful weeping shape of a well-grown Japanese maple looks good in leaf and in winter, when the plant has a beautiful skeleton of twigs. It does not outgrow a small garden; a perfect framework plant.

Left: Make use of the larger shrubs to complement the shape of hard features, such as paths, and make a year-round outline to the garden. In really good framework planting, the shapes left between key plants and hard landscaping also create interesting shapes, as here, to be filled in with small details.

Right: Architectural features, such as a pergola clad in climbers, (this is rambler rose 'American Pillar') help to create the internal shape of the garden. They can represent a much more imaginative way of using space than a border of evergreens in the same situation.

Above: Topiary is invaluable for adding detail. Small-scale potted topiary, such as these box swans, can be stood in a border of low plants, at the end of a dwarf hedge or on paving to help provide year-round shape to the garden. Being portable, they are also versatile.

Left: Although it makes a medium-sized tree in time, *Robinia pseudoacacia* 'Frisia' can often be accommodated in a relatively small garden, as its light canopy of gold, feathery foliage does not cast much shade. The tree has a good structural shape that makes it a valuable part of the garden.

Trees in containers

Trees and shrubs restricted in pots will stay much smaller than those in open ground but need frequent watering, particularly in warm weather. Dwarf conifers in pots around the patio provide height and winter interest. Clipped evergreens in pots on either side of steps or an ornamental seat look good in a formal garden setting.

Formation pruning of a young tree

Nurseries often sell 'feathered' young trees, meaning that all the side shoots have been left on the plant so that the customer can choose whether to grow it as a multistemmed tree, a bush or as a normal standard tree on a single trunk. It is cheaper than buying a trained tree, as you do the training yourself. This is Liquidamber styraciflua.

1 For a standard, choose a strong young tree with one upright stem and vigorous side shoots at the top of the stem.

2 Working up from the base, using sharp secateurs, cut away all unwanted 'feathers' (side shoots) flush with the stem.

3 Leave five or seven strong side shoots round the top of the tree. Remove the tip of each one to encourage branching out. Cut out the tip of the main upright shoot growing from the top of the tree to divert all the tree's energy into the branches.

4 A short stake prevents roots rocking but lets the trunk flex and develop, so that it can stand without support after a year or two.

Growing lavender hedging

1 In summer, choose strong, non-flowering shoots 5-7.5cm(2-3in) long to make cuttings. Take them from a lavender plant in the garden, or buy one plant from a nursery.

2 Strip off the lower leaves by running your thumb and finger down the stem. Leave about four full-sized leaves at the tip. Remove any flower buds with their stalks.

3 Nip out the growing tip using your finger and thumbnail. This helps to produce a bushy plant. Hedging plants must branch from the base to avoid a gappy effect.

4 Make a clean cut just below the bottom leaf joint, which can be seen as a scar on the stalk. This removes any tissue that might rot, causing the cutting to die.

5 Prepare all your cuttings at once. Take about 30% more than you need to allow for failures. You can also then select only the best for planting later. Push each cutting individually into a small pot filled with seed mix.

DWARF EDGINGS

Dwarf hedges are a good way to divide up the interior of a small garden into compartments, without creating a lot of shade or taking up much room. Since a dwarf hedge is 30cm(12in) tall at most, it also makes the perfect edge for a formal flower bed, knot garden or traditional, geometric herb bed. The idea here is to outline beds, paths and borders with a continuous row of plants, clipped hedge-fashion. Team them with small topiary box balls, to add architectural detail to the ends of rows or at corners. The best plants for dwarf edgings are naturally upright, evergreen kinds that take close clipping. Dwarf box *(Buxus sempervirens* 'Suffruticosa') is ideal for a foliage hedge. This grows easily from cuttings and you can start trimming plants into a flat linear shape as soon as they are potted. Alternatively, plant young pot-grown dwarf box bought from a nursery, about 15cm(6in)apart, and clip them to shape in situ. Once established, clip dwarf box hedging once or twice per year, in late spring and late summer, to keep it in shape. Compact, flowering evergreen herbs, such as dwarf varieties of lavender or rosemary, are often used for a less rigidly formal look. Choose upright rather than sprawling kinds, as they are the easiest to keep in shape. Clip over flowering hedges immediately after flowering. Plants with small leaves make the best dwarf edgings, but if you do not mind pruning with secateurs, then larger-leaved plants such as purple- or gold-variegated sage make a good dwarf hedge. Trim them in late spring to tidy the shape and remove dead and frost damaged foliage. For an even more informal look, try low hedges of potentilla, cistus or hebe. Trim them in late spring. Like ornamental sages, they need a little more width than formal, close-clipped edging. Use them to edge paths in an informal or cottage style flower garden or herb feature.

6 Water the cuttings well and stand them in a sheltered spot out of direct sun. Check daily. Water when the mix starts to dry out. They will root in six weeks; move them to a sunnier spot and gradually increase watering.

7 Eight to ten weeks after taking the cuttings you should have many young plants with plenty of vigorous branching shoots that are just beginning to flower. The pots will be filled with roots and are ready for planting.

8 Now prepare the soil for planting and mark out the row. Tap down the pots to loosen the plants and knock out the cuttings without disturbing the rootball. Plant them firmly, about 15cm (6in) apart.

9 Straight after planting, cut the plants back by a third to a half. This reduces water loss through the leaves and also encourages further branching. Plants will respond to this by making new growth fast.

Right: A dwarf lavender edging makes an attractive, colourful, scented feature. Annual trimming is essential, as lavender gets straggly after a few years and old plants are killed if you have to cut them back into old wood.

Box hedges

If you cannot wait to grow your own box edgings from cuttings, look for a nursery specialising in box. They may sell pot-grown plants already trimmed to shape. Simply plant them at the right distance to achieve a perfect dwarf edge instantly. A specialist nursery is also the place to find unusual kinds of box, such as those with gold or silver variegations. The best known, 'Gold Tip', with yellow ends to the young leaves, is more widely available. Although not dwarf in the same way as Buxus sempervirens *'Suffruticosa', variegated box can still be trimmed to about 15cm(6in) for low hedges or used to make topiary.*

Right: *Dwarf edging hedges are easily trimmed 'by eye' or use a string guide to help you. Trim them before they lose their shape so that the structure of the hedge creates its own cutting guide. Trimming also encourages plants to thicken out and form a more solid outline.*

Above: *As well as giving the garden year-round structure, dwarf hedges also help to support plants grown in beds behind them and shelter them to some extent from the wind – ideal for early flowers such as spring bulbs.*

BEDS AND BORDERS

Beds and borders are the parts of the garden reserved for plants; borders go round the edge of the garden and beds are cut into the lawn. The precise shapes you choose depend very much on the style of your garden. In formal gardens, edges are straight and borders surround the edge of a geometric-shaped lawn or run parallel to a straight path, while beds are squares, circles or oblongs cut into the lawn. In informal gardens the opposite is true; there are no straight lines at all, borders have gently curving edges and beds are irregular shapes, such as teardrops, or may even follow the contours of an undulating garden to create a more natural impression. Beds and borders are often planted on a particular theme. This could be something traditional like a rose bed or a herbaceous border, but often the theme will be suggested by some aspect of the site and situation. For instance, if the soil is damp, a border surrounding a pond may be filled with damp-loving or bog garden plants. In a hot, dry spot, Mediterranean plants are a good choice; in a raised sunny site, a rock garden would be ideal. In this way, the work of running a garden can be much reduced, since plants are only grown in the situations that suit them best and you are not constantly struggling to grow them in less than ideal conditions. And by growing plants with similar requirements together, whole beds can be given the same treatment at the same time, thus cutting down on individual plant care. Beds can also be planned to peak at particular seasons, so that the centre of interest gradually moves round the garden from season to season, which again adds to the charm of a small plot.

Above: Plants that naturally enjoy the same growing conditions, normally associate well together, too. This dry garden features dianthus, sedum, lavender, nepeta, yucca and helianthemum. One large shrub – here elaeagnus – makes a good background without taking up too much room.

Left: To create a cohesive look, borders need to be planted in a style that suits their surroundings. This very natural pond is flanked by beds filled with iris, campion, digitalis, mimulus and ranunculus. Logs help to stop soil going into the pond, keeping the water clear.

Above: A rose bed improves the view from this window, while the wall of the house makes the perfect frame for the border when seen from the front garden. It is a good idea to blend roses with low carpeting foliage and taller flowering perennials for variety.

Above: Conifers interact to make a shapely, year-round centrepiece in an island bed surrounded by lawn. They mingle attractively with the annuals, which are accessible and easily replaced for seasonal interest.

Right: Maximise space by tiering the planting, with spring bulbs under perennials and perennials under shrubs. Vary hard surfaces by filling cracks in paving with gravel or alternating cobbles with slabs.

Below: Cottage gardens are traditionally packed with plants. Include old favourites, such as nepeta, with the poppy-like flowers of eschscholzia. The result should look completely spontaneous.

Planting a perennial

1 Dig a hole about twice the size of the plant's rootball. Put the excavated soil next to the hole. Add a spadeful of well-rotted organic matter and mix in.

2 Sprinkle a handful of general-purpose fertiliser into the hole and mix well. Add half a handful of fertiliser to the soil alongside the hole and mix it in well.

3 Slide the plant carefully out of its pot. Lift it by the rootball into the hole so that the top of the rootball is level with the soil. The best side should face forward.

4 Surround the rootball with the improved soil excavated from the planting hole. Firm in lightly. Add more soil to bring it up to the level of the surrounding bed.

5 Trickle plenty of water around the edge of the rootball. Mulch with 2.5-5cm(1-2in) of bark chips or rotted organic matter. Keep well watered.

USING MULCHES

Mulching is a useful technique to use all round the garden to avoid routine weeding. It works by starving germinating weed seedlings of light, because they are buried under the mulching material. (Mulching also reduces moisture loss and insulates roots from extremes of heat and cold.) There are various mulching materials. Organic mulches, such as garden compost or well-rotted manure, improve the soil, since worms drag the material down into their burrows and virtually do your digging for you. With this type of mulch, weed seeds carried by the wind soon start to grow on the surface of the material. However they are easy to remove since the mulch is soft, so hoeing is quick and easy. Cocoa shell and chipped bark are available in bags at garden centres, so are cleaner to handle. They last longer than manure or garden compost mulches, but also break down in time. The larger the chippings, the slower bark is to break down; coarse material can last five years. For a really long-lasting effect use gravel, which only needs topping up occasionally. To be effective, spread any loose mulch of this sort 5cm(2in) deep. None will prevent strong perennial weeds, such as bindweed and nettles, growing through. Spot treat these with a glyphosate-based weedkiller, taking care not to spray surrounding plants. For a totally effective mulch, cover the ground with landscape fabric or a plastic film mulch. Lay this down after preparing the soil in a new bed or border, so that you can plant through it. With existing beds, lay it in strips between shrubs and perennials, leaving a large overlap. Tuck it carefully around the base of the plants to avoid weeds growing in the gaps. Once down, hide a plastic mulch with 2.5cm(1in) of gravel or bark.

1 Cover the soil with perforated black plastic or landscape fabric. Secure it with pegs sold for the purpose or bent wire prongs to prevent billowing in a breeze.

2 Spread a 5cm(2in)-thick layer of pea gravel with rounded edges evenly over the plastic. If the gravel comes from the seabed, wash it first to remove the salt.

3 Decided where you wish to put in a plant and scrape back the gravel to reveal the plastic. Leave the spare gravel nearby as it will be replaced after planting.

4 Make two cuts crossing each other in the middle of the planting site, each one about twice the diameter of the pot to allow room for working.

5 Peel back the corners of the plastic to expose the soil beneath; place stones or gravel on the flaps to hold them back while you put in the plant.

6 Scoop out soil from the planting hole with a small trowel. If the soil was not first prepared for planting, dig a larger hole and add organic matter.

7 When the plant is out of its pot, make sure that the planting hole is large enough to take the rootball. Sit it in position, with its best side to the front.

8 Fill in the space around the rootball with soil and firm down lightly. Water well and then push back the plastic flaps, so that they fit snugly around the plant.

9 Holding the plant over to one side, sweep the spare gravel back round the plant with your hand, so that all the plastic is completely hidden.

10 Continue adding plants in the same way, including some prostrate kinds that spill forwards over the gravel, so that it looks as if they had seeded themselves.

Soil improvers

Well-rotted garden compost made up of kitchen and disease-free garden waste.

Sedge peat or old growing bag mix lightens clay soils and increases the moisture-holding capacity of light soils.

Gritty sand contains a mixture of particle sizes. Dig it in to 'cure' clay.

Composted horse manure. Stack in a heap until soil-like or layer it between waste to help compost heaps rot down faster.

Coir. Use it alone as a soil improver or as ready-made sowing and potting mixtures.

Below: A low-maintenance gravel garden makes the most of a warm sunny spot. A deep covering of gravel leaves a firm pathway through the plants and keeps borders weed-free.

Left: This scheme would look equally at home in a cottage garden or a car parking area covered with gravel. In the latter case, roughly surround the plants with large stones as an early warning!

A RAISED LOG BORDER

In a shady situation under a light canopy of trees, a slightly raised woodland style bed looks most attractive. It also provides an ideal environment for growing shallow-rooted plants, such as rhododendrons and hostas, that like a moist humus-rich soil, especially if the surrounding soil is not entirely ideal for them. In very natural surroundings such as woodland, the hard manmade bricks and straight lines of a formal raised bed would look out of place, so use natural materials. You may have your own logs that can be cut to suitable lengths to edge a bed. If not, buy them from log merchants or timber yards. However, look out for interestingly bent and angled shapes to create natural curves, and use straight logs only for the back of a bed that runs alongside the edge of the garden. Elsewhere you can make island beds that look as if you have merely encircled a naturally occurring plant-studded knoll with logs. If the garden soil is reasonably good, fork it over to loosen it before laying out the log surrounds and filling the shape to the rim with a mixture of rich woodland soil and leafmould from under your own trees. Elsewhere you may need to buy good-quality topsoil, and add organic matter – composted bark or fairly small bark chippings are ideal in a woodland situation. Use them also as a mulch after planting to retain moisture and deter weeds, and top up the level each spring so that the worms constantly improve the soil. Bark chippings make a good surface for a woodland path that complements log-edged beds like this perfectly.

1 Start by preparing the ground well. Lay two courses of straight logs in a row to make the back of the raised bed. Save the very best lichen-encrusted logs for the front of the bed, where they will be most noticeable.

2 Use attractively curved or angled branches for the front of the bed.

3 Fill the bed with good-quality topsoil. If you have some spare soil from elsewhere in the garden, mix this with plenty of well-rotted organic matter before filling the bed.

4 Position the biggest plant first, after removing the pot. This rhododendron can be planted even though it is in full flower as it has been grown in a pot all its life and has a firm rootball that can be planted without any disturbance.

5 Divide up the remaining planting area into smaller 'cubicles'. Sprawling plants can ramble attractively over the logs, which also provide some support.

6 Fill the planting compartments with more of the soil and organic matter mixture. The logs acting as 'dividers' will be slightly higher than those edging the bed.

7 Choose a striking plant that contrasts well with the logs and the rhododendron, and enjoys similar growing conditions. Hostas are ideal for a woodland garden.

8 After planting the whole bed, spread a 5cm(2in)-deep layer of bark chippings or composted bark as a mulch all over the surface, tucking it under the hostas. The mulch helps to retain vital moisture.

A woodland feature

The finished bed makes a most attractive feature. All the plants are relatively slow-growing, but look good together and virtually look after themselves. Since the plants all enjoy light, dappled shade and some shelter, construct the feature under a canopy of birch or similar trees.

Under trees, the soil is often poor, dry and full of roots, so nothing grows well. By making a slightly raised bed like this, you create an 'island' of rich leafy soil in which woodland plants can thrive. They need humus-rich soil that stays moist but drains freely after rain. Before planting, dig out any weeds and add plenty of well-rotted organic matter to the soil.

You can pile up the soil in the planting compartments slightly higher than in the main area. This is a useful way of increasing the depth of good available soil for plants to grow in.

A mulch adds an authentic-looking woodland-style finish to the bed and sets off the plants to perfection. Lacy fern foliage contrasts with the craggy log bark and helps to blend the feature into the scenery.

*Good plants for a woodland bed include large-leaved hosta varieties, epimedium, dog's tooth violet (*Erythronium *sp.), hardy cyclamen, hellebores, dwarf narcissi, cultivated violets,* Corydalis flexuosa, Kirengeshoma palmata *and lily of the valley* (Convallaria majalis) *– the variegated version is particularly attractive. Since many woodland plants are spring flowering, add* Liriope muscari *for late-season interest. If the bed is large enough, use lilies that tolerate light shade, such as the heavily scented 'Mabel Violet'.*

9 Plant a hardy fern just outside the raised bed to conceal a congested corner where several logs join. Aim for a natural look, as if the fern has grown spontaneously.

Acer palmatum dissectum 'Atropurpureum'

Rhododendron 'Rosy Dream'

Matteuccia struthiopteris (shuttlecock fern)

Hosta fortunei var. *aureomarginata*

Hosta 'Frances Williams'

Colchicums

1 Colchicums flower in autumn; buy the bulbs in late summer. Plant them in groups, 10cm(4in) deep, in well-prepared soil in sun or light dappled shade.

2 Water the bulbs thoroughly. Colchicums soon flower but produce their foliage later. Do not expect to see any until the spring, when it should be left to develop.

3 *Colchicum* 'Waterlily' is a spectacular plant, with large double flowers up to 20cm (8in) across. Plant it in a well-sheltered spot protected by trees, as strong winds or early frosts can spoil the flowers overnight.

Tulips

Above: Tulips lend themselves well to formal bedding schemes. Plant them in a single row in a narrow border against a wall. To soften the effect, mix with spring bedding.

Right: Large-flowered tulips are best used as spring bedding. Dig up the bulbs after flowering to avoid rotting. Store in a dark, dry place to replant the following autumn.

BULBS IN THE GARDEN

Bulbs are invaluable for small gardens, as they provide a useful extra tier of colour under trees and shrubs. They also add seasonal colour to beds of perennials that normally peak in summer. As well as spring bulbs, you can also get autumn-flowering bulbs (colchicum, sternbergia and autumn crocus) and various summer-flowering ones, many of which are frost-tender. There are two ways of using bulbs. You can plant them as temporary bedding. This is mostly done with spring bulbs, which are dug up when the flowers are over and discarded to make way for summer bedding. However, frost-tender summer bulbs, such as tigridia, are used as summer bedding in much the same way as tender perennials. Plant them out after the last frost as dry bulbs, then dig them up after flowering and keep the dormant bulbs in a frost-free place to replant the following year. The other way of growing bulbs is to naturalise them by planting them in informal groups or as a random carpet. Once planted, the bulbs are left in the ground to increase naturally, and only dug up when they need to be divided. To achieve a natural effect, scatter bulbs on the surface of the ground by hand, dropping them in handfuls from about waist height, and then plant them where they land. To ensure that naturalised bulbs flower well each year, plant them at the right depth (as a rule, covered by three times their own depth of soil), feed generously by sprinkling bulb fertiliser or general feed around them after the flowers are over, and let the old foliage die back naturally.

Choosing bulbs

Choose clean, healthy, undamaged bulbs. If you buy them in late summer there should be no green shoots, but as their natural growing season approaches, short stocky shoots are acceptable.

Hyacinths

1 Hyacinth (and tulip) bulbs are naturally late to start rooting. Store them in a cool, dry spot until mid- to late autumn and then plant. If planted too early, dormant bulbs of these species are more likely to rot, especially if the soil is cold and wet.

2 A bulb planting tool is useful for planting bulbs in small groups. Press the tubular base into the soil to the right depth for the type of bulb and lift out a core of soil.

3 Place each bulb in position the right way up and screw it down into the soil at the bottom of the hole so the base plate of the bulb makes firm contact with the soil.

4 If you do not have a bulb planter, use a trowel to plant individual bulbs. Always mark the position of buried bulbs with a label marked with the name.

Below: Hyacinths are the most strongly scented of anything in bloom at this time. Group them close to doors and windows to appreciate their perfume.

Planting bulbs in grass

If you only have a few bulbs to plant or when planting in isolated clumps, cut holes through the turf with a bulb planter. Plant bulbs at the correct depth for their type. Some bulb planters have depth markings; if not, use a permanent marker pen to show the required depth.

1 Scatter bulbs, then lift each one to make a hole. Press the planter into the ground and twist to remove a core of turf and soil, which stays inside the planter.

2 Place a single bulb in each hole. Press it into the soil at the base to ensure it remains upright. If the hole is too narrow and deep, drop the bulb down it.

3 Reinsert the planter into the hole and squeeze the handle to drop the core of turf and soil back into place over the bulb. Firm the soil down to level the turf with the surrounding grass.

Left: *Daffodils are perfect for naturalising in grass. Mow the lawn in midwinter so that the flowers are not swamped by long grass. Then delay mowing again until six weeks after the flowers are over.*

PLANT ASSOCIATIONS

To keep a small plot filled with an ever-changing tapestry of colour through the seasons, you need many different plants. Compact ones are the best for creating fine detail. But it makes a garden difficult to plan, as the end result can look uncoordinated and messy. The secret is to make good plant associations. This is a way of organising plants into groups so that each one stands out individually, instead of getting lost in a solid mass of colour. It takes practice to master the art, but there are a few guidelines. Always choose an odd number of plants – three or five, for instance – each with something in common (perhaps a similar colour), but all contrasting (different heights, textures or shapes). They might include a plant with yellow flowers, one with gold foliage and another with yellow spots or stripes on the leaves. Plan a number of plant associations and then link them together to make a border, using a low, spreading plant as a carpet throughout the border. In a conifer bed, for instance, you could use heathers to connect 'islands' of architectural shapes visually. You do not have to keep plant associations for entire beds. In the same way, you can team a small specimen tree with two smaller plants, or underplant it with a contrasting coloured carpet of ground cover. You can bring hard architectural features, such as paving, gravel or ornaments of various kinds into play. A chimney pot, chunk of gnarled tree root or old rhubarb forcing pot is the perfect way to break up a large area of plants into visual, bite-sized chunks, each with its own mini focal point.

Left: Spiky leaves, circular flowers and soft fluffy foliage make a winning combination when the ingredients all enjoy the same growing conditions.. These are *Anthemis* 'Sauce Hollandaise', *Phormium tenax* and *Santolina incana*.

Above: Planting in narrow bands is a good way to bring out the contrast between different plant textures. This association of silver foliage pyrethrum and orange tagetes looks good edging a path or around a border.

Below: Subtropical plant associations are great fun, as the plants are big, bright and bold with bags of charisma. Giant banana leaves *(Musa basjoo)* combine here with stripy canelike *Arundo donax* 'Variegata' and tall spikes of colourful canna flowers.

Above: Many popular border plants make great natural partners. Blend spherical allium flowers with feathery fennel foliage, chunky box, colourful sage, architectural iris and euphorbia, frothy filler alchemilla and spiky lavender for an eyecatching update on a traditional look. They would look good with a box edging.

The right plant for the right place

To create plant associations on the spot, pick out plants at the nursery and stand the pots together while you build up the group around one key plant. In the garden, find the best place for a new plant by standing it – still in its pot – in various places and view it from different aspects to judge it alongside its neighbours. To compare several possible places at once, cut some flowers, each with a sprig of foliage, and stand them in jars of water round the border. Although it takes time to choose the right spot, it is much more satisfactory to do this than spend a season with a plant that is obviously in the wrong spot and which you then have to dig up and move at the end of the season.

Moving pictures

Plan perfect plant associations using pictures cut from catalogues and magazines. Even though the plants will not be in scale, you can gauge the effect of the colours and shapes next to each other. Start with two or three that go together, then build up a group of any size you like.

Left: *With care, you can easily find plants that bring out the best in each other. You can experiment to find the best planting positions simply by moving the pictures around.*

Left: *When buying an architectural feature, such as a seat, arch or gazebo, use plant pictures to find the best climbers to co-ordinate with it. The ones shown here all contain tiny touches of each other's colouring.*

DECORATIVE DETAIL

Making the most of a small garden is all about detail. In a large garden the main concern is to fill the big picture: creating a landscape with giant shapes, big blocks of colour and broad sweeps of grass; fine detail would never be noticed. In a small garden, it is the little things that count. Borders should be as varied as possible. Because you only use one plant of each kind, it is vital to make good plant associations so that each individual looks its best. And dwarf edgings of lavender or box visually unite even the widest mixture of plants. Raised beds provide opportunities to grow compact and miniature plants in scaled-down surroundings where it is easy to enjoy them. Containers are always on show so they must look immaculate all year round. Evergreens can be clipped, and shrubs trained as standards to save space and add interest. Every plant needs to look well groomed for the whole garden to shine. And that even means giving the lawn regular 'beauty' treatment. On the other hand, if you like a small garden to look clean and tidy but without making much work, just use a few specimen shrubs and trees that will not outgrow their welcome. A few suitable garden ornaments do much to bring out the character of a small group of plants, or a particular area within the garden. Avoid anything too large or fussy for the situation, and make sure it follows the general theme of the plants around it. Ideally, choose the ornament and plants at the same time, but if this is not possible try to take a photograph of the garden with you when shopping. In a small space, simple, natural-looking props made from everyday objects picked up from the ground often create a better effect than expensive ornaments.

Right: These simple decorations made from bits and pieces collected from around the garden break up a plain white wall very effectively. It is easy to alter or replace them whenever you feel like a change.

Below: Old items of garden equipment are good for themed decorations. They should look as if they have been casually abandoned and overgrown by plants, not deliberately placed in a border.

Left: A small group of flagons and interestingly shaped bits of wood bring this corner to life. The secret is to apply the same rules as for plant associations. Here, the three main objects are all similar but differ slightly in shape and size.

Right: Terracotta pots can be used in all sorts of creative ways around the garden, both with and without plants. This flowerpot man is held together by a metal plant support, and makes a striking centrepiece among the low leafy plants.

Right: You need not pay a lot for garden ornaments; these stones have holes through the middle and have been threaded onto a cane pushed into the ground.

Below: Wind chimes are a good way of drawing attention to a taller plant in a low background. This bamboo version makes a low, hollow sound in a light breeze.

Below: A layer of pebbles over the potting mix in a container adds decorative detail and helps to keep the mix cool and moist. Pick a colour that matches the pot.

Rustic plant supports

A little light support props up tall plants and those that fall forward or lean over the edge of the lawn and get in the way of the mower. Rustic supports made of woven or bent twigs not only do their job, but also make more of the plants. They are easy to make yourself from prunings.

Right: *Bent hazel stems, wired or tacked together, make decorative low plant supports. They usually last two or three years if taken under cover in winter, but are cheap to buy and easily replaced when past their best.*

Left: *An even simpler support like this can be pushed into a border temporarily at any time of year. You cannot hide the support, but this does not matter as it becomes part of the display, adding a touch of rustic style.*

Below: *Low sections of willow or hazel hurdle keep the lawn edge clear without looking unduly fussy – ideal for a country or cottage garden. Taller sections will discourage pets from taking short cuts through borders.*

GARDEN GROOMING

Good garden grooming means attending to little details that make all the difference between a garden that just looks alright and one that is immaculate. In a small garden, everything is on show all the time, so the little extra effort is well justified. Having a well-groomed garden naturally means keeping up-to-date with all the routine chores such as weeding, mowing, hedge-trimming and lawn edging. But it also means finding the time on a fairly regular basis to sweep paving, dig weeds out of the cracks between slabs on the patio, rake over bark mulch and gravel paths to restore a smooth level surface, and snip the dead flower heads off container and bedding plants. You will notice that a water feature with stones in it or a birdbath containing water turn green after a time and look better if scrubbed clean occasionally. (You can add an algicide to the water in a fountain or pebble pool where there are no fish or plants to be affected by it. Do not use it in a birdbath.) Garden ornaments that are left out all year also benefit from an annual spring clean; use a semi-stiff brush and warm water with patio cleaner to wash terracotta urns, stone statues, cast aluminium furniture and similar items. Rock plants and small shrubs, such as potentilla, heather and lavender, can be clipped lightly after flowering to reshape them and remove dead blooms before they turn brown. Many evergreens also benefit from a light trim. Provided you chose compact plants suitable for a small-scale garden, they should not need heavy pruning, but they stay looking much smarter if you periodically snip off any shoots that have grown too long and spoil the shape. Also remove plain green shoots from variegated plants whenever you see them. Clip trained plants, such as box spheres or topiary trees, twice a year in early and late summer to maintain a sharp outline, and twist or tie in climbers to their supports to prevent them looking straggly.

Left: Lavatera dies back to ground level in winter. Old stems protect the plant in winter, but remove them in spring to leave the shrub tidy. As new growth appears near the base, cut off the old stems close to ground level.

An ivy rope path edging

An edging of ivy makes a neat way of outlining garden beds and borders or steps, giving them structure and winter interest. It is a novel alternative to a dwarf box or lavender hedge, and does not need any clipping.

1 Plant ivies 45cm(18in) apart. Use all the same kind or a mixture of green and variegated varieties. Wait until the plants grow together and start to creep out onto the path before training them. No framework is needed.

Caring for patios and paths

Routine care: Regularly sweep up dead leaves, dirt, spilt soil or organic debris. They cause weeds and moss to establish, even over the top of cement. At the start of the summer remove mud and stains with a stiff brush and warm water with a drop of detergent.

Moss: Weedkillers will not kill moss, nor is it a good idea to use proprietary mosskillers unless they state that they can be used on paving – most do not. Dig out moss with an old knife or trowel instead.

Weeds: Dig out weeds with a narrow-bladed knife or eradicate them using a proprietary path weedkiller. This will kill any plant it touches, so keep it well away from any plants overhanging the paving or planted in it. (Remove large weeds by hand first, as woody stems persist, even after the weed is actually dead.) You can also use long-acting path weedkillers on a clean patio in spring to prevent weed growth for the rest of the season.

Liverwort and algae: Keep paving especially clean in autumn to prevent the surface becoming slippery. Treat it with tar oil wash or a suitable liquid mosskiller specially recommended for this use.

2 Untangle the ivy trails, combing them with your fingers. Remove any dead, brown or damaged leaves to tidy the plants as you work. Lay out all the trails in roughly the same direction.

3 Beginning at one end of the row, gather up trails from either side and a strong one from the centre to plait together. This holds all the stems together like a horizontal sheaf.

4 Work back along the row, tucking all the short shoots under the longer strands to hold them in place. Peg down the rope with some U-shaped hoops of stiff wire, leaving a neat outline.

5 As the ivies grow the rope thickens out. You can either tuck the new shoots in amongst the mass of others or snip off the tips. This makes sideshoots develop from the main stems and thickens the rope.

Clipping lavender

Soon after the flowers have faded, reshape the plants by clipping them lightly. This removes the dead heads and flower stems, plus the tips of young growths. Do not cut back into the old wood. New side shoots sprout within a few weeks, giving the plant a more natural look.

Left: *Using sharp shears, round off the shoulders of the plant to make a neat, even bun shape. Clear away all the cuttings to avoid fungal infections building up.*

Right: *Nip out the dead flowers of rhododendron between your fingers. Take care not to break off the soft buds on either side of them from which the following year's flower shoots develop.*

Variegated foliage

1 With golden or variegated shrubs it is vital to remove any shoots that revert to the normal green colour and soon dominate the bush if allowed to do so. Cut them out with secateurs

2 In the case of this Spiraea japonica *'Goldflame' you could also shorten the shoot on the right to improve the shape. Prune the whole plant fairly hard in early to mid-spring to keep it neat.*

Moving plants indoors

Tender perennials, such as pelargoniums and fuchsias, are killed by frost, so about two weeks before the first frost is anticipated in your area, pot them up and move them into a frost-free greenhouse, sunroom or porch or keep them on a cool windowsill indoors for the winter.

1 Once tender plants are past their best, dig them up with their roots, but shake off as much soil as possible. Do not worry too much about damaging the plant.

2 Use sharp secateurs to cut the oldest, woody stems back to about 2.5cm(1in) above the top of the roots. This gets rid of any fungal spores and leaf pests.

3 Trim away the longest roots, leaving the short fibrous roots close to the base of the stems. Since the plant has lost most of its top growth, you can safely remove more than half the roots. Aim to leave a fairly compact fist-sized rootball that will fit easily in a pot.

4 Put the plant into a suitably sized pot, using good-quality potting mix. Keep it in a well-lit, frost-free place for the winter. Tender perennials need a cool rest with just enough water to keep them alive. Warm, wet and humid conditions cause mildew.

TIDYING-UP IN AUTUMN

Autumn is the natural time for a big end-of-season clear-up, and especially in a small garden, it is a good opportunity to ensure that the winter view over the garden is tidy when seen from the house. Clear the borders of weeds that were previously smothered by foliage and cover the soil with a mulch of well-rotted garden compost. (Stack weeds and dead leaves ready for the compost bin.) Today, the trend is not to over-tidy perennial beds in autumn. Aim to make the garden look cared-for and to reduce the spring workload, but leave some plant stems to help wildlife through the winter. Leave the seedheads of bronze fennel, ornamental grasses and thistles for birds to feed on and only clear them when the last of the seeds have been eaten. And delay clearing the back of a border around the edge of the garden till spring, as the plant debris provides hiding places for overwintering beneficial insects, centipedes and money spiders. These useful creatures can then get straight to work on garden pests when they emerge in spring. Lawns need some attention now. A small lawn that gets heavy wear will benefit from raking, spiking and an autumn lawn feed to set it up for the spring. Expect to give the lawn its last main cut in mid-autumn, but while the weather stays mild you may need to cut it every three to four weeks until a sharp cold spell stops it growing completely. Leave the grass slightly longer than usual in winter, as this keeps it in better condition. Remove dead leaves that settle in drifts on the lawn or they will smother it, turning the grass yellow.

Storing dahlia tubers

1 When the first frost blackens dahlia foliage, cut off all the stems about 10cm(4in) above ground level and remove them.

2 Lever out the plant in one clump. Avoid spearing the large underground tubers, which may rot in store if damaged .

Tidying up perennials

When perennial plants reach the end of their yearly growing cycle, the leaves and stems die off naturally leaving the roots safely dormant underground. New shoots appear from the base next spring. Clear away the old material before then, so that all you see is the fresh new growth.

1 Collect up plant support frames and canes, cut away any plant debris and clean before storing for the winter. Throw away broken canes; treat sound ones with preservative.

2 In beds that are on show within the garden, cut off the dead foliage of perennial plants close to ground level. Soft healthy leaves and stems can be composted.

3 Spread a good layer of compost or manure around the crowns of perennial plants. If you have enough material, spread it 2.5cm(1in) thick all over the bed.

3 Remove as much earth as you can by hand. Then lift the plant into a container of water and wash off the remaining soil.

4 Turn the tubers upside down for a week to dry. Dust lightly with green sulphur powder and store in a dry, airy, frost-free place.

Plant labels

When tidying plants in autumn, make it a habit to check the labels. Plastic labels become brittle in sunlight and are easily snapped off or buried when mulching round plants. If labels are missing, replace them while you remember what the plant is, or rewrite the name if the writing has faded. (Use a permanent marker pen on plastic labels.) Longer-lasting systems, such as metal labels (write on them with a soft artist's pencil) or copper tags that are etched with a ball-point pen, are more secure.For an invisible way of identifying plants, push metal labels into the ground alongside plants where they can be easily retrieved if necessary, or make a paper plan of each bed with the positions of plants and their names safely marked, and keep it indoors.

Above: *Prune ornamental grape vines in midwinter. Remove most of the new growth, cutting back to one bud from an older stem.*

Garden maintenance

The end of the season is a good time to repair fences, treat timber sheds or fence panels with wood preservative, service the mower and clean and oil garden tools. Then everything is in order and ready to use the following spring.

Above: *Some perennials, such* as Sedum spectabile, *produce small shoots at their base that remain dormant all winter. Take great care not to damage these when tidying up borders. In a cold region, delay cutting back old shoots until spring, as they protect the plant.*

Garden equipment

Put away upholstered garden furniture and portable barbecues. (Waterproof covers are only intended for summer.) Hardwood benches and built-in barbecues benefit from cleaning and appropriate timber treatment. Clean cushions and other soft furnishings, dry them thoroughly, then store them indoors – not in a shed or garage, even if they are wrapped in plastic, as they will get damp and go mouldy.

Above: *Gather up woody perennial herbs in a handful and trim back the stems to about 7.5cm(3in) above ground.*

BUILDING A COLD FRAME

A cold frame is a useful addition to any garden. It is basically a bottomless box with a glazed lid and is used like a miniature greenhouse to grow seeds and cuttings and to acclimatise tender plants that have been raised under cover before they are finally planted out in the garden. It can stand on a hard surface, such as a patio or path – the best idea if you intend to fill it with seed trays and plant pots - or it can be placed directly on the soil so that you can plant things in it. You can buy ready-made cold frames, but making your own is a simple and satisfying project that allows you to tailor-make the frame to just the size you want. You can make the cold frame entirely from softwood, or build up the base in brickwork and add a wooden-framed lid. The lid can be glazed with glass, but plastic glazing materials are safer and easier to work with. Hinge it to the base so that you can open it during the day for ventilation and fit a simple catch to the front edge to keep it closed at night; strong winds could lift and damage it otherwise. If you want a larger planting and growing area than a single frame provides, simply add further bays to the basic structure as the need arises. Site the completed frame in a sunny position, ideally sheltered from the prevailing winds, and keep the lid clean to allow the maximum amount of sunlight to reach the plants inside. Cover it on cold nights with sacking or some old carpet to cut down on heat loss.

1 Cut the planks that will form the front, back and sides of the frame to length. Mark angled cutting lines on the two top side boards and cut along them.

Take care to keep the saw cut vertical as you saw along the marked line.

2 Cut front legs to the height of two full boards, plus the thinner end of the top side board. Drill clearance holes and screw the bottom two boards to one leg.

3 Interlock the grooved edge of the second full board over the tongue on the first one. Tap it down along its length to close up the joint. Screw the board to the leg.

4 Cut the back legs to match the height of two full boards plus the thicker end of the top side board. Continue to build up the box; attach the second set of boards all round.

5 Offer up the two tapered top side boards, interlocking the tongued and grooved edges as before. Attach them to the legs with two screws at the back and one screw at the front.

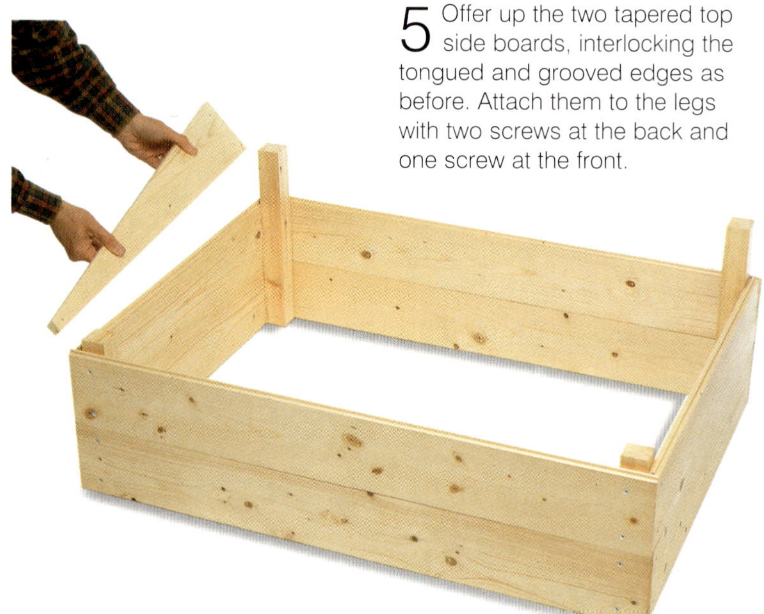

6 Cut down the top back board to match the height of the thicker end of the tapered top side boards. Include the tongued edge. Plane or sand the cut edge.

7 Cut down another board to create a narrow strip the same height as the thinner end of the top side boards. Screw it to the front legs to complete the base.

8 Measure the width and depth of the base as your first step towards constructing the glazed lid for the frame. Make it from 25x50mm(1x2in) planed softwood.

9 The two side pieces overlap the cut ends of the front and back pieces. Drill and counterbore holes for fixing screws; glue and screw the frame together.

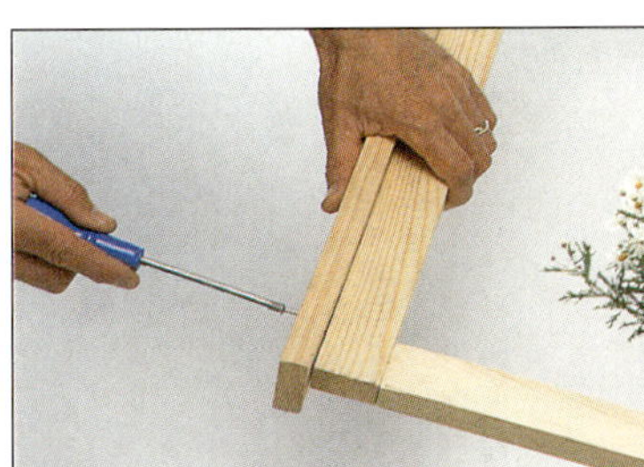

10 Glue and screw strips of 25x50mm(1x2in) softwood to the side edges to protect the edges of the glazing material and cover the corner fixing screws.

Finishing off

11 Cut the glazing material – here tough, twin-wall polycarbonate – to size. Use a fine-toothed saw and make cuts that run parallel to the internal ribs.

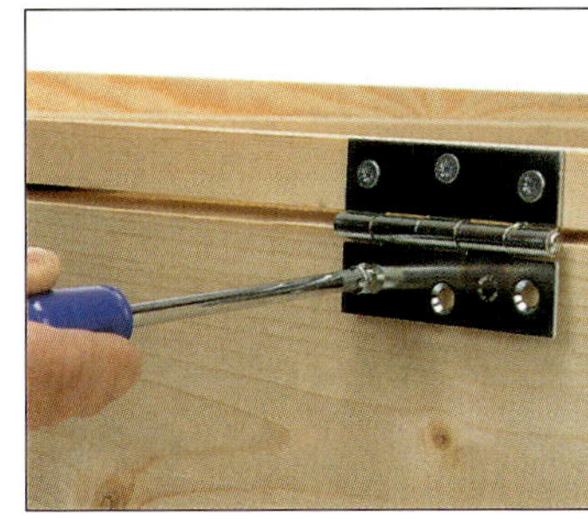

12 Lay the lid on the base. Position hinges about 230mm(9in) in from the corners, and attach them with 19mm(¾in)-long countersunk screws.

13 Treat the frame and lid with two coats of a preservative stain that is not harmful to plants. Leave it to dry with the lid propped open.

14 Place the plastic sheet on the lid and drill evenly spaced clearance holes through it. Screw it down, using plastic screw cups with snap-on covers.

You can buy special tape for sealing the cut edges of polycarbonate sheet.

15 Complete the screw fixings and check that all the screw caps are snapped in place. Use two small softwood offcuts to prop the lid open for ventilation.

A mirrored archway lends extra depth to a small but stylish courtyard.

PART FIVE

THE PATIO GARDEN

One of the most important features of a small garden is somewhere to sit. A patio can be any size; barely big enough for a couple of seats and a small table, or an entire garden. The secret of success is sun, privacy and plants.

THE PATIO BONUS

A patio is a tailor-made environment for both people and plants. The same conditions that make it a nice place for us to sit and relax also provide perfect growing conditions for container plants. Its close proximity to the house means that hanging baskets and pots do not get forgotten; as a tap is never far away, watering is quick and convenient. The sort of plants that suit patios best are those that naturally put people into a holiday mood – plants that thrive in sun and shelter and provide plenty of colour. So make the most of valuable container space to grow sun-shaped daisies, exotic climbers and subtropical-style bedding. It is a waste of a choice situation to grow plants that would do just as well in the open garden. And since patio plants are on show all the time, make the most of the space for plants that put on a long and spectacular show of flower all season long. Bedding plants, such as lobelia and verbena, and half-hardy perennials, such as fuchsias and gazanias, are favourites for pots. In hanging baskets, petunias and Swiss balcon geraniums (a type of trailing pelargonium with huge numbers of narrow-petalled flowers that hide the plants) cannot be beaten for their long, continuous flowering season. On walls and up trellis or over a pergola, annual climbers, such as ipomoea or *Thunbergia alata*, provide strikingly shaped flowers in bright colours. At the end of the summer replant the same containers with a fresh set of plants to provide winter or spring colour. If you want to avoid replanting containers in spring and autumn, you can also grow permanent plants on the patio – long flowering evergreens and climbers are the best value.

Above: When sitting out is too chilly to consider, all-year-round plants such as this phormium, plus seasonal bulbs and wallflowers, create an attractive cameo on a patio in spring.

Right: Morning glories (ipomoea) are among the most versatile annual climbers for a sunny sheltered patio. Use them in hanging baskets, in large pots with obelisks or on trellis screens.

Right A patio is an outdoor living room that you can use to entertain your family and friends al fresco. Choose from the wide range of outdoor furniture available to create a style that suits both the house and your garden.

Above: Permanently established containers of hardy plants provide a year-round display on the patio without making the regular work associated with annual flowers. Frost-proof containers are a 'must' and certain plants may need protection in long freezing spells.

Below: You can make an outdoor room as sophisticated as you like, just by varying the furnishings. If space is short indoors, creating an elegant outdoor dining room like this may be the perfect solution. Use lanterns on the table if the unshielded candles blow out.

Siting a patio

Observe your garden during the course of the day to establish which areas are the sunniest at certain times. You could plan for two or even more patio areas, each serving a different purpose or designed to catch the best of the sun at different times of the day.

***Left:** Here, the house shades the area immediately beyond the back door for most of the day. A spot like this is unlikely to make a successful patio. A pergola would be better here, with the patio located at the far end of the garden to catch the sun.*

***Left:** An adjoining or nearby building may cast unwelcome shadows on certain parts of the garden. Here, an irregularly shaped patio at the opposite side of the house and extending out into the garden is the practical solution.*

***Left:** In this situation, the whole garden is enjoying the benefits of full sunshine and only the front of the building is in shade. A conventional patio running across the back of the house is ideal here.*

LAYING SLABS ON SAND

The quickest way to lay a garden path or patio surface is to bed paving slabs on a sand bed. The slabs are relatively large, so once you have prepared the site you can quickly cover a sizeable area. First choose your slabs and make a note of their size and thickness. Most slabs are squares or rectangles; square slabs range in size from 230 or 305mm (9 or 12in) up to 610mm(24in) across, while rectangles measure from 455x230mm(18x9in) to 685x455mm (27x18in). The larger slabs are quite heavy and you may need help to handle them. Some ranges of paving also offer interlocking hexagonal slabs, complete with two types of half hexagon for finishing off the edges of the paved area, and slabs with a quadrant cutout in one corner; four of these placed together create a circular opening to fit round a tree or other feature. Most slabs are made in shades of buff, red and grey; the surface texture may be smooth, textured, riven to resemble natural split stone, or embossed in imitation of stone setts or paving bricks. Once you have selected your slabs, mark out the site with pegs and string lines so that you can take measurements and draw up a simple scale plan. This will be invaluable for estimating materials accurately and is a useful laying guide if you intend to create a pattern using slabs of different colours.

1 Unless the subsoil is firm, spread and compact a layer of solid material over the site. Gravel or crushed rock is ideal.

2 Excavate the site, level the subsoil and spread a 75mm (3in)-thick layer of filling. Compact it with a length of fence post.

3 Shovel out the bedding sand on top of the compacted filling and rake it out evenly to a depth of 25-50mm(1-2in) across the site.

4 If you have edge restraints, level the sand so its surface is just less than the slab thickness below the top of the edging.

5 The paving should have a slight fall (away from the house if this is adjacent) to help rainwater to run off it. Use a batten and spirit level to check the direction of the fall.

An edge restraint around the excavated site will prevent sand from leaching out.

6 Lay four slabs in one corner of the site, setting small wooden spacers between adjacent slabs to ensure an even gap for the pointing. You can remove the spacers as soon as each slab is surrounded by other slabs.

7 Lay a batten across the slabs and check the direction of the fall. If necessary, tamp the slabs further into the sand bed using the handle of a club hammer. Check the fall regularly as you work your way across the site.

Above: Yorkstone paving has a rough, craggy look and is the 'ultimate' paving for decorative uses, but do not use it for serious paths that you will need to use regularly in the winter as it is very slippery when wet or icy.

Below: Natural stone paving complements plants of all sorts and suits any style of garden. Use it for paths, paving and steps. It teams well with other natural hard surfaces such as gravel and cobblestones, bricks and terracotta edging stones.

8 Continue laying slabs across the site, kneeling on a board on the sand bed if you cannot reach right across the area from the edge. Be sure to check the fall regularly as you work.

9 Remove the last spacers and spread some fine sand across the surface. Brush it into all the joints with a soft broom, then sweep off the excess.

PLANTING IN PAVING

One way of livening up a large area of paving is to make sunken beds by removing occasional slabs and planting in the spaces, or to plant low-growing plants into the cracks between slabs. You could even combine the two ideas for a bigger, more imaginative planting scheme. Decide where you want to create a bed and stand the plants, still in their pots, on the slab you have decided to remove so that you can judge the effect.

If you are laying a new patio, it is simple to plan for such beds in advance. Instead of laying the usual rubble and concrete base over the whole area, leave the soil clear where your bed is to go. Improve the existing garden soil (assuming it is reasonably good) with organic matter, such as well-rotted garden compost, and pave round it. If you want to take up slabs from an existing paved area, chip away the cement from between the slabs and lever them out with a crowbar. If they are completely bedded into cement, you may not be able to avoid cracking them, and you may need a power hammer to remove them, together with the foundations beneath them, until you reach bare soil. Once the slabs are out, excavate as much rubble as you can from underneath and then refill with good-quality topsoil, enriched with some extra organic matter. You could leave the bed 'flush' with the paving, or make a low raised edge to it using bricks or rope-edged tiles. Plants growing in paving thrive because the surrounding slabs keep their roots cool and prevent evaporation, which means that the soil dries out much more slowly than potting mixture in containers. The plants have a bigger root run, too.

Above: Sempervivum plants are about the same size as pebbles, but instead of being smooth and round they have a spiky texture and may be bright red, purple or green. Use an occasional row in soil-filled cracks between paving slabs to contrast with real pebbles, but try to avoid putting them in places that will be walked on.

Planting in a paved area

1 Lever out the slab – this one is easy as it is loose-laid over soil. Excavate the hole so that there is room to put in plenty of good soil.

2 If the existing soil is fairly good, simply add suitable organic matter to improve the texture and help moisture retention.

3 Put the largest plant in the centre of the new bed. This compact, bushy potentilla will flower all summer. It spreads quickly and could fill the space left by a single slab in one growing season. Clip it the following spring to keep it tidy

4 Planting compact rock plants in the corners 'ties in' the bed with rock plants growing in cracks between other paving slabs nearby.

5 Plant all four corners for a neat look. Choose plants that contrast in colour and shape, and that will spill out over the paving.

6 Tuck some gravel around and under the plants for decoration and to improve drainage. Use the same gravel to cover gaps in the rest of the patio.

Sowing seeds

Sprinkle seeds of alpine flowers, alyssum or creeping thymes thinly in the cracks between paving slabs. Do this instead of using ready-grown plants or to fill gaps. Sprinkle a little fine grit over the top, barely burying the seeds, then water well. Keep the area watered until the seedlings grow into small plants. Thin them out – do not transplant them. Once they reach a fair size, undisturbed rock plant seedlings are more drought-tolerant than transplants.

Above: Tip the tiny seeds into your hand and sprinkle the barest pinch of seed very thinly into the crack in the paving.

Plants between paving stones

If possible, improve the soil before you lay the slabs, otherwise you will need to lever up the slabs around the cracks to work on the soil. If you do lift a slab, replace it carefully in order not to damage any plants. Use an old fork or spoon to make planting holes in a confined space.

1 Choose a mixture of low, mound-forming and compact, low, spreading plants. Plant them in the 'crossroads' between slabs.

2 Arrange plants of contrasting shapes next to one other. Lift the straggling ends of trailing plants onto the slabs as you plant.

3 Plant up several adjacent corners. In time, the plants will almost cover those slabs, so leave the main walking areas fairly clear.

4 Sprinkle pea-sized shingle over the cracks and under the necks of plants. It aids drainage and helps prevent rotting.

5 Water plants in well and do not allow them to dry out during the first growing season. After that, they should be able to survive, except in unusually long, hot, dry spells.

1 Place edge restraints – pegged boards or kerbstones – all round the area you intend to pave. Then cover it with sand and level it roughly with a straightedge.

2 To get the blocks level with the top of the edge restraints, measure the block thickness and tamp down the sand to this depth, with a slight fall across the area.

3 Decide on the laying pattern you intend to follow and start placing the first blocks on the sand bed. For a patio or path, simply tamp the blocks down level with each other using a hammer handle.

4 Most patterns have a plain border. Here, a single row is laid along each edge. Use a batten and spirit level to check that the second edge is level.

BLOCK PAVERS ON SAND

Block pavers are relative newcomers to the world of garden building, but have rapidly become extremely popular because they are small and easy to handle, are designed to be dry-laid on a sand bed and need no pointing. Unlike other dry-laid paving, they can even withstand the weight of motor vehicles thanks to the way they interlock once laid, so they can be used for all hard surfaces around the garden. However, for large areas you must lay the sand bed with a continuous edge restraint to prevent the sand from leaching out. Be sure to use concreting sand for the bedding layer, as building sand is too soft and may stain the blocks.

The blocks are made in a wide range of colours and generally rectangular in shape, measuring 200x100mm (8x4in) and about 65mm(2½in) thick. This shape allows you to lay the blocks in a variety of patterns, from a simple stretcher-bond arrangement resembling brickwork to herringbone and basketweave designs. You can also lay them diagonally across the area you are paving, filling in the edges with cut-to-size pieces. If the pattern requires many cut blocks, it is well worth hiring a hydraulically operated block splitter that cuts cleanly through the dense aggregate. You can split them with a bolster chisel and a club hammer, but they may not break cleanly. The small size of pavers means they are excellent for creating paving in non-standard shapes. You can make small paved areas anywhere around the garden where they are needed, to support a heavy ornament, for example. Even when loose laid on sand, they make a much firmer foundation than gravel.

6 Build up the paving by adding more blocks, working away from the first corner. Check constantly that the pattern is correct as you work.

5 Start laying the blocks in your chosen pattern; this will be a simple basketweave design with pairs of blocks placed at right angles.

7 After completing a small area, use a straightedge to check that the blocks are level with each other. Then check the fall with your spirit level. Tamp down any pavers that stand proud

8 When you have completed all the paving, spread some fine sand over the surface and brush it well into all the joints between the blocks. Sweep off the excess.

Rope twist edging

Strong retaining edges are vital where pavers are bedded onto loose sand, as otherwise rainwater would slowly erode the base away, making a path collapse along its edges. One of the most attractive ways to fix the edges are to use rope twist tiles. Mark out the position of the path first, carefully calculating the width based on the size of the pavers. Then excavate the area to a depth of 10cm(4in). Position the rope tiles along the edge, bedding them into a shallow trough filled with cement to hold them in place. Spread a 4cm(1.5in) layer of sand over the base of the path and lay the pavers in place.

Right: You can use pavers to create attractive dog-leg shapes like this good solid path, which looks equally at home in any type of situation, including a cottage garden, a traditional formal design or a modern contemporary setting.

Herringbone pattern

1 A contrasting border is one of the simplest effects you can create. Here, the border pavers are laid side by side and the infill is added in herringbone style.

2 Tamp the pavers into the sand bed, using a wood offcut and a club hammer to set them level with their neighbours. Lift and relay any that sink down or stand proud.

3 Use a long wooden straightedge and a spirit level to check that there is a slight fall across the paved area. This will ensure that heavy rain can drain freely off the surface of the paving.

Below: The continuous pattern begins to build up as you work across the area. The cut blocks at the edges of the area maintain the herringbone bond.

PATTERNS WITH PAVERS

The block paver is ideal for creating paths, patios and other paved areas in the garden, because it is light and easy to handle and quick and simple to lay. Most people choose a monochrome effect, laying pavers of just one colour and relying on the way in which they are placed for extra visual interest. However, as pavers are made to a standard size there is no reason why you should not use pavers of different colours to create distinctive patterns, or even mix them with other paving materials or cobbles. Pavers now come in a wide range of shades, from yellow and red to buff and brown and various shades of gray, so you can choose complementary or contrasting effects as you prefer. The only limit to what you can create is your own imagination. One of the simplest options is to use a band of different-coloured pavers along the edges of the area. If you prefer to mix the colours across the whole area, you can simply insert pavers of the second colour regularly or at random. The basketweave pattern – pairs of pavers laid at right angles to the adjoining pair – allows you to create a chessboard effect, while the popular herringbone pattern can feature zigzagging bands of different-coloured pavers. If you are prepared to cut blocks in half, there is even more scope for creating attractive patterns. Keep an eye open for unusual effects created with block pavers in public spaces; you can then copy any ideas you like in your own garden.

Cutting bricks and pavers

To cut a brick, mark a line on the brick and score it all round with the tip of a bricklayer's chisel. Place the brick on a bed of sand and drive the chisel with blows from a club hammer to break the brick at the marked position.

To cut a paver, score a cutting line deeply across its face by drawing the corner of a bolster chisel against a straightedge. Place the paver on a sand bed and cut it with a chisel and hammer.

Mixing block pavers and paving slabs

Small paving slabs can look particularly attractive when combined with block pavers. Be sure to choose your slabs with care, so that their size coordinates with a whole number of pavers, or you will end up either with unacceptably wide joints or impossibly intricate block trimming.

Left: If you are mixing pavers and slabs, choose slabs with sides equal to a whole number of pavers. Experiment with designs on paper. Place extra sand beneath the slabs to keep them level with the pavers.

A squared pattern

Left: First work out the pattern you intend to lay on squared paper, so that you can order the right numbers of each colour. Start building up the pattern from one edge, checking it against your plan as you work.

Above: Here, half blocks in a contrasting colour have been used to fill in the open centre of a square formed by four full blocks. The repeated motif creates a striking visual effect.

Diagonal zigzag pattern

Mixing pavers of different colours can create even more dramatic effects if you are prepared to work to a diagonal grid rather than a square one. It allows you to create straight lines or zigzags running at an angle to the edge of the paved area, according to the laying pattern you adopt. However, designs of this sort involve a great deal of block cutting at the perimeter of the area, so allow for this when estimating quantities and add some extra pavers to cater for the occasional cutting blunder. Plan the layout and pattern on paper first, so that you can check your progress as you work and avoid costly mistakes.

Right: *With the edge restraints and border pavers in place, build up the diagonal pattern. Move a line across the area as the pattern extends, and include pavers cut at an angle as necessary to maintain the design.*

Left: *The simple grey zigzag perfectly complements the straight border. Here it is about to be repeated at the near edge of a path. Hire a block splitter to make light work of cutting the angled infill pieces neatly.*

Using weathered bricks

Left: *The colours and textures of old or recycled bricks vary even within the same brick. To make the most of them, use them very simply for paving, raised beds or a plinth for a garden ornament. Brick colours team well with red flowers.*

LAYING SLABS ON MORTAR

A patio designed to support nothing heavier than, say, a loaded wheelbarrow and patio furniture, can safely be laid on a sand bed. However, if a patio surface is intended to support a considerable weight it will be necessary to prepare a concrete base on which to lay the paving slabs. Excavate the site to a depth of at least 150mm(6in) – more if the subsoil is unstable – and lay a concrete base a minimum of 100mm(4in) thick. You can use ready-mixed concrete or mix your own with one part of cement to five parts of combined sand and 20mm(¾in) aggregate. Set up wooden shuttering around the area to give the base a neat square edge, tamp the concrete down well, level the surface with a long straightedge laid across the formwork and remove any excess material. Give the base a slight fall across its width, and incorporate full-width vertical expansion joints of hardboard or similar material every 3m(10ft) to prevent the base from cracking. Cover the concrete with plastic against rain or frost, or use damp sacking if it is hot and sunny. Leave to set for at least three days.

Above: Paving slabs set in concrete might seem more suitable for a formal garden, but it all depends what sort of slabs are chosen and how they are used. Here, steps and a patio with violas growing in the crevices, make a successful transition into a wildlife garden.

1 To give the slabs adequate support, place the mortar on the concrete base in a square beneath the edges of the slab and add more mortar beneath the centre of the slab.

Use a concrete mix of 1 part cement, 2½ parts concreting sand and 3½ parts 20mm(¾in) aggregate or a mix of 1 part cement to 5 parts of combined aggregates.

Use a fairly sloppy mortar mix (1 part cement, 1 part lime, or a measure of plasticiser and 6 parts building sand), so that it is easy to spread beneath the slabs.

2 Lower each slab gently onto its mortar bed and tamp it down evenly with the handle of a club hammer to compress the mortar and make the paving slab level with its neighbours.

3 After placing the slab, bedding it down and setting it to the correct fall, insert small wooden spacers between it and its neighbours to ensure an even pointing gap.

A pointing guide

If the pointing mortar stains the slab surface as you work, reduce the problem by using a guide made from a plywood offcut. Cut a slot into the plywood to match the joint width and lay the offcut on the slabs. Fill the joints through the slot.

4 Continue laying the slabs in this way, checking that the surface has the correct fall. Tamp down out-of-line slabs a little more if necessary.

Use a spirit level and a long straightedge to check level and fall.

5 When all the slabs are laid and levelled, remove the wooden spacers and point the joints with a fairly dry mortar mix. Force it well into the joints with the edge of a pointing trowel. Alternatively, brush dry mortar into the cracks between the slabs and water it with a fine rose. This washes in the mortar, wets it enough so it can set and cleans the slabs.

Mixing mortar

Mortar is used as an adhesive to bond bricks and blocks together when building walls or steps or to bed paving on a solid substrate. A standard mix consists of one part of ordinary Portland cement, one part hydrated lime and six parts of fine sand. You can use masonry cement instead of cement and lime, or replace the lime with a chemical plasticiser.

1 Measure out dry ingredients by volume on a smooth hard surface. Mix them together, from the edges towards the centre.

2 If the sand is at all damp, lumps will form. Break them up as you work, using the edge of the shovel in a chopping motion.

3 When the mix is a uniform colour and free from lumps, form a crater in the centre of the heap and add a little water from a watering can or hose.

4 Shovel the dry mix into the crater to absorb the water. Turn the mix over and add more water as necessary, but take care not to make the mix too sloppy.

5 The mix should hold its shape when formed into smooth ridges. If it is too sloppy, add one small measure of cement and lime and five measures of sand.

6 Compact the mix into a heap so that it does not dry out too quickly. To test its plasticity, take a slice of mortar onto a trowel; it should stick readily to the blade.

Preparing stones

If you are using slabs from different manufacturers, make sure they are all the same thickness, or it will be difficult to get a level surface to your finished paving.

Right: To break up a stone or improve the fit, lodge it between two stones and crack it cleanly with a firm hammer blow.

CRAZY PAVING

Crazy paving aptly describes the effect created when pieces of randomly shaped stone are interlocked to create a hard surface for drives, paths and patios. It is economical to buy, making use as it does of broken pieces of square or rectangular paving that would otherwise go to waste. The stones fit together like the pieces of a jigsaw and the gaps between them are pointed with mortar, which bonds the stones to a stable base layer. An old concrete surface would make an ideal foundation for a driveway or parking place; well-rammed coarse aggregate is suitable for light-duty areas, such as a patio or garden path. Crazy paving can look very attractive if you fit the pieces together carefully and neatly detail the pointing. You can achieve interesting decorative effects by mixing stones of different hues and textures or by using mortar pigments in the pointing that contrast with the colours of the stones. Having trimmed the stones, if necessary, to improve their fit, piece them together one by one, tamp them down into a mortar bed and level them. Start at the perimeter, using stones with one straight side, and use a long wooden straightedge as you lay down more stones to ensure that they are level. If necessary, check that the stones are laid to a slight fall to allow surface water to drain off. Only spread as much mortar as you can cover with paving pieces within the time it takes for the mortar to set.

1 Sort stones into groups: corner stones with two adjacent square edges, perimeter stones with one straight edge, large, irregularly shaped stones and smaller infill pieces.

2 A solid foundation is essential for crazy paving. Spread a bed of fairly sloppy mortar along the perimeter of the base layer.

3 Choose relatively large stones with two adjacent straight edges to form the corners of square or rectangular paved areas.

4 Set the corner stone in place, tamp it down into the mortar bed using a wood offcut and check the levels in both directions.

5 Place the next perimeter stone on the mortar bed in line with the first, tamp it down and check that it is level with its neighbour.

6 Complete one edge of the area, including the next corner stone. Then start building up the jigsaw effect with large and smaller stones.

7 As you extend the paving, use a spirit level and a long straight-edge to check that the stones are level (or have a constant fall).

Allow a slope of 1 in 40 away from adjacent buildings or across free-standing paths and drives.

8 Allow the mortar bed to harden overnight before filling and pointing the joints. Draw the trowel point along the joint to leave a ridge and two sloping bevels.

Left: Well-designed, carefully constructed crazy paving makes a practical and economical path. Remove the bare look of a new path by encouraging adjacent plants to sprawl over it or plant new ones. Here, *Helleborus argutifolius* is used as an edging plant.

Informal mixed paving

You can use almost any durable material for informal paving as long as it looks good, is laid with care and is an integral part of a whole area. If you have a large quantity of one or two materials – say, old bricks and pieces of flat rock – group them so that they appear at intervals throughout the whole space and fill in with patches of scarcer pieces.

1 Rake the ground to remove any debris and loosen and smooth the soil. Tread it down firmly and evenly, taking care not to leave 'pits' in the surface.

2 Lightly rake over a thin layer of clay crocks or pebbles and tread them down well. All the hardcore must be bedded in, not overlapping and loose.

3 Space out and bed in the larger pieces first. Fill some of the gaps with cobbles at the same depth as the bricks and slabs laid across the area.

4 Use shingle to fill the last gaps. Many low-growing plants thrive in these conditions. This lovely Oxalis adenophylla *furls its leaves when not in sun.*

5 When planting up the spaces in a path or patio, keep to tiny mat-forming subjects and crevice-dwellers, and plan a route that can be followed easily and naturally among them. Surround tiny plants with some grit; it protects them from slugs and keeps them well drained.

Laying pebbles and cobblestones

It is best to bed pebbles and cobblestones in mortar, especially if they form a surface that will be walked on or are used to line a watercourse or surround a fountain. Within decorative areas they can be loose-laid.

1 To outline a pebble path with a border of paving bricks or granite setts, spread a generous mortar bed, set the bricks in place and point neatly between them.

2 Place pebbles on the mortar bed, butting them up closely to the border and to each other. Select stones for fit and the colour contrast with their neighbours.

3 Use an offcut and a club hammer to tamp down the pebbles into the mortar bed. It is important to ensure that they cannot subsequently work loose.

4 Check that the stones are reasonably level across the surface. If any of them project too far above their neighbours, tamp them down further.

5 Water enhances the natural colours and textures of pebbles with dramatic effect. Create this look artificially by coating the finished bed with a clear silicone masonry sealant.

PEBBLES AND COBBLES, EDGES, TILES AND SLABS

Naturally rounded pebbles and larger cobblestones are a good way of introducing varieties of shape and texture to your paving. You can use them to create paths and patios, but they are more commonly used as a visual counterpoint to flat surfaces – perhaps as a border or to highlight a garden feature, such as a sundial or statue. Their advantage over other garden paving materials is their relatively small size, which makes it easy to fit them round curves and irregularly shaped obstacles. However, because of this, they do take much longer to lay than other materials. You can buy pebbles and cobblestones from builders' suppliers and garden centres, in a range of sizes and colours. Small quantities – enough for an individual garden feature – are usually sold in bags, but for larger areas it will be more economical to buy the stones loose by weight. Ask your supplier for advice about coverage, and have large quantities delivered; more than two or three sacks will wreck your vehicle suspension.

Frostproof terracotta pavers, embossed tiles and decorative edging are becoming increasingly popular. They can be used alone or mixed with other paving and edging materials for strong visual contrast. Terracotta pavers and tiles are not as strong as other paving materials, so bed them on a continuous mortar bed for solid support.

Left: You can make a most attractive pathway by blending contrasting surfaces, such as gravel and brick, with creeping plants. Creeping thyme is excellent in this situation, as it does not mind being crushed occasionally, and being fragrant, it creates its own pleasant atmosphere.

Laying tiles and edging

Secure terracotta edging strips in place with a strip of mortar along each side. Slope it as shown and check that it is low enough to allow the paving slab to butt up against it. Terracotta rope edging is sold in lengths of about 610mm(2ft). Use a strong mortar – 1 part cement to 3 or 4 parts sand, plus added plasticiser – to bed the edging in place.

1 Set the rope edging and corner posts in place. Spread a bed of sloppy mortar over the area to be paved. Place the corner tile first, then add further tiles.

2 With a few tiles in place, check that they are level when viewed against the edging. Use a spirit level to ensure that each row is level across the tiled area.

3 Here, decorative tiles form a border to plain terracotta pavers, each equivalent in size to four tiles. Place the paver on the mortar bed, tamp it down and check the levels.

4 This completed module shows how the edging, tiles and pavers are coordinated in size. The edging length matches three tile widths.

Mosaic pattern

Left: *Mosaics are easy to make from almost any hard flat ingredients, though broken ceramic tiles are always popular. To make a mosaic work, first fit the pieces together to make the pattern, then push them down into a bed of damp mortar.*

Splitting tiles

1 To cut a paver, score a cutting line deeply across its face. Draw the corner of a bolster chisel against a straightedge for increased accuracy.

2 Place the paver on a sand bed and cut it with a chisel and hammer. Move the chisel along the line until the paver splits cleanly in half.

WOODEN DECKING

1 On firm ground, support the joists on bricks. Space them evenly, using a plank to align the joist ends and to check that the tops are level.

2 Cut a fascia board to the width of the decking and secure it to the joist ends with galvanised nails. Fix a batten across the tops of the joists at the other end of the deck.

3 Cut and position the first plank across the joists so that its front edge projects over the fascia and forms a projecting nosing. Secure it to each joist with two nails.

Wooden decking is a natural alternative to hard paving in formal and informal gardens. The raw material is widely available and costs broadly the same as paving (unless you choose an exotic hardwood instead of softwood). It is much easier to cut to size than paving slabs or blocks, quickly blends in with its surroundings as it weathers and is more forgiving to walk or sit down on than hard paving. The only disadvantages of wooden decking are that it will need occasional maintenance work and that it can be slippery in wet weather. Make sure that all the sawn joists and planed planks for decking have been pretreated with preservative and apply a preservative stain to the completed structure, paying special attention to any cut ends you have sawn during construction. To keep the decking clear of damp ground and reduce the incidence of rot, set the joists on bricks, ideally with a pad of damp-proof membrane or roofing felt between bricks and joists. Clear the ground beneath the decking and apply a long-term weedkiller first.

Wooden decking looks particularly good in modern surroundings or teamed with a woodland or oriental-style garden. To make the most of the timber theme, use wooden containers and furniture and choose plants that suit a timbered background, such as hostas, hardy ferns, camellias, lilies and miniature rhododendrons in wooden tubs. Try the striking shapes of yucca, phormium and Chusan palm with exotic-looking half-hardy plants such as agave, aeonium or abutilon. And for an oriental feel, go for a few well-shaped, clipped conifers and bonsai shapes in oriental ceramic pots.

4 Leave a slight gap between adjacent planks so that rainwater can drain freely. Set a slim batten against the first plank, then position the second plank against the batten. A temporary batten on the other side holds the joists parallel while you fix the planks.

5 Secure the plank to each joist, punching two galvanised nails just below the wood surface. A string line will help to align the nail heads across the decking.

Finishing touches

Below: Treat the decking with a preservative stain or wood dye to improve its resistance to rot and insect attack.

Above: Butt-join planks as necessary over the centre line of a joist. Sand the cut ends first to prevent splinters.

6 Set the decking on bricks or blocks bedded in the subsoil so that the joists are held clear of the ground. Hide the supports with pebbles or low-level planting.

Wooden decking tiles

You can buy small, preassembled wooden decking tiles made from preservative-treated softwood. Some also have a non-slip grooved surface. You can lay them directly on the soil, but it is a good idea to support them on joists to create whatever area of decking you require.

1 The tiles have closely spaced slats held together by two stapled-on support battens. Start by making up a framework of preservative-treated joists to support the prefabricated tiles.

2 Space the joists to allow the tiles to meet along the centre line of each joist and then lay in the individual tiles in the desired pattern.

3 Nail the tiles through the slats into the joists beneath. If you prefer invisible fixings, drive screws between the slats through the support battens.

'Traditional' planked decking can cover as large an area as you need.

4 In this case, all the tiles have been laid with their slats running in the same direction, but you can create different patterns with them.

1 Use preservative-treated sawn softwood for joists. Space them evenly and nail a transverse joist to their ends to hold them in position.

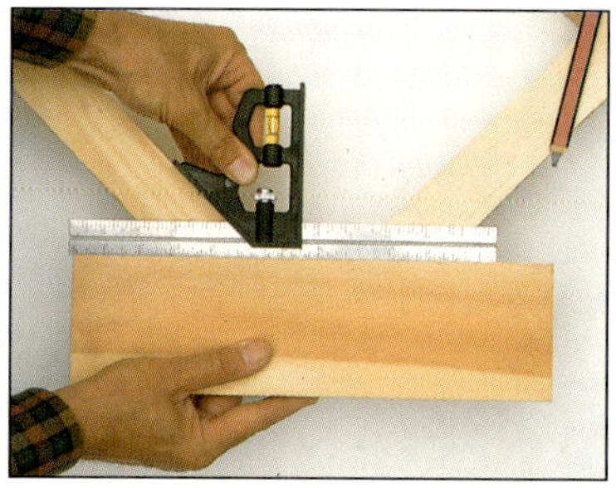

2 To set planks at a 45° angle to the joists, use a combination square to position the first plank at the corner of the joist framework.

3 Once you have positioned the first plank accurately, remove the square and mark the plank position on the joists below.

4 Use the square with its 45° face against the plank edge to mark a guideline for the nails above the centre line of the joist beneath.

5 Nail on the first plank. Drive in the nail nearest the corner first, check the alignment of the plank with the pencil lines, and secure it with two more nails.

6 Use a slim batten as a spacing guide to ensure that the gaps between adjacent boards are the same across the decking surface. Offer up the next plank.

DECKING DESIGNS

Since wood is easy to cut to size and shape, you can create any number of decorative designs. Carefully work out the design on paper first, adjusting the spacing between the planks to ensure that a whole number will fit the area you want to cover. You can create chevron and diamond patterns by reversing the direction of the planking on adjacent areas of the decking. Round off cut edges slightly with sandpaper to ensure that they are free from splinters. Provide additional protection for the perimeter of the decking by nailing on edge battens all round.

Wood is a material that allows your inventiveness full rein when it comes to creating walkways and sitting areas in the garden. Set alongside a garden pond or other water feature, it conjures up images of sturdy wooden jetties on a boating lake. Placed amongst an overflowing border, it creates a natural-looking pathway that blends in with the informality of the planting far more sympathetically than any masonry path can. The structures you create with it can be assembled from small modules put together in your workshop and then arranged – and rearranged – in the garden. However you decide to use it, remember the two essential rules. Firstly, all wood that spends its life in contact with the ground must either be a naturally durable species, or else be thoroughly pretreated with wood preservative to keep rot and insect attack at bay. Secondly, wood can become slippery when wet since moss and algae will grow on its surface, so be prepared to scrub it down once or twice a year to keep it in a safe condition and looking good.

7 Repeat the procedure with the square and pencil to ensure that the nails securing the second plank are in line with those holding the first one. A combination square (or adjustable try square) is an excellent tool for checking and marking angles.

8 Use the spacer batten to position subsequent planks, nailing them to the joists one by one. Punch the nail heads just below the surface of the wood.

9 When all the planks are nailed down, place a straightedge over the projecting ends, align it with the outer face of the joist below and mark a cutting line.

10 Use a panel saw to cut off the projecting ends of the planks. Saw just on the waste side of the cutting line, taking care to keep the saw blade vertical as you work.

11 Sand all the cut ends of the planks to remove splinters. Nail on edging battens for a neat finish and to protect the exposed end grain against rot and damage.

Above: *Raised hardwood decking with a built-in bench surround. The furniture, too, is hardwood so it can safely be left outdoors all year round. From this vantage point, you have a perfect bird's-eye view of a woodland garden.*

12 You can treat the finished decking with clear wood preservative (as here), a coloured preservative stain or wood dye. Avoid varnish, which will soon blister and crack.

Wooden decking makes a natural background to many plants and sets of containers perfectly.

SEATING IN THE GARDEN

Mention garden seats and people think either of traditional wooden chairs and benches or lightweight portable garden furniture. Both can be surprisingly expensive to buy. Portable items have to be set up before use and then stored away under cover when they are no longer required, while traditional pieces (usually left outdoors in all weathers) are becoming an increasingly popular target for thieves. One inexpensive, permanent and thief-proof solution is to build your own seating using bricks, mortar and preservative-treated wood. You can site a seat like this anywhere in the garden, but the best positions will allow you to catch the sun while you rest from your labours and admire the view. This simple bench consists of two piers of brickwork, built without the need for any cut bricks, and a slatted seat that is screwed unobtrusively to the masonry to create a sturdy, good-looking and surprisingly comfortable garden structure. You can build it directly on any existing paved or concrete surface; if you want to site it down the garden, set two paving slabs on some well-rammed subsoil to provide a stable base for the masonry. Choose bricks that match those used to build your house if you plan to site the seat close by. If you prefer to build it further down the garden, you could use garden walling blocks to create a seat with a more rustic appearance. The seat can be left with a natural finish (protected by clear preservative), or can be stained or painted if you prefer a coloured finish. The slats allow rainwater to drain away freely, but if you prefer a solid seat, simply close up the gaps between the slats and glue them together with waterproof woodworking adhesive before screwing it to the supporting framework.

1 Build up the piers, positioning two bricks side by side and a third at right angles to them in each course. Check that each face is truly vertical.

2 Decide on the width of the bench and build up the second pier in the same way. Use a spirit level on a timber straightedge to check that the two piers are precisely level with each other.

3 Cut two support blocks from 50mm(2in) square softwood, slightly longer than the depth of the piers. Fix one to the outside of each pier with screws and wallplugs.

4 Cut two seat edge slats to length and attach them to the ends of the seat support blocks. The overlap at each end helps to conceal the support blocks.

5 Screw on the first seat slat so that it rests on top of the front edge slat. Use a spacer slat to position the next one. Countersink all screw heads. Add more slats.

Stone seats

Stone seats are a permanent part of the garden. They last for ever and if anything look better as they age, due to the natural encrustation of lichens they acquire in an area with clean air. However, if necessary, scrub them annually with a stiff brush and soapy water. Do not use chemicals.

Above: A stone bench surrounded by pebbles lends a Mediterranean air to a paved area against a colour-washed wall. A matching statue or plant container plus some aromatic plants would strengthen the theme.

6 Apply two coats of clear preservative to keep rot and insect attack at bay, or use paint or stain if you prefer a coloured finish to the natural look.

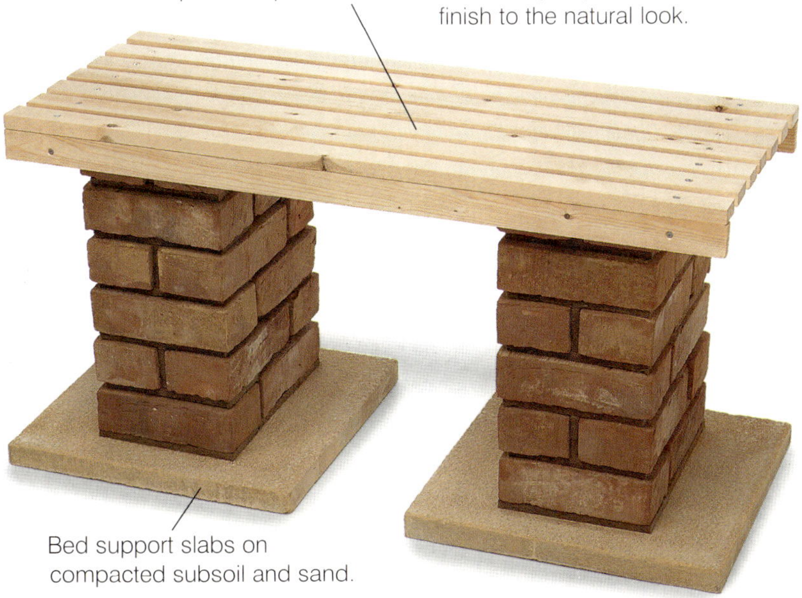

A seat around a tree

A tree seat turns a bare tree trunk into an attractive garden feature that provides generous seating even in a small garden. Seats are available in various sizes to match a range of different tree diameters. Use curved moulded edging stones as a sturdy base for the legs.

1 Buying a prefabricated tree seat avoids the need for fairly complex carpentry. Treat the seat with a preservative stain before assembling it.

2 Cut away the turf, compact the subsoil and lay a bed of sand in the excavation. Put each moulded edging stone in place and tamp it down to get it level.

3 Stand the first prefabricated seat section in place on its stones, then offer up the second section. Raise or lower the stones slightly as necessary.

4 Thread the bolts through the predrilled holes. Add another washer before fitting the nut so that it does not bite into the wood. Tighten the bolts well.

5 Give the seat a new coat of preservative paint when necessary. Wood is ideal for garden use; it is both warm and comfortable to sit on and dries off quickly after rain. Durable hardwoods are dearer than softwood.

Vivid flowers and bold plants displayed to perfection in clay pots.

PART SIX

GARDENING IN CONTAINERS

Container gardening is the ultimate in compact horticulture. Pots, tubs and troughs let you grow plants anywhere, even where there is no soil. And by using windowboxes, hanging baskets and wall pots, you can make the most of wall space, too.

USING CONTAINERS

Containers are probably one of the most important ingredients in a small garden. The type you choose makes it easy to identify the general style of the garden instantly; clay pots equal cottage garden, patterned terracotta says Mediterranean, while hand-painted pots state fashionable 'designer garden', and expensive lead or stone planters suggest formal gardens. Containers make natural focal points, drawing attention to key places such as porches and entrances. In groups, they form the main decoration for patios, while a single large container makes a striking centrepiece for a courtyard or garden room. Because they are so important to the garden, they must look good all year round. For most gardeners, this means filling them with colour. Several changes of annuals, planted for short-term seasonal effects, is the very best way to make the most of containers. True, this creates extra work, but planting and replanting containers involves much less effort than using bedding plants in a garden bed. There is virtually no soil preparation or weeding to do in containers and very little pest control. Deter slugs and snails by applying anti-pest 'glue' around pot rims, and take advantage of special potting mixtures with added pesticide. However, feeding, watering and deadheading are regular vital chores that you must make time for, but even these do not really take long compared to the spectacular displays that containers create in a garden. And by choosing suitable plants and products such as automatic watering systems, you can enjoy the benefits of glorious containers without most of the work.

Above: Now that dwarf sunflowers 30-60cm(12-24in) tall are available, you can grow these delightful plants in terracotta pots on the patio. Raise your own from seed or buy ready-grown plants in spring.

Self watering containers

Self-watering containers, such as the trough shown here, have a reservoir in the base. These containers can keep plants watered for up to a week before the reservoir needs refilling, even in summer.

Potting mix in this indentation acts like a wick to draw up water from the reservoir.

Perforated plastic base plate.

Water reservoir

Generous size and plastic construction both help to conserve moisture.

The hole at the top of this moulding allows water to overflow just before it reaches the main potting mix.

Above: Choose several good-sized plants for a large container. They should be one-and-a-half to two-and-a-half times the height of the container to look in perfect proportion. These are abutilon, *Lobelia cardinalis* and helichrysum.

Left: Hanging baskets are the most popular containers. For stunning results, fill them with fuchsias, pelargoniums and brachyscome, as here. Kept well-fed, regularly watered and deadheaded, they flower prolifically all through summer.

Above: A striking container often looks more spectacular when planted all with the same species. Use as many plants as it takes to create a well-filled display straightaway. This is *Lotus berthelotti.*

Right: Windowboxes are the containers most likely to miss out on frequent watering, so plant drought-tolerant sunlovers such as pelargoniums. But try not to forget them!

Ideas for using pot shards

1 Part-fill a shallow terracotta pan with potting mix. Lay curved pieces of clay pot in a circular pattern. Plant a lewisia in the centre, with a shard around it.

2 Add more small alpines with similar growing requirements – full sun and good drainage. Leave space to see the pattern made by the shards. Finish with a layer of fine gravel to prevent neck rot in wet weather. Stand the container in a sunny spot.

Recycling a broken pot

1 Lay a broken pot on its side and bank up potting mix to form a slope from back to front. Plant a large sempervivum in the deeper mix at the back of the pot.

2 Plant a low spreading sedum on its side in the shallow mix, so that the stems and flowers spill out towards the lip. Add more mix between the rootballs.

3 To prevent it rolling, bed the finished container into loose soil or, better still, gravel (which is more decorative). Set the back of the pot slightly deeper so that water does not run straight out.

MAKING A WINDOWBOX

Wooden planters and windowboxes are versatile and easy to build yourself in virtually any shape or size. The aim of this project is to make a wooden surround that will enclose a standard-sized plastic trough; these are widely available in a range of colours and sizes. Tongued-and-grooved cladding is an ideal material to make the sides of the windowbox; simply use as many planks as necessary to give the height of container you want. You can choose from several cladding profiles, but be sure to use the heavier weight 'structural' cladding rather than the thinner type supplied for facing surfaces. The one used here has a more detailed profile that gives the finished box more 'style'. There are two good reasons for using a plastic trough inside a wooden window-box. One is that the interior of the box is not in direct contact with the planting mixture and is therefore less liable to rot. The other is that it is very easy to change the display simply by replacing the trough with another one planted up in a different way. The plastic trough featured here is 60cm (24in) long and a convenient size for a small windowbox that will not be too heavy or unwieldy to fix up. The box is particularly sturdy around the end panels and these are the ideal points for support when attaching it to a wall or balcony railing. Treat the windowbox with preservative stain or paint before using it. You can also add stencilled motifs and decorative mouldings. The possibilities are endless and it is easy to match existing house or garden colour schemes.

1 Measure and mark the pieces of cladding that will form the end panels of the box. For a snug fit, make these 17cm(6.75in) wide.

2 Saw the end panels to length and sand the cut edges for a smooth finish. Each end panel will consist of two pieces of cladding.

3 Using a tenon saw, cut off the thinnest part of the tongue on the piece of cladding chosen to form the top of each end panel.

4 Squeeze some woodworking adhesive in the groove of the top piece of cladding and carefully push the two pieces together.

5 Using panel pins or fine nails, attach the bottom edge of the end panel to a batten cut to the same width. Use adhesive to create a firmer bond.

6 Nail and glue battens along each side edge of the end panels. Punch the nail heads below the surface. Wipe off any excess adhesive with a damp cloth.

7 Cut long pieces of cladding and assemble them in pairs to make up the side panels. These should measure 63.5cm(25in).

8 Add adhesive and attach the side panels to the end panels with nails, creating a bottomless box that will fit around the trough.

9 Cut two pieces of roofing lathe to fit inside the box, sawing notches at each end so that they rest on the battens.

10 Push the support rails down onto the end battens. Screw them in place or leave them loose for removal when cleaning the box.

11 Drop the trough inside the windowbox so that it rests on the two rails. Drill holes in the plastic base to let water drain out.

Staining a wooden windowbox

Some years ago, the only options for staining wood were varying shades of brown. Today, the range of stains and preservative paints is quite staggering. And what is more important, many are water-based, making them more pleasant to apply and safer to use with plants. Coordinate your plant displays with the colour of the container.

Above: *Translucent, water-based wood stains such as these are available in a range of bright colours. They allow the grain of the wood to show through.*

Below: *Here, the yellow daffodils echo the cheerful colour of the windowbox. The centres of the primroses pick up on it, too.*

Stencilling with masonry paint

Masonry paint is ideal for decorating terracotta containers. Since it is designed to protect brickwork and house walls, it forms a weatherproof finish. The only drawback is that the colours are usually in the pastel range, but you can create new, brighter shades by adding colourisers. Add a few drops of pigment to a little paint and apply to the pot with a stencil brush.

1 Attach the stencil securely to the pot with tape and apply the first colour by dabbing carefully with a stubby bristled stencil brush.

2 The first colour dries quickly and then you can add the second one. Make this by adding blue colouriser to basic white paint.

3 To create a contrasting central ring in each flower, simply dab in some white paint. Ensure that the stencil does not move.

4 The final touch in this floral decoration is to add a yellow blob that reflects the pollen-bearing stamens of a real flower.

DECORATING CONTAINERS

Decorative paint effects, such as stencils, have been fashionable indoors for some time. Now they are moving outdoors; painted flowerpots are the latest patio accessories. But there is no need to spend a fortune because you can paint your own. Use stencils, handpainted patterns or colour washes to make new pots look much more expensive than they really are, or to give old pots a new look. You can also make raw new terracotta pots look weathered by dabbing shades of green, grey and yellow onto a colour-washed pot with a sponge, to simulate moss and lichen growth. After painting, add a coat of varnish to make the colours weatherproof. But since repainting is so simple, why not just repaint them every year or two? Clean the pots well and remove loose or flaky paint, then cover them with a light colour wash (use two coats if needed to cover the old pattern) and redecorate when completely dry.

Painting is also an effective way of overcoming the grey drabness of cement and concrete containers. You can buy paints formulated for concrete surfaces or use those sold for masonry and house exteriors. The latter are also available with added grit to produce a textured finish, which may suit some containers. The range of colours available is very wide, although generally speaking the more natural 'earth' shades will suit containers better than some of the sweeter hues destined to adorn a country cottage or a seaside home. Follow the manufacturer's instructions when using these paints – some require protective gloves, for example.

You need not limit yourself to conventional pots. Wicker baskets, cane picnic hampers and woven log baskets all make good containers, first lined with plastic and treated to protect them from the elements.

This terracotta pot has a rough-textured finish that is ideal for masonry paints.

5 When all the colours have dried, peel off the stencil to reveal the finished pattern. You can reuse the stencil, but wash it before applying it again.

Decorating a concrete wall planter

1 Painting and gilding can transform a humble cast cement planter. Start by applying a coat of exterior wall paint all over – here lovat green. Choose from a huge range of pastel tones.

Make sure that your paint reaches into all the crevices.

2 Lightly brushing with gold paint emphasises the intricate detail of this wall planter. Filled with suitable plants, this planter would grace the walls of a stylish conservatory.

3 Fill the painted wall planter with compact plants such as primula, pansies and trailing ivy. Attach it securely to the wall.

The patterns on the cement casting are ideal for picking out in gilding.

Painting wicker baskets

New or secondhand wicker baskets need treating to protect them from rotting when left outdoors in all weathers. Since their natural colour soon fades in the sun, stain or paint them in natural or bright colours, depending on your planting scheme. Line them before planting.

Left: *Wicker baskets with loop handles are available in many styles and sizes. Treated with water-based wood stain, they make charming planters, ideal in a country garden.*

Right: *An informal mixture of pink flowers in various shapes give this well-filled basket its air of country charm. They include drooping fuchsias, flaring petunia trumpets and snapdragons.*

Using coloured washes on pots

Terracotta can look raw and orange when new. You can 'age' the surface quickly, using a dilute colour wash of artist's acrylic. As the water is absorbed into the terracotta, an uneven and natural-looking covering of white pigment remains. This is how to create a pink finish.

Left: *Using diluted white artist's paint, roughly apply a wash to a dry container. Mix your colours together, here ultramarine and crimson, with some more white paint. Apply in downward strokes to create darker and lighter 'weathered' streaks. Apply the darker colours cautiously.*

WATERING AND FEEDING

The secret of successful containers lies in regular watering. Check containers daily by testing them with a fingertip or a water meter, and water whenever the potting mixture starts to dry out. Keep it as evenly moist as possible for optimum growth. In a hot summer, well-filled containers in full bloom may need watering twice a day. Morning and evenings are the best time to water; during the middle of the day water simply evaporates before plants can take it up. Use a watering can or slow-running hosepipe to water. Hanging baskets pose the biggest problems, but fortunately there are various products and devices to help, such as self-watering containers and water-retaining gel crystals.

A good brand of potting mixture will provide all the food a plant needs to start with, but after a time all the nutrients will be used up. From then on, regular liquid feeding is needed. This restores nutrients to optimum levels, essential for the plant to grow and flower or fruit well. But even regular liquid feeding is not enough to keep the balance of trace elements in the soil exactly right, and potting mixtures lose their open texture in time. So plants that are grown in the same pots for a long time need completely fresh potting mixture every few years. Either repot them into a container one size larger or put them back into new mix in the same container after shaking off the old mixture.

Water-retaining gel crystals

1 Gel crystals absorb water that is slowly released back into the potting mixture. Mix the dry crystals with water as directed and stir thoroughly to make a thick gel.

2 As they absorb water, the crystals swell up to many times their original size. When the gel is fully expanded, add it to your potting mix in a suitable tray.

3 Once the gel is combined with the potting mix, use it in the normal way. Mix with added gel is ideal for hanging baskets, which are prone to drying out rapidly. The gel lasts the whole season.

Feeding

Right: Keep powdered feeds in a closed container, as they take up moisture from the air. To keep your feeding programme simple, find a good general-purpose product and use it for everything.

Left: Do not be tempted to exceed the dosage levels advised for liquid feeds. It is better to feed plants at half strength twice a week than to overdo it.

Below: Slow-release fertilisers are available as tablets and pellets. Add them to the potting mix at planting time. They release feed when the plants are watered.

Reaching high baskets

1 Easy-to-operate pulley systems clip onto the hanging hook or bracket and give access to baskets for feeding, watering and essential maintenance.

2 Reach up to the base of the hanging basket and pull it down to attend to plants. Nudge the basket up to release the lock and push it back into place.

Right: Long-handled attachments that fit onto a hosepipe for watering hanging baskets have an on/off switch on the handle, so you only need to squirt once the nozzle is in position. They are invaluable if you have a lot of high baskets.

Left: An empty plastic bottle is also a useful aid to watering, especially if you just have one or two baskets. It is lighter and easier to direct than a full watering can. A slow steady stream of water has the best chance of soaking in.

Self-watering containers

Being small and more exposed to drying breezes, both solid-sided and wire wall planters dry out very rapidly. However, self-watering wall planters have a reservoir in the base that can keep plants watered for up to a week before the reservoir needs refilling, even in summer.

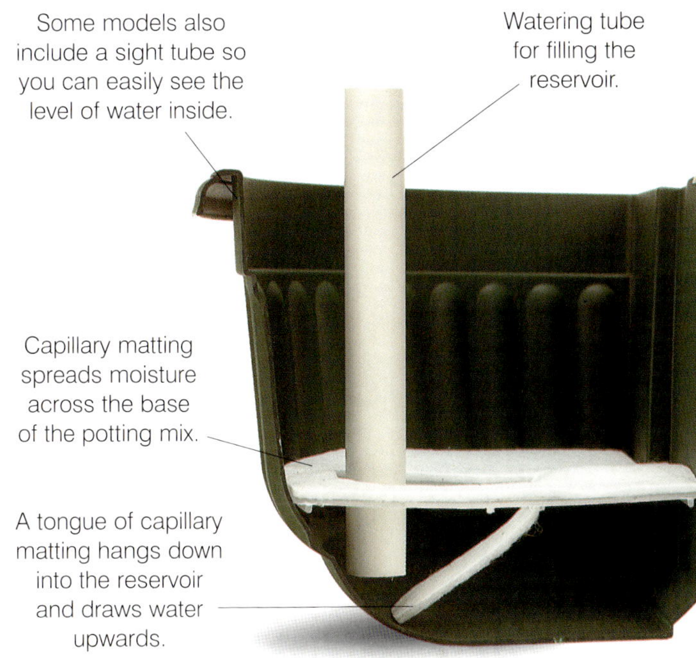

Self-watering hanging basket

Immediately after planting, water the basket in the normal way to ensure that the potting mixture is thoroughly wetted. Thereafter, water will be drawn up from the reservoir, as and when the plants require it. Self-watering hanging baskets are ideal for busy people.

1 Feed the wick through the plastic base plate. It draws water up from the reservoir at the base of the basket and keeps the capillary matting damp.

2 Push the watering tube through the hole in the base plate before adding the potting mixture and plants. You should be able to camouflage it easily.

CONTAINER CARE

In summer, the main concern of container gardeners is keeping tubs and baskets adequately fed and watered in hot, dry weather, especially at holiday times. But now that year-round container planting schemes are so popular, winter care is just as important. From autumn until well into early summer of the following year, plants grow slowly, if at all, and rarely need watering (but check them weekly in dry spells). During wet weather, containers need protection from excess wet. Raise floor-standing containers up on pot feet or bricks. Strong winds are another problem; if tall plants keep blowing over they may be bruised or broken and their containers damaged. In autumn, group together all planted-up containers to make new seasonal displays in a sheltered spot. If necessary, secure tall plants to wall ties to keep them upright. During the coldest spells, containers need extra protection to prevent the potting mixture freezing solid. If a cold or frost-free greenhouse is available, move the most susceptible plants under cover during the worst weather. If this is not possible, protect them with fleece and bubble plastic as shown here. In extreme conditions, plants can even be moved temporarily to a shed or garage where they are in the dark, but only for a few days at a time.

Protecting plants in winter

Protect the roots of plants in pots from the dehydrating effects of freezing.

Above: In a hard frost, the tender 'hearts' of plants such as cordyline palm will die, but new shoots may grow from lower down the stem.

1 Using raffia, tie the leaves into a loose cone. The foliage creates an insulated layer around the delicate central growing point.

2 Wrap fleece loosely around the top of the plant – this is good for extra protection, but avoids the risk of excess humidity.

3 Wrap several layers of bubble plastic round the sides. Leave the bottom uncovered so that after the thaw, moisture can drain away.

Maintaining a good display

Summer displays may need watering once or twice daily when the container fills with roots and plants are standing in sun; the plants also need regular heavy feeding as they grow in such restricted root-room. Make both jobs easier by adding water-retaining gel crystals and slow-release fertiliser granules to the mix before planting up. Where possible, group containers together so that the roots are shaded, to reduce overheating and hence watering. And if you have a large collection of containers, it may be worth putting in a drip watering system to make watering quicker. These systems can be connected to an outdoor tap fitted with a timing device that automatically turns the water on and off every day.

Right: To make a funnel, cut a plastic bottle in half. Remove the stopper. Push the neck into the mix. When filled with water, the soil in the neck prevents water running out too quickly.

Protecting pots from frost damage

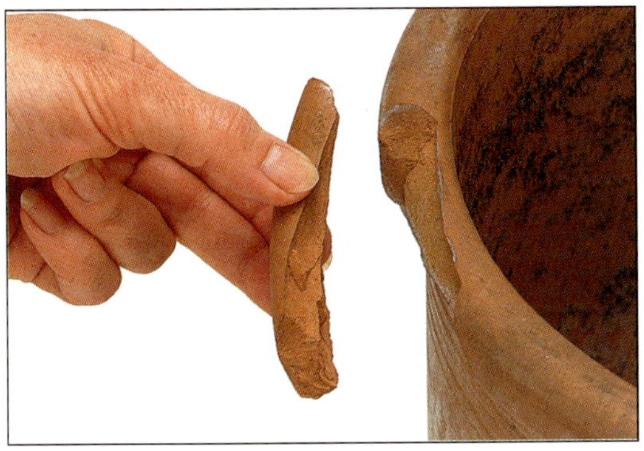

Left: Porous pots, especially terracotta ones, can crack, chip or shatter if left outside in freezing weather, because water within the walls of the pot expands. Frostproof terracotta is less likely to be damaged. Check the labels on pots.

Right: Place pot feet under containers left standing outdoors in winter to help surplus water run out of the potting mixture. It also avoids any risk of a container standing in a puddle of water. If too wet in winter, plant roots may rot.

4 The plant can be left like this for several weeks, but unwrap it and let the air in as soon as the severe conditions have passed.

Above: Another way of insulating containers is to sink them to their rims in a sheltered spot in the garden, and let the soil act as insulation. Make a hole slightly larger than the pot. Sink the pot in and add loose soil around the edges. A layer of bark chippings over the surface acts as a mulch.

Watering dried-out potting mix

Potting mixes that have dried out, particularly peat-based ones, can be difficult to rewet because they shrink, allowing water to trickle down the sides of the pot instead of being absorbed. This is often a problem in hanging baskets, as they dry out quickly and it is difficult to examine the potting mix, but it can be a problem in all containers in hot or windy weather or if plants have been neglected. The quickest solution is to stand dried-out pots in a deep container of water for several hours, until the mix is completely rehydrated. Do not leave them overnight as roots can drown. If containers are too large or heavy to move, make a shallow depression in the centre of the mix and fill it with water. It soaks in slowly; top it up several times so that moisture spreads throughout the mix. Do not feed plants that have dried out badly until they have recovered.

1 When potting mixture dries out it forms a hard crust that does not absorb water easily. The water forms into large droplets and runs away across the surface.

2 A drop of liquid detergent breaks up the surface tension, preventing water making large droplets. Instead, it stays where it is applied and soaks in.

3 Once slightly damp, the potting mix readily absorbs more water. Avoid repeating the treatment too often, as the plants will not like too much soap.

SPEEDY TOPIARY

Classic topiary shapes include domes, pillars and spirals, right through to more fanciful shapes, such as peacocks and teapots. On a smaller scale, any of the free-standing forms and many other currently fashionable shapes such as teddy bears, are suitable for growing in pots. Topiary specimens are traditionally created from box, yew and bay, which are ideal due to their evergreen foliage, dense bushy nature, slow growth and ability to withstand tight clipping. For quicker results, try euonymus and lonicera. The foundation of most shapes is a frame to which the plant's main stems are secured. Frames can be made of wire, wire netting or timber and can be bought preformed or you can make your own, which allows you to create more individual designs. Where a chunky pillar is topped by a crown or peacock, only the decorative device on top needs a framework. This is held up by a post driven into the pot through the foliage, which hides it from view.

1 Gather the stems loosely and fit the frame over the top. With all the stems inside, press the cone gently into the mix until it is stable.

2 Tuck any stray shoots behind the wires. This thickens up the shape and ensures that protruding stems will not be snipped off.

3 Working all round the plant, secure strong upright stems to the frame with ties. This makes the shape more solid right away.

4 Snip off any protruding straggly shoots. Remove the very tips of thin straight shoots to encourage them to branch out.

5 As the shape of the cone emerges, work your way round the plant, lightly 'tipping'. Cut close to the framework at this stage.

6 When the horizontal side shoots start to make the outline look rather shaggy, the plant is ready for its final shaping.

7 Tie a string to the base of the frame. Sweeping the stems up with one hand, bind them in place with the other to fill out the shape.

8 At the top, tie the string firmly to the frame. Snip off any protruding stems, leaving the cone with a neatly pointed tip.

9 Sheep shears are used with one hand. They are ideal for trimming off any stems that stick out from the sides of the cone, leaving the sides tidy.

10 The finished cone has taken less than three months to complete. The same feature made in box or bay would take over a year.

11 *Lonicera nitida* is very fast growing. Trim as often as necessary during the growing season to keep the shape neat and to encourage it to thicken out.

12 Using sheep shears, clip to about 2.5cm(1in) beyond the frame. Start at the base of the topiary, using the top of the pot as a guide, and work your way up.

Topiary in context

Topiary trees suit a huge range of situations. They originated in formal gardens, and on a small scale, geometric spheres or spirals make a good way to end a row of dwarf box edging to a herb garden or formal flower bed. Potted topiary peacocks look good standing next to a doorway, and a row of different potted topiary shapes looks very decorative along the top of a wall or up a flight of steps in a country garden.

Right: A pyramid is one of the easiest topiary shapes to create and maintain. If wide enough at the base, you may not need a frame for a small pyramid.

13 Use the frame as a guide when clipping the sides, but keep standing back to check that they slope by the same amount and that the outline is symmetrical. Leave the top till last; trim it to a sharp point.

SHAPING IVY AND BOX

Traditional topiary takes years to perfect, but for quicker results try 'instant' topiary, made by training ivy round a light framework of wire or willow. Preformed wire topiary frames – usually two-dimensional animal shapes – are sold in garden centres or you can create your own hoops and spirals by bending stiff fencing wire into shape. Make more complicated shapes, such as teddy bears, from wire netting. Plant several climbers in a large tub all round the shape and peg out the stems to ensure complete coverage. Ivy is the usual subject for instant topiary; small-leaved forms are best for modest-sized topiaries; experiment with the many variegated or gold forms, and also the arrowhead-shaped *Hedera helix* 'Sagittifolia'. For even greater variety, try other evergreen climbers: *Euonymus fortunei* varieties such as Blondy or Emerald 'n' Gold can be trained in this way although they are not normally regarded as climbers. For a bigger topiary, use larger climbers, such as *Jasminum nudiflorum*. Grow it on the same frame as a strong-growing ivy for an interesting effect, or choose the variegated evergreen honeysuckle, *Lonicera japonica* 'Aureoreticulata'. For a scented topiary, grow *Trachelospermum jasminoides* or *T.j.* 'Variegatum', both of which have fragrant white flowers in summer, as well as evergreen foliage. Do not overlook plants that need greenhouse protection in winter, such as passion flower, plumbago and bougainvillea, all of which make good flowering topiary shapes for summer patios.

1 Push a spiral training frame into a large pot, plant two climbing ivies and twist the stems up round the frame. You can sometimes buy ivy 'topiary' at this stage.

2 By the time the ivies reach the top, side shoots lower down start to make the shape 'fuzzy'. The topiary will need trimming three to four times a year to keep it neat.

3 Twist in all the overhanging stems around the base. Avoid cutting them off while the topiary is young, as they help to thicken the shape. Tie in place if necessary.

4 Working up, twist wayward stems firmly round the frame to keep the shape well defined. Use long new shoots to 'bind' existing stems close to the framework.

5 Hold stems in place with plant ties – as many as you need to achieve a tight shape. Do not worry about the appearance; ties soon disappear under the foliage.

6 At the apex, twist the top stems together before winding them round the tip of the spiral. This creates a neater finish with more leaves and fewer visible stems.

7 Secure the top of the ivy firmly in place. This is very important, because if it comes adrift, the rest of the plant will slacken on the frame and the topiary will 'relax' out of shape.

8 About 20 minutes work restores the shape to mint condition. Repeat the process at the start of the growing season (late spring) and thereafter at regular intervals two or three times every summer.

Planting a narrow-necked jar

Left: To avoid filling the whole jar with potting mix, wedge a hanging basket into the neck, plant it with ivies and simply lodge it in place.

Right: Some containers have a strong character of their own. Here, evergreen trailers, such as ivy, accentuate the shape of the jar without competing for attention.

Growing a box ball

Box is a very popular and easily managed topiary subject. Use Buxus sempervirens, *not the miniature cultivar 'Suffruticosa'. Take cuttings from established plants in late spring and summer.*

1 Start with a strong, rooted box cutting. Nip off the growing tips of the shoots using forefinger and thumbnail. Repeat when the side shoots are 2.5cm(1in) long.

2 Use secateurs to nip back the tips of the next crop of side shoots. Each time new growth reaches 5cm(2in) long, shorten it. Pruning encourages bushiness.

3 As the first pot fills with roots, move the plant into a larger pot with fresh potting mixture. Clip the plant regularly using small shears instead of secateurs.

4 When it reaches the required size, clip back to the previous outline each time. By then, clipping three or four times each year should be enough.

5 It is possible to create a good box ball about 23cm(9in) across by this method in three years. Clip it two or three times a year to retain the shape and size.

SPRING CONTAINERS

Spring container displays get the season off to a colourful start; the perfect antidote to a long dull winter. Once the worst of the weather is over, nurseries and garden centres stock up with plants just coming into flower, ready to give instant results. Choose from coloured primroses and polyanthus, ranunculus with their large turban-shaped flowers, double daisies, forget-me-nots, and dwarf spring bulbs, all sold growing in pots. Give plants a weak feed (use quarter-strength liquid tomato food) to replenish nutrients just before planting. If you have summer containers still filled with the old potting mix, there is no need to empty them. Simply cut out pot-sized holes and sink the new plants pot-and-all to their rims in the old mixture. In this way, individual plants can be lifted out when the flowers go over and new ones dropped into their places. This is a specially useful technique for prolonging the life of a large display or if you are growing different kinds of plants with overlapping flowering seasons together. For smaller displays or ones with plants that all 'peak' together, knock the plants gently out of their pots and plant them as normal. However, try not to disturb the rootball, as plants in bud resent any root damage. Spring bedding plants and bulbs do not have a long flowering season, but in a sheltered spot they usually continue up to early summer, leaving just enough time to empty tubs and refill them with fresh potting mixture ready for the start of the main container planting season.

A self-watering spring basket

The dark green basket used in this display has solid sides, so all the planting has to go in the top. Pick at least one plant with long trails to soften the edge. Hang the basket in a lightly shaded, sheltered spot.

1 Assemble the basket and add a layer of moist potting mix. Try the largest plant for size and adjust the level as necessary.

2 If the rootball is too big to fit into the basket, open out the base of the rootball so that it fits into the space available.

3 Plant two primulas and then fill in the gaps left on one side with the variegated euonymus. Put in more potting mix as you go.

4 Plant two hardy primroses, one on either side of the watering tube. Leave space around the rim for trailing plants. As well as ivy, you could try variegated periwinkle, aubretia or silver lamium.

5 Split apart a couple of pots of rooted ivy cuttings and fit them around the edge of the basket. Fill any gaps with soil. Water thoroughly in the usual way.

Below: This unusual container has only a small planting area, so choose compact bushy types of plant that do not look overpowering. Here, orange pansies and yellow primroses team attractively with variegated ivy.

6 Hang the basket in a sheltered spot and water via the tube. Remove individual blooms as they fade; cut off drumsticks when the whole head has finished flowering.

Miniature roses, primroses and ivy

In spring, the houseplant sections of garden centres often stock miniature roses that have been forced into bloom early. They can be hardened off and used outdoors once they have become acclimatised.

1 Put in a layer of gravel followed by potting mix. Fill the back of the box with miniature roses. Feed with a liquid fertiliser for flowering plants and remove dead heads regularly.

2 Plant a row of equally spaced double primroses in front. The colour of these tones with the windowbox. When they are over, replace them with, say, double red busy Lizzies.

3 Fill the gaps between the primroses with a compact, small-leaved ivy. Trim back long trails. For a flowering cascade, try blue trailing verbena or lobelia.

4 Remove fading flowers and leaves from the primroses. Deadhead the roses and feed and water the box regularly.

A temporary display of primroses

1 This homemade windowbox has a deep plastic trough inside to protect the wood from damp. Part fill with lightweight peat- or coir-based mixture.

2 Choose a selection of cultivated primroses just coming into bloom and stand the lightest or darkest one in the middle, plunging the pot to its rim.

3 Continue to add more pots to the windowbox. Carefully arrange the leaves so that they hang over the sides and mask the hard edges.

4 The finished display takes only a few minutes to make, yet in a cool spot protected from strong sun the plants will keep flowering for six to eight weeks or more.

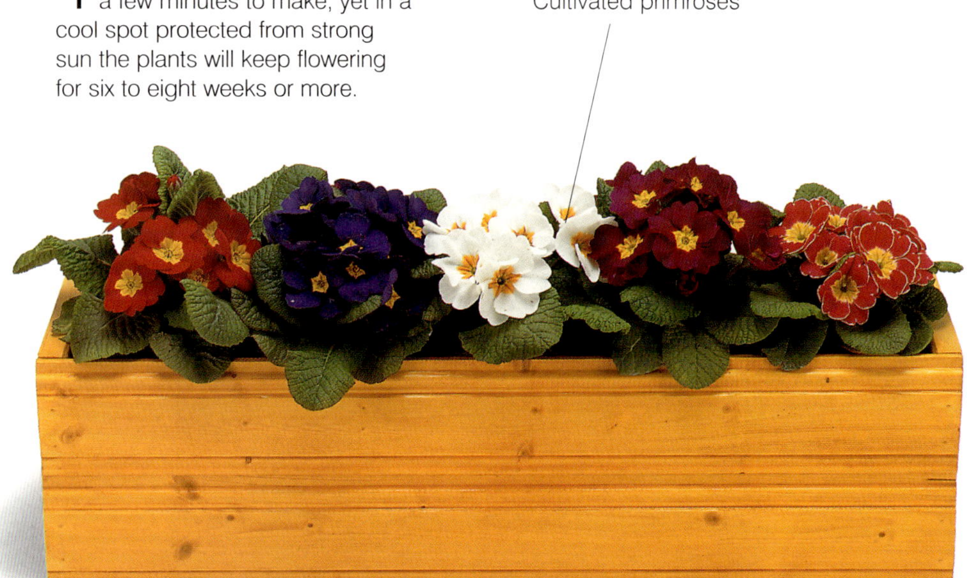

SPRING DISPLAYS

When spring arrives you just want to make the most of it with plenty of containers around entrance doors and on the patio where you can see them. Of all the seasons, spring is the one in which you can afford to take liberties. Do not worry about teaming seemingly hostile colours such as pink with yellow. They are the top two spring colours in nature and though you might not put them together in summer, at this time of year they do not seem to clash in the same way. You can dilute the effect using ivy or euonymus foliage, but most spring flowers have enough foliage of their own to do the trick. Unlike summer bedding, spring flowers are quite shortlived, so refresh or replace displays once or twice between early and late spring with the new range of plants appearing in nurseries. To make the most of 'spring fever' in the garden, team bulbs with bedding. The rather formal symmetrical shapes of tulips or narcissi make the perfect foil for charming cottage flowers, such as double daisies, violas, forget-me-nots and polyanthus. Once bulbs are over they do not produce a further flush of flowers, although bedding should continue for a while if it is regularly deadheaded.

Choose colourful baskets and stained timber troughs in spring to match the exuberance of the flowers. Yellow is particularly seasonal, and looks extra good when planted with flowers that include bicolored violas or golden-eyed polyanthus that pick out the same shade as the container. One good thing about containers like these is that you can quickly change the colour to suit the season or your planting scheme, at the burst of a spray can!

5 If there is room, substitute the central primrose for a taller plant as a centrepiece, and balance it with two similar plants in smaller pots.

A basket of pansies

1 Containers with a handle convert easily to hanging baskets. To prevent waterlogging, add a layer of pebbles as drainage material to a lined wicker basket.

2 Cover the pebbles with potting mixture, but make sure that there is still room for the plants on top. Check the level with a plant and adjust as necessary.

3 Split up the ivy to make a foliage edging with trails overhanging the basket. Wind some pieces around the handle. Plant the pansies close together, fill in any spaces with potting mix and firm in.

4 Add just enough water to settle the soil. Thereafter, allow the soil surface to dry out slightly between waterings.

A spring display in a manger basket

1 Line the basket with black plastic and a thick layer of moss. Plant bedding violas and fill the gaps with potting mix.

2 Put three pots of tulips along the back, breaking the roots apart so that the bulbs can be planted in more of a straight line.

3 Add the yellow polyanthus and double daisies. Firm in potting mix around the plants, cover with moss and water in.

4 Once the tulips fade, replace them with more potgrown bulbs and spring-flowering herbaceous plants.

1 If your container does not have drainage holes in the base, drill some. It is vital that containers that will be standing outdoors in winter can drain freely.

SPRING BULBS IN TUBS

With daffodils, tulips and hyacinths in containers, a patio can be a riot of colour from early spring onwards. There are two ways to use spring bulbs. The slow but cheap way is to plant dry bulbs in autumn using peat- or soil-based potting mixture. Choose compact varieties. Buy daffodils as soon as they are available and plant them straightaway, as they start rooting earlier than many spring bulbs. The bulbs should be plump and healthy, without cuts, bruises or mouldy bits; the biggest bulbs will bear the most flowers. You can plant containers entirely with one kind of bulb, but if you want to mix them, choose bulbs that flower at roughly the same time. After planting, stand portable containers outdoors in a cool, shady spot protected from heavy rain. When the first shoots appear, move them to the patio. Plant heavy tubs where they are to flower. While bulbs are flowering, feed them weekly with general-purpose liquid feed. When they are over, tip them out and plant them in the garden. Buy new bulbs for the following year's container displays, as they will flower better than the old ones.

For instant results, use ready-grown spring bulbs sold just as they are coming into flower. By waiting until spring and buying plants in bloom, you can choose those at the same stage for a truly perfect display. When creating temporary seasonal displays, there is no need to remove the plants from their pots; just plunge the pots to their rim in a suitable medium. Put them as close together as possible to maximise the display. You can lift out individual pots and replace them as flowers go over, or renew the whole display.

2 Place 2.5-5cm(1-2in) of coarse gravel over the base of the tub to aid drainage. Bulbs can easily rot if the potting mix is too wet.

3 Add 2.5-5cm(1-2in) of potting mix. In pots, it does not matter if bulbs are not planted with twice their own depth of potting mix.

4 Press each daffodil bulb gently down into the mix, giving it a half turn. This ensures that the base of the bulb makes good contact with the soil – essential for rooting. Plant the bulbs close together, but do not allow them to touch each other or the sides of the tub.

5 Cover the bulbs with enough mix to leave the tips on show so you can see where they are when you plant the next layer.

6 Gently press in *Anemone blanda* corms between the tips of the lower layer of bulbs. Cover these corms with more mix.

7 Dot another layer of *Anemone blanda* over the surface, about 2.5cm(1in)above the last. Fill the tub to the rim with potting mixture.

8 Leave the potting mixture roughly level on top. Take care not to knock over the bulbs, as they are still quite unstable.

Right: This cross section shows the layers of bulbs in the container, with popular 'Golden Harvest' daffodils below and *Anemone blanda* 'Blue Shade' above.

Below: Daffodils do best in the sun, but tolerate light shade. *Anemone blanda* grows to 15cm(6in) It is usually sold in mixed colours but single shades are sometimes available.

Narcissi 'Golden Harvest'

Anemone blanda 'Blue Shade'

A spring display in a plastic cauldron

Inexpensive containers are ideal for brilliant spring displays; the secret is to pack them with plants. Spring bulbs and bedding plants just coming into bloom will not have time to make much more growth, so they must create immediate impact. Choose plants at roughly the same flowering stage, and with varying heights and shapes.

1 Part-fill the container with potting mix and knock plants out of their pots. Avoid breaking up the rootballs or the plants may wilt and fade rapidly.

2 If the container will be seen from the front, plant the tallest flowers at the back with shorter kinds in front. This hides foliage and gives a fuller display.

3 Complete the display with a low spreading plant such as this winter-flowering heather at the front to soften the hard line created by the container rim.

4 Leaving plants grouped together instead of splitting them up randomly throughout the display creates a stronger effect. Their foliage sets off each clump.

PLANTING UP A SINK GARDEN WITH ALPINES

Few people have room for conventional rockeries and there is also growing concern about the removal of rock from natural habitats for use in gardens. The most practical alternative, especially where space or funds are limited, is to grow alpines in containers. This way you avoid using any natural rock at all, as the hard surface of the container provides a suitable backdrop. The traditional container for alpines was an old-fashioned stone butler's sink, but you can adapt modern sinks by covering them with hypertufa, or create a sink entirely from hypertufa. Sink-type containers must have drainage holes in the bottom. Most alpines will thrive in a free-draining mixture with some organic matter to hold moisture. You may need to prepare this at home, as suitable mixes are normally only sold by specialist alpine plant nurseries. More moisture-loving plants, such as tiny alpine primulas, dodecatheon, ramonda, etc., are happy in a mixture of equal parts soil and peat-based potting mix. Be sure to group plants that will happily share similar growing conditions. Most alpines will thrive in a situation where they get direct sun for at least half the day, although very drought-tolerant, sunloving kinds such as sedum and sempervivum need a very sunny spot. Few alpines are happy in shade; go for ramonda, haberlea and dwarf ferns. Water sink gardens in dry weather, and feed plants occasionally in spring and summer with weak tomato feed.

1 Cover the drainage holes with crocks. These prevent soil from running out but allow excess water to drain away freely.

2 Almost fill the sink with equal parts of lime-free gritty sand, soil-based mix and coir, coarse peat or sterilised leafmould.

3 Decide on the arrangement and start from the centre. Tip each plant out of its pot and use a small trowel to scoop out a hole.

4 Nestle plants into the corners so the sink has a well-filled but natural look. Make sure a few plants trail over to soften the sides.

5 Choose a few small pieces of attractive stone and tuck them in amongst the plants as you work. These add contours, trap condensation in hot weather and help to keep plant roots cool.

6 Use plants with long flowering seasons and some, such as mossy saxifrages, that make good background foliage when not in bloom. Mix plants with contrasting shapes and textures.

7 Use a narrow-bladed trowel to make holes for plants and pieces of stone. Avoid damaging the rootballs of nearby plants.

8 Drape sprawling plants over pieces of stone to set them off. Lifting leaves and stems clear of the soil also prevents rotting.

9 When all the plants and rocks are in place, spread a generous layer of gravel or granite chippings over the whole surface as a stone mulch.

10 The sink garden looks good straight away, but will improve as plants blend together and spill over the sides. Water well and raise up on bricks for extra drainage.

SUMMER DISPLAYS

Summer is the main season for container gardening, and a huge range of bedding plants and tender perennials are available in nurseries and garden centres especially for this use. The best kinds are colourful and compact, with a long and prolific flowering season. Pelargoniums, petunias, argyranthemums and fuchsias are traditional favourites as they are particularly free-flowering and reliable. For the most striking display, team plants with contrasting flower shapes and sizes together, for instance daisy flowers and tiny fillers like lobelia, or fuchsias and petunias. This is specially important when creating a container using all one colour. However you should choose plants that suit your site and situation, and the amount of time available for looking after them. In a hot sunny spot, real sunlovers such as zonal pelargoniums, osteospermum, mesembryanthemum and gazania, do well as they are naturally fairly drought-tolerant, and the flowers of many only open properly in direct sunlight. In shade, impatiens are best for a long show of colour. Container plants with large flowers need regular deadheading to prevent them setting seed and to encourage them to produce more blooms. Busy people who do not have time to give container displays so much regular attention often prefer small-flowered plants, such as lobelia and nemesia. With these, the dead flower heads do not look so untidy if they are left, and they do not inhibit the production of the next crop of flower.

Left: Patio roses do not need much pruning. Just remove dead twigs in late spring and tidy straggly stems that spoil the shape.

Right: Lilies are normally bought as dry bulbs in spring. Plant them deeply in soil-based potting mix. Once in flower, stand them in shade or sink the pot in a border.

Below: You can use all kinds of containers outdoors. This black wire basket was intended to hold eggs, but lined with black plastic it is ideal for a bright summer display.

Easy-care perennials for containers

Bedding plants and tender perennials need frequent feeding and watering to keep them looking their best. An easier alternative is to plant perennials in containers instead, and this is becoming increasingly popular. Plants that grow slowly, remain compact and have natural drought tolerance are specially useful. Festuca grasses, shrubby evergreen herbs, such as lavender, rosemary, golden marjoram and thyme, and the more succulent rock plants, such as sempervivums, sedums and thrift, are ideal and look superb teamed with terracotta containers. Although these have less flower than bedding plants, they create a more subtle effect and flower in sequence over a long season. Plant the sunloving species listed here in a potting medium made by combining soil-based and soilless potting mixture in equal volumes. The result is a free-draining mix that retains just enough moisture to prevent the roots being damaged by shrinkage when it dries out.

Geranium palmatum is a slightly tender plant that needs winter protection in colder areas. It has an elegant symmetrical shape.

Below: Grow perennial Mediterranean-style plants in individual pots and then group them together to make summer displays. They can be regularly rearranged to suit what is in flower at the time.

Festuca glauca, a compact evergreen grass that looks good all year round.

Rhodanthemum hosmariense makes a compact hummock, studded with daisy flowers all summer.

Salvia officinalis 'Tricolor' holds its leaves all year round, although their colour fades in winter.

Lavandula stoechas pedunculata 'French' lavender has aromatic foliage and long-lasting flowers.

SUMMER CONTAINERS

In summer, old and new wicker baskets make superb temporary plant containers, either to conceal plastic pots or to create an instant display. Treat them first with two coats of yacht varnish or apply a coloured stain and allow it to dry thoroughly. If you intend to plant directly into a basket, line it with black plastic before filling it with potting mix to protect the wicker from discoloring or rotting. Natural baskets look particularly good filled with exuberant country garden flowers. For a tall upright basket, choose plants that are one-and-a-half times to twice its height to maintain the correct proportions. In a wide shallow trug, a low display of trailing annuals would look good; add a climber to grow up over the handle. In shade, try alternate green and gold varieties of *Soleirolia soleirolii* or fill generously with *Duchesnea indica* (false strawberry) for an artistic 'still-life' effect. In the garden, always stand a basket up on bricks to permit the air to circulate underneath and prevent rotting. Do not leave baskets outdoors in winter, as they quickly deteriorate in bad weather, even when protected by varnish.

1 Loosely line a wicker basket with black plastic and make a few holes in the bottom. Place 5cm (2in) of clean gravel into the base.

2 Part-fill the basket with good-quality potting mixture. Leave the top of the plastic liner rolled over the top of the basket for now.

3 Put the tallest plants – here lythrum – at the centre-back of the display in order to create a graduated effect. This allows all the plants to be seen properly.

4 Use a mix of flower shapes; contrast spires of astilbe with the chunkier, flat-topped shapes of verbena. Contrast is important in displays that use mainly one colour.

5 A phygelius at the front makes a strong focal point and penstemon adds a finishing touch. Flower shapes add variety to a limited colour scheme.

6 Top up with potting mixture, then roll the liner over to make a firm edge and tuck it just inside the rim of the basket.

7 A chipped bark mulch looks decorative, teams well with the natural cane basket and helps to keep plant roots cool and moist.

8 If the finished basket is too awkward or heavy to move easily and you do not have help, use a small wheeled trolley or even a skateboard to manoeuvre it into its final position.

Terracotta wall planter

A terracotta wall planter suits all kinds of planting schemes. The main thing is to pack it full of plants and water it often.

1 A pot with a rounded base will not stand upright, so fix it to the wall before filling it almost to the brim with soilless potting mix.

2 The centrepiece is a rose-pink tuberous begonia. Plant it in the middle of the pot without damaging the rootball.

3 Add trailing lobelia to fill the rest of the space. The blue of the lobelias makes a bold contrast to the deep red begonias, and both colours are set off by the warm tones of the terracotta container.

4 By midsummer, the container will be a mass of flowers. Be sure to water it often, as this type of porous terracotta container does not hold much soil and dries out quickly.

SUMMER BASKETS

Hanging baskets are probably the single most popular kind of summer container. Yet to grow a really superb example means daily or even twice daily watering and feeding 'little and often'. It is often better to have one outstanding basket, perhaps coordinated with a nearby trough or windowbox planted in a complementary scheme, than a big collection of containers that look less impressive but actually take longer to look after. Although it is slow to make up, the 'double' basket used here creates a stunning display. Yet because it contains a larger volume of potting mix, the plants stay in better condition and roots remain cooler and moister than in a conventional basket. And by building in a funnel at the top, watering is no more difficult than for a normal basket. To make a 'ball of bloom' you need two 25cm(10in) wire hanging baskets, a large bag of moss (or synthetic moss), a bag of potting mix and about 20 plants. The impatiens used here enjoys light shade; in this situation a hanging basket does not need watering as often as one in full sun. Since the finished result will be twice the weight of a conventional basket, check that the bracket and supporting chains are strong and firmly fixed. When making up a matching hanging basket and trough display, use some of the same plants in each container to link them visually. Or if one container is in shade and the other in sun (so that the same plants would not be suitable) use a similar colour scheme in each.

1 Prepare two identical moss-lined wire baskets. Plant a row of busy Lizzies as close as possible to the base of each basket. Use a bucket for support.

2 Tuck moss around each plant to prevent leakage of potting mix. Place a second row of plants about halfway up one of the two baskets, but not too near the top.

3 Fill each basket to the brim with more potting mix and firm it well down. Add more mix to both baskets if necessary; it is vital that the surface is level afterwards.

4 Water the potting mix well; this helps to hold it together and also makes it stick to the moss. If watering causes sinkage, top up the baskets before proceeding.

5 Place a piece of wood or firm card over the basket planted with just one row of plants and hold it firmly. Invert this basket over the second one. The plants should be randomly arranged over the surface of both baskets.

6 Make sure that the two baskets are perfectly aligned. Then prevent the top basket from sliding as you gently pull out the board. An assistant is helpful here.

7 Use plastic-coated wire to secure the baskets together at several points round the rim. Green-coated wire shows up least. Twist the ends tightly with pliers.

8 Hang up carefully. Trickle water from a can onto the top of the basket; you could tease apart some of the moss to make an opening for easier watering.

Deadhead regularly for best results.

9 After just a few weeks, the basket is completely smothered in flower. Keep it well fed and watered all summer and site it out of strong midday sun to keep it looking this good all season.

Below: This fine hanging basket is packed with pansies, lobelia, begonia and pelargonium. The tougher foliage houseplants, such as chlorophytum, can also contribute to a summer display.

Windowbox display

In this plastic windowbox, an interesting mix of textures has been created by blending the rounded pelargoniums and pansies with the upright shoots of rosemary and low mounds of golden oregano.

1 A perforated base plate separates the plants from the reservoir below. Add a layer of soil-based potting mix, plus extra grit for the herbs; plant a row of pelargoniums along the back.

2 Interplant the pelargoniums with rosemary and plant five equally spaced golden oreganos along the front edge to soften it.

3 Add sparkle to the display with cream-coloured pansies, fitting as many as you can into the gaps at the front and back.

4 Keep the trough in a sunny spot. Pinch back rosemary shoot tips to keep it compact. Feed, water and deadhead.

AN INSTANT BORDER IN CONTAINERS

The art of small-scale gardening lies about halfway between landscaping and flower arranging. This is especially true of a garden that is covered by hard surfaces, where you have to do most of your gardening in pots. As a change from the usual patio display, where each container houses a single shrub or a traditional mixture of bedding plants, try using containers as modules in a border-style display that just happens to be growing in pots. Good plant associations are the secret of success. In a conventional garden border, what 'makes' a really eye-catching display is the way plants are grouped together by a common theme – say, colour – to make a series of arrangements within a bigger picture. The same technique works even better in pots, because you can plant each container with one complete group of plants and then stand several together to make your display. Since each element of the display is in its own pot, the scheme can be rearranged or partially replaced as flowers go over or when you feel like a change. It is as easy as moving accessories around indoors to give a room a new look. For a really versatile potted display, use a mixture of variegated plants, long-lasting perennial and annual flowers, scented plants, evergreens and seasonal bulbs. Include a few striking pots as focal points, and some containers of small filler flowers. These will link together the stronger elements of the display.

1 Choose three matching pots of different sizes and stand them on bricks to make a more 'staged' display. Part-fill each pot with good-quality soil-based potting mix (best for plants that will stay in the same pot for some time) and begin planting.

2 You can put two or three plants in each pot, as long as they associate well together and all enjoy similar growing conditions. The aim is to recreate a border that just happens to be growing in a series of containers.

3 Choose a different colour scheme for each pot, so that each one 'stands up' in its own right. That way, you can use them separately later on or move them to another planting scheme. Each container is like one element of a border, but with the benefit of being portable.

4 Drought-tolerant grasses are ideal for small or shallow pots. With their geometric shapes, they make good specimen plants for pots when they grow bigger.

5 For instant impact, surround the grass with gazanias. Being tender, they will have to come out in autumn, leaving the grass room to fill the pot.

Above: *For a garden where there is no soil, make a potted border with containers. Group a mixture of shrubs and perennial plants closely, with the smallest at the front, just like a real border.*

6 The final 'potted border' makes a good group, but each element can be re-cycled independently to create new planting schemes so that you can 'redecorate' your patio endlessly.

Above: *Use billowing containers to bulk up a border that looks rather sparse or to replace a plant that has died. The container is soon lost amongst foliage.*

AUTUMN CONTAINERS

It is all too easy to let summer displays linger on long after they have passed their best. Do not wait for the first hard frost to finish them off; instead, replant them with a new autumn display straight away. There is no need to replace the potting mix; simply pull out the old plants and roots, shaking the old mix back into the tub, and top it up with fresh material. Suitable autumn plants include compact varieties of chrysanthemums in a wide colour range. Choose plants with a few flowers open but plenty of buds to follow and they will remain in flower for eight to ten weeks. Most are frost-tender; if you want to keep them, move them to a frost-free greenhouse after flowering. You will also find some hardy plants, such as *Campanula carpatica,* which have been grown as houseplants and forced into flower out of season. These can also be used in containers outdoors, but since they have been grown in 'soft' greenhouse conditions, give them a well-sheltered spot and harden them off for a week or so before putting them outside, otherwise the sudden change of climate will finish off the flowers prematurely. Similarly, some of the hardier houseplants, such as ivy, solanum and pot chrysanthemums, can also be used for a temporary seasonal display in a sheltered spot. And in a mild city centre microclimate, indoor cyclamen, indoor azalea and asparagus ferns can be added to a display that often lasts well into winter.

Basket of campanulas

Campanulas suit a rustic wicker basket. Many other hardy herbaceous plants or tender perennials would create a similar 'cottagey' effect.

1 Line the basket with some black plastic to protect the wicker. Make small drainage holes in the plastic and put some gravel in the base.

2 Add more gravel or pieces of broken polystyrene plant trays to cover the base of the basket for extra drainage.

3 For seasonal displays, use a peat-based mix. For alpines or perennials, use a soil-based mix or add coarse grit to a peat mix.

Houseplants in a sheltered windowbox

1 Cover the drainage holes with crocks. Add 2.5-5cm(1-2in) of coarse gravel and stand the most striking plant centrally. Adjust the gravel so that the pot is just below the rim of the windowbox.

2 Place a pair of matching plants one at each end of the windowbox, with their best sides facing forward. Plunging the pots in a box of potting mix provides valuable insulation from the cold.

3 Fill the spaces between the pots with potting mix and add a gravel topping. This sets off the plants and adds extra drainage.

4 Arrange the longest trails of variegated ivy so that they create a rim of greenery that spills out over the basket's dipped edge. Make the composition asymmetric.

5 Fill the centre of the basket with the campanulas. Try not to hide the handle, as it is very much part of the overall design. Fill any gaps with soil and firm in lightly. If necessary, add more rooted ivy cuttings around the edge.

Campanula carpatica 'Blue Clips'

Hedera helix cultivar

6 Water the basket and hang it in a sheltered spot. Pick off dead blooms regularly. Harden off the campanulas after flowering and plant them in the garden.

Autumn crocus

1 A terracotta pan or half-pot is ideal for small bulbs. Start by placing a piece of broken pot over the drainage hole.

2 To ensure good drainage, put a layer of grit in the base before half-filling the pan with potting mix. Smooth it down.

3 Position the corms about 2.5cm(1in) apart, with the tiny flowering shoot uppermost. If in doubt lay them on their sides.

4 This 23cm(9in) diameter pan will hold 20 evenly spaced corms. They are about 5cm(2in) below the rim of the pot.

Right: Crocus medius *is an autumn-flowering species that will do well in a sunny, well-drained spot and is ideal for containers or rock features. The light purple petals contrast vividly with the branching orange stamens.*

An autumn display in an urn

When selecting plants, do not just pick those with flowers of a colour that will coordinate with their container; aim for a mixture of strong shapes that work well together, so that each flower stands out from its background.

1 Place 2.5cm(1in) of washed gravel or crocks into the urn for drainage. It already has small holes to allow water to run out.

2 Fill the urn to within 5cm(2in) of the rim with good-quality potting mixture. Leave the mixture loose and fluffy for planting.

3 Begin planting from the back, starting with the tallest plants. Choose those that tone well together in colour, but provide varied shapes and textures for added interest and impact.

4 As this is only a temporary display, feel free to use a mixture of whatever plants look good together, are the right size and peak at the same time. Shrubs, perennials, trailing and bedding plants are all suitable and provide plenty of choice.

VIVID AUTUMN DISPLAYS

In autumn, garden centres stock up with all sorts of plants just approaching their peak, ready for making instant displays. The cream of the autumn bedding is ornamental cabbage. At their best, each plant resembles a giant flower, with a frill of wavy-edged, glaucous blue-green leaves surrounding a mauve-pink or greenish-cream filled centre. You can also find decorative varieties of kale, which have narrower leaves and often deeper blue or almost purple foliage – the two look superb put together. Ornamental cabbages and kales only develop their full colour when the weather starts turning cooler at the start of autumn, so plants are often not available until the season has already begun. But they do not grow any more after you buy them, so containers need to be well-filled to make a good display. Given a sheltered spot and well-drained containers that prevent the plants rotting in a wet autumn, the plants can remain looking their best well into winter, before eventually starting to run to seed. A cluster of ornamental cabbage and kale makes a good display on its own, but they can also be teamed with other plants. Choose some that echo the shades of the cabbage, if making a mixed display, to keep the result looking harmonious. And if teaming them with other plants with shorter display lives, then leave the latter in their pots so they can be lifted out and replaced.

5 Bold ornamental cabbages provide solid colour that makes a good focal point to the display. Lean them over at an angle (even over the side of the urn) so that they make the most impact.

Late-flowering perennials for autumn displays

As a change, try planting late-flowering perennials. Buy *Liriope muscari* or *Sedum spectabile* just as the buds are showing their true colours, or look out for pots of compact dahlias. Since any of these are only going to stay in flower for six weeks or so, stand the pots inside empty containers or group several together inside large tubs and hide the top of the pots with a layer of bark chippings. The perennials can be planted out once the flowers are over, but leave dahlias outside till their foliage is just touched by a frost. Cut off the tops, dry the tubers and store them in the same way as garden varieties to replant next year.

6 Finish off by tucking a few trailing ivies around the front of the urn to soften the edge. They also help to frame the focal point, thus drawing attention to the heart of this colourful display.

7 Combining the ornamental cabbage with flowers, berries, and foliage produces a varied end result that will remain attractive for a long period. Replace the sedum when it looks past its best.

Dahlias in a wicker basket

In late summer, garden centres offer a good choice of bedding dahlias. These remain short and compact – ideal for containers. Feed them regularly and do not allow them to dry out. Deadhead as necessary.

1 Line the basket with plastic and add some gravel to improve drainage. Fill the basket with moistened peat-based potting mix. Firm lightly and offer up the first plant – here Thunbergia alata *– to see if the level is right.*

2 You may need to weigh down the opposite side of the basket while you decide where to plant the dahlia. Lift up the dahlia foliage and tuck in the ajuga, arranging the trails so that they fall over the edge.

3 Add two pots of euphorbia between the dahlia and black-eyed Susan. Take care, as all euphorbias exude a milky-white irritant sap if damaged. Hang the display out of the midday sun.

WINTER CONTAINERS

Containers used outdoors in winter must be durable and frost-proof. The best choices are timber or good-quality plastic. You can use the more expensive frost-proof ceramic and terracotta pots, but this does not mean that they protect the plants from freezing; rather that the pot is less likely to crack in freezing conditions. However, even frost-proof pots are not infallible, so anticipate occasional accidents. The most reliable plants for winter containers are winter-flowering heathers and small shrubs that flower or have berries or good evergreen foliage, such as skimmia, santolina, lamium, ivies and dwarf conifers. Winter-flowering pansies make a colourful combination when planted with them, but must have a well-sheltered spot. In this situation pansies will bloom non-stop all winter and late into spring, but in hard freezing weather they stop and may even be killed if the potting mixture freezes solid. If this happens, replace them in spring with daffodils or spring bedding, such as primroses and polyanthus just starting to flower, to continue the display. In mild regions or city centre gardens where the microclimate prevents proper frosts, you can grow a range of the hardier houseplants such as winter cherry, cyclamen and Indian azalea outside in winter, perhaps alternated with ivies or tiny dwarf conifers for foliage effect.

A winter display

Evergreens and small pot-grown conifers make a good backdrop for winter-flowering pansies. These stop flowering in severe conditions, so a sheltered site is essential. Put drainage material and potting mix into the base of the box.

Place the most striking plant – here, variegated euonymus – in the middle, towards the front. Add a matching pair of small flame-shaped conifers. They will not outgrow their space as this box will be replanted in early summer.

Below: Balance the colours of the pansies evenly. Water the box thoroughly and do not let the mix dry out thereafter.

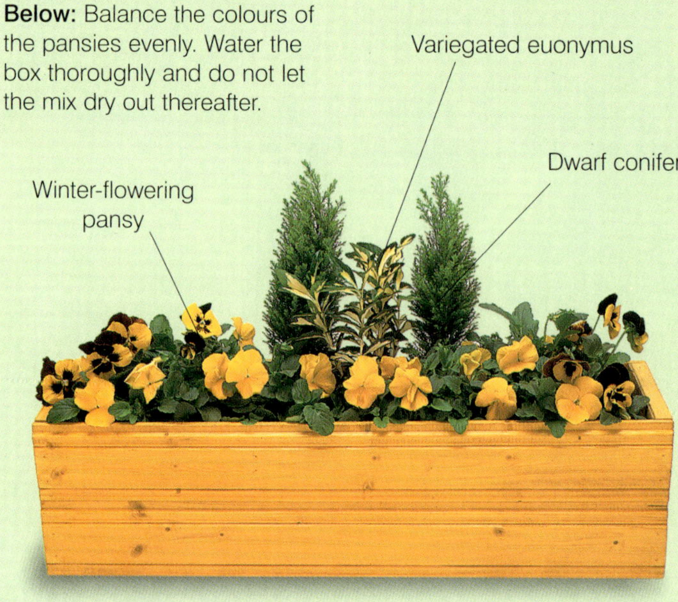

Planting up a winter tub

1 Assemble a variety of suitable plants and, with a crock covering the hole in the base of the pot to prevent soil running out, fill the tub to just below the rim with good-quality soil-based potting mix.

2 Put the largest plant in the centre. Keep the rootball intact, as space will be short and there are several other plants to put in.

3 A large plant, such as ivy, trailing over the tub softens the straight edges and helps the ever-green to blend in with the display.

4 Fit in as many flowering plants as possible. They will not grow any more, so the finished result must provide the full impact.

Above: Wooden barrels make ideal winter containers, because unlike terracotta or ceramic pots, the wood does not crack if it gets frozen. This barrel has been planted with *Skimmia japonica*, ivy, *Euphorbia amygdaloides* 'Rubra' and red-flowered cyclamen to give a long season.

A heather basket

The compact shape and free-flowering habit of winter-flowering heathers makes them ideal for hanging baskets. Since they are able to withstand the weather, they do not need a particularly sheltered site.

1 Six heathers in small pots and a large variegated ivy with long trails will fill a medium-sized hanging basket; this is a self-watering type. Roughly half-fill the basket with potting mixture.

2 Plant the ivy, plus stake, with the top of the root-ball 1.25cm(0.5in) below the rim of the pot. Firm in gently.

3 Plant the flowering heathers so that the shoots cascade over the edge without swamping the smaller gold-leaved heathers.

4 Arrange the ivy trails around the edge of the basket and in the heather. This looks best where the inside of a low hanging basket will be easily visible.

5 Pull out strands of ivy for a wispy effect. Site the display in a prominent position. Water well. Apply a weak feed in mild weather.

COLOUR IN WINTER

Festive holly and ivy foliage forms the basis of this winter container display, backed up by traditional berries and evergreen foliage, plus an ornamental cabbage, which makes a good alternative to winter flowers. If you cannot find a standard holly, you could remove all but one of the stems of a poorly shaped bush to convert it into an instant standard. Alternatively, use a bushy holly with fewer surrounding plants. For a formal entrance, make a pair of matching pots and place one on either side of a porch. For a less formal look, team a single container with smaller but matching pots of evergreens, winter-flowering heathers and early spring bulbs. Keep winter displays in a well-sheltered spot, with containers raised up on pot feet and in as much light as possible. Even plants that normally prefer partial shade will thrive in better light during the dull winter days.

To help insulate the roots of plants in smallish pots, stand each one inside a decorative container and pack the space between the two pots with bark chippings. Check containers regularly, even in winter, to see if they need watering; normal rainfall may not be able to get through dense foliage and into the potting mixture. Feed plants during mild spells in spring. Pick off discoloured leaves and generally tidy up container displays every week.

A festive winter tub

1 Assemble the plants and remove them from their pots before planting. Despite its name, 'Golden King', the standard holly, is a female that bears red berries provided it has been pollinated.

Hanging baskets

Given a reasonably sheltered sunny spot, it is possible to keep hanging baskets looking good all winter. Choose 'Universal' pansies and hybrid primroses with plenty of ivy, euonymus, santolina or periwinkle (the variegated versions are especially pretty). Use the trailing kinds around the edge of the basket for a fuller, softer effect.

Right: A basket of ivy, winter cherry and cyclamen needs a sheltered, frost-free location. Keep the potting mix just moist at all times but never soggy.

Above: Hang a basket of Universal pansies, ivy and hybrid primroses in a sunny spot. Check to see if it needs watering every week and apply a weak liquid feed in mild weather.

2 Cover the drainage hole with a crock and part-fill the pot with an ericaceous potting mix, but leave enough room for the plant roots.

3 Stand the holly in the centre; add the golden tree heather at the base to soften the upright line of the trunk. Firm in gently.

4 Plant gaultheria and heather towards the front so that they overflow the edge. Tuck potting mix around their roots and firm in.

5 Add a tall ornamental cabbage at the back. Plant the ivy, so that it curls round the sides of the pot for an instantly mature effect.

6 Fill any gaps with potting mix. Stand the display on pot feet, water it well and do not allow it to dry out. Do not feed until spring.

Wicker wall pots

1 Cut a large square of plastic (here we have used bubble plastic for insulation) and press it loosely down into the basket. Add potting mix and firm gently down.

2 The weight of the potting mix will make the plastic sink into the crevices. When it is bedded down, trim it tidily, leaving an overlap of about 2.5cm(1in).

3 Roll the edge of the liner over for a neat finish, and tuck it in down the sides of the basket. When the basket is planted up, the plants will disguise the plastic.

4 Put in the largest plant, placing it centrally at the back. Slightly mound up the soil around it to make it stand out from the plants that will go in front.

5 Tuck in as many small plants as possible around the heather. Choose plants with a complementary colour, and angle them outwards for a fuller look.

Two varieties of clematis growing through a climbing rose create a stunning vertical feature.

PART SEVEN

VERTICAL GARDENING

Double the space available for gardening by using the vertical space above your garden as well as the room inside it. Grow plants against walls, pillars and pergolas, use fashionable obelisks, trellis and rustic plant supports – or make your own!

3-D GARDENING

When every single scrap of space has to count, you cannot afford to overlook the third dimension. Gardening upwards takes advantage of the space over your garden as well as that inside it. Naturally, you will want to take advantage of all your walls fences and outbuildings to grow climbers and wall trained shrubs. But what about adding extra vertical features deliberately to add extra opportunities for growing them? Arches, pergolas, trellis 'garden dividers' and arbours, all act as creative space for climbers. And fashionable willow and rustic 'twig' plant supports or classic iron obelisks add a designer touch to borders. You can add to the vertical element in your garden by training climbers up into trees. Or create living screens as a fast alternative to hedges, by growing climbers over wire mesh, chain link fences or posts and wires. Great for hiding distant eye-sores. And have fun converting plants that are normally too big for your garden into something more suitable. You can train wisteria as a standard tree, thus turning a potential problem into a beautiful feature that not only looks good, but flowers much sooner and is far easier to prune than the same plant on the side of a house. Or transform large shrubs into small, space-saving trees, using much the same technique you would use to train a standard fuchsia. Instead of occupying a space 2.5m(8ft) in all directions, you can then plant right up to the trunk, freeing valuable space for extra perennials or ground covering plants. And by training large shrubs or trees flat against a wall and keeping them properly pruned, they take up virtually no space at all.

Right: Obelisks are one of the smartest ways of raising the interest in borders without using large spreading plants. This one shows off *Clematis* 'Madame Julia Correvon', a late-flowering cultivar. Cut it down hard in early spring to keep it compact.

Left: The pewtery-purple foliage of *Rosa glauca* always looks particularly good with clematis, such as 'Silver Moon'. Thalictrum flowers at about the same height, making a superb eye level plant association with room for short perennials below.

Left: An arch planted with climbing roses makes a good frame for a focal point, adds height to a border and is a good way of getting more plants into the space. Here a rose and euonymus are growing on the same arch.

Right: Climbing roses add vertical colour to brick walls and since the framework of main stems remains permanently in place, you can use it to support annual climbers or clematis that bring a second crop of flowers in new colours or shapes.

Right: The weight of its large double flowers gives *Fuchsia* 'Royal Velvet' an almost weeping shape. This type of growth may need support, such as tying the branches to a central cane.

Growing squashes decoratively

1 About six weeks before the last expected frost, fill 9cm (3.5in) pots with seed mix. Press one seed into the middle. Plant more than you need. Water well.

2 Label the pots. Keep them in a propagator, greenhouse or at a sunny window at 16-21°C (61-70°F). Seedlings appear within a week. Water as needed.

3 In a small area, squashes look attractive trained up over an arch in a decorative potager, or grown up strong trellis or along a chain link fence. Support large, heavy fruit with a net. Left to trail on the ground, squashes take up a great deal of space.

Growing ipomoea (morning glory) up a rose

1 Cover the bare stems at the base of some climbing roses by planting annual climbers such as ipomoea close to the base of the plants. Improve the soil first and plant after the last frost.

2 The climber starts flowering within a few weeks, covering the base of the rose in bloom. For best results, choose climbers with contrasting shapes or colours, but not too much foliage.

FIXING UP TRELLIS PANELS

Trellis panels are available in a wide variety of styles and materials. Trellis framework is attractive in its own right and its impact can be accentuated by painting it in different colours. Bright blue, yellow and terracotta water-based wood stains, which double as timber preservatives, are an increasingly popular and fashionable option. Natural wood finish and white are traditional choices, the latter conveying a 'classic' style to the garden. You can fix trellis panels to free-standing posts to create simple 'walls' that climbers can clothe with foliage and flowers, or you can build up arches, arbours, bowers and pergolas to suit your space and budget. In fact, you can buy many such trellis features as self-assembly kits. You can also buy perspective trellis panels to attach to walls. These create the impression of a niche, which is ideal for framing a mirror, statue or urn.

One of the main ways of using trellis panels is to fix them directly to a wall. You can do this simply by drilling through the battens and screwing directly into the brickwork. Do make sure that heavy panels are securely fixed and bear in mind that the climbers will add more weight to the structure. If you are using heavy duty, square-mesh trellis you will need to decide whether to place the horizontal or vertical battens closest to the wall. One way might be better for the plants you use, giving you room to tie in the stems to the framework.

Above: Stylish terracotta wall pots attached at various heights onto a rustic screen made from dried heather stems create a delightful display in which the plants are almost a bonus.

Right: Use soft string to tie honey-suckle stems to a trellis panel or a cane. The stems are delicate so take care when handling them and tie knots loosely.

Below: Expandable cedar trellis panels need support. Try screwing them to cedar stakes on the wall. This also creates space behind the panels.

Above: A wooden trellis panel with the horizontal battens fixed directly to the wall. This leaves the vertical pieces free, but plant growth may be restricted behind the cross pieces.

Above: Turn the panel round and the cross pieces form a series of rungs held away from the wall by the vertical battens. This might give climbers the best chance to develop.

Above: To save deciding which way round to fix the panel, simply space the whole thing away from the wall by fixing a suitable batten down the sides. This gives plants plenty of room.

Making wooden brackets

Below: You can make a support that fits over the horizontal lathes of a trellis panel with two pieces of 50x25mm(2x1in) planed softwood and a piece of 25x25mm(1x1in).

Above: Attach a hanging basket bracket to the support and simply hang it onto the trellis. The horizontal lathes are at the front here so the wooden hook fits well.

Left: Make a simple wooden bracket with an overhang on the top section and attach a piece of 25x25mm (1x1in) so that it will hook onto the trellis.

Right: Use one bracket to suspend a hanging basket or two brackets to support a windowbox or any suitable type of trough.

Attaching plants to supports

Plant support systems range from small nails or screws driven into the wall to a more permanent system of wires stretched horizontally across the wall at about 30cm(12in) intervals. There are various products for tying plant stems to wire or trellis, from soft green string to plastic and paper ties. Every year, check that plants have not outgrown their ties.

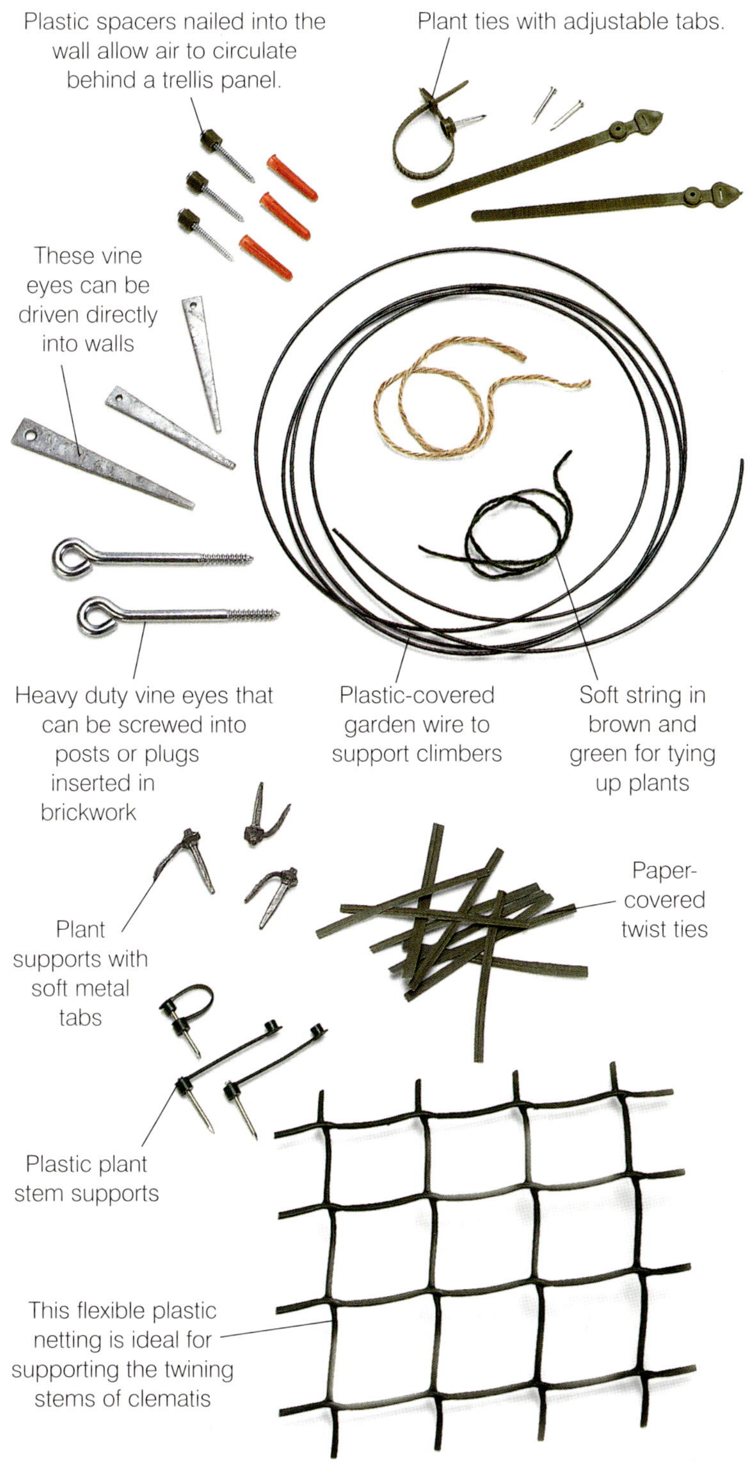

GROWING CLEMATIS AGAINST A WALL

Growing clematis against a wall is just one way to display the flowers. If appropriate for the variety, choose a wall that faces the sun, as this helps the plant to grow and the flowers to look radiant. The heat reflected and retained by the bricks aids growth and promotes a more vigorous plant. Do not plant clematis too close to the base of a wall as this will cause the plant to dry out. The wall provides good support for clematis stems to climb, but they will still need some assistance. You could tie them to trellis, attach them to a loose netting support or to wires stretched between vine eyes. It is the nature of the clematis plant to have seemingly dead stems lower down when it is mature and a burgeoning mass of foliage and flowers on top. On a wall, the natural growth habit can be encouraged to suit your design needs, with a mass of plant high up or hanging down, arranged along the top of the wall or spread sideways across it. A trellis against a white wall not only draws attention to the plant and its flowers, but also acts as a good plant support.

Preparing the plant

Before planting, plunge the plant in its original pot into a bucket of water and soak it for at least ten minutes so that the roots and rootlets are completely saturated. Clematis will grow in a wide range of soil types, providing they have adequate supplies of water and nutrients. If necessary, improve the soil before planting. Mulching with bark or manure in early spring helps to conserve water during the summer and improves the soil structure.

1 Dig a hole about 30cm(12in) away from the wall and deep enough to put in the clematis below the soil level in its pot.

2 Break up the sides and bottom of the hole. Sprinkle in a handful of slow-release fertiliser to boost the plant's growth.

3 Remove the plant plus stake and place them in the hole, so that the surface of the rootball is about 10cm(4in) below the surface.

4 Replace the soil around the plant and firm it down with your knuckles. Take care not to break the delicate stem.

5 Be sure to plant the clematis sufficiently far away from the base of the wall to clear any dry spots or accumulated rubble.

6 Arrange the plant and flowers against the trellis and tie them in. Leave the existing ties in place around the stem and cane.

Above: *Clematis* 'Jackmanii' is one of the larger hybrids, here adding a purple background to the red blooms of *Phlox* 'Starfire' and the emerging white flowers of *Sedum spectabile*. Cut it back close to the ground every spring.

7 Apply a small amount of slow-release fertiliser around the base, but do not allow it to touch and possibly burn the plant's stem.

8 Water the plant in well to help it become established. Do this every day for about a week, depending on the local conditions.

Growing clematis on trellis around a drainpipe

1 This hardwood support is designed to fit around a drainpipe. Start by laying out three trellis panels side-by-side.

2 To interlock the edges securely, slide one section slightly forward of the other and create an angle between them.

3 Hold the middle section as you interlock the edges of the third piece. The structure is now rigid enough to support itself.

4 Stretch two rubber bands across the protruding edges of the panels to hold the pieces together as you move them.

5 Place the support around the drainpipe and against the wall. When it is in position, fix it firmly to the pipe with plastic ties.

6 A clematis will soon cover the trellis support. Remember that the base of walls can be very dry, so feed and water the plants.

Training plants to a wall with wire

1 Drill a hole for the wall support. This is much better than knocking in the eye with a hammer, as there is no risk of splitting. Short cuts don't work!

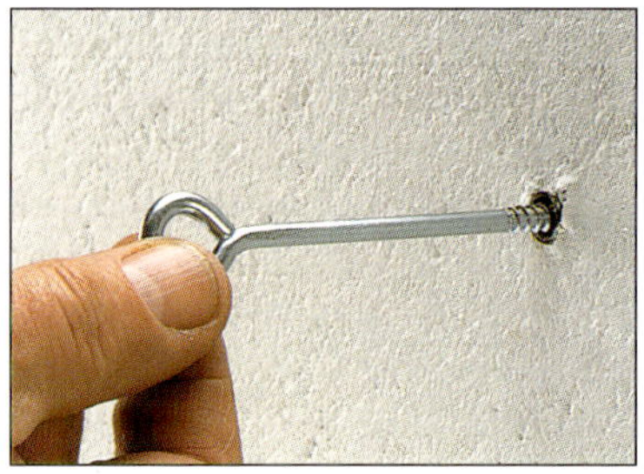

2 After pushing in a wall plug, screw in the screw-eye, leaving the eye about 2in(5cm) out from the wall. This allows room for tying shoots to the wire.

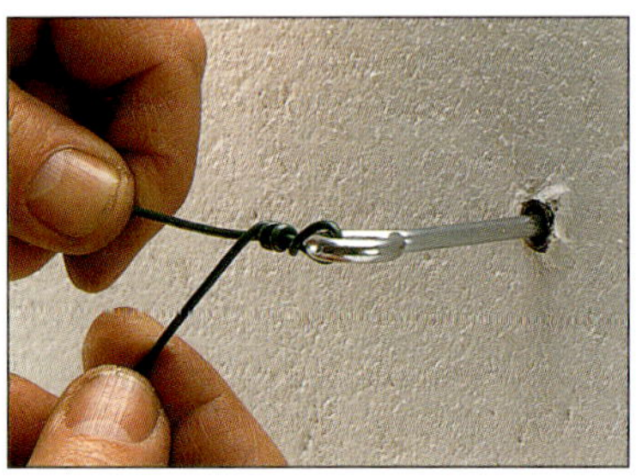

3 Pass one end of the wire through the eye and twist it around itself several times. This is another reason for keeping the wire away from the wall.

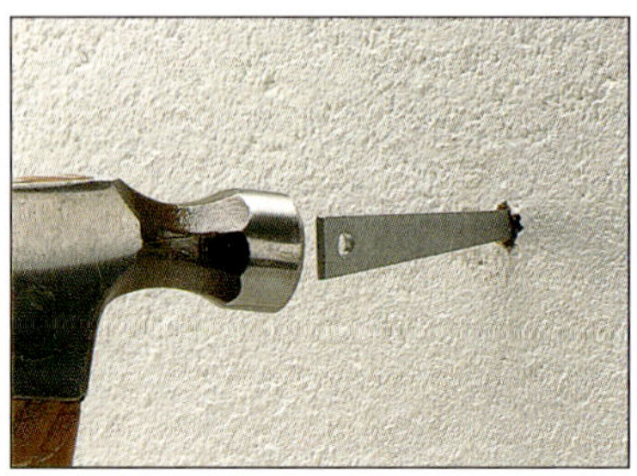

4 To stop the wire sagging or coming away, drive in vine eyes every 1.8m(6ft). Draw the wire across to the next screw eye to give a straight line.

5 Only attach the far end of the wire temporarily; once the vine eyes have been driven in, it will have to be detached and passed through each eye.

6 To train a chaenomeles against a wall, spread out the main stems and tie them to horizontal wires secured to wall nails. Tie in any shoots growing out over the wall. They increase the branch structure and create extra flowering space.

WALL SHRUBS

There are two definitions of a wall shrub. It is either any shrub that is not a climber but which is planted against a wall for support, or it is a shrub on the borderline of hardiness that is grown against or close to a wall for protection from the weather. In the first category you find a few shrubs, such as *Cotoneaster horizontalis*, which, in spite of its name, looks very attractive when grown against a wall instead of on the flat. *Forsythia suspensa* and winter jasmine could also be included in this category. Because these plants, and others like them, are perfectly hardy, a wooden fence would serve as well as a wall. However, true wall shrubs form quite a large group of plants that actually need the extra warmth or shelter from cold winds that a wall provides. A house wall that receives the sun at midday faces the sun for a long time and is sheltered from cold winds. The brickwork also warms up and it is the heat given off by a wall at night that can be just as beneficial to the plants growing near to or against it. Thus, a warm, sunny wall is an excellent place for early-flowering shrubs and small trees, including fruits such as peaches and nectarines, that are perfectly hardy in other respects. The warmth stops the flowers being frosted and killed.

Because you could be dealing with many different kinds, shapes and sizes of shrubs, there is no one training system that does for all. However, you can use the wall to advantage by making it a form of support for trees and shrubs that, in a warmer climate, would be fully in the open. By training them to a warm wall, you are showing them off better, as well as giving them more favourable growing conditions. The prime example of this is the glorious *Fremontodendron* 'Californian Glory', which needs the warmth of a house wall and is seen at its best when trained fairly formally against it.

7 Immediately after flowering, shorten outward-growing shoots close to the wall. Make sure your secateurs are sharp. Chaenomeles produces suckers from the base. They spoil the shape of a wall-trained shrub, so remove them.

Training forsythia

Although you would not normally grow *Forsythia* x *intermedia* against a wall, it makes an excellent subject. It flowers on the previous year's shoots, so prune it straight after flowering to give the plant the longest possible time to produce long vigorous shoots for the following year.

1 Plant the forsythia about 15cm(6in) away from the support. Tie in the stems loosely with string or plastic-covered wire. A tight tie will soon bite into the vigorous shoots and damage them.

2 Tie in the main shoots (here there are four), so that they cover a wide area of the frame. Cut out any weak, out-of-place shoots and unneeded branches.

3 Cut away any shoots that are growing straight out from the plant, as they will not be suitable for bending back towards the frame later on.

4 Lightly cut back the remaining branches to encourage side shoots. Spring-flowering shrubs need to make plenty of growth to produce flowers the following year.

5 Do not allow young shrubs to flower too much at this tender age otherwise growth will suffer and the plant will take longer to cover the frame.

Training pyracantha

Pyracantha makes a lovely sight when trained to a wall and carrying its familiar berries. Train it formally, with branches spreading horizontally from the central stem, or informally, with less regimentation. Prune pyracantha in mid- and late summer, cutting just above the berries.

1 Train the best side shoots along a trellis panel. Cut back any shoots growing straight towards or away from the frame.

2 Tie the central stem to one of the vertical struts with soft string. This plant is intended to grow informally against the frame.

3 Tie in side shoots so that they point in the right direction. Do not tie them horizontally; it is too formal and reduces plant vigour.

4 Tied to the frame like this, all the retained shoots form the basis of a larger plant that will cover the trellis completely in three to four years.

***Left:** Trained wall shrubs make a natural frame around a window. Prune them once or twice a year to keep them neat and to prevent them obscuring the light.*

ERECTING A PERGOLA

Self-assembly pergolas are available from garden centres and mail-order suppliers. Following the instructions, you should be able to put one together in just a few hours. The one featured on these pages has four uprights, two side beams, four cross beams and two trellis panels. The wood is treated with a preservative stain that will protect it from rotting and will not harm plants growing on it. When you have unpacked the kit and are ready to begin, it is a good idea to have someone to help you and you will also need a hammer, nails, gloves and a stepladder. Wear gloves to prevent splinters and as protection against the preservative stain applied to the wood. If you prefer to build a pergola from scratch, you can buy the wood and cut it to size at home. You will need to stain and preserve the wood as well. Naturally, this is a cheaper option than buying a ready-to-assemble kit. Whichever method you choose, you need to decide where to site the pergola and how to support the uprights. You could sink them in concrete or fix them to metal post holders driven into the ground. This last method requires shorter uprights and, as they are not sunk into the ground, they will not rot. Once the pergola is completely constructed, mark out the bed running along the side or just prepare a square of soil around each of the uprights, ready to take the climbers.

Left: This simple pergola has been embellished with attractive trellis, a great foil on which to display a fine specimen of *Clematis* 'Ville de Lyon', a very fine, free-flowering summer hybrid.

Right: You can make a living gazebo by training four trees to form a roof. Start with young flexible 'whips' of a compact but decorative tree. After planting, bend the trunks over a framework of metal tubes and tie them in place. In time they 'set'.

Building a pergola

1 Support two of the uprights and lower one of the unnotched side beams into the groove. Decide on the spacing of these uprights before securing them into the ground.

2 When you are happy with the overhang at each end of the side beam, secure it to the uprights with galvanised nails as shown. You may choose to use two nails at each end.

3 Once the two sides of the pergola are complete, join them together by dropping in one of the four cross beams. Put the end ones 'outside' the uprights for a stable structure.

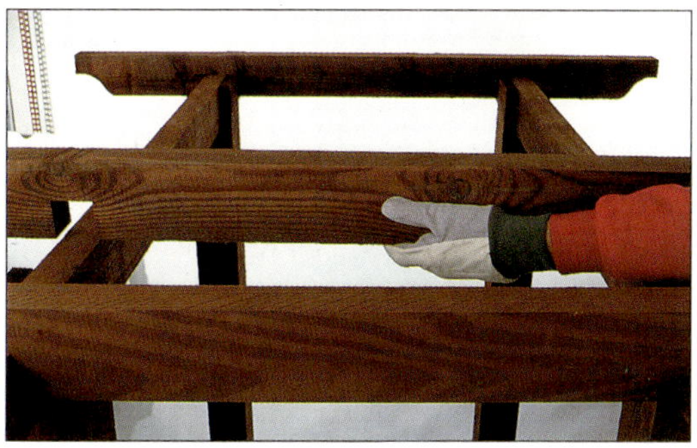

4 With the far end cross beam also in place, space the other two out equally. The width of the pergola is set by the notches in these cross beams.

5 Nail the cross beams to the top of the side beams. Then position and nail the first trellis panel in between the uprights. Raise the panel 15cm (6in) off the ground to protect it from soil moisture and rain splash.

6 With the second trellis panel in place opposite the first, the pergola is complete. This demonstration sequence has not included the vital task of fixing the uprights securely into the ground.

Above: If you want to grow a large climbing rose such as this 'Paul's Himalayan Musk', use it where it has room to develop and can take over the whole of a pergola.

Climber or rambler?

It is important to know whether you have a climbing or rambling rose, as it affects the way they are pruned later. Ask the nursery which kind they are when you buy them. If in doubt, check the name and habit in a reliable reference book. If you buy a young climber during the dormant winter season, prune it quite hard after planting. This encourages strong new shoots that you tie to the wall or fence. If a new rambler has a few strong, young shoots, keep them, but cut out all the others.

VIGOROUS CLIMBERS

Large vigorous climbers should clearly be treated with caution in small gardens. The wrong climber in the wrong place can quickly swamp surrounding plants and overwhelm obelisks, gazebos or pergolas. One giant creeper can easily dominate the whole garden, when the balance would be better shared amongst more, but smaller plants that between them have a longer flowering season. However, in the right situation, large climbers can be useful. For instance, if you have a small garden surrounded by walls and want a fairly low-maintenance garden, then growing one climber that acts as a continuous backdrop to a simple planting scheme may look better and be easier to look after than a fussier style. Large self-clinging climbers are also a good way of covering a mesh screen in a hurry to provide instant privacy or hide a distant eyesore. They take up less space than a hedge and need no clipping. Unlike a hedge, they stop at the required height – in this case the top of the climbing frame – so you avoid future problems. You can also use a large climber to conceal chain link fencing in a new garden, converting it quickly into a living green boundary that needs much less clipping than a hedge. Many climbers can also be trained as standards which converts them into small trees; wisteria are specially successful trained in this way. Some large climbers – notably late-flowered clematis – can conveniently be cut back to ground level each spring, which limits their spread. Growing large climbers in containers restricts their roots naturally.

Above: *Clematis montana* var. *rubens* does not need regular pruning, but can be cut back hard every few years in early spring to reduce the size. Remove the tangle of old woody stems that builds up to rejuvenate the plant. Here it is growing through a large ceanothus shrub.

Below: *Clematis* 'Niobe' and 'Comtesse de Bouchard' both flower from midsummer onwards. These kinds are seen at their best if they are cut back hard, to within 15cm(6in)of the ground, each year in early spring. Left unpruned, they grow tall and lanky, with flowers only at the top of the stems.

Pruning late-flowering clematis

Clematis that bloom from midsummer onwards, flower on shoots that grew earlier in the same growing season. Prune them hard in early spring just before growth starts. Cut the whole plant down to about 15cm(6in) above ground level. This severe treatment will not harm the plant; on the contrary, it encourages a reliable show of flowers where you can see them. On unpruned plants they are all up at the top of long stems.

Below: Using sharp secateurs, always cut back to a live bud to avoid leaving unsightly snags that may become infected by fungal diseases.

Above: Separate two climbers with different pruning needs by growing them on either side of a doorway. Cut the blue *Clematis* 'Perle d'Azur' close to the ground in spring, while *C. tangutica* can either be cut back hard then or just tidied up.

Below: *Clematis viticella* 'Alba Luxurians' can reach 6m(20ft). In a small garden, grow it into a tree or large shrub. Cut it down to 15cm (6in) in spring and clear old stems.

Drastic pruning

Occasionally, large 'no-prune' climbers, such as *Clematis montana,* outgrow their space and need attention. Prune them hard in mid- spring, just as they are about to start making new growth. Cut back to about half the required size, or clip the plant back closely leaving little more than a main framework of stems. If severe pruning is essential, take the risk and cut it back to about 30cm(12in) from ground level, again in mid-spring. Although flowering will be affected for a season or two, the plant will soon return to normal. From then on, keep new stems trained in to the area to be covered.

A standard wisteria

1 Remove the side shoots from the base of a strong healthy young plant, leaving the main stems twisted around the cane.

2 Cut the side shoots flush with the main stems until 30cm (12in) from the top. Shorten long shoots at the top to form a head.

Above: Trained as a standard, *Wisteria floribunda* makes a spectacular small weeping tree suitable for even a tiny garden.

3 Train any long shoots close to the base around the cane in the same direction to thicken up the trunk of the plant

A WILLOW PLANT SUPPORT

Rustic willow plant supports are fun and fashionable. They are available ready-made, sold by craftspeople from their stands at flower shows or by mail order direct from their studios. A limited range is sometimes available in garden centres, too. The basic material is versatile and easy to work with, so provided you can find a source of suitable willow stems, you can create your own designs. The long, slender, one-year-old willow stems (correctly called withies) are sometimes available in winter by mail order from basket makers in willow-growing regions (look for advertisements in craft or gardening magazines). Willow plant supports do not have a long life compared to synthetic materials (perhaps one to three years), but their natural charm is more than compensation - and any imperfections only add to their attraction. They are so quick to make, you could easily replace them every year or two.

Preparing the willow

With care, an upright willow support in a patio pot, with two 'bands' for tall climbing plants, should last for two seasons or more in the garden. It is cheap and easy to make.

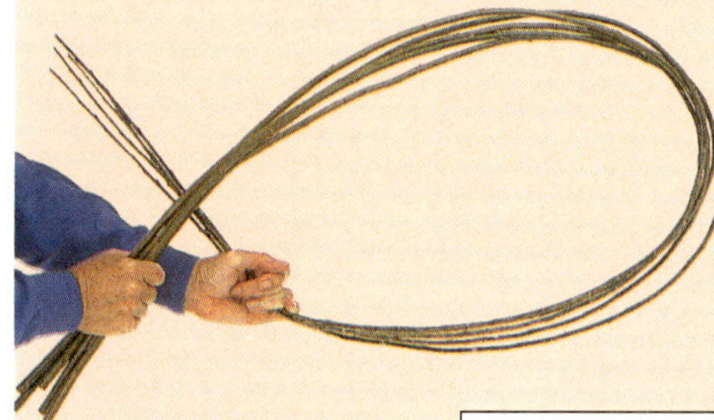

1 Lay short willow wands out flat in a bath of water to soak. Tie up and loop long withies into large circles, so that they fit into a water butt or large bucket.

2 Secure the ends so that they do not spring out, and wedge the hoops into the container. Leave them to soak for 12-24 hours (overnight is fine) immediately before use. It will not do any harm to leave them in the water longer.

1 Choose a container heavy enough to support a tall structure. Fill it with potting mix and push an odd number of tall, straight willow wands evenly around the edge to form the uprights of the plant support.

2 Take a prepared willow wand and tie the thick end firmly to one of the uprights above the rim of the pot. Weave the wand in and out between the uprights, keeping the uprights evenly spaced.

3 Once the first wand is in place; press the layers close together to tighten the weave. Tie or tuck in the loose end to secure it. Do not try to weave with the very thin material at the tip of the stem.

4 Weave in a second wand as before. Continually check that the uprights remain evenly spaced; it takes a long time to put things right later on if you overlook this essential monitoring.

5 To neaten the thin end of the withy, hook it round an upright, bend it back in the opposite direction and tuck it into the weave, down the edge of an upright.

6 Only tie in the first withy. Then weave in new stems leaving a long 'tail' inside. When both bands are complete, cut off the excess stems with strong secateurs.

7 Gather together the tops of the uprights and tie them well with strong string. Do not worry if this looks untidy; it will be hidden by a decorative willow covering later on.

8 Take a very thin, flexible piece of willow 60-90cm(24-36in) long, and push it down between the tops of the stems. If the string is secure, it should be a tight fit.

9 Bind the new piece of willow around this section, working neatly from bottom to top. At the top, bend the tip of the willow and push it firmly inside the 'collar' so that it cannot work loose.

Planting sweet peas

1 Annual climbers, such as these sweet peas, make a fine show in summer but do not outgrow the pot. Morning glory or trailing nasturtiums are also good.

2 Sweet peas need help to start them off in the right direction. Tie each stem loosely to an upright, so they are spaced evenly out all round the container.

3 Water the container. Stand it in a sheltered spot with direct sun for most of the day, but not exposed to scorching midday sun.

4 Team the finished container with similar materials, such as rustic hurdles. Slight imperfections are normal and even desirable in craft work; other people never notice them as much as you do.

Sweet peas cling on to suitable supports using their own tendrils.

A HONEYSUCKLE POLE

Climbers offer plenty of creative possibilities, and when you garden in a small space it is worth investigating unusual vertical solutions. For example, growing a honeysuckle as a standard allows you to fit a potentially large plant into a small space. Once it has grown and formed a dense ball, the head of the plant will be completely covered with flower for three months or more every summer. And even when not in flower, the striking shape acts as a stylish topiary that would enhance any border. A certain amount of training and pruning will be needed to keep the shape of the standard. Simply tie in new shoots to the ball as they grow, and as soon as the plant finishes flowering for the year, trim back excess growth to within 15cm(6in) of the ball. Other climbers with a similar natural growth habit can be trained in this way. Clematis are particularly successful. Choose one of the varieties that starts flowering after midsummer, as these can be hard pruned in early spring every year. But do not prune it right back to the ground; instead, just prune all the stems back to within 15-30cm(6-12in) of the top of the support frame. And since clematis cling on to their supports with their leaf stalks, tuck the new growth back into the ball to make a dense solid head to the plant. Do not try to form the top by pinching out the tips of the shoot, or honeysuckle and clematis will not flower.

1 Hammer a strong pole into the ground where the climber is to grow. Or push it into a large container filled with potting mix. Hammer in a large metal staple.

2 Take a long, slim, flexible willow or hazel wand about 90cm(36in) long. Push it through the hoop and adjust it until both ends protrude the same amount.

3 Do the same with another three willow wands. Separate the stems so they open out like the spokes of a wheel, with the hoop as its centre. It is helpful to have someone else to hold them roughly in place at this point

4 Holding both ends of one stem, bend them down until they cross about a 30cm(12in) below the top of the pole. Tie both ends to the pole with soft string.

5 Bend all the stems in the same way so they form a globe. Do not risk breaking the stems to achieve an ideal shape; the climber will hide any irregularities later.

6 Use several rows of soft string, knotted to each stem in turn, all round the middle of the sphere, to space them equally apart. This not only looks good but also gives stems something to cling on to as the head forms.

7 Plant the climber close to the base of the pole. Knock it out of its pot, but leave the stems tied to their cane. Water thoroughly and wait for the soil to settle.

8 Remove the cane. Untangle the stems and holding two at a time, twist them round the pole in opposite directions. Hold the top of the stems in place with soft string.

9 Keep the plant well fed and watered. Each time the stems grow another 15cm(6in), tie them back up to the pole. When they are long enough, train some stems around the sphere.

Below: Flowering honeysuckles look equally good growing through hurdles made from hazel twigs and other screens and supports made from natural materials.

Using wicker plant supports

Wicker plant supports are fashionable, and whether you buy them or make your own, they make a good way to show off naturally sprawling plants such as trailing nasturtiums, turning them into novel displays in the border. Expect natural wicker, willow or hazel twig structures to last for two or three years; a little longer if you treat them with a plant-friendly wood preservative, although this can be a laborious task.

1 Press the plant support into level ground so its legs leave a mark. Remove it. Knock the plants out of their pots and plant them well inside the cage shape.

2 Fill the space well. Two or three pots of well-grown plants should fit underneath a 30-38cm(12-15in)-diameter cage. Firm and water them thoroughly.

3 Fit the cage carefully over the top of the plants. Tuck the flowers and foliage inside to avoid damaging them. Then push the legs firmly down into the soil.

4 The growing plants scramble up and over the wickerwork, forming a loose, rustic-looking mound. The bare twigs contrast well with the plant material.

A METAL OBELISK

Climbers are fashionable and colourful, but if you have a garden without many walls or fences, it can be difficult to find places to grow them. One popular solution is to choose from the wide range of decorative climbing frames suitable for beds, borders and containers. But suit your planting to the type of support. Rustic-looking climbers look better grown on rustic supports. Clematis is ideal for a formal, metal obelisk. For the best effect, plant two or three clematis with differently shaped flowers and colours, for instance a viticella variety, a texensis and a later-flowering large-flowered hybrid. All three can be hard pruned in spring. Clematis combines well with coloured foliage. *Ampelopsis brevipedunculata* 'Elegans' is specially good, as the cream-green- and pink-variegated leaves team well with clematis flowers, and the plant is naturally compact but also dies back close to ground level in winter, so will not get overgrown. *Vitis vinifera* 'Purpurea', with its pewter-tinged purple leaves, is another good candidate. Cut back this stronger-growing plant close to the ground each spring.

Planting clematis

Clematis are best planted deeply, with the surface of the rootball up to 15cm(6in) below soil level. In this way, large-flowered hybrids, which are susceptible to clematis wilt, are able to regrow from underground buds if the tops of the plants are killed off. But even wilt-resistant species, such as *C. viticella* cultivars can regrow if damaged when hoeing. Before planting, prepare the site well. Remove any weeds and dig in plenty of well-rotted organic matter. When planting clematis, do not break up the rootball unless the plant is badly potbound; lower it carefully into the prepared planting hole and firm it down gently.

Left: Fill the planting hole with a mixture of topsoil and well-rotted organic matter, taking great care not to bruise the stem of the plant.

Planting up a metal obelisk

1 Prepare the planting site well. Dig a hole about 2.5cm(1in) narrower than the diameter of the base of your obelisk, position the frame and press it down firmly.

2 If you are using a variety of plants, put in the clematis first, as it needs to go in deeper than other climbers. Plant everything well inside the base of the obelisk.

Above: This *Clematis* 'Jackmanii' looks very attractive grown against an ornamental frame, but will need coiling around an obelisk to stop it outgrowing the support. This also encourages flowering, as the stems are more horizontal.

3 Add a plant with colourful foliage. If space is short and the soil is deep, rich and fertile, you can safely plant later climbers above the clematis rootball.

4 Fill the gaps between the rootballs with more garden soil, firm gently and water so the soil sinks before you secure the stems to the climbing frame.

5 Starting near the base of the plant, lean the stems up and around the obelisk and tie them in a loose spiral around it.

6 Once the tips have been tied in place, the new growths of clematis will hold on to the frame for themselves, by their leaf stalks.

7 Already the base of the obelisk looks well-clothed. Twist the new growth around the frame every week or two, otherwise the new shoots rush straight up to the top and will not flower so well.

Perfect partners

Clematis are perfect plants to grow on an obelisk as the airy foliage does not swamp the shape of the frame or smother anything else you plant with it, and the large, symmetrical, rosette-shaped flowers complement the formal effect. By choosing varieties that can be cut back almost to ground level in early spring each year, the obelisk never looks overgrown. If you want to grow earlier flowering clematis, choose naturally more compact varieties, such as Clematis alpina *cultivars, and leave them virtually unpruned except to tidy the shape back close to the framework of the obelisk shortly after flowering finishes. In this case, avoid mixing them with climbers that need different pruning, as the stems intertwine making the job almost impossible.*

Right: *'Arctic Queen' has two flushes of double white flowers. To keep the first flush of flowers, cut back the plant close to the shape of the obelisk after flowering finishes in late summer.*

8 Together, *C. texensis* 'Etoile Rose', *C. viticella* 'Etoile Violette' and *C. v.* 'Polish Spirit' make a good display of flowers in complementary colours from mid- to late summer.

A wide range of plant textures surround a stylish water feature in a small garden.

PART EIGHT

SMALL WATER FEATURES

Bring a small garden alive with the sounds and sparkle of moving water, or relax at the end of the day beside a tranquil fish pond – but all in miniature. However small the space, there is a water feature to suit you, right down to tiny potted ponds.

MAKING THE MOST OF WATER IN A SMALL GARDEN

Water is an essential feature of many gardens, but in a small plot 'conventional' ponds and water gardens are rarely practical. A pond needs to be a reasonable size for the water temperature to remain stable and the biological balance to 'work', keeping the water clean. A normal pond on a tiny scale needs a lot of maintenance to keep the water from turning green, and to prevent pond and waterside plants clogging it. Otherwise, it soon disappears from view or just looks a mess. There are, however, several ways you can use water successfully in a limited space. Pebble pools, fountains and wall masks all avoid any standing water so maintenance is low, and this type of feature is perfectly safe where small children have access to the garden. Birds and other wildlife can still drink and bathe, and the units are so compact and versatile they can be incorporated into even tiny or highly 'designed' gardens. Simply choose a style that goes with the rest of the garden; you can buy ready to install features that include a decorative architectural feature such as a statue or urn complete with pump, reservoir and plumbing, or you can create your own design from the basic components using a pedestal or base of your choice. Another option is to make a small pool in a container. This can either be moved under cover in winter, or dismantled so that plants plus any fish can be kept indoors or in a heated greenhouse in winter to protect them from freezing. A potted pond is much easier to clean and restock every spring than a normal pond, and is perfect for growing some of the fascinating, small frost-tender floating water plants.

Left: A water pavement is a most attractive semi-formal 'walk-through' water feature, where you step onto raised paving in the water. It needs a reasonable space to do it justice and, as it is quite complicated to build, is probably best left to a construction company unless you are used to creating water features.

Left: A bubbling water feature provides the focal point in a courtyard garden. This type, where the water runs over the sides of the jar, has an underground reservoir into which water trickles back through the cobbles at the base of the container. Sit the jar absolutely level, otherwise the water only runs out down one side.

Maintenance

Features that do not include plants, fish or standing water are easy to keep clean. Simply add an algicide to the water in spring or immediately after construction. This should keep the water and the cobblestones or ornaments it runs over completely clean for a whole season. Each spring, partly drain the system by running the pump and diverting the water away from the feature. Then refill it with fresh water and add a new dose of algicide.

Left: This novel fountain makes a good alternative to a more formal spout for a water feature in two containers. A small submersible pump in the base of the lower container circulates water back to the face in the upper one. Floating plants, here duckweed, hide the mechanics. A display like this attracts attention to a shady corner, and the fountain adds light, sound and sparkle.

Above: A potted lily pond makes a complete container that needs nothing else; any open water provides good reflections of overhanging plants. To help the container blend into a patio or deck, team it with a grassy-leaved plant, such as carex, festuca and ophiopogon.

Left: This Japanese style fountain is very child friendly, as there is no standing water. For the same reason it also stays clean. Water from the bamboo spout runs into the hollow stone and then into an underground reservoir, which is hidden by cobblestones. From there it is recycled via a small submersible pump.

SETTING UP A WATER PUMP

A submersible pump is quite powerful enough for most small water features. The smallest models are little bigger than a fist and as long as they can be covered by water, can run in as little as half a gallon. You will need a larger, more powerful pump if the water has to be raised any height to run a waterfall or a fountain raised up on top of a statue. Some types of fountain jet (such as the popular bell jet) need more power to provide sufficient through-flow of water to run them. Check before buying a pump that it is capable of powering the sort of feature you have in mind. Many water features, such as a simple pebble pool where the water simply wells up through the centre of a millstone, do not need any extra fittings. If you want a fountain, you will need to fit a special jet to the outlet pipe from the pump to create the desired spray pattern. Various kinds are available from the very natural looking gusher type to formal kinds with fine droplets forming tiered wedding cake shapes. Basic fountain jets are sometimes included with the pump, but otherwise you need to buy them separately, always ensuring that they are suitable for the power of your pump. Most small pumps are low-voltage models, but it is a good idea to plug the pump into a residual current device (RCD) that will cut the power if there is any risk of a fault causing a shock. For safety, always use a pond pump with the electric cable supplied; do not attempt to extend it. Most pumps are supplied with quite enough cable to reach a pond from the house, garage or greenhouse.

Setting up a pump for a fountain

1 If you want to use the built-in filter simply push it over the inlet pipe of the pump until it clicks into place. It is easy to remove for cleaning. The built-in filter houses a block of plastic filter foam

2 If you plan to run a fountain and perhaps a waterfall as well, push the T-piece adapter onto the outlet pipe of the pump.

3 Screw on a blanking cap if you decide not to run a waterfall from the adaptor. If you change your mind, fit a tube instead.

4 The pump is ready to have a fountain head fitted on top of the outlet pipe. The built-in foam pad will filter the water as it is sucked through the vents in the casing.

5 Fit the T-piece into the top outlet and select a fountain head. The one with three circles of holes produces a three-tier pattern with a wide spread of water.

A bubble fountain head

Below: Correctly adjusted, a bell fountain head produces a smooth, symmetrical dome of water at the size you want

Above: To change the shape, push in the cone at the top of the head. Start with a reduced water flow and gradually increase it.

A geyser fountain head

Below: The geyser head produces a strong jet of aerated water. To get the best effect, operate the pump at its most powerful setting.

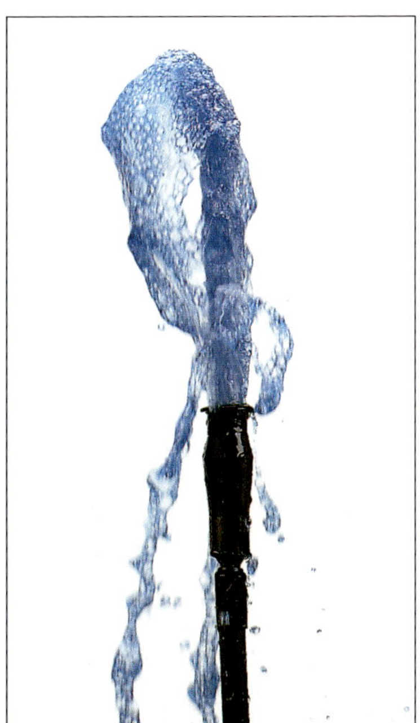

Above: Push the geyser head firmly onto the extension tube. You can alter the angle of the head to create different water flow patterns.

Waterfalls

A waterfall or cascade is an excellent way to add movement and height to a garden scheme.

***Right:** If you just want to run a waterfall, simply connect a suitable length of plastic tubing directly to the outlet of a submersible pump (as here) and direct the water flow as you wish.*

***Left:** You can make water spill from a jar into a pond. The moving water helps oxygen to dissolve, which is helpful to fish. To reduce the sound of the running water, plant a water plant, such as* Lysimachia nummularia *'Aurea' or watercress in the jar and let the water run down its stems.*

Waterfall and fountain

1 Remove the blanking cap from the T-piece adapter. Push on plastic tubing to supply the waterfall. This tube has a bore of 2.5cm(1in). Use one of the adapters to fit plastic tubing of a different diameter.

2 Use the adjuster to control the flow of water. Fully screwed in, all the water will go to the waterfall; fully out, it will split the flow both ways. Make sure that your pump is powerful enough to supply both outlets.

Setting up a small water feature

1 Use a tiny pump that will work in a small quantity of water. Attach clear plastic tubing to the nozzle and sit the pump in the pot.

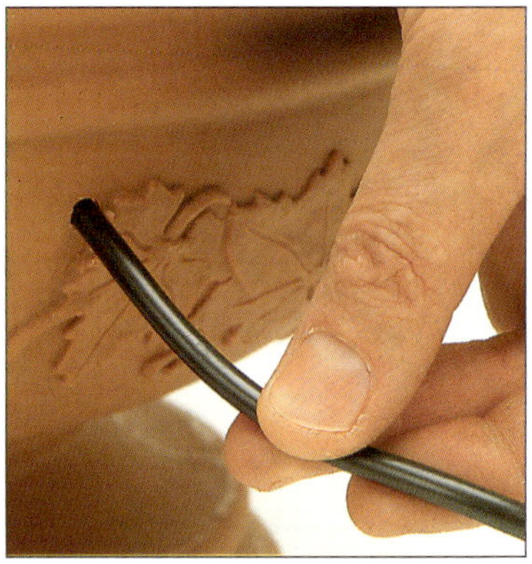

2 Drill a hole under the pot rim, thread the wire through and reconnect the plug. This will leave the rim of the container clear.

A wire hanging basket makes an ideal support for the pond pump.

3 Find a hanging basket frame the right size to sit inside the pot, covering the pump. Remove the chains and fit it firmly in place so it will not slip when weighted down with pebbles.

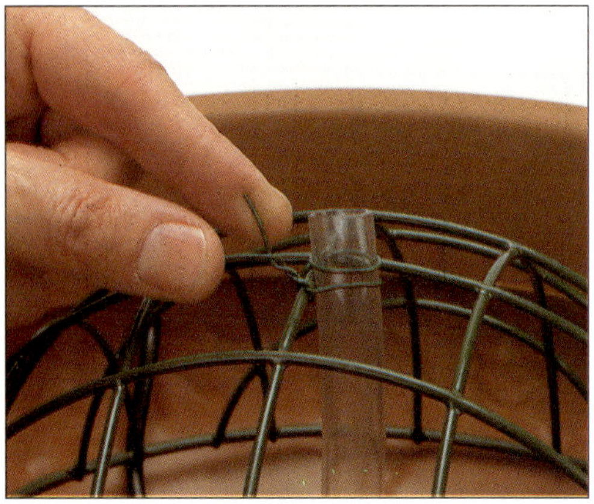

4 Wire the tip of the nozzle to the framework of the basket to hold it securely. There is no need to fit a spray head as the nozzle alone will produce a clean fountain-shaped jet of water.

5 Part-fill the container with water, covering the pump completely, with 5cm(2in) to spare. This ensures that the pump will remain covered with water when the fountain is in operation.

PEBBLE POOLS

Fountain features make striking and unusual ingredients for a container garden. Team a bubble fountain, like either of the ones shown here, with two or four 'potted ponds' of different sizes to make a complete patio water garden. (As in all container displays, they will look best if an uneven number of elements are grouped together.) It is the ideal way to add moving water to a display of potted 'water lily ponds', since these plants cannot be grown under fountains – they do not thrive if the tops of their leaves keep getting wet. And in a garden used by small children, a feature filled with pebbles where there is no standing water – however shallow – is a safer option.

Set up a potted fountain with care. Make sure that the pot, stones, etc., are all perfectly clean, as any dirt and grit will soon clog the pump. The submersible pump must be covered by water at all times. Adjust the jet so that the water trickles back into the pot and is continuously recycled – if too high, much of the water will go over the sides of the container. If the container empties, the pump runs dry and will be damaged. Top up the water level at least once a week, since evaporation will gradually lower the water level. A small bubble fountain like this only needs the smallest type of submersible pump; choose a low voltage one, and plug it into a residual current device (RCD), which automatically cuts the power and prevents shocks in case the power cable is damaged. In a mild location with plenty of shelter, water features in weatherproof containers can be left outside in winter. But if the water is at risk of freezing solid (ceramic or terracotta containers are most at risk as they crack if this happens), either move them under cover for protection or drain out the water, clean and dry the pump and store it in a dry place until the feature is reassembled in spring.

6 Hide the pump and the hanging basket pump cover completely under a layer of smooth clean pebbles; choose a size of pebble that is in proportion to the size of the container.

7 When the pump is switched on, a simple fountain effect trickles water over the pebbles. Adjust the pump valve to make the fountain jet a suitable height.

Left: You can add a special jet to the outlet at the top of the pump to produce a formal bell fountain. Although its wall of water is more wind-resistant than a spray fountain, choose a sheltered spot or the bell blows out of shape.

Variations on a theme

With a little imagination, it is possible to create several novel variations on the fountain in a container of pebbles theme. Once you have made one version, all sorts of other ideas will present themselves, so instead of simply recreating the same idea each spring, why not take the opportunity to add a few subtle alterations?

Right: *Water from this small raised pond is pumped up through a pile of pebble-filled pots, so that it spills down attractively over them to make an unusual waterfall. So the water runs smoothly instead of just trickling down the sides of the pots, you need to make a shallow lip for the water to run from.*

Above: *A smooth rock with a hole drilled through the centre makes a classic bubble fountain. The rock rests above a small underground reservoir containing the pump; the water appears to run away through cobbles but actually runs back into container. Adjust the pump to produce a low trickle of water, not a jet.*

Planting up a metal trough

1 Part-fill the trough with good-quality potting mix. A shallow trough with waterloving plants needs no gravel drainage.

2 Choose a mixture of upright plants with contrasting shapes, textures and colours, but of roughly similar height. Knock them out of their pots and plant them in a row.

3 Plant several of the same kind of low, spreading plant along the front and at each end of the container. Here we have used a purple-leaved form of ajuga.

WATER PLANTS IN METAL BUCKETS

Shiny metal buckets make superb containers for waterside plants. A group of different shapes and sizes, planted with marginal and bog garden plants, looks good in an informal cottage-style garden, outside a back door, or by an outbuilding. Stand the display on a base of gravel, cobbles or pebbles; it looks good in front of a pond, a large glass door or a white-painted wall where sunlight will be reflected between the various surfaces to create a sparkling effect. Suitable plants include those that grow naturally in shallow water or boggy ground that never dries out. To make a good display, plant some containers with a single large specimen foliage plant and others with a group of smaller flowering plants, then team them together. All water plants associate well together, but for a more 'designed' look, allow one colour, say yellow, to run through the scheme in each container. It only takes a small amount in each to link the display together visually, since they are already in matching containers. Ideal plants would be compact or slow-growing subjects with a long flowering season. In practice, however, few water plants fall into this category. It is best to choose plants with a long flowering season, and either plant them out in a damp part of the garden after one season in containers, or else to divide and replant them the following spring.

4 Use a narrow trowel and a little potting mixture to fill any gaps between adjacent rootballs. Fill the trough almost to the rim, as the mix will sink when watered.

5 Trickle water around each plant to settle the mixture around the roots. Add more water, leaving the mix wet but not sloppy. Keep it wet, as bog plants dislike drying out.

Growing invasive plants in buckets

1 Place a layer of clean gravel in the bottom of a watertight bucket to give it a firm base and to support the finished display.

2 If the plant is large, stand it in its pot in the bucket. If it is small, fill the bucket with potting mix and plant as normal.

Planting an astilbe in a metal bucket

A tall, narrow, metal flower bucket suits a tall, graceful plant such as astilbe. The plant can be left in its pot or removed – it will only be left in place for one summer as it will soon grow too big.

1 Fill the base of the container with gravel to act as 'ballast' to keep it upright, and to provide some drainage for the plant.

2 Position the plant on top of the gravel bed, so that it rests 2.5cm(1in) below the rim of the container.

Suitable plants

Caltha palustris, *Cyperus*, *Filipendula ulmaria* 'Aurea', *Hosta*, *Iris laevigata*, *Iris versicolor*, *Lysimachia nummularia*, *L. punctata*, *Juncus effusus* 'Spiralis', *Mentha aquatica*, *Mimulus*, *Schoenoplectus* 'Zebrinus', *Typha minima*, *Zantedeschia aethiopica*.

PLANTING MARGINALS IN A WOODEN BARREL

Marginal pond plants make fascinating container subjects. Any container that holds water is suitable, but a wide half barrel is best as it has a large water surface that makes the most of the plants' reflections – one of their best assets. Marginal plants are the sort that can be grown in 0-20cm (0-8in) of water (measured over the top of the pot). This includes all the popular water irises, marsh marigolds and rushes, as well as many of the bog garden plants, such as zantedeschia. Avoid plants that merely grow in damp soil; although they are sometimes sold mistakenly as marginal plants, subjects such as hosta and astilbe do not enjoy standing in water above their necks and do not last long under these conditions. Marginal plants are often imposing specimens that grow quickly; to keep them at a suitable size for a half barrel, lift them out and divide them every spring, just as they are starting into growth. Once planted up, keep the barrel topped up with water; in hot weather it can lose 2.5cm(1in) of water each week due to evaporation.

Potting up a marginal

1 Knock the plant out of its pot or cut away the plastic very carefully. Put 2.5cm (1in) of pond plant mix or garden soil with no added fertiliser into the bottom of a net-sided pond pot.

2 Sit the plant in the centre of the pot and fill round the roots with more of the same mix. If it trickles out through the holes, line the pot with hessian.

3 Cover the surface with 2.5cm(1in) of well-washed gravel. This weights down the soil to prevent it floating away when the pot is in the water.

Planting up the barrel

1 Line the tub with butyl pond liner. Drape the material loosely inside and arrange the slack in folds. Put 2.5-5cm (1-2in) of well-washed gravel into the bottom of the tub to bed the marginal plants into later.

2 Using a hosepipe, half-fill the barrel with water to weight the liner down into the bottom of the container. Rearrange the folds so that surplus material is evenly distributed around the edge.

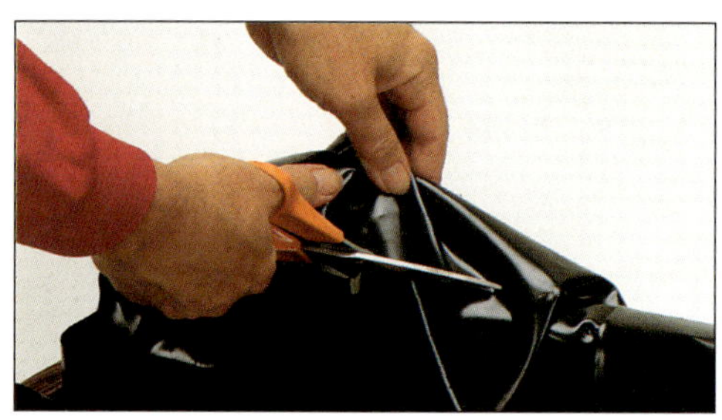

3 Trim away the excess liner, leaving enough spare material to turn over the edge. Make small tucks to even out large folds around the rim.

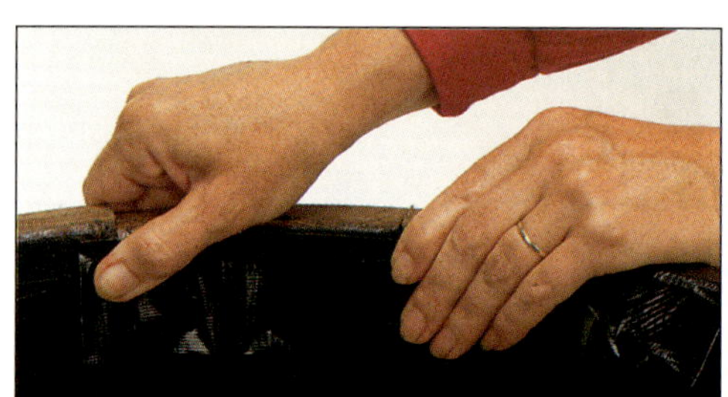

4 Turn the liner edges under, smoothing out tucks in the material as you work. Use waterproof tape, ideally black, to secure the liner firmly inside the rim.

5 Begin adding plants, choosing a mixture of striking flowering and foliage marginal plants that contrast well in shape. Leave the plants in their net-sided pond pots.

6 Upright, reedlike shapes are typical of many waterside plants. These are *Butomus umbellatus* (flowering rush) and *Typha minima* (miniature bulrush).

7 Pickerel weed has striking heart-shaped leaves and blue flowers from early midsummer to early autumn. It works well with the tall linear leaves of the other plants.

8 Three plants are enough, as they will grow quite a bit over the summer. Top up with water and float a handful of azolla or other floating plant over the surface.

9 Choose a sunny site for the barrel, perhaps standing on paving slabs in a low border or herb garden. Best of all, group it with other containers planted with a watery theme in a patio or courtyard.

A WATER GARDEN IN A WOODEN BARREL

A miniature pool in a barrel, pot or other suitable container can have all the features of a large pond: water lilies, marginal plants, fish and even a tiny, sparkling fountain. Any waterproof container is suitable, from a large cut-down barrel to a small terracotta or plastic patio pot. The only real proviso is that the container has not been treated with any poisonous or fungicidal chemicals that might damage plants and fish. Paint it inside with a sealant and line it with butyl rubber or plastic pond liner to make it watertight. Remember that once filled with water, a few plants and an ornament or fountain, the feature is going to be extremely heavy, so decide on its final position while it is empty and plant it up in situ. If you are going to have to move it, place the container on a low platform with lockable casters for mobility. A water feature in a tub makes an excellent focal point for a dull corner of the garden or patio, where it might be raised up on such a platform or a few bricks for extra prominence. Alternatively, stand it on a bed of pebbles or gravel, or surround it with large stones and pots of lush plants to reinforce the watery effect. To show off the tub at its best, position it against a suitable backdrop, such as a wall, fence or plain greenery. Large pebbles or a wall behind are also useful for installing concealed spouts for moving water effects to enhance the feature.

1 Since the wooden barrel is not waterproof, line it with a large piece of pond liner. Push the liner firmly down inside. Trim off some of the excess but leave plenty around the edges to allow for it to settle as you add the water and bricks.

2 Stand the pump on a hard brick for stability and to raise it up to the right level. This is a small mains-powered model ideally suited to such a display. Add more bricks to support the plant pots and stones.

3 Add some cobbles to fill in the spaces between the bricks. These will help to stabilise the piles of bricks and will also stop the pump moving around once the feature is operating.

4 Now add the large stones that will form the visible part of the feature. Rounded boulders not only look attractive but will also stand continuous immersion in water.

5 Add water until it reaches the base of the boulders. This will leave enough expansion room to add the plants and final stones. Do not dislodge the pump.

Now you can trim off more of the pond liner. The weight of the water will have pushed it into its final position.

6 Add the plants, potted into plastic mesh pond baskets. Plan the planting in advance. A low-growing water forget-me-not towards the front will work well with the tall water buttercup at the back of the barrel. Fill in any spaces with more stones or boulders.

7 Add cobbles and pebbles to match the colour range and shape of the boulders. This helps the feature to look more like the bank of a natural stream. By now the barrel is very heavy and should be in its final location.

Moisture-loving plants around the barrel

If there is room, you could grow moisture-loving plants around the barrel pond to add atmosphere. The iris family is a large one whose members enjoy a wide range of growing conditions from well-drained soil to shallow water, although all need plenty of sun. Moisture-loving iris include Iris laevigata, I. ensata, I. versicolor *and* I. 'Holden Clough'. *All grow in 0-15cm(0-6in) of water round the margins of ponds.*

Right: Iris ensata *is a spectacular water iris, given the right conditions. It does not do well in pond baskets, so plant it in the ground in lime-free soil. Stand it in water in summer, but provide drier conditions in winter to avoid rotting.*

Below: *Many primula species suit moist soil; choose* Primula florindae *and candelabra primulas, such as* P. pulverulenta, japonica *and* beesiana *(shown here). All hybridise freely.*

Ranunculus flammula

Iris versicolor 'Blue Light'

Lysimachia thyrsiflora

Myosotis palustris

Epimedium x *youngianum* 'Roseum' (Not a marginal but would look attractive close to the barrel.)

Primula veris (Not suitable for inside the barrel, but this bog garden plant thrives in damp soil.)

8 Neaten the edge of the liner. Fit a three-tier spray fountain head or, as here, a bell-shaped head. Be careful not to pull out the central tube of the pump when changing the fountain heads.

CREATING A MINIATURE WATER LILY POND

If you do not have room for a conventional pond, then a potted pond could be just the answer. Put the container in position first, as it will be difficult to move once filled. You can use normal tap water, but if possible fill the tub and allow it to stand for 48 hours before introducing plants. This allows much of the chlorine to disperse. When choosing plants, opt for those with a long season of interest. A single miniature water lily could be used alone; it will quickly fill a 45cm(18in)-diameter barrel with foliage, and flowers all summer. Or add up to two other plants, as we have done here. Choose good foliage plants to contrast with the lily; go for bold architectural shapes that will look good all summer. Or why not make a group of potted ponds? Use matching containers in various sizes, each with a different planting theme. You might have a water lily pond, a marginal plant pond of water irises, zebra rush and miniature bulrush, a potted bog garden, a 'pond' of fountain and pebbles, and a floating garden of water hyacinth, azolla and water lettuce. If you want fish, choose the largest container possible and only a few small fish, or there will not be enough oxygen in the water for them.

1 Use a waterproof wooden barrel, or line it first with thick black plastic or butyl rubber pond liner. Half fill it with water and add a tall, strikingly shaped, leafy plant.

2 Choose a second plant that complements the first; foliage types look good all season. Slowly submerge the planting baskets until they sit on the bottom.

3 As there are going to be fish in the pond, add a spray of Canadian pondweed, *Elodea canadensis*, to oxygenate the water. Being evergreen, it keeps working in winter, too. Anchor the clump down with a clean pebble.

4 Top up the pond to just below the rim of the barrel. Now there is only the water lily to plant; if the barrel is overfilled at the start, water will spill over the edge each time a new plant is added.

5 Lower the water lily slowly, protecting the leaves and flowers, which become weak and floppy out of water. They easily tear if snagged on the edge of the barrel. Stand the pot on the bottom of the barrel.

6 Four small fish are plenty for a barrel this size. Float their bag on the surface for 30 minutes so that their water reaches the same temperature as that in the tub.

7 Open the neck of the bag underwater, allowing the fish to swim out in their own time. Do not tip them out as this might injure or frighten them.

8 After a few hours, the lily leaves shrug off water and emerge floating on the pond surface. Water lily flowers only open fully in direct sun, so make sure the pond is correctly sited from the very start.

Plants for potted ponds

In a sunny spot, the most miniature water lily varieties will thrive in a potted pond. Other suitable plants include:

Callitriche stagnalis *(starwort) is a submerged aquatic oxygenating plant that makes masses of small green rosettes at the surface of the water.*

Azolla caroliniana *(fairy moss) has floating ferny fragments that turn red in cool weather.*

Eleocharis acicularis *(hairgrass) is a small plant with grassy foliage. It provides some oxygenating effect and needs 7.5cm(3in) of water over the top of the plant to thrive.*

Houttuynia cordata *'Chameleon' has variegated leaves in red, green and cream, plus white flowers. Needs 0-7.5cm (up to 3in) of water over the plant.*

Pistia stratiotes *(water lettuce) and* Eichhornia crassipes *(water hyacinth) are both exotic-looking tender floating plants that are ideal outside in summer, but be sure to keep them in a jar of water in a frost-free greenhouse, conservatory or at a windowsill indoors during the winter.*

Left: Nymphaea pygmaea *'Helvola' is a delightful, free-flowering miniature water lily, with tiny star-shaped flowers and red-marbled olive-green leaves. Ideal for shallow ponds and tubs.*

Below: Nymphaea *'Laydekeri Purpurata' is a good water lily for a container. Small marbled leaves set off deep pink flowers all summer.*

A BOG GARDEN IN A TUB

Bog garden plants make ideal subjects for containers. This is a good way of growing them if you garden on dry soil, where they would not be happy in the open ground. It is perfect for a small garden, since many bog garden plants are large and invasive, spreading rapidly given a free root-run, so that they soon become a nuisance. Use a watertight container; if yours has drainage holes in the bottom or leaks, simply line it with butyl rubber pond liner or heavy duty black plastic before filling and planting. Since the soil will be kept permanently damp, this type of container suits all sorts of bog garden plants, including houttuynia and *Lobelia cardinalis*, as well as border plants that enjoy moist to boggy conditions, such as hostas, lythrum and astilbe. Since space is limited, restrict yourself to plants with a long summer flowering season and those with good architectural foliage. Those that have both, such as zantedeschia, are doubly valuable. Bog garden plants are often sold growing in special net-sided pond pots. They are best left in their pots; the roots are intended to grow out through the sides so that you can lift them out later if they grow too big and you want to replace them. Otherwise, the whole container becomes over-run with roots, and you have to empty the whole tub and replant it all at once.

1 Line a large half barrel with butyl pond liner, loosely cut to shape, and put half a bucketful of washed gravel in the bottom.

2 Fill the container to just below the rim with pond planting mixture or garden soil with a high clay content but no added fertiliser.

3 Place a tall plant at the back. This striking *Lobelia cardinalis* 'Queen Victoria' produces spikes of red flowers in mid- to late summer.

4 Choose plants that contrast well with each other. Use drooping or trailing plants round the sides and shorter plants towards the front to make the best possible display in a small space.

Zantedeschia aethiopica (arum lily) grows 45cm (18in) high and makes a bold statement in the middle of the display.

5 Add a trailing plant at the front; this is a gold-leaved form of creeping Jenny, *Lysimachia nummularia* 'Aurea'. Top up the soil level to within 2.5cm(1in) of the rim. Add at least a full watering can of water, leaving the soil boggy.

6 Leave the barrel for about 30 minutes and then water it again if the soil has absorbed so much moisture that the surface is no longer boggy. Level it roughly and then scatter 2.5cm(1in) of washed gravel over the surface.

7 Decorate the surface with a small cluster of attractively coloured, smooth rounded pebbles. When watering in future, trickle water over the pebbles to avoid soil splashing up onto the gravel or plants.

8 Now that the weight of the soil and water have pulled the liner down into the barrel, neatly trim the excess butyl liner with sharp scissors. Roll the edges over and tuck them out of sight below the gravel.

9 These plants will thrive in a sunny spot on a patio or by a pond and look good all summer. They die down in winter but come up again the following year.

Creating a bog garden feature

Excavate an informally shaped depression, about 30cm(12in) deep, and lay a sheet of thick black plastic over the depression, holding it in place with stones at each corner. Perforate the lowest part of the liner with a garden fork to allow surplus water to drain away.

1 Place a 2.5-5cm(1-2in) layer of gravel in the base to facilitate drainage. Bog garden soil needs to be moist but not totally under water. Fill the bog garden up with a mixture of border soil and organic matter, such as old growing bag potting mixture or garden soil.

2 Make a hole for each plant the same size as the pot in which it is growing. Remove the plants from their pots and group them together in small 'cameos'.

3 Choose plants with a wide range of shapes and a mix of flowers and foliage. Tuck smooth, rounded pebbles between the plants for colour and texture.

Below: *After about three years, dig up the groups of plants and divide them in early spring.*

A LOG ROLL POOL

This raised pond, based on a large, strong rigid plastic container, is the quickest and easiest way of making a water feature and also costs a lot less than using a preformed fibreglass pond shape. It makes a striking and unusual centrepiece for a patio, tiny courtyard garden or a themed garden within a garden. Being small and self-contained, the pond can be dismantled in a few minutes and moved. This alone makes it an asset for a small garden water feature, and is ideal for anyone planning to move house in the near future who wants to take their pond with them. The basic idea is extremely flexible and can easily be adapted to suit many different styles of garden. The log roll used here can be bought ready-made from a garden centre or made from timber offcuts. For a designer look, use planed timber and a coloured water-based wood stain, as here, that will team well with matching coloured trellis in a modern garden. Using rough, bark-clad timber, the pond acquires a natural woodland style that would go well with potted ferns and hostas to add sparkle to a shady spot. For an ultra-modern effect, substitute the log roll with a sheet of mirror acrylic bent around the container to form a complete cylinder. You could use outdoor adhesive to glue mosaics or pebbles to the outside of the container, or even apply acrylic paints to create a mural on a sheet of flexible plastic bent around the pool. For a more traditional effect, try building a surrounding dry stone wall or use bricks; unless the wall is to be used as seating, it is not essential to cement the stones together, so the pond remains portable. Unlike many potted ponds, this one holds quite a large volume of water, making it practical to include fish, plants and even a normal water lily suitable for a small pond instead of one of the real miniatures. But do not mix fish and/or a water lily with a fountain in such as small space, since the turbulence created by the fountain will not suit the fish, and waterlilies will not grow where the foliage is always getting splashed.

1 As an alternative to a preformed pool shape, you can use any large, strong, rigid plastic container like this to make a formal style pond. It need not be black.

2 Encircle the container with log roll. The roll should be the same height as the container; saw it to size if necessary, then treat it with coloured wood preservative.

3 Stand the container in its final position before filling it with water. Position the log roll around it when the paint is dry.

4 In early spring, fill the tub with water to within about 15cm(6in) of the rim to allow room for displacement when you add the plants and pump. Let the water stand for a few weeks before adding the plants.

5 Place a clean plastic flower pot or net pond pot upside down in the bottom of the container, close to one side. Check that it is the right height to raise your water plant to the correct level in the tub.

6 Cyperus enjoys standing in water. Sit it on top of the upturned flower pot. The top of the rootball should lie just below the water level when the tub is full.

7 Add a small, low-voltage submersible pump. It can sit on the floor of the pool as there will be little sludge inside. Add water to within 2.5cm(1in) of the rim.

Right: The floating annual *Trapa natans*, or water chestnut, is grown for its novel triangular leaves. In a warm climate it produces white summer flowers and edible 'nuts'. The plants are killed by frost, so do not float them on the pond until early summer.

8 Adjust the fountain head until it is flush with the water surface, and alter the flow rate so that it produces a gentle gush of water.

Winter care

Where the water will not freeze solid in winter, this pond can be left outside all year round. Alternatively, unplug the pump in winter and replace it with a small electric pond heater to prevent the water freezing. Otherwise, bale out about half the pond water to reduce the weight and move the container carefully under cover for the winter; an unheated sunroom, car port or frost-free greenhouse should be sufficient protection in all but the very coldest areas, but good light is essential.

Colourful and useful herbs surround a bay tree planted in a terracotta container.

PART NINE

SMALL HERB GARDENS

Herbs earn their keep in any garden, adding fragrance, culinary value and colourful foliage and flowers, as well as attracting butterflies and bees. Plant them in formal geometric beds, flower borders or containers for all-round ambience.

SMALL-SCALE HERBS

In a small garden, the first rule for selecting plants is to choose those that really earn their place. Herbs fit the specification perfectly. Besides being naturally compact, many kinds are also aromatic or evergreen, and some of the most popular have other uses – mainly culinary – as well as being decorative. Herbs are also very versatile and can be grown in all sorts of ways. In a formal small area, they could make a complete, traditional geometric garden. Elsewhere, thymes and other herbs make good edgings for a path or for growing in cracks between paving slabs. Many make good container plants. Aromatic herbs are ideal, as their fragrances are released when the leaves are bruised or crushed. Plant them where you can best appreciate them. As an unusual novelty, it is interesting to see that medieval-style herb seats are making a design come-back. Although many herbs enjoy hot, sunny, Mediterranean conditions, some prefer moister or shadier conditions, so use plants such as mints to perfume a flower or shrub border; the eau-de-cologne variety is delightful used this way. You can also use a selection of the prettier herbs such as lavender in a border. Many, including marjoram, attract butterflies and bees. Herbs can also look very decorative grown with flowers and vegetables in a potager. Leeks or red cabbage plants look superb with nasturtium trailing through them, and dill looks wonderful naturalised amongst deep blue winter brassicas while they are growing in summer. Flowering chives make a pretty edging, as does curled parsley.

Right: A collection of informally planted herbs make a good multi-purpose edging to paths or steps. As well as being compact, decorative and fragrant, they are also easy to pick from a firm, non-slip surface in all weathers.

Above: Herbs with a Mediterranean style enjoy hot, dry, sunny places and soil that is low in nutrients and organic matter. In borders, they team well with perennials that enjoy the same conditions. Here, origanum, chives and tricolour sage are growing with verbascum.

Right: Lavender-lined paths are a traditional feature of old cottage gardens, but they suit all styles of garden from ancient to modern. A naturally compact variety, such as 'Vera', makes the best semi-formal dwarf hedge, but for a more abundant flowery path you can use taller varieties with more scent.

Above: Make the most of steps to raise up potted plants above the surrounding borders to make small cameo displays. Herbs are superb plants for this situation, as foliage invariably sprawls over the treads and when stepped on, releases herbal fragrance into the air.

Below: Massed together, herbs tend to look predominantly green, so the plants need contrasting textures and colours to bring out the best in them. Team them with willow wands, basketry (as shown here), wood, stone and terracotta pots or old brick.

Thyme path

Thyme is a most useful garden plant. Its tiny leaves and dense habit create a carpet, cushion or low hedge according to variety, and are ideal for softening harder landscaped features, such as walls, paths and edges of containers. Creeping thyme roots where the stems touch the soil, so plants are very resilient.

1 To plant a creeping thyme beside a path, first dig a planting pocket in the soil the right size for the pot.

2 Press in the plant, leaving no gaps around the rootball. All the foliage should remain on the surface and not be half-buried.

3 A creeping variety of thyme is perfect for growing between patio slabs or alongside a path. It spreads and softens the edges of the stones and survives being trodden on occasionally. The pungent scent of fresh thyme perfumes the air each time you do so.

HERBS FOR SUN AND SHADE

Few gardens have perfect soil and ideal growing conditions, but fortunately, there are herbs that will flourish in a wide variety of situations. Hot dry areas will suit many plants and you can help the soil to retain sufficient moisture by mulching it with a top dressing of potting mix, gravel, bark or similar material. A garden that is full of sunshine and has plenty of moisture at root level will suit many herbs.

A shady garden is no bar to growing a variety of herbs. Indeed, many prefer dappled shade and well-drained soil, especially those with light or golden variegation on the leaves. Curly gold marjoram, golden marjoram, golden sage and variegated melissa (lemon balm) are good examples. If you have an area of damp shade in your garden, the bright golden leaves of golden feverfew and golden meadowsweet provide bright splashes of colour. Add wild strawberry, sweet violet and primroses for flowers and fruit. For interesting foliage textures, try curled wood sage (*Teucrium scorodonia* 'Crispum') and sweet woodruff *(Asperula odorata)*, which smells of new-mown hay when cut and dried and was used as a 'strewing' herb on the floor. In dry shade, you can allow the variegated herb ground elder to take over!

Herbs for damp sunny places

Angelica needs damp soil to grow tender stalks for crystallising. The leaves and stalks of this biennial plant are at their best in the first year. Coriander also thrives in sunny, damp locations. Choose one of the named varieties selected for leaf production, unless you want to use coriander seeds for grinding as a spice. The leaves of self-heal *(Prunella vulgaris)* form a useful ground cover mat. It has deep blue, 10cm (4in)-tall flowers. Bergamot *(Monarda didyma)*, with red, white, pink or purple flowers, is good for flavouring tea. Mace *(Achillea decolorans)* has white flower-heads and leaves with a flavour reminiscent of the tropical spice of the same name.

Add small pieces of angelica leaf and stalk to fruit during cooking for a delicate fragrance and flavour.

Fresh carraway leaf is mild and used for flavouring many foods and pickles.

The strong celery, yeasty flavour of lovage enhances many soups and stews.

In damp soil, comfrey produces abundant leaves for cropping and a profusion of beautiful flowers in a range of colours.

Add young, tender rocket leaves to salads and eastern dishes. The pale cream flowers have a mustard flavour.

Remove the flowering heads of salad burnet to encourage tender new leaves for salads.

Plant marsh mallow at the back of the border; it may grow to 2m6(5ft).

Herbs for dry sunny places

Different varieties of thyme provide a range of leaf textures and patterns. There are many varieties of lavender, with flowers that range from pale blue to deep purple, white to deep pink. Dry, sunny gardens are ideal for the grey-leaved curry plant. The hyssop family develop flowers from midsummer onwards, attracting bees and butterflies. Rock hyssop has rich, blue, upright flowers. Other varieties have pink, blue, purple or white flowers. The larger hyssops look beautiful on raised beds. Do not forget the marjoram family, the purple, green and variegated sages, aromatic winter savory and rosemary – if you have space for them in your garden.

The sweet, spicy leaves of alecost, or costmary, are used in stuffings and potpourri.

Dry the stalks and leaves of catnip to make catnip mice.

The long-lasting, pretty pink flowers of calamint are enhanced by bright green scented leaves.

Once established, most of the thyme family will cover a dry bank and provide welcome colour.

Herbs for damp shade

Suitable herbs include curled and plain-leaved parsley, creeping and upright pennyroyal, ginger mint, flat-leaved golden marjoram, sweet and dog violets, celandine, centaury and hedge hyssop.

Curled parsley (*Petroselinum crispum*)

Ginger mint (*Mentha x gentilis* 'Variegata')

Pennyroyal (*Mentha pulegium*)

Corsican mint (*Mentha requienii*)

Herbs for dappled shade

Suitable herbs include French sorrel (Rumex acetosa) *and buckler-leaved sorrel* (R. scutatus), *bugle* (Ajuga reptans) *and golden feverfew, with its pretty white flowers. Herbs found at the edge of woodlands include primrose, wild strawberries and sweet violet* (Viola odorata).

Left: *Golden feverfew, with its masses of flowers, retains its bright gold leaf colour even in the shade. Deadhead it regularly to encourage fresh flowers to develop until late autumn.*

Herbs for seaside gardens

A seaside garden will thrive if there are sheltering walls and hedges to provide protection from a strong prevailing wind, especially in winter. In this atmosphere, rosemary *(Rosmarinus officinalis)*, which literally means 'dew of the sea', will flourish. A carefully planned seaside garden could enjoy a range of lavender flowers from early summer until late autumn. Evening primrose *(Oenothera biennis)* does well by the coast, and thrift is a seaside plant that is often seen on clifftops. Overhead watering to wash off salt deposits helps all plants to recover after stormy weather. Many people have created beautiful coastal gardens using herbs of all kinds – sheltered garden 'rooms' with their own microclimate.

HERBS NEAR WATER OR IN HEAVY SOILS

Plants vary in their ability to live in really 'wet' soil. Many will flourish, but some may not survive if the water is stagnant, so it is far better if there is some flow of fresh water. There are various ways of improving the soil conditions: one solution is raising a bed so that the plants can send down taproots for water while leaving the rest of their roots in drained soil. Wet clay soil can be improved by installing proper drainage pipes and introducing plenty of grit and bulky natural compost. All these measures will help to provide the air spaces in the soil that plants require in addition to water. Many beautiful herbs will thrive in damp, even marshy, situations, producing a succession of flowers in a wide range of attractive colours. In the case of heavy clay soils, it is a good idea to leave them weeded but 'rough' in the autumn to allow frost to break down the clumps. Dig in some rough, gritty compost when the soil is workable to improve the texture.

Herbs for the seaside

Herbs with wet feet

For an interesting contrast of flower colour and leaf shape, try planting purple loosestrife, with its upright foliage and flowers, spiky figwort, which has unusual tiny red-fringed flowers, and pink soapwort. Sweet cicely is pretty all year round, with its soft, ferny, aromatic leaves and white flowers, followed by large mahogany-coloured seeds.

Left: Buy plants of sweet cicely, as seed must be sown very fresh or it does not germinate. Stewing the leaves with rhubarb or apples flavours the fruit so you do not need to use so much sugar.

Meadowsweet *(Filipendula)*, with its clouds of fluffy white flowers on slender stalks, has flat rosettes of green, gold or variegated green-gold leaves.

The bright golden-yellow flowers of Elecampane (*Inula helenium*), which can grow up to 2m(6.5ft) high, are very dramatic.

Dwarf forms of comfrey *(Symphytum)* are available for small gardens.

Marsh mallow (*Althaea officinalis*) needs moist soil to produce edible tender young shoots and roots.

Herbs for chalky sites

Suitable herbs include red and green fennel, borage, chives and garlic chives and marjoram. All the origanum family are worth gathering and drying for winter use; there are many variations in flavour.

Chives *(Allium schoenoprasum)* are attractive in groups or as an edging.

Oregano *(Origanum vulgare)*

Borage *(Borago officinalis)* has sky-blue flowers.

Compact marjoram *(Origanum* 'Compactum')

Below: *Tansy* (Tanacetum vulgare *var.* crispum) *is a rapid spreader, best restricted in the same way as mint.*

Herbs for clay soil

Comfrey *(Symphytum officinale)*, Elecampane *(Inula helenium)*, Golden rod *(Solidago virgaurea)*, Horseradish *(Armoracia rusticana)*, Jacob's ladder *(Polemonium caeruleum)*, Tansy *(Tanacetum vulgare)*

Fresh or dried, the flowerheads of tansy (here the curly variety) make it popular with flower arrangers.

MAINTAINING HERBS

Herbs are generally easy to maintain, even in summer. Most aromatic herbs tolerate dry, sunny conditions and a poor, stony soil, while woodland herbs flourish in the kind of damp, shady positions many other garden plants hate. Herbs do not suffer much from insect attacks. Use natural pesticides, such as soft soap and sulphur, to control pests and diseases organically. Even though you have been cropping plants for the kitchen or for drying, at the end of the season there will still be dead flowerheads to remove and diseased or damaged foliage to snip away. By cutting or pinching off dead or shrivelled leaves, you also discourage disease and prevent a proliferation of slugs and snails. Older plants also tend to become woody or shapeless after a while. Cut back any dead or straggly stems almost to soil level. This may seem a little drastic, but will encourage stronger, more vigorous growth and a healthier plant. Trim small, mat-forming plants, such as thyme, with a pair of sharp kitchen scissors, but use secateurs for taller, shrubby herbs, such as lavender, tansy and santolina, or even hedging shears for mature growth. Do not cut lavender or santolina into old woody growth; instead, clip over lightly just after flowering. In the informal garden, an annual cut-back and trim to remove unsightly stems helps plants to keep their shape.

Below: An informal herb garden, where a scented patchwork of plants almost smothers a winding path of stone stepping stones, and completely disguises the garden's underlying, rectangular shape.

Feeding and watering

All but the moisture-loving herbs can survive with little or no watering, even in prolonged hot conditions. The only exception applies to herbs in containers, where the soil dries out more quickly. Here, regular watering is essential – but good drainage too, as herbs hate a waterlogged soil even more than a parched one. Patio and windowbox herbs will need regular feeding. Try to use an organic fertiliser, preferably a herbal feed, such as an infusion of nettles, yarrow, coltsfoot or comfrey. Heavily cropped garden herbs also benefit from an occasional feed during the growing season.

Above: Add soluble fertilisers to make up a quick-acting liquid feed. Use high-potash formulations for all herbs

Below: Tomato fertiliser diluted to quarter the usual strength makes a good liquid feed for herbs growing in containers.

Mulching

Left: A mulch of small stones around young plants helps conserve moisture and deters weeds. Pull out weeds in spring as the herbs are establishing themselves and you should have no problems later on.

Right: Mulching between plants with coloured pebbles or chipped bark helps to maintain the shape of each herb. Bark chips make an excellent mulch, as they are attractive to look at and eventually rot down to enrich the soil with valuable compost.

Trimming shrubby plants

While plants are young and still being shaped, they may need trimming several times a year. To speed up the thickening process, prune out any strong woody branches growing horizontally from the main shape, trimming them back into the main canopy of the plant.

1 In late summer, trim back the old flower stalks, top twigs and shoots of tall, shrubby plants, such as *Lavandula angustifolia* 'Munstead'. Keep a rounded outline.

2 Reduce the plant by two-thirds. In spring, remove any winter-damaged twigs or branches to ensure a fine summer display of flowers on the neatened bushes.

Left: Deadheading flowering herbs throughout the summer encourages new blooms to develop. If the herbs are being grown to harvest the leaves for cooking, remove the flowerbuds before they open.

Right: Trim back all sages, including this *Salvia officinalis* Purpurascens Group, in early spring to encourage new shoots with good leaf coloration. Trim the tips on young plants; reduce older plants by one third to prevent them becoming straggly.

Taking soft semi-ripe cuttings

Many herbs, including sage, marjoram, pineapple sage and lavender, will root well from cuttings taken at any time from late spring to early summer. Select healthy shoots that are starting to harden at the base. On sage plants, the central growth on each branch is usually more advanced than the side shoots. If you are propagating from one of the coloured sages, select the shoot with the best coloration on the plant. In this way, you will maintain good, well-coloured plant stock.

1 Select undamaged young branches, free of pests or disease, for best results. This bushy branch of purple sage will provide good material for cuttings.

2 Remove all the leaves except for the tip leaf buds and two leaves beneath. Leaves left on the cutting will delay or prevent roots forming for the new plant.

3 Cut through the stem at the point where the 'wood' is beginning to harden, just above the small stalks of the previous year's growth. Use a sharp knife to make a clean cut. Ragged ends may encourage rotting and disease.

4 Make a hole with a dibber and insert the cuttings into an open gritty mix in pots or a deep seed tray. Rooting in pots allows the cuttings plenty of room for root growth. Cuttings in trays will need potting on at an earlier stage, once roots are established.

HERBS IN CONTAINERS

Troughs, pots, chimney pots and flue liners are ideal containers for growing a selection of culinary herbs in a limited space. Choosing the right blend of herbs can be great fun. Even taking into account soil compatibility and whether the plants need sun or shade, there is plenty of scope to create pleasing contrasts of colour, foliage and size. Regular cropping or trimming is important to ensure that the herbs remain small and leafy. Keep the containers adequately watered and apply a liquid feed during the growing and cropping season. Potting mix soon runs out of essential nutrients in the confines of a container, especially where plants grow prolifically and where rain washes constantly through the mix. A mulch of small pebbles conserves moisture and reduces the effect of heavy rains.

Experimental cooks often prefer to grow a variety of herbs in small quantities; growing them in containers is the perfect way to do this. Keep herbs close to the kitchen for maximum convenience; if you only want a few sprigs, you may not want to bother going down to the bottom of the garden. If you grow herbs in the kitchen, keep spare pots of herbs in the garden to bring in when the first batch need a rest. If you grow herbs outdoors in a trough on the windowsill, make sure that the container is firmly secured (check brackets and ties regularly for wear and weathering) and that you have ready access for watering.

Herbs in flue liners

1 Use an open-ended flue liner, 23-30cm(9-12in) in diameter. Settle the base into the ground and fill it two-thirds full with good-quality soil-based potting mixture.

2 Place the plant in the flue liner and water it. Top up the soil until it is 5cm(2in) below the rim of the liner to retain moisture when the plant is watered.

A trough of herbs

1 Choose a selection of herbs and place a few crocks in the bottom of the trough to prevent the potting mixture washing away.

2 Add 5-15cm(2-6in) of washed gravel or pea shingle to make a well-draining layer at the bottom of the box. Top up with potting mixture.

Flat-leaved parsley has a better flavour than the curly-leaved variety.

Purple sage has attractive foliage and spikes of blue flowers in early summer.

If chives are left to dry out the plant will collapse. The flowers bloom in varying shades of lavender-pink in early summer.

Thymus doerfleri 'Bressingham Pink'

3 Plant the herbs, maintaining a pleasing balance of appearance, height and habit. Tip them gently out of their pots and into your hand, supporting the stem lightly between your fingers.

4 Top up with soil, making sure it settles between the plants. To allow for watering, do not fill to the top of the box. A sprinkling of gravel or small stones around the plants looks good and helps to slow down moisture loss.

5 The finished trough looks good and includes a useful blend of flavours for the cook. If you use plenty of herbs in cooking, reduce the number of plants in the box to two or three bigger plants.

Bay in a terracotta pot

Bay looks particularly good in a Mediterranean-style terracotta pot. Stand it in a sunny, well-sheltered spot and bring it under cover at the first signs of frost. Bay produces small yellow-green flowers in late spring or early summer, followed by black berries. A layer of small stones or gravel on the surface of the soil not only helps to retain moisture, but also looks attractive. In addition, it discourages weed growth. The leaves of bay add a deep and lasting fragrance to potpourri, as well as being ideal for culinary use.

A display of mint

An ingenious way of growing a collection of mints is to plant them in a variety of terracotta pots of different sizes, thus displaying their range of colour, shape and texture. The mints included here are: spicy ginger mint, variegated apple mint, pennyroyal, peppermint, spearmint and red raripila.

Creeping forms of pennyroyal make a scented carpet of small leaves. This is not an edible herb.

A parsley pot

Parsley is such a popular culinary herb that it is well worth growing to ensure a constant supply. A multi-pocketed container provides plenty of parsley for picking within a small planted area. A partly shady spot is ideal for parsley and give it plenty of moisture. Pinch off flower stalks as they appear. Sow a fresh supply each year in spring and late summer.

A BASKET OF EDIBLE HERBS

Herbs can be grown in all sorts of containers, but where space is short a hanging basket is the ideal choice. And by combining culinary herbs with a few decorative types – which can often be used for garnishing as well – you can create a stunning and useful display. A large basket is best, as there will be enough room to grow a good selection of your favourite herbs. Start by choosing herbs that you use regularly in cooking, such as basil, thyme, chives, mint and oregano. Choose interesting varieties of each, such as lemon thyme, Greek oregano (a specially fiery-tasting form), curly mint or red-leaved basil 'Dark Opal', which is decorative as well as edible. Include a few scented herbs, such as pineapple sage and lavender, and add a few unusual herbs that you use occasionally and which add a touch of colour to the arrangement. These need not only be leafy herbs; petals of calendula and red clover can be sprinkled in salads. Snip small sprigs from the plants little and often; it encourages plants to grow bushier and improves their appearance. Turn the basket round once a week so that no plants are always shaded by others, and all grow evenly.

1 The mesh used to line this basket is sold as windbreak material. It provides free drainage (ideal for herbs) and a pleasant green background. Drape it inside the basket. Place a circle of plastic cut from an old potting mix bag into the base, black side down.

2 Fill the basket loosely with soil-based potting mixture. As the basket fills, the netting sinks into the shape of the basket. When the basket is full, trim the mesh.

3 Leave a 2.5cm(1in) rim to stop potting mix spilling out; this will soon be hidden by the plants as they grow and start to trail over the edge of the basket.

4 Place the most striking or colourful plants in the centre. This is red orache, *Atriplex hortensis* 'Rubra'; its deep red triangular leaves make a colourful, unusual salad ingredient.

5 Add borage, red clover and purple basil. Borage and red orache usually grow tall, but in a container are naturally dwarfed. Nip out stem tops to make them bushier.

6 Calendula flowers look pretty in salads, drinks or sprinkled over rice. Separate the petals from the green calyx first or use whole heads as buffet decorations.

7 Heartsease is another popular edible flower. Whole blooms are good for garnishes and salads. They can also be crystallised for decorating cakes and trifles

8 Plant up a herbal basket in early summer, as some plants are frost-tender. In autumn, prune and pot up perennial species or plant them in the garden. Replant the basket with fresh herbs the following spring.

Culinary herbs

Use herbs for cooking, drying and freezing, in salads, and as attractive garnishes.

1 This elegant terracotta pot makes an ideal container for a range of scented herbs. Cover the drainage holes with crocks and add a 2.5cm (1in)-layer of gravel for drainage. Add potting mixture to just below the rim of the container.

A POT OF SCENTED HERBS

Aromatic herbs enjoy hot, sunny, dryish conditions, which concentrate their scents, and a well-sheltered spot where their perfumes can linger on the air. Place a large container such as this on the patio, by a doorway or outside a window that is often left open in summer. Alternatively, put it by a sunny seat anywhere in the garden. Since it is the leaves that are scented, aromatic herbs are perfumed all the time, but the leaves need to be bruised lightly to release their fragrant oils, so brush them lightly with your hand. Choose eau-de-cologne mint, pineapple sage and scented-leaved pelargoniums; those with citrus, rose and spicy scents have the most pleasant perfumes; save culinary or medicinal herbs for elsewhere. Aromatic herbs in general do not have colourful flowers, but offer a range of foliage shapes, textures and sizes. If more colour is needed, include a few edible flowers, such as heartsease or compact nasturtium. Otherwise, add a few related flowering plants that are happy in similar conditions and will not outgrow the display. Miniature pelargoniums, dwarf lavender, gold marjoram, rockery pinks or *Salvia grahamii* (which has blackcurrant-scented leaves) are good choices. Many scented herbs are not frost hardy, so bring scented-leaved pelargoniums, *Salvia grahamii*, *Lippia citriodora* and pineapple sage indoors for the winter months. Otherwise, take cuttings and keep them at a sunny window until after the last spring frost.

2 Knock each plant gently out of its pot and plant it without breaking up the rootball. This is a variegated, scented-leaved pelargonium, 'Lady Plymouth'.

3 Scoop out a hole for each herb, planting the outside row close to the edge of the tub. This scented-leaved pelargonium is called 'Chocolate Peppermint'.

4 Add a lemon-scented verbena *(Aloysia triphylla)* and include at least one good prostrate plant to soften the edge. This is *Pelargonium tomentosum*, which has soft, furry, strongly peppermint-scented leaves.

5 Fill the container well, especially if you plan to pick from it. Tuck in as many plants as possible. This is *Salvia officinalis* 'Tricolor', a red, cream and green-variegated form of culinary sage (also edible).

6 Once all the plants are in, fill any gaps between adjacent rootballs with potting mix. This provides extra root-room as plants grow, and helps prevent the pot from drying out too quickly.

7 Finally, water well to settle the potting mixture around the roots. If it sinks slightly, top up to within 2.5cm(1in) of the rim. This still leaves enough room for watering later on, but take care not to overfill the container with potting mixture.

8 As the plants fill the container; finger-prune wayward stems. To concentrate the fragrance, grow in full sun, avoid over-watering and place the container where you can brush gently against the plants.

The various plant perfumes combine to create a living potpourri.

Some scented herbs

Grow scented herbs in containers near seats and windows where you can enjoy their fragrance.

A MEDICINAL HERB POT

In the past, people relied on medicinal herbs as home-grown remedies for a wide range of problems. Today, true herbal medicine should be left to trained practitioners, but since many culinary and decorative herbs have mildly beneficial effects, it is fun to use them as a natural tonic or for minor problems. Purple sage has natural antiseptic properties; an infusion makes a good gargle for treating sore throats. Thyme is a mild antiseptic, too; make an infusion for coughs or upset stomachs. Use an infusion of rosemary for rinsing hair to make it shine, or add it to the bath for a scented herbal bath. In cookery, the herb is believed to improve the memory. Any of the usual culinary herbs, chopped in small quantities into salads or used in normal cooking, have a mildly therapeutic influence. For instant first aid, grow aloe vera, also known as the burn plant. Cut a piece from one of the thick succulent leaves and squeeze the clear gel inside onto minor burns, scalds or sunburn. Houseleeks have been used in much the same way, with the juice from the leaves applied to burns and skin complaints – it was once believed to cure warts. Several herbs make pleasant herbal teas: use hyssop, chamomile or black peppermint in this way. The latter is good for the digestion, while chamomile tea is very relaxing and often used as a caffeine-free bedtime drink.

To maximise their therapeutic properties, grow herbs in a warm sunny spot and avoid overwatering or excess feeding. When planted in normal soil-based potting mixture, plants should not need feeding for about three months. Then use a general-purpose liquid plant feed (preferably organic) at about half the normal dilution rate.

1 Choose a container capable of holding a large volume of potting mixture. Cover the drainage holes with pieces of broken clay pot and cover the base with 2.5cm (1in) of gravel so that excess water can run away quickly.

2 Add soil-based potting mixture to within 5cm(2in) of the rim. Soilless mixes are less suitable for herbs as they retain more water, which can lead to roots rotting.

3 Tuck the outermost plants up against the edge to use every bit of space in the container. This plant is variegated lemon balm, which can be used in salads.

4 Heartsease has edible flowers that look like tiny cream-and-purple pansies. It makes an attractive plant in a herb container, especially since so few herbs have such pretty flowers.

5 Add more herbs, making sure that neighbouring plants have contrasting shapes, leaf colours and textures for best effect. This is houseleek, or sempervivum.

6 Fill the container well; once you start picking, plants are unlikely to grow faster than they can be used. Plant prostrate kinds around the edge of the display.

7 When all the plants are in place, top up any gaps with potting mixture. For a more ornamental look, surface the top with a thin layer of pea-gravel or granite chippings.

Even if you do not use them, a pot of medicinal herbs makes a good conversation piece.

8 Water well to settle the potting mix around the roots. Leave the tub until it is nearly dry before watering again and allow surplus water to drain away. Over-watering 'dilutes' the beneficial oils in the foliage.

9 Keep the container regularly fed and watered. When cutting, nip off sprigs from the back of the plants or take shoots hidden behind other plants to avoid spoiling the display.

Some medicinal herbs

Enjoy the tonic properties of herbs in refreshing drinks, but do not treat yourself for anything beyond minor problems.

MAKING A HERB SEAT

Traditionally, herb seats were planted with turf or sweet-scented herbs to make a pleasant place to sit and enjoy the garden long before the days of upholstered garden furniture. Various types of herb seats have been used throughout history. They were invariably substantial, permanent features built with a brick or timber base filled with soil, with a solid backrest and arms like a conventional bench. The modern version we have created here uses renewable natural materials. It is small and easily portable, unlike the 'real thing', but looks much more at home in today's small garden. It is based on the design of a bentwood dining room chair and made in a container with a rustic back. Like the original herb seats you can actually sit on it, but because the backrest is decorative rather than functional, use it more like a stool than a chair. If you wanted a more glamorous effect, you could plant the backrest with annual climbers, such as morning glory or black-eyed Susan, although the slightly rustic, minimalist look of herbs and hazel is more authentic. Any creeping herbs can be used to plant the seat. Creeping thymes and rosemary are often used in this way, although if you actually intend sitting in the seat, the non-flowering chamomile is probably better as it makes a dense, cushioned surface that does not attract bees. Sitting on the herbs crushes them gently so that they release their scent, but as long as you do not do it too much, you will not harm the plants. Stand pots of upright herbs nearby for added fragrance.

1 Choose a half barrel, about the same diameter as a chair seat, and a bundle of 15cm(6in) hazel sticks (beanpoles are ideal). Fill the barrel with potting mix, bend one of the sticks in half to make an arch, and push both ends in on opposite sides of the barrel.

2 Cut two other beanpoles in half, and push in three straight sticks, evenly spaced around the back between the ends of the arch. Angle them so that they all meet up above the centre-back of the container. Push all the sticks down firmly as far as they will go.

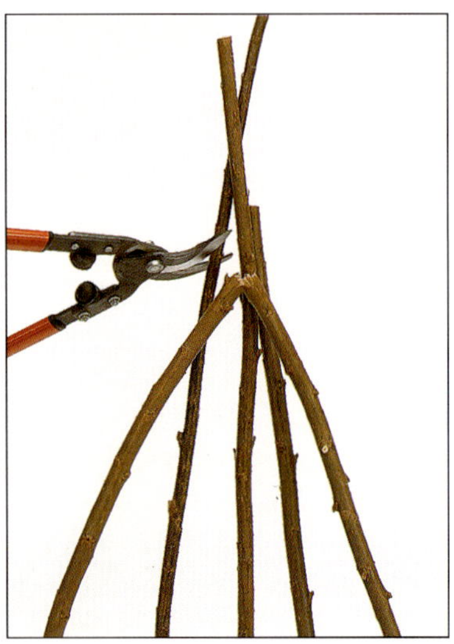

3 Use loppers (long-handled secateurs for thick branches) to cut the three straight sticks roughly level with the top of the arch. Take care not to cut the sticks that form the arch as the bark 'bridge' that connects the two ends makes the 'gothic' shape.

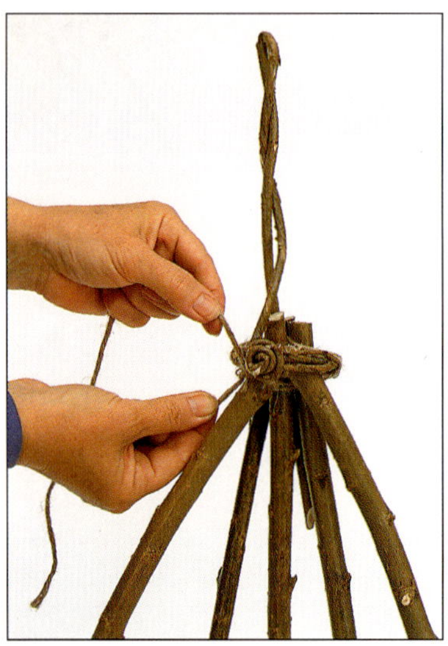

4 Tie all the sticks and the top of the arch firmly together with string. Use a decoration to hide the string; this is a piece of twisted willow that was wound round a bundle of willow withies to hold them together. It was saved for just such a use.

5 Now plant up the seat. For a traditional effect, use the non-flowering chamomile 'Treneague'. Three plants will fill a container of this size, as they quickly spread to form a dense mat. They enjoy the good drainage in a container.

6 Space the plants out evenly, so that they spill attractively over the edges, as well as filling out the centre. Once they are all planted and firmed in lightly, water the container thoroughly to settle the plants. If the potting mixture sinks, top it up.

7 Keep the plants well watered in summer so that they grow lushly to form a thick cushion of bouncy, aromatic foliage. Although chamomile likes good drainage, if the plants go short of water some of the older leaves turn yellow or brown which spoils the seat.

Chamomile in containers

Chamomile is a very versatile plant, ideal for containers of all sorts. Use the non-flowering 'Treneague if you want apple-scented, dense, low, feathery foliage to be the main source of interest. However, the double-flowered Roman chamomile (Chamaemelum nobile *'Flore Pleno') stays fairly compact and has most attractive small shaggy flowers; this is the best variety for small containers. Grow both from softwood cuttings taken from the tips of new growth in late spring and early summer. Root them in pots of gritty mix (made by combining seed mix with 25% sharp sand). They take about eight weeks to root, but wait till they fill the pot with roots before planting them out. Normal chamomile grows much taller and looks unruly, though it is cheap to raise from seed. Chamomile needs a sunny situation and very well-drained conditions to thrive. If kept too wet or shady, the plants grow sickly and rarely survive the winter.*

Above: *The almost ferny foliage of chamomile makes it useful for planting in natural-looking containers such as a hollow log.*

If you sit on the herb seat, do not lean against the backrest.

8 Stand the herb seat in a sheltered, sunny spot. Once the plants have covered the potting mixture, you can sit on the seat if you want.

MAKING A HERB WHEEL

All sorts of unlikely items can be rescued from secondhand shops and recycled as garden ornaments, given a good imagination. You can even use them as the starting point for a complete mini-feature. A metal wheel from a piece of farm machinery provided the inspiration for this unusual raised herb bed. The spokes divide up the wheel naturally into segments similar to those found in old-fashioned designs for traditional circular herb gardens. It would have been easy to restore the wheel and lay it on the ground as a template for a small formal garden bed. But, being made of cast iron, if the wheel were left in contact with damp soil all the time it would quickly rust, needing regular treatment to stop it deteriorating. And the unique patterns of cogs around the rim of the wheel would soon be lost as the shape was obscured by spreading plants. Add to this the fact that herbs grow best in sunny, well-drained situations and need to be very accessible and it seemed logical to design a special container-bed to make the most of the wheel's unique character. From there it was only a short step to adding the divider, so that spreading herbs can be kept separate. Teamed with other metal containers in matching colours, it would make a most unusual attraction.

1 This rusty old iron wheel was once part of some farm machinery. You can sometimes find old wooden cart or wagon wheels in similar places. You could also use a container with internal dividers on its own, though it would not look so decorative.

2 Prepare the wheel for painting by thoroughly removing all the loose rust with a stiff wire brush. Wear gardening gloves and spend time getting into all the crevices

3 Paint the wheel with one coat of a rust-inhibiting paint for use on metal surfaces. You may need a special base coat if the wheel will be in contact with damp surfaces.

4 Saw up sufficient pieces of 5x5cm(2x2in) pressure-treated timber into 30cm(12in) lengths to make a base for the wheel. You can also buy log-roll ready made.

5 Paint the timber with a water-based wood stain that is harmless to plants. Allow it to soak in well and dry completely. Be creative with your colour scheme!

6 Lay down the timber sections close together in a row. Lay three lengths of strong plastic packaging tape over the timber and tack the tape to the timber with a staple gun. Use plenty of staples.

7 Lay the wheel on the ground and offer up the 'log roll' to make sure that there are enough wood sections to go right round. It bends easily round the curve. Add extra pieces if necessary until it fits.

The internal sections

Use 30x2.5cm(12x1in) pressure-treated timber planks to make the dividers. Cut three equal lengths slightly shorter than the diameter of the wheel, with angled slots so that they fit loosely for later adjustment. Fit the pieces of plank together as shown here.

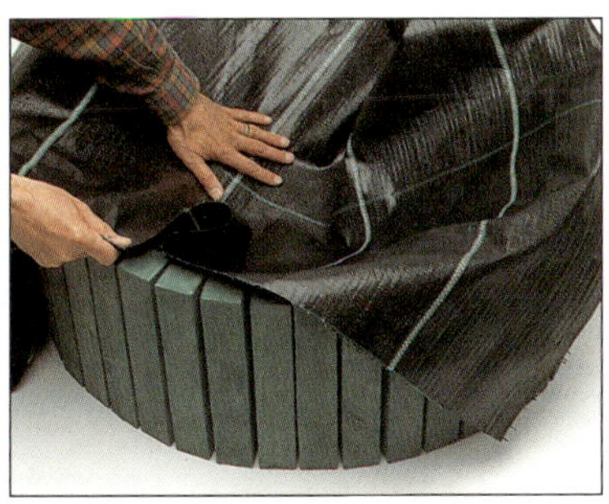

8 Complete the 'log roll' circle by stapling the tapes where they overlap. Finish off neatly, leaving no stray ends. You do not need the wheel in place at this stage.

9 Line the 'container' with a piece of plastic mulching sheet. It is strong enough to hold in potting mix later, but the weave allows excess water to drain out.

10 Assemble the components with the wheel in its final position. First, arrange the divider. Since it was made to fit loosely, you can shuffle it about to get a good fit and to ensure that the log-roll wall makes a perfectly circular shape.

Finishing off the herb wheel

The finished container will have six equal-sized planting compartments. The 'liner' keeps out worms and pests, contains the potting mix but lets water drain away, and stops roots escaping into the open ground – ideal for invasive herbs, such as mint, tarragon and horseradish.

11 Trim off the excess woven liner, leaving 2.5-5cm (1-2in) of plastic hanging over the sides to make a neat edge.

12 Neatly fold under the spare fabric and staple it firmly round the rim, leaving a level surface for the wheel to rest on.

13 Set the wheel in place, with the rim over the rim of the log-roll wall, hiding the liner, and the spokes resting on the divider. If necessary adjust the divider so that the spokes rest directly on the partitions.

14 The finished container is an attractive feature in its own right, as well as a practical container for a display of herbs.

These compartments are deep enough for planting herbs.

PLANTING A HERB WHEEL

If you enjoy using herbs for cooking, part of the satisfaction comes from growing your own basic ingredients. The trouble is that a lot of the best culinary herbs spread rapidly, and within a year or so, what began life as a very attractive herb feature becomes overgrown and untidy. Plants such as mint, tarragon and horseradish are particularly notorious, but it is amazing how even relatively 'tame' herbs, such as sage and thyme, 'run' all over the place if you give them the chance. The herb wheel feature shown here combines the benefits of a container and a small bed. Because the herbs are kept isolated from both the soil, by a weed-proof plastic membrane, and each other by the dividers that support the spokes of the wheel, they cannot spread. And because it contains its own soil, it can be sited in any convenient sunny spot, regardless of whether the area is covered by soil, gravel or paving. The patio or somewhere close to the back door are ideal situations, so that herbs are readily at hand when you are cooking; you will not want to walk the length of the garden to gather a few sprigs. Once the planting has been done, maintaining the wheel is simple. Just keep the herbs watered and remove any weeds (you could mulch the surface with gravel to reduce both jobs further).

1 Cover the base of the container with a good layer of gravel, which must be clean, salt-free (wash well if necessary) and not previously treated with weedkiller.

2 Fill the container almost to the rim with potting mix. Garden soil has insufficient nutrients for a restricted root system, and you may introduce pests or diseases.

3 Plant only one kind of herb in each 'cubicle'. This way, each herb is kept separate from potentially invasive neighbours. With most herbs, a single plant will soon spread to fill all the available space.

4 As far as possible, choose plants that contrast with each other in shape, colour or texture to create an interesting effect. Herbs tend to look very 'green', with little flower colour, so make the most of their other main features, and remember to include some for scent.

5 Choose perennial herbs to avoid having to replace plants frequently. Remove the pot and set the herb in a planting hole, leaving the top of the rootball roughly level with the surface of the surrounding potting mix. This is rock hyssop.

6 Parsley will not grow much bigger than this, so if you use a lot, plant three plants close together in a triangular shape to fill one complete segment.

Making the most of a herb garden

The essence of a good herb garden is to grow many different kinds of plants in the quantities you are most likely to use. A good strategy is to concentrate on culinary kinds where you have the space for them, and use the more decorative, scented or medicinal kinds for containers, raised beds and similar features.

Salvia officinalis 'Icterina', a compact green-and-cream variegated form, also good for culinary use.

Allium schoenoprasum. Chives have a mild onion flavour. Chop the leaves or use flower petals in salads.

Hyssopus aristatus. Rock hyssop, a creeping species with blue flowers loved by bees and butterflies. Use it in stews or as a tea for coughs.

Variegated applemint, a mild-flavoured dwarf mint.

Thymus 'Porlock', a good evergreen flowering and culinary variety.

Curled parsley. Use it fresh, frozen or dried.

7 The completed container is productive, pretty and perfumed. The herbs are good culinary kinds that combine variegated foliage with flowers to make a pleasant mauve, cream and green colour scheme that will last from spring until autumn.

1 Herbs need good drainage; on heavy soil spread 2.5-5cm (1-2in) of grit or gravel over the planting area and dig in. Remove weeds and debris and rake level .

2 Shovel gravel onto the areas where the paving slabs are to go. Compact the soil down first by treading it well with your feet. Avoid walking on the planting areas.

3 Sit the paving slabs in place so that alternate slabs and soil make a pattern like the black and white squares on a chessboard. Wriggle the slabs down into their gravel bases as you lay them, so they are firmly bedded down and will not move later once you start walking on them.

4 Surround the feature with contrasting bricks laid on their narrowest edge and sunk to about half their depth into the soil. This is enough to hold them firmly.

5 Tap down each brick as it is laid, using the handle of the trowel. For the rest of the time this is only used to take out the flat-bottomed 'bed' for each brick.

A CHESSBOARD DISPLAY

This contemporary version of a traditional geometric herb garden is more in keeping with the style of a modern home, and can be adapted for a space of any shape or size. It is based on the alternate black and white squares of a chess-board and could easily be created in a quiet corner of a patio by removing some of the slabs and improving the soil underneath. It also makes a good form of flooring for a small fragrant courtyard garden, but could also become an attractive herb feature in a family garden, especially if linked with a seat and taller potted herbs. The combination of herbs and paving is a particularly effective one, since the paving reflects heat and light, which provide ideal growing conditions for the plants. In this situation, herbs produce more concentrated essential oils, which in turn perfume the air when the plants are crushed if you step on odd sprigs overhanging the paving. The most suitable species to use are the more decorative but naturally compact bushy herbs that will not get overgrown quickly, such as purple sage, double flowered Roman chamomile, purple basil, orange thyme, and pineapple sage. Choose a mixture of evergreen, flowering and coloured foliage plants for a 'chessboard', that looks varied and interesting all the year round. To accentuate the chessboard idea, why not trim potted box plants into the shape of chessmen to stand on some of the paving slabs; if you are feeling ambitious you could even have a game!

6 Plant up the soil squares. This formal bed resembles those of a historic geometric herb garden, but on a scale in keeping with today's modern gardens.

7 Choose low spreading herbs for this style of bed, as they will billow out over the slabs, releasing their scents when they are crushed. Take the pots off before planting and avoid breaking up the rootball.

8 A small sphere-trained box tree in each corner suits the formal style. This gold-variegated box is slower-growing than the green forms, but looks more distinctive.

9 Snip off the tips of any long shoots that spoil the outline. Sideshoots will soon grow and thicken out the shape. Box balls may take a year or two to fill out.

10 Spread a 2.5-5cm(1-2in) layer of gravel over the surface as a mulch. These pink granite chippings set off the plants and tone in with the brick surround.

Maintaining a herbal chessboard

A feature like this is very quick and easy to maintain as the gravel mulch helps to retain moisture. After the plants have been watered in they should not need much more water except in dry spells. If it is deep enough (at least 2.5cm/1in and ideally 5cm/2in thick) the mulch will also prevent weeds growing from any seeds that may be present in the soil. However, in time, new weed seeds will blow onto the surface of the mulch from other gardens, so to stop them spoiling the appearance of the bed, rake the gravel over briefly every week. This way, germinating weeds are disturbed before they can take a hold, and any footprints or dead leaves, etc are removed so that the bed always looks neat and well cared for.

Suitable plants

Most non-invasive Mediterranean-style herbs that like well-drained soil and sun will thrive in a bed like this. Choose the most decorative of the low-growing bushy kinds or creeping varieties. Good ones include purple sage, gold-variegated sage, golden marjoram, or prostrate rosemary. Choose well-scented kinds and/or those with good flowers for the container in the middle; French lavender, a purple frilly-leaved variety of basil such as 'Fluffy Ruffles', pink lavender, gilded rosemary (silver- and gold-variegated varieties are both available), pineapple sage or a trimmed bay tree are ideal.

11 A decorative terracotta urn with lavender makes a good centrepiece. A feature like this could be inset into a patio or lawn, and would make a good focal point in a small enclosed garden or 'garden room'

Swiss chard and bright red pelargoniums make a striking and productive combination.

PART TEN

SMALL-SCALE VEGETABLES

Even the smallest garden can 'grow its own'. Use the latest techniques for intensive vegetable cultivation and specialise in fast, fresh, fashionable gourmet crops. Planned like a formal flower garden, the results can be as pretty as they are productive.

GROWING VEGETABLES

A vegetable garden is the first thing small-scale gardeners imagine they must do without, but this is not true. In fact, a compact vegetable plot can be more productive and easily run than a large one, where much of the effort is wasted and a proportion of produce does not 'make the grade'. The secret is to make a deep bed system. Here the ground is dug deeper than usual, with large amounts of rich organic matter mixed in. Once the initial soil preparation has been done, you never dig again. All cultivation, planting and harvesting is done from the path around the bed so you never stand on the soil, which remains uncompacted, allowing roots to penetrate deeply. Plants can therefore be grown closer together, so they quickly cover the ground and smother out weeds. Not only does this mean less work, you also get a lot more crops from the space as you do not leave paths between the rows, as you would with a conventional vegetable plot. Produce is better quality, too, as plants get more individual care instead of being 'farmed'; you should be able to use everything you grow. If you prefer to grow your vegetables without chemical pesticides or fertilisers, the deep bed system is ideal for organic growing. You can recycle all your crop debris and kitchen peelings, along with other soft garden refuse, via a compost bin or wormery, to make your own rich soil improvers. Tack paper mulches to the wooden edges of the beds to suppress weeds or fit wire hoops over the bed to support insect-proof netting that shields crops from insect pests, rabbits and birds. Increase yields by using cloches to extend the growing season.

Above: The secret of a small vegetable plot is to grow plenty of different crops, but only small quantities of each. Choose only your favourite crops. By sowing fast-maturing crops little and often, you always have something to cut without a surplus that goes to waste.

Harvesting vegetables

Pick regular croppers, such as courgettes and beans, every two days, If you do not need to use them straight away, keep them in the refrigerator for up to three days. Left on the plant, they would grow too big and spoil.

1 Keep courgette plants at peak productivity by cutting the crop regularly, as soon as they are big enough to use. If you forget, plants put all their effort into one huge marrow and even after it is cut it may be several weeks before you have a new crop of courgettes.

2 Lettuce are ready to eat as soon as the pale, tender heart forms in the centre of the leafy rosette. To cut, slide a long knife under the plant just above soil level, then trim off the outer leaves.

3 A trug is not just for show; it is designed for gathering delicate crops or flowers without bruising or crushing them. The wide, flat, base makes it possible to carry quite a lot of produce.

Right: In a small garden, a vegetable plot needs to look decorative. Use naturally pretty plants, such as fennel, and coloured versions of popular vegetables, such as red lettuce and red (actually purple) cabbage, which taste even better than the green kind.

Left: Trellis and arches make a good frame for a decorative vegetable plot. The vertical surfaces are ideal for growing climbing beans, such as these runner beans, or trailing crops such as squashes that normally take up plenty of space.

Organic gardening

Organic gardening means cultivating plants without chemicals. True organic gardeners would not use an artificial fertiliser or pesticide anywhere in the garden, but many gardeners merely want to avoid using them on crops they are going to eat. The main principal is that instead of boosting crops with synthetic feeds, you use natural organic matter, such as manure or garden compost, to improve the soil structure, and add concentrated animal, mineral or vegetable nutrients to feed high-yielding crops. Instead of chemical sprays you find natural alternatives for tackling common pests and diseases, such as removing pests by hand.

Below: Very fine plastic netting can be draped permanently over brassicas and carrots to keep out rootfly and caterpillars.

Making a compost heap

Garden compost is one of the most common and effective forms of bulky organic matter that you can add to the ground, and it is also the cheapest. It is made from plant remains, including annual weeds, vegetable trimmings, lawn mowings, hedge clippings and soft prunings.

1 Start a new compost heap with a layer of coarse, woody material, such as hedge clippings, for drainage and aeration.

2 When the foundation layer is firmed down and 15cm(6in) deep, add soft materials such as grass mowings that will heat up.

3 Sprinkle on an activator to speed up the composting process. Add more raw material, such as these potato tops.

4 A layer of shredded prunings will assist the decomposition process by aerating the heap. This in turn leads to heating up.

5 Put in more activator for every 25cm(10in) of vegetation. To stop the generated heat escaping, cover the bin with a substantial covering. It will also stop rain from cooling the heap.

SETTING UP A WORMERY

A small garden that is kept well hoed during the growing season will not generate a large quantity of weeds, so it may not be practical or necessary to have a compost heap. In this situation a wormery makes a good alternative, allowing kitchen scraps and small amounts of vegetable waste to be continuously recycled to make rich organic compost, which is technically pure worm casts. This is ideal for enriching a vegetable plot, for combining with potting mixture and for topdressing plants grown in containers, A wormery is especially useful for organic growers; as well as providing a natural source of chemical-free plant food, it also produces a rich liquid feed as a by-product, which drains out of the base of the unit. A wormery takes a bit of getting used to. The 'multistorey' type shown here is a great advantage over the 'bin' design, as you can remove finished compost just by lifting out the bottom chamber without having to tip out the whole bin and starting again.

Keeping a wormery is almost like having a pet. Unlike a compost heap where you just throw in barrowloads of weeds when you feel like it, a wormery needs small amounts of suitable material added to it little and often – every day or two. As it contains living creatures, it must be sited with care. Shade it from the summer sun otherwise it will get too hot, and protect it from freezing in winter. And if the contents get too wet or too acid, the worms die and you have to start again. The secret is to avoid overfeeding; increase the amount given at each 'feed' as the worms get more active and breed.

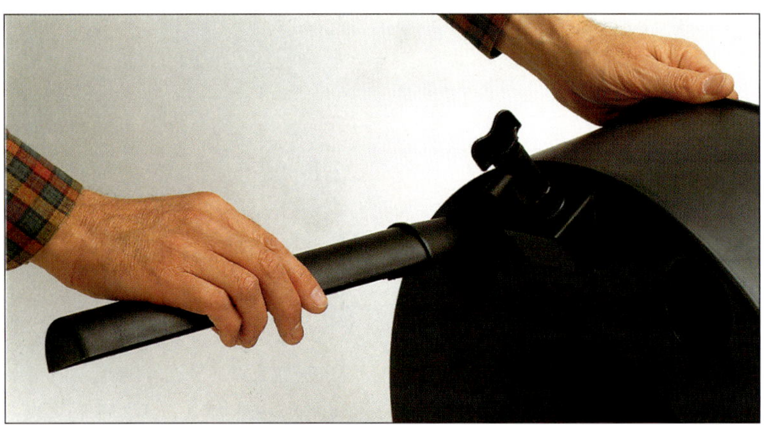

1 This model is a sophisticated multistorey design. Assemble the bottom compartment by screwing on the legs. It acts as a stand and has a tap in the side to drain off excess liquid. Do not put anything into this part.

2 Sit the first tray on top of the base unit. It will become the powerhouse of the unit in its early days, as this is where you add the worms. Since you have no worm compost yet, you must add some suitable bedding material.

The plastic trays look like sieves. Place a circle of newspaper or natural fibre in the bottom tray to stop material falling straight through into the base unit.

Use the tap to drain off liquid that collects in the base of the wormery. Do this every week, or more often after heavy rain, to prevent the compost becoming soggy and the worms drowning.

The base unit of the wormery is raised on legs to provide clearance for a watering can or other container to go under the tap.

3 As part of the kit, the makers also supply a block of concentrated coconut fibre (coir) as bedding material. Following the instructions, place it in a bowl of water to soak for about 15 minutes. There is no need to remove the wrapping, since evidently worms like paper, too.

4 When the coir bedding block has soaked for long enough, it will have absorbed a great deal of water and will have expanded enormously. Break it up with your hands (it is not harmful) and rub it together to a fine, uniformly moist consistency that looks a bit like potting mix.

5 The wormery kit includes a cardboard circle. Lay this over the base of the tray. It acts like a filter, keeping the bedding and worms in, but letting moisture drain through. Spread the bedding mixture evenly over the cardboard in loose handfuls.

Adding the worms

1 Open the bag that contains the worms. To keep them happy and healthy in transit they are delivered in moist bedding material. (It is important to unpack and set up the wormery kit as soon as possible.) Spread the worms and bedding over the material in the tray.

2 Fit the next tray in position over the top. The base should rest on the bedding material in the tray below. Add a small quantity of suitable material to feed the worms, and cover it with damp newspaper. Every few days remove the paper and add a little more food. Do not overfeed.

How many worms?

You need at least 1000 worms to get a wormery started efficiently. If anything goes wrong with the wormery and large numbers of worms die, perhaps due to excess cold or wet conditions, then it is worth buying more; if worm numbers are low, the wormery will work very slowly to start with. Once set up, worms will breed and you will find slim pale-coloured baby worms that grow and feed. Within a few years you could have 20,000 worms or more at work, and by this time the wormery will be working fast and need proportionately more food.

MAINTAINING A WORMERY

A multistorey wormery, as shown here, makes harvesting the worm casts very easy, as you need never wait for the container to fill. The worms move up from one tray to the next. Eventually, the lowest tray is full of pure worm casts, but virtually no worms, as they have all moved 'upstairs' to the feeding trays containing vegetable waste in various stages of decomposition. Lift off the upper trays and remove the lowest one with its 'harvest' of worm casts. When you have emptied this, return it to the top of the stack. This type of wormery takes about a year to get into full production, but from them on production speeds up as the number of worms 'at home' increases, and you can harvest a trayful of casts fairly regularly. Meanwhile, you can run off the liquid that drains out of the base of the wormery (all types) and use it as organic liquid feed. If you have a traditional bin-type wormery with a single compartment, you need to fill it up to the top, which can take two years. When you cannot add any more vegetable material due to the build up of worm casts beneath, it needs to be emptied. Tip it out and separate the pure worm casts in the bottom of the container from the partly or totally undecayed material nearer the top. Sift the material through a soil sieve with a 1.25cm(0.5in) mesh to remove the worms, and then use the worms to restart the bin. Begin by putting a layer of drainage material in the base, cover it with a little of the old, well-rotted material, add the worms plus the rest of the undecayed material, and continue 'feeding' as before.

1 Sprinkle a thin layer of suitable worm food all over the surface of the new tray and spread it out evenly. Worms will soon make their way up from the tray below, as they consume the remaining food there. Add a little more food daily.

2 After 'starting' the new tray, cover the layer of food with damp matting (provided by the makers of the wormery kit) or a newspaper cut to fit, soaked and squeezed partly dry. This stops the food from drying out. Replace it over the top each time you add more food.

Acidity regulator. Make your own by mixing equal parts of calcified seaweed and sharp sand or fine grit (grit helps worms digest their food).

Concentrated worm feed. Make your own by mixing equal parts of flaked maize, wheat bran and layers pellets sold for hens.

3 Concentrated food gets a new wormery off to a quick start, is useful when worms are breeding most actively in late spring and makes a top-up when fresh food is short. Sprinkle a handful evenly over the surface. Do not overfeed.

4 When vegetable waste breaks down, it becomes slightly acid. To counteract this and to prevent the wormery contents becoming too acid for the worms, sprinkle a handful of acidity regulator over the surface occasionally.

5 When the second working tray is filled with compost, add the third and proceed as before. Once the top tray is getting full, you can lift out the bottom tray and harvest the first crop of worm compost.

6 Tip the contents into a bucket and recycle the empty tray as the new top tray. Sprinkle worm compost along rows of vegetables in a deep bed to provide nutrients and valuable trace elements.

7 A relatively large amount of liquid builds up in the base. Expect more after heavy rain if the wormery stands in the open. Run it off periodically to prevent waterlogging, or the worms will drown.

Suitable foods

Fruit and vegetable peel. Shredded newspaper, kitchen paper and cardboard soaked in water, wrung out till damp, then fluffed out. A few crushed eggshells (to neutralise acidity). Tea leaves, tea bags, coffee grounds. Dust and fluff from vacuum cleaner. Pet hairs.
Do not add: garden waste, weeds, lawn mowings, citrus peel or rinds (too acid), onion peelings.

8 The liquid is a rich natural source of nutrients and makes a superb liquid plant food. Dilute it with water and apply it evenly around any plants, although it is most valuable as a homegrown organic feed in the vegetable, fruit and herb patch.

9 For feeding vegetables and plants in containers, use a 50/50 mix of 'wormery liquid' and water. Fruit and shrubs can have neat worm liquid. As a precaution, do not use it for seedlings or cuttings as they are more delicate.

10 The great advantage of a tiered wormery over a one-piece bin is that once set up, it runs continuously, without ever needing to be emptied completely. Neither do you have to sieve out the worms from the compost.

MAKING A CLOCHE

A cloche is like a miniature greenhouse, but instead of moving plants under cover, you move the cover over the plants. Cloches make a vegetable garden more productive by extending the growing season and getting newly planted seeds or young plants off to a faster start. To use cloches, stand several together in a row to make a continuous tunnel. Close off both ends with a sheet of glass or rigid plastic held in place with two canes pushed into the ground. Remove the ends as needed during the day for ventilation or to harden off tender plants, and replace them at night if frost or cold weather threatens. Start using cloches in early spring, placing them over prepared soil to warm it up for several weeks before sowing or planting. Leave it over the earliest crops until they fill the space under the cloche. Throughout spring, move the same cloches over each newly planted row of crops to provide one or two weeks of temporary shelter while plants recover from the shock of transplanting. Cloches are also useful for protecting newly sown pea or bean seed from pigeons, and later they enable you to plant out frost-tender crops a week or two earlier than usual. Around harvest time, use cloches to cover onions and shallots that have been pulled up and laid on the soil to dry. And if you have outdoor tomatoes with a lot of unripe fruit two to three weeks before the first frost is expected, untie the plants from their canes, lay them down flat on the soil (ideally covered with straw) and, leaving the roots in the ground, cover the top of the plants with cloches. The fruits ripen much faster. Towards the end of the growing season, cover late crops that might otherwise not have time to reach maturity before the onset of cold weather.

1 You can make a cloche by cutting a pair of sides from stiff white plastic sheet. These can be any size you like, but about 30x45cm(12 x18in) works well. Alternatively, make the cloches the full width of an existing deep or intensive vegetable bed.

2 Use a pair of special cloche clips (various makes are sold in garden centres) to hold the two sides together at the top. Similar clips can also be used to hold two pieces of glass together if you prefer, but avoid glass cloches in windy areas in case they break.

3 Set the cloche over a row of slightly tender crops, here a double row of dwarf French beans. The cloche's main function is to speed up growth, so that the plants grow faster and crop sooner than those in the open. Unless it is very hot you could leave French beans covered until the flowers open. Uncover them then so that insects can pollinate the flowers.

4 Since the ends of cloches are open, cut two squares of plastic to cover them. Hold these in place with a horizontal stick pushed into the ground. On hot days, you can slide out the panels at both ends of a row to provide ventilation. Replace them at night. To hold the cloche down in a breeze, slide a cane through the special apertures in the clips.

5 Cut the cane so that it sticks out just beyond each end of the cloche, and tie it firmly to the uprights holding the ends of the cloches in place. In a windy site, you could also secure cloches by 'guy ropes' to long, large-headed nails hammered halfway into sides of the beds. In a very windy site do not risk using cloches and find another form of protection instead, such as a heavy wooden cold frame with a well-fixed glass lid.

Right: Cloches are functional plant protectors intended for use in a vegetable garden where looks are not the top priority. However, for a more decorative alternative, you can buy bell jars in glass or clear plastic, which are ideal for an ornamental potager or even a garden border. The one shown here is covering a single strawberry plant in a decorative potager.

Making a glass cloche

Make glass cloches smaller than plastic ones due to the extra weight and safety considerations. Use two pieces of glass 45x30cm(18x12in) Wire cloche clips were traditionally used to secure flat sheets of glass together to make a simple tent cloche, but nowadays plastic clips are a widely available substitute. Lift glass cloches carefully, and do not use the clips that hold the two sheets of glass together as a handle as the glass slips out easily and can cause an accident.

1 Slightly bevel the edges of each pane with a flat carborundum stone to remove the sharp cut edges. Alternatively, bind around the edges for protection, using a special clear outdoor sticky tape designed for repairing cracked panes of glass in a greenhouse.

2 Holding the glass firmly, fix one cloche clip a short distance from each end of the glass. Plastic clips are quite stiff as they are designed to grip tightly, so take great care.

3 Bring the second sheet of glass up to the first and make sure the two corners line up perfectly before attempting to get the new sheet into the jaws of the clip. It is often helpful to have someone else hold the other end of the glass while you do this.

4 The completed cloche makes a tent shape ready to use. To complete the greenhouse effect, use a square piece of glass held in place with a couple of short canes to close off each end of a row of cloches covering a crop or newly-sown seeds. This also prevents cats sunbathing inside and flattening crops, stops pigeons and other pests taking plants or seeds and prevents wind funnelling through to chill new plants.

USING A PAPER MULCH

A loose surface mulch of bark chippings, weathered manure or garden compost is not practical in a vegetable garden, where individual rows of crops mature at different times. It would mean mulching small sections of a bed each time it was turned over to a different crop – perhaps several times within the same growing season. However, biodegradable paper mulches are quick to put down and let moisture soak through. They prevent weeds, reduce water evaporation and provide a safe home for many beneficial creatures that will provide biological pest control. You can also write on a plain paper mulch, rule out straight rows, mark planting distances or give variety names. Tuck complete newspapers folded in half lengthwise to make double thickness paper wads between existing rows of vegetables. You can adjust the fold to provide 100% ground cover between rows of other widths. Or lay whole newspapers out, opened along their centrefold and just overlapping, so that they cover the soil completely. (A single sheet of newspaper is not thick enough.) Plant through crosses cut in the paper, then damp the entire newspaper with a hosepipe; it will cling to the ground. To keep the paper flat in a windy area if it dries out, secure the edges with stiff wire pins. You can also buy rolls of paper mulch from organic gardening equipment suppliers. It is specially useful in a raised bed where it makes a good anti-weed seal over the soil. Avoid wallpaper and lining paper, as they would not let rain soak through to the soil.

1 Prepare the soil well. In spring, unroll the paper mulch across the bed, starting at one end. If you do this in advance of planting; the paper will allow the soil to warm up and weed seeds will not be able to germinate underneath.

2 Cut the paper a few inches longer than the width of a raised bed with wooden edges and tack or pin them to secure the edges. On beds with brick walls or deep beds made at ground level, cut the paper 30cm(12in) or more wider than the bed and bury the edges.

3 Cut a cross where you want to put the young pot-grown plants or transplanted seedlings. This is the very easiest way to grow through a paper mulch.You can even use a pencil to make a row of dots to make sure the planting distances are correct.

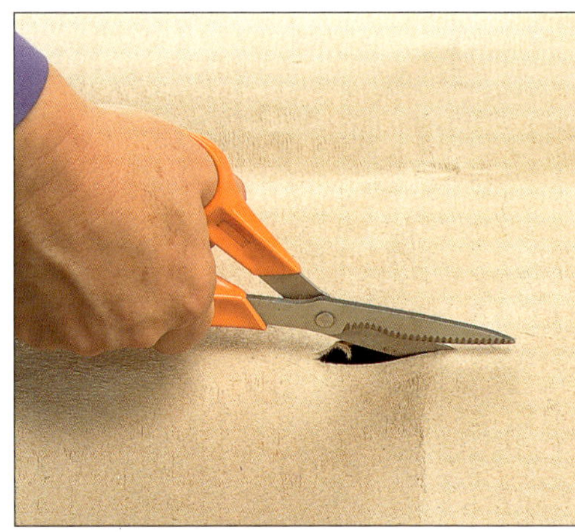

4 Lift the flaps and peel them back to expose the planting hole. Make this too small rather than too big; it is easy to enlarge if necessary. In time you will find it simple to gauge how big to cut the cross for any given pot size to get a neat finish.

5 Use a narrow-bladed trowel if working with small planting holes. A large hole would leave bare soil around the neck of the plant in which weeds can grow. Push the soil back to make a planting hole and then drop in the plant.

6 Tuck the flaps neatly back around the stem. As the stem thickens, it gradually pushes the paper aside. The slits also funnel rainwater around the roots, where it is most needed.

Right: The reward of attentive gardening is a fine crop of beans for immediate use or for freezing. Do not let them become tough and stringy.

Sowing seeds through a paper mulch

Although paper mulch is mostly used in conjunction with young plants, it is possible to sow seeds through it if you are careful. This avoids much of the tedious thinning and weeding within the rows usually associated with rows of vegetable seedlings growing in the open soil.

1 Rule a straight line and mark the distances you want your vegetable plants to be at their final spacing. For broad beans grown on a deep bed system, the ideal distance is about 15cm(6in) between plants.

2 Use the tips of the scissors to make the smallest possible hole for the seeds. Push one seed through at each mark and press it in to the correct depth with your fingertip. Seedlings will find their way through the hole to the light and fill the gap.

3 Water thoroughly. Much of the water will flow through the sowing holes, but the paper also soaks up moisture which then passes through it. Rain-water will wet the ground, but very heavy rain may bounce off raised beds covered with paper.

Hints and tips

Use paper mulch in conjunction with leaky hose-type irrigation lines. Run the irrigation under the paper. This prevents water wastage due to evaporation, and also avoids having to remove irrigation pipes to hoe weeds growing around them, as happens when they are used on unmulched soil.

Paper mulch lasts up to a year if used to grow a long-term crop such as winter broccoli. However, it is often so badly damaged when the first crop is cleared, that the best strategy is to lay a new strip across that part of the bed when planting a replacement row. If you can cleanly cut the lettuce, or other crops growing through the paper, simply clear away the debris and make new holes in the paper to plant the next crop through. The paper breaks down and can be dug into the ground or put on the compost heap.

MAKING PAPER POTS

The secret of a successful deep bed vegetable garden is to keep the ground fully occupied all the time. The best way to maximise yields and minimise weeding is to have young plants in pots waiting to occupy the space as fast as the ground is cleared of a previous crop, or as soon as the soil warms up in spring. Starting vegetable plants off in pots has many advantages. Planting fairly well advanced seedlings means they cover the ground quickly, so they soon smother out weeds. Crops that have completed part of their growing cycle in a cold frame or greenhouse mature more quickly, so you get more crops through the beds every year. You can start plants off earlier, so you harvest the rewards sooner. And in the case of plants such as peas and beans, whose seeds are at risk of being eaten by pigeons or mice or liable to rot in cold damp ground, you get better germination by sowing under cover in pots. This in turn means less wasted seed and no wasted space due to gappy rows. But even quite a small vegetable garden will need a large supply of pots if you are going to raise plants in this way. You could use plastic pots, but – especially vital for vegetable seedlings – these must be thoroughly washed and disinfected each time they are reused to prevent root diseases and other organisms attacking the young plants. It also takes time to know young plants out of their pots and collect up the empties afterwards. The simple solution is to use disposable pots. You can buy preformed paper pots, peat pots or fibre pots, or make your own, as shown here.

Below: Paper pots are made from recycled paper, pulped and formed into pot shapes and dried. They have a soft fibrous texture and are used just like peat pots but without the peat.

1 It is not difficult to make your own paper pots. Use the sort of paper sold for paper mulches, or you can use newspaper or paper kitchen towels. Avoid non-absorbent paper, such as writing paper or wallpaper, since these will longer to break down in the soil.

2 To make pots for vegetable seedlings, cut the paper into 20x10cm(8x4in) shapes. It is a good idea to cut a stack of these before starting to assemble the pots, but experiment first to check that the pots turn out a usable size. The necks must not be too narrow.

3 Roll one piece of paper into a tube 2.5-3.2cm(1-1.5in) wide. If too wide, it will not hold together when in use. If too narrow, you will have difficulty filling it with soil or pricking out a seedling. Do not try to slope the sides like a plastic pot, or the pots will not stand up

4 To form the base, make an inward tuck at the point where the edges overlap. This way, the pot will be stronger and less likely to spring apart. Hold this tuck down, and make a second one opposite it.

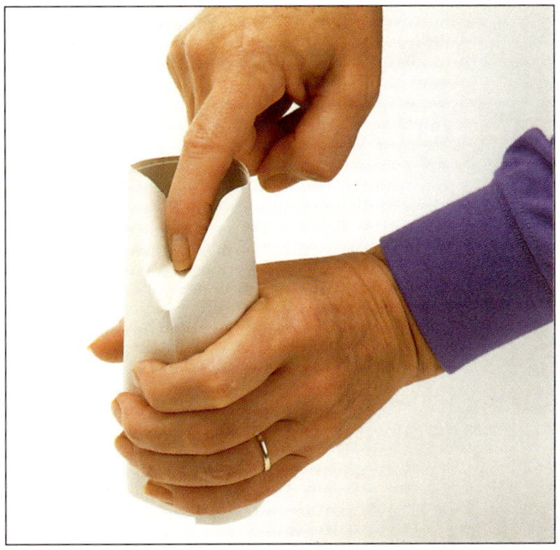

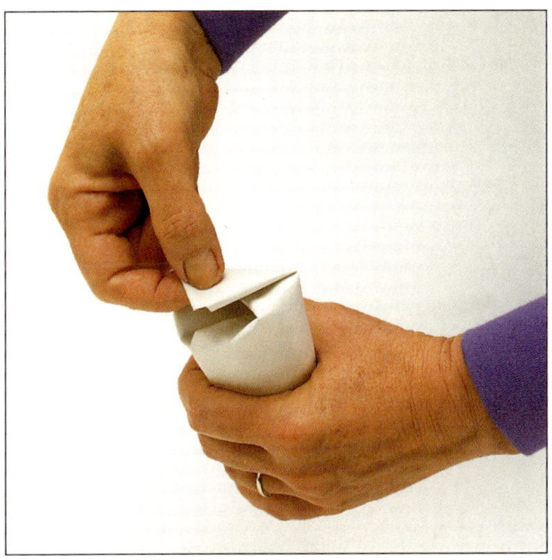

5 Continue folding. Three or four folds are normally enough. The last fold makes a neat flap that you can tuck under the end of the first fold or secure with a paper clip or staple. The latter is stronger, but takes time to do, especially if you are making many pots.

6 Fill the pots with seed mix and stand them on end in a seed tray. Pack them close together, so they hold each other upright and remain firmly folded. Once watered, the paper holds its shape.

Sowing and planting vegetables in paper pots

Spring cabbage: *Sow in late summer to plant in autumn.*
Cauliflower varieties: *Sow in late summer, keep in the greenhouse in winter and plant the following spring (or grow in greenhouse border or polytunnel).*
Courgettes, outdoor tomatoes and cucumbers, French and runner beans, sweet corn and squashes: *Sow in early summer to plant out after the last frost.*
Oriental vegetables: *Sow in early midsummer.*
Early beetroot: *Sow in a heated propagator under glass in early spring to plant outdoors in late spring.*
Summer- and autumn-cropping brassicas: *Sow mid-spring to plant out six to eight weeks later.*
Winter brassicas: *(eg Tuscany black kale) Sow in late spring.*
Early crops of lettuce, broad beans and peas: *Sow in early spring to plant outside mid- to late spring depending on the weather.*
Greenhouse tomatoes, peppers and aubergines: *Sow in early spring to plant out late spring in a frost-free or unheated greenhouse.*
Greenhouse cucumbers and melons: *Sow in mid-spring to plant late spring in a frost-free or unheated greenhouse.*

Below: *Sow individual sweetcorn seeds in tubes filled with seed or multipurpose potting mix and supported in trays. Plant out the seedlings about 45cm(18in) apart, complete with their tubes.*

The advantages of homemade pots

They are quick and cheap to make, and free if you recycle paper that would be wasted.
Planting is quick. Since paper biodegrades in the soil, you plant the pot as well.
Because there is no root disturbance during planting, plants grow away better.
The paper from the pot retains moisture while the roots establish themselves in the soil.
Save valuable time during the growing season by making a supply of paper pots during the winter and storing them until they are needed – a nice indoor job for a winter's day!

SALAD CROPS IN A WOODEN PLANTER

Even if you do not have space for a vegetable plot in your garden, you can fill a large container with salad plants and keep it by the back door where the crop will be convenient for picking. Nowadays, a whole range of edible leaves are popular as garnishes and ingredients for green salads; planted together, they make a decorative and useful container display. The best 'ingredients' for a container salad garden are those that can be picked little and often: sorrel, purslane, rocket, land cress, salad burnet and cut-and-come-again lettuce, such as 'Salad Bowl'. Planted in spring, the same plants can be picked over lightly for most of the summer. If the container is large enough, add a few hearting salads, such as Chinese cabbage, cos and normal lettuce and radicchio-type chicory. Where available, choose miniature varieties, as they take up less room and are faster-maturing than full-sized varieties. As soon as a plant forms a heart big enough to use, cut it, remove any remaining foliage, pull the root out carefully and put in a new plant. In this way, you can obtain quite a regular succession of salads from a very small space.

1 Loosely fill a wooden planter (with drainage holes) with rich potting mixture. There is no need to add fertiliser. Choose plants with a floppy or low, semi-trailing habit for the edges and corners.

2 Place the plants as close to the edge as possible to make full use of the space. Turn plants so that their best sides face forward.

3 The low plants allow light to reach all parts of the container. Add an edible-flowered plant, such as nasturtium, in the centre, where it will make a focal point.

4 French sorrel is a leaf-salad, with large, lemon-flavoured leaves. This perennial plant can be cut little and often over several years, but dies down in winter.

5 Chinese cabbage grow quickly and are safer from slugs and snails in a raised container, but make sure that the potting mixture does not dry out, otherwise they are likely to run to seed. Plants form chunky hearts.

6 Put in all the remaining plants 15cm(6in) apart. Water well after planting, and check daily, as the potting mix will start drying out fast when the tub fills with roots, and in hot weather. Begin liquid feeding after four weeks.

7 Although the tub will soon look crowded, plants around the edge will spread out over the sides, while plants such as sorrel and purslane are picked regularly.

Sowing lettuce seeds

Sow lettuce 'little and often' in summer and early autumn. Raise young plants under glass and transplant for early crops. In summer, sow in situ and thin out. Lettuce seedlings do not transplant well in summer.

1 Fill a suitable size pot with a good-quality seed-sowing or multipurpose potting mix. Gently level and firm the surface.

2 To aid seed germination, dampen the soil with a fine-rose before sowing until water runs out of the holes in the base.

3 Sprinkle the seeds evenly and thinly over the surface of the soil. If you sow too thickly, the seedlings will be lanky and weak.

4 Cover the seeds with sifted potting mix. Firm the surface lightly to ensure that the seeds are in contact with the soil.

5 If you prefer to water after sowing, stand the pot in a bowl of water until moisture soaks up to the surface.

6 Cover the pot with glass or plastic to maintain a damp atmosphere. Label it and stand it in a warm, but not too sunny, spot.

GROWING TOMATOES

One of the best ways of growing tomatoes, in a greenhouse and outdoors, is in a growing bag – a long plastic bag filled with a specially formulated planting medium. Growing bags are free of pests and diseases and the plastic isolates plant roots from any diseased soil. Tomatoes are susceptible to root diseases at the best of times and greenhouse plants are especially vulnerable. Both cordon (single stem) and bush varieties grow well in bags. Generally speaking, grow one less plant of a bush variety than a cordon, because a bush type takes up more room. Follow the general rules for watering growing bags; wait until the surface of the soil has dried out and then give at least 4.5 litres(1 gallon) of water at a time. Feeding is not necessary for the first few weeks, but once the first fruits are pea-sized, feed according to the instructions on the bag or the feed packaging. To allow sun and air to reach the bottom fruits, remove the leaves from the base of the plant up to the lowest truss that has fruit showing red. A container arrangement is another good way of growing a few tomatoes in a small garden. Compact, bushy varieties are ideal for hanging baskets, as they have a prostrate growth habit and you need not remove their side shoots. For best results, use a large container (which holds more potting mix than a small one and takes longer to heat up or dry out) and insulate it with a thick liner. To keep moisture levels even, add water-retaining gel crystals to the mix and water up to twice daily in hot weather. A sunny spot and frequent feeding with a high-potash liquid tomato feed are essential for tomatoes. Leave the tomatoes on the plants until they are completely ripe to develop their full flavour, but do not leave them until they become soft.

1 A good way of preventing an opened bag from spreading is to cut off the end beyond the heat seal to form a plastic ring.

2 Slip the ring over one end of the unopened bag and move it into the centre. Do not be rough with the strap if it is not very wide.

3 Make a V-shaped cut at each end of the bag, with the point of the V towards the centre. Join the points of the two Vs with another straight cut running under the strap.

4 Fold under the edges of the single planting compartment and work the mix down the sides and into the corners of the bag.

5 Put in three plants per bag in a greenhouse. Outdoors, plant four single stem or three bush plants per bag.

6 Apply up to 6 litres(1.5gallons) of water at the first watering to rehydrate the mix fully. Delay the next few waterings until the mix dries out slightly to avoid lush growth.

When to plant out tomatoes

Do not plant out tomatoes until you see yellow petals in the bottom truss of flower buds. This takes about ten weeks from sowing seed.

Above: Extra growth induced by overwatering young plants will lead to an unfruitful bottom truss.

Below: This tomato is ready to plant out. Turn it upside-down, tap the pot rim and drop the plant into one hand.

The rootball should be full of healthy roots at this stage.

Left: As the fruits mature on this bush variety, they provide an array of attractive colours, ranging from pale green to bright red.

7 The same growing bag some weeks later. Being a bush variety, the side shoots have not been removed from the plant. After a few weeks, there are plenty of flowers and the promise of a good crop.

Tomatoes and French marigolds in a basket

Several kinds of edible plant make attractive hanging baskets, especially when teamed with complementary ornamental flowers. Marigolds attract beneficial insects that help prevent pests attacking tomatoes, so you should not need to spray, which is ideal for organic gardeners.

1 Line a large hanging basket with a thick coco-fibre liner for insulation and an inner lining made from black plastic to hold water.

2 Loosely fill the basket with potting mixture and firm the mix down gently. The weight will settle the liner into all the curves.

3 Trim the edges of the liner. Space three plants of a compact bush tomato variety evenly around the basket, angled outwards. Fill the spaces between them with a few French marigolds.

4 Water the basket well. Use diluted liquid tomato feed to encourage heavy fruiting and avoid excess leafy growth.

5 Ripe tomatoes hanging below the basket rim are easy to pick. Harvest them regularly and deadhead marigolds to maintain the display all summer.

PRODUCTIVE CROPS FOR SMALL-SCALE GROWING

Some summer crops are particularly productive for small-scale growing. Aubergines and sweet peppers both make compact bushy plants, but being very cold-tender are best grown in pots or tubs on a sheltered sunny patio. The plants can easily be protected with plastic covers at night and on cold days; these act as individual mini-greenhouses and bring crops on faster. Plants take several weeks to get established, after which they need frequent feeding and daily watering. If allowed to dry out they often shed their flowers, causing a delay before the next crop of fruit; they are heavier yielding and easier to care for when grown in a rich, intensive garden bed. Early potatoes also make good crops for tubs and deep beds; buy tubers in early spring and 'sprout' them to prepare them for planting. Plant in late spring, after the worst frosts are over. Early potatoes produce a lot of small tubers early, and you can start gathering small crops in early summer without digging up the plants, just by rummaging in the soil around them. Courgettes and French or runner beans also produce huge crops from a very small space; climbing varieties can be trained over an arch where they look decorative as well as being easy to pick. Put plants out after the last frost, keep well fed (liquid tomato food is ideal) and water generously in dry spells. Pick courgettes and beans regularly while they are small; besides being better for cooking this encourages the plants to greater productivity.

Left: An aubergine and French parsley growing in the same pot provide a stylish display as well as an edible harvest.

Broad beans in a tub

Dwarf-growing varieties of broad beans do well in containers on a sunny patio. Being short and sturdy they generally need no support. Sow them in the early spring and keep them outdoors, so that the flowers are adequately pollinated by bees.

1 Fill the container almost to the top with good-quality multipurpose potting mix. Firm it down gently to make a good seedbed. This dwarf variety, 'The Sutton', is suitable for tubs. Sow the seeds individually on the surface of the mixture about 10cm(4in) apart.

2 Push the seeds about 4-5cm (1.5-2in) down into the potting mixture. Move some soil back over the seeds and firm in gently.

3 Water thoroughly. Do the initial watering in easy stages but do not stop until some drains out of the base of the container.

4 The young plants grow away well and flower. When grown outside (cooler than under cover), this variety should need no support. The plants stay short and are suited to containers.

Growing potatoes

In a small space, it is perfectly possible to grow new potatoes in large plant pots or tubs filled with used soil-based potting mixture or old growing bag mix. New potting mix can lead to rather too much top growth.

1 To cause potatoes to sprout, stand them on end in a warm, well-lit place, with the eyes uppermost until shoots are 2.5cm long.

2 Fill the pot or tub with potting mix until it is one third to half full. Firm it down gently. This tub is about 45cm(18in) in diameter.

3 Lay in the chitted seed potatoes, leaving 15-20cm (6-8in) between them. This produces a good crop without overcrowding.

4 Cover the potatoes with potting mix and fill the container to within 2.5cm(1in) of the rim and level the surface.

5 Water thoroughly and stand the container in a warm place. If you can obtain, or save, seed tubers, you could grow potatoes all year round.

Aubergines in a growing bag

Sow aubergine seeds singly in small pots. For best results, plant them into a growing bag in a greenhouse or conservatory when they have made a good root system. Cut two compartments in a growing bag.

1 Plant three aubergines in the bag, with the top of the rootball just below the soil. Firm in and add at least 4 litres (1 gallon) of water. Do not feed at this stage.

2 When the stem is 15-20cm (6-8in) tall, nip out the top. Add supporting canes once the weight of fruit bends the branches.

3 In temperate climates, in a good summer, aubergines will succeed outdoors if grown in a sunny, sheltered spot.

Growing courgettes

When all danger of frost is past, plant out young courgettes, two to a growing bag, with the top of the rootball 1.25cm(0.5in) above the soil to help prevent collar rot fungus disease. Water the plants thoroughly.

Right: *Always grow a proper courgette variety, not a marrow. Pick courgettes regularly. Not all varieties continue fruiting if some are allowed to grow into marrows, as here.*

MAKING A DEEP BED

Deep beds are the best way of growing a lot of vegetables in a limited space. Although it takes time to make the beds in the first place, once you have done the hard work, you need never dig the soil again and the routine workload is very much less than in a conventional vegetable garden. The idea is to prepare the soil very deeply to give roots the greatest depth of moist, rich, organic, loose fluffy soil to grow down into. This is the whole secret of the unique success of this growing method. The greater root depth means that plants can be grown much closer together than usual; about two-thirds the usual spacing. Furthermore, there is no wasted space, as you do not leave paths between rows in deep beds; the space is completely filled with vegetables. All the work on a deep bed is done from the paths around the edge, so that you never stand on the soil, thus compacting it. Because it stays soft and fluffy, water soaks in, worms can work, and roots can grow freely. And because vegetables are planted close together without any gaps, they quickly cover the soil so that weeds are unable to grow; without light their seeds cannot germinate. Provided you keep newly sown or planted crops carefully hoed for the first few weeks, you rarely need to do any more weeding until after the crop has been cleared. At this point, the ground just needs clearing and minimal preparation before the next crop goes in. Naturally, the whole system depends on very good preparation in the first place, so allow plenty of time. It is heavy work so take frequent breaks to avoid straining your back, and do not feel you have to do it all at once. Begin in autumn or winter so that the beds are ready for use in spring.

1 Deep beds should allow you to work from each side without treading on the soil; 90-120cm (3-4ft) wide is about right for most people, and 3-4.5m (10-15ft) long is ideal, as you need to walk round to get to the other side. Strip off the turf.

2 Dig out a trench, removing the soil to the full depth of the spade. Take out two rows of soil to make a wide trench. You can see how badly compacted this soil is; the light colour indicates that it is short of organic matter, too. Both these problems will be remedied during digging. Only deep digging is capable of thoroughly improving the lower layers of soil.

3 Throw the soil from this trench into a barrow and, if possible, tip it near the end of the last bed you intend to make. As you dig each bed, the soil will move one place forward, so that the soil from the first trench will be used to fill in the last trench as you complete the digging. The idea is to avoid moving soil further than necessary; it makes sense as you do it!

4 Loosen the soil at the bottom of the trench with a garden fork. If the subsoil beneath appears a different colour (particularly if it is heavy yellow or blue clay) avoid mixing it with the soil above. If the topsoil is deep, dig the fork in to its full depth to create a deep, loose bed that vegetable roots can penetrate easily.

5 Once it has been well forked over, spread a layer of well-rotted organic matter over the base of the trench. Use as much as you can – up to 15cm(6in). Mix it lightly into the loose layer beneath with the fork. This is the only chance you will have to improve root conditions this deeply, so make the most of it.

6 Dig the next row of soil, turning the soil over into the previous trench. Take this opportunity to break up the clods as you work; smash them up with the back of the spade or, if the soil is heavier, slice into them with the edge of the blade to chop them roughly up into cubes before smashing them.

7 Continue working in this way down the length of each bed, using the soil from each trench to fill the last.

8 You can see how the firm soil quickly becomes more crumb-like when it has been turned over and the clods have been broken up. Worms will help to distribute the organic matter throughout the soil besides aerating it, and their numbers will increase due to the extra humus in the soil.

9 As you dig, keep the spade at 90° to the ground so that the blade goes in to its full depth, otherwise the beds will not be sufficiently deeply prepared. And do not skimp on the organic matter; if you get tired, take a break.

Making an all-weather path

Since you do all the work on deep beds from the paths, it is a good idea to lay firm, all-weather paths that stay dry and do not harbour weeds. Grass paths make a lot of work as they need mowing and edging to keep tidy, and in wet wintery weather they soon turn to mud. However, weed-proof matting laid under gravel or bark chippings is very practical. You can also make the soil even deeper, and thus more productive, by making raised beds above the areas you have already deeply dug.

10 Use the soil from the first trench to fill the last trench to complete the bed. If you are making several parallel beds close together you can save a lot of soil shifting by using the soil from the first trench of the first bed to fill the last trench of the final bed. By now the soil is light and fluffy. To keep it that way, do not walk on it.

11 To prevent weeds and stop earthworms mixing your gravel or bark chip path into the soil, unroll heavy-duty woven plastic matting over the ground. Hold the edges down firmly with special pegs or metal skewers.

12 Nail together four planks the same length and width as the bed. Sit this in place so it rests over the weed-proof matting, leaving a small overlap. This will be fixed inside the beds later, so that there is no gap where weeds can grow along the edge of the path.

13 The timber surround will form a low wall around the raised bed, and will be filled with soil. Use treated timber or paint it with preservative to prevent rotting. Untreated timber only lasts a season or two in permanent contact with damp soil.

14 Tack the overlapping edges of the matting around the inside edge of the timber surround. The timber will prevent the soil in the bed from spilling onto the path and acts as a firm edge so that the sides of the bed do not break down when you use the paths.

15 Hammer a square peg, bevelled to a point at the bottom end, into each corner. Nail the adjacent planks into it. This gives the low wall greater strength and stability and stops it moving if you happen to tread on it when working on the beds later on.

Preparing the beds for planting

For the best results, it pays to prepare the ground well for planting. The soil should end up as a fine tilth, ideal for seedlings and small plants. You can apply the fertiliser several weeks before planting or on the same day, whichever suits you best.

1 Sprinkle a good-quality, general-purpose fertiliser evenly over the soil, following the recommended application rates.

2 Rake over the ground several times to mix in the fertiliser, break down lumps and remove any debris. The soil should be roughly the same texture as breadcrumbs.

3 Cover the weed-proof, woven plastic barrier with a thick layer of bark chippings. This makes a soft, all-weather path that drains quickly after rain and can be raked tidy.

EARLY VEGETABLES IN A DEEP BED

To get the most out of a deep bed, start sowing or planting as early as possible in spring. By growing early varieties and protecting them under cloches, they will be ready weeks before similar plants grown out in the open. Instead of cloches you could drape garden 'fleece' over plants to keep them warm. Hold down the fabric with stones around the edge or bury the edges in slit trenches. Some people like to warm up the ground first by covering it with sheets of black polythene (which also prevent weeds growing) for a few weeks before planting. This is a good idea if the winter has been a cold one, as the soil temperature has a major effect on early growth. However, if you use cloches, you could simply stand them in place for a few weeks before planting. Do this after preparing the soil and then put in the vegetable plants when conditions are suitable. Wait until after the worst frosts are over and water the rootballs thoroughly before planting.

Vegetables for sowing in early to mid-spring

Beetroot (bolt-resistant)
Broad beans
Carrots (early)
Leeks
Lettuce
Onion sets
Parsley
Parsnips
Peas (early)
Radish
Shallots
Spinach
Spring onions
Swiss chard
Turnips (forcing)

Young plants to put out in mid- to late spring

Broccoli (sprouting)
Cabbage (summer and autumn)
Calabrese
Cauliflower
Endive
Kale (black Tuscany)
Mangetout and snap peas
Radicchio

Right: Planting spring cabbage. Firm the plant in well to ensure that the roots will quickly get established. Water thoroughly.

1 The tallest crops, here mangetout peas, go at the back, so that they cannot cast shadows on shorter crops in front of them. Before planting or sowing, push in a row of twiggy pea sticks.

2 For early crops, plant out pea plants raised under cover in pots. Space the plants 10-15cm (4-6in) apart, and plant a single row on each side of the supports and close to them. This will make it easier to weed later on.

3 Water in very well. Newly prepared ground is likely to have dried out quite a bit due to all the preparation, so expect it to take more water. Raised beds also need more water than those that are flush with surrounding soil.

4 Allow 30cm(12in) between the last row of peas and the next crop. A fast-growing crop, here rocket, will mature before the peas take up their maximum spread.

5 The next row can be a crop that takes longer to mature. Plant these leek seedlings deeply, 2.5cm(1in) apart so they become 'pencil' leeks, eaten when young.

6 Continue adding potgrown young plants. The solid red hearts of this radicchio are used as salad leaves. Plant early so that plants can mature before autumn.

7 Space 'Lollo Rosso' lettuce plants 23cm(9in) apart. Pick individual leaves as needed. The same plants last several months, ensuring a continuous supply.

8 Plant another lettuce variety. These are 'Webbs Wonderful', whose, big solid hearts take longer to mature than the leaves of 'Lollo Rosso'. By planting the two together, it should be ready after the latter has been picked once.

Extending the season

Make the most of a deep bed by getting the season off to an early start. Prepare the soil for planting during the autumn or winter, while it is moist, crumbly and easy to work. Then cover it with a sheet of heavy duty black plastic to create ideal conditions for early sowings and plantings. Protecting with plastic not only warms up the soil, using the heat of weak winter sun, but also keeps it weed-free, since weed seeds cannot germinate in the dark. It also keeps the soil dry so that it remains light and friable. Otherwise, exposed soil (especially clay types) may become waterlogged and muddy. The soil is ready to use as soon as the cover is removed. All that remains to be done is to add fertiliser and rake it in. To keep up the early advantage, cover the crops with cloches or fleece after sowing or planting.

***Right:** Stand a few bricks around the edge of the bed to hold the plastic in place. (In windy areas you may need some bricks in the middle of the sheet, too). Alternatively, tack it down to the wooden edges of the beds. Do not use clear plastic; weeds grow rampantly underneath it.*

9 Water everything in very well immediately after planting so that young plants do not wilt. Wilting checks the growth of vegetable plants and can be the reason for them bolting later on.

10 Keep the newly planted bed well watered at all times. Until the young plants cover the soil, smothering out weeds naturally, keep the soil hoed.

SPRING VEGETABLE SOWING

Not all vegetables are suitable for very early planting; some, such as beetroot, 'bolt' (run to seed) if put in too early and others, such as courgettes and French and runner beans, are killed by frost. The greatest range of vegetables can be planted in late spring and early summer, so do not completely fill a deep bed with early crops; save some space for those that need to go in a bit later. You will also find that by early summer, some of the fastest early crops, such as spinach or lettuce, will have been picked, leaving rows vacant ready for new crops to be sown. Root vegetables, such as beetroot and carrots, do not like being transplanted, so they are always sown by scattering the seeds thinly along shallow rows. When the seedlings come up, thin them out by carefully pulling out the surplus ones. Leave the strongest young plants correctly spaced along the row. Large seeds, such as peas and beans, can be sown in pots under cover and then planted out later, or sown by planting each seed spaced out exactly where you want the plants to come up. Frost-tender vegetables are best raised early under glass and planted out after the last frost. Brassica crops can also be sown under glass and pricked out into individual pots to plant outside later, as space becomes available. To get the maximum productivity from an intensive deep bed system, plant out pot-grown plants as much as possible. The time saved by not waiting for seeds to germinate in situ is enough to get an extra crop from the space every year.

1 Rake the ground to a fine tilth. Run the edge of a hoe or rake along a straightedge to make a 'drill', a shallow depression about 1.25cm(0.5in) deep, for the seeds.

2 To sow small seeds, such as this lettuce, tip a small quantity of seed into your palm and use your finger-tips to take small pinches of seed. Sprinkle these thinly along the drill. It helps to imagine each one growing into a small plant. This avoids wasting seed.

3 Trickle water evenly along the drill. Avoid 'flooding' the seeds, which washes them all down to one end, where they come up in a clump that need separating and transplanting later. Keeping the water where you want it also discourages the growth of weed seeds.

4 Use the teeth of the rake to cover the seed. Pull the soil very gently from each side of the drill to cover the seeds with just 6mm(0.25in), but sealing in moisture. This is a particularly good technique to use in hot dry weather as it reduces the loss of water by evaporation.

Sowing dwarf French beans

1 Presoak French bean seeds in tepid water for 12 hours before planting. If you cannot sow straight away, leave them on damp kitchen paper but do not let them dry out.

2 Make two 2.5cm(1in)-deep, straight drills about 15cm(6in) apart. Sow the beans in a double row, which leaves just enough room to run a hoe through later.

3 Trickle water slowly along each drill, so the soil around the seeds is thoroughly damped. If seed is too wet or dry during the crucial germination period, it dies.

4 Rake dry soil over the seeds. Bury dwarf French beans to two to three times their own depth. If too shallow, they push up out of the ground while germinating.

5 As the beans grow, train the courgettes away in the opposite direction so that they do not smother the beans in foliage. It will take 12-14 weeks from sowing to picking the beans.

Planting courgettes

1 Keep vigorous plants, such as these courgettes, at one end of the bed. They will spread over the path without swamping other crops. Plant two seedlings close together in case one dies; if both survive, remove one when they get overcrowded.

2 Courgette plants need lots of water, but are susceptible to 'neck rot' when first planted. To avoid this, make a shallow 'moat' round them. When you water, the neck stays dry but the excess is held where the roots can use it; it cannot run away out of reach.

3 Fill the moat every few days, so roots are encouraged to grow deep into the moist soil below. Feed courgettes with a high-nitrogen liquid added to the water once a week. Change to tomato feed when the first baby courgettes start to set.

Weeds

Wherever there is freshly turned over soil, weed seedlings will follow. They compete with growing crops for water and nutrients, and if left unchecked can smother vegetables, which grow more slowly. Keep the soil between rows of crops weed-free by hoeing regularly while the weeds are small. A narrow hoe is precise and good for working in confined spaces.

Above: Run a hoe between rows once a week, which only takes minutes. It takes much longer if weeds are overgrown.

Thinning out seedlings

1 Crops sown in rows often need thinning to give each plant room. Do this in several stages; the first time leave seedlings about 1–2in(2.5–5cm) apart; if any die there will be enough replacements.

2 After about a week, thin again leaving plants 3in(7.5cm) apart. At the final thinning, leave them 6 or 9in(15 or 23cm) apart depending on the ultimate size of the variety. Use thinnings in salads.

Harvesting radishes

If radishes are sown fairly thinly they will not need thinning. After about 10–12 weeks, depending on the weather and the variety, you should find the roots marble-sized and ready for pulling. Do not leave them too long or they will taste too hot, get tough, and begin to run to seed.

HARVESTING CROPS

The secret of getting peak productivity from a deep bed is to keep it full. As soon as one crop is harvested, the next one should be ready to go straight in. The sort of crops that are sown straight into the ground, such as radishes, can be put in as soon as the ground has been "recycled" ready for use. In the case of crops such as broccoli, which are put out as plants, make sure they are sown on time so that they are ready to plant as soon as a space becomes available. With experience, it becomes easy to tell how long to allow. You can also buy most popular vegetable plants from a garden center, ready for planting immediately. One problem people often find when they start growing their own vegetables is that they end up with too much of the same thing all at once, so a lot goes to waste. If you plant too many lettuces at the same time, they will all be ready at once and you cannot even freeze the surplus as you could with vegetables such as broccoli. Deep beds help here because being narrow, you can only have short rows. Aim to grow many different crops, each in small amounts. And only put in one row of lettuce and spinach at a time to avoid a glut. Wait three to four weeks before sowing another row of fast-growing crops such as these, so that you have time to use the last row before the next one is ready. And start picking the first vegetables in a row as soon as they are just big enough to use; do not wait until they are enormous, or you will never keep up. In any case, vegetables are tastier and more tender picked young. If they are left to grow huge they will just be tough and tasteless. The secret is keeping a fast turn-over.

Harvesting arugula leaves for salads

1 Start picking arugula once it has a reasonable number of leaves so you can pick without denuding the plants. Choose fully expanded young leaves, free of holes or pests.

2 When the plants look untidy and become unproductive, rejuvenate the row by cutting the plants off just above ground level. New leaves will soon regrow.

Planting broccoli

1 After early crops have been cleared, plant winter brassicas, such as purple- or white-sprouting broccoli or brussels sprouts, 12in(30cm) apart in deep beds.

2 The plants produce heavy crops when there is not much else around. Water them in, and keep them well watered in dry spells to prevent them bolting.

Harvesting lettuce

1 A lettuce is ready to cut when it has formed a large solid heart within the dark, coarse outer leaves. Slice through the stem close to the soil, and trim away the outer leaves before taking it indoors.

2 Once the first lettuce is ready, the rest of the row will soon follow. Cut them as soon as they are ready. If lettuce stands too long once mature, it starts to run to seed and tastes bitter.

3 Once the whole row has been cut, clear the remaining dead leaves and dig out the old stumps including their roots, to avoid encouraging pests such as slugs.

4 Shake the old soil of the roots, take out weeds, and tidy the ground. If you find soil pests, such as root aphids, do not put them on the compost heap.

Preparing the ground for a new crop

As soon as one row has been used up, get the ground ready for the next crop. Use fertilizers with care; in strong concentrations they can scorch plants or prevent seed germination. If any fertilizer gets onto neighboring crops, wash it off with water to avoid scorching.

1 Once the old leaves, roots, and weeds have been pulled out sprinkle a little general fertilizer evenly along the row, keeping it off adjacent crops.

2 Use a small hand trowel, fork or hoe to mix the fertilizer into the soil—this avoids a strong concentration accidentally occurring all in one place.

3 As you mix in the fertilizer, you could loosen up the soil where it has become compacted between crops. However, provide a firm seedbed for brassicas.

4 From midsummer onward, sow early varieties of peas and carrots as they mature the fastest. Sow peas in a wide shallow drill instead of in rows.

5 Sow the pea seeds about 2in(5cm) apart in three staggered rows. This is a dwarf variety that makes a productive, self-supporting "pea hedge."

6 Cover the seeds with 1–2in (2.5–5cm) of soil, taking care not to bury them too deeply or leave any exposed, as this encourages birds to forage. Water in as usual.

A glass bell-jar makes a mini-greenhouse for a single strawberry plant.

PART ELEVEN

THE COMPACT FRUIT GARDEN

Modern fruit trees and bushes are tailor-made for small gardens, producing useful crops of fruit that look decorative and, when eaten fresh-picked, have a superlative flavour. Grow them in containers, beds and borders, over arches or up fences.

SMALL-SCALE FRUIT

You would probably not have room for many traditional apple or pear trees in a small garden, though nowadays, thanks to dwarfing rootstocks, they are compact enough to grow in a lawn or border. Their blossom is as good as any ornamental malus, and the ripening fruit better than that of crab apples, with the bonus of being edible, too. And nowadays you can also get self-fertile varieties that do not need a partner for pollination, which makes them specially suitable for small gardens. Peaches and cherries are also available as ultra-dwarf trees.

You can also find room for soft fruit, if you train them to save space. Cordon-trained redcurrant bushes take up virtually no room when grown against a wall, and gooseberries make pretty standards good enough to grow in a border. Even loganberries and similar large cane fruit could be trained around a fence, where they provide blossom and ripening fruit for color. Thornless varieties have attractive "finely cut" foliage as an extra bonus, while the better-tasting thorny varieties turn a wire fence into a barrier against livestock and intruders.

Above: Heavily cropping, but less tasty, thornless blackberries have attractive ferny foliage and look good trained along a chain link fence or over a good-sized wall.

Right: Autumn-fruited raspberries only grow to about half the height of the normal kind, so you need not tie them to wires. Plant them 12 x12in(30 x 30cm) apart in a small bed. Cut down all the canes to ground level in early spring.

Left: Apples on dwarfing rootstocks make good plants for containers. Upright cordons, such as this 'Red Pixie', take up less space. Pot the tree into a larger pot or half barrel and tie it to a stake.

Below: Cordon pears grow slightly bigger than apples trained in the same way. A row planted 18in(45cm) apart makes a productive decorative screen, or train two cordons over an arch so they meet in the middle.

Above: The hybrid jostaberry looks like a gooseberry bush that produces giant blackcurrants. Although not the most compact bush, it can be trained and is decorative enough to use as a garden shrub with the bonus of edible fruit.

Above: Cultivated as cordons, redcurrants and their colorless cousins the white-currants, take up very little room and will grow either in the open garden trained to canes or against a wall or fence.

Left: Choose a pot 12–15in(30–38cm) in diameter and partly fill it with good-quality, soil-based potting mix. Remove the fruit bush from its container and sit it in the center of the new pot. Fill the gap around the edge with more potting mix, barely covering the surface of the root-ball. Water in. Start feeding after the first week, using diluted tomato feed.

Growing fruit

Above: *Pears look attractive grown as espaliers in a sheltered, sunny spot. In a small space, choose a self-pollinating kind. 'Conference' is also a very reliable heavy cropper.*

Above: *Oblique cordons are a most economical way of growing pears. Most varieties readily form fruiting spurs, which develop all along the sloping stem from bottom to top.*

Above: *A stepover apple tree is a normal cordon grown horizontally. It makes a productive and decorative edging to a fruit garden.*

Left: *Ballerina apple trees naturally grow into upright shapes with plenty of fruiting spurs. They do not grow branches and need no pruning.*

PLANTING CORDON TREES

In a small garden, you might think that there would not be enough room for fruit trees. That is true of conventional trees, which grow as wide as they are tall, and create heavy shade underneath. But thanks to modern dwarfing rootstocks and new training methods, it is now possible to grow fruit trees that take up less room than a small shrub. The most space-saving form of all is the cordon tree. This consists of a trunk with many knobbly clusters of short shoots called spurs growing all along its length. Apples and pears are most commonly sold trained as cordons, but you sometimes find cordon plums too. Cordon-trained trees can be planted as a hedge only 45cm(18in) apart, and are incredibly productive, as each spur produces one or more fruit, and even young trees crop reliably each year. They are often planted on the slope, supported by a row of posts and wires. By sloping the cordons you can have a trunk 2.5 or 2.8m (8 or 9ft) long, but still be able to reach the top to pick the fruit, since it will only be 1.5 or 1.8m (5 or 6ft) from the ground. However, you can also grow upright cordons, which need less supporting; a simple stake and tree ties are enough, but they will need staking throughout their life. Cordon trees make a good, productive 'garden divider' that also makes a decorative screen, ideal for separating a vegetable plot from the ornamental part of the garden without wasting space.

1 Apple trees need well-drained, fertile soil and a reasonably sheltered sunny situation. Prepare the ground well before planting by digging organic matter into the whole bed the previous autumn or winter. Then dig out a planting hole slightly bigger than the pot the plant arrived in.

2 Lift the plant out of its pot, and sit it in the hole without breaking up the rootball. Do not plant it too deeply; the top of the rootball should be roughly level with the surface of the surrounding soil. Do not bury the graft (this is the bulge you can see near the base of the stem).

3 Hammer in a stake alongside the rootball. Use a stake 45cm(18in) taller than the tree and secure the trunk to it with two proper tree ties. These have a rubber buffer that fits between the trunk and the stake to prevent chafing.

4 Mix some well-rotted organic matter, such as old potting mixture or garden compost, into the topsoil excavated for the planting hole. Use this to fill in round the roots. This is done after staking the tree to avoid hammering the stake through the roots and damaging them.

5 Shovel the prepared mixture all round the tree, making sure it trickles between the rootball and the sides of the planting hole without leaving any air pockets. Firm gently down with your heel, but do not trample the soil down hard. Leave a circular shallow depression for watering.

A family tree

You can buy fruit trees made up of more than one variety of the same fruit. This family apple tree is in full flower and clearly shows the three varieties grafted onto the same rootstock. Ideally, they should all flower together for good pollination, but an overlap of a few days is enough. The three varieties here are 'Fiesta', a late-keeping Cox-like variety with an excellent flavour, 'Discovery', a reliable early dessert apple and 'Sunset', a prolific mid-season apple with small fruits.

Above: The cordon tree bearing fruit. Apples are ready to pick when they come away from the tree easily as you lift them in the palm of your hand.

6 Shorten the leader – the new growth at the top of the tree – by half to encourage the development of sideshoots lower down, which will bear future crops. Do not let the tree carry fruit in its first year as it needs to get established first.

Dwarfing rootstocks

A fruit tree consists of two plants grafted together just above ground level. The trunk branches (and fruits) are the named variety you have chosen. The roots are a different but related variety – the rootstock. This has been chosen by the nurseryman, and different varieties of rootstock have different effects on the named variety grown on them. Dwarfing rootstocks are available in various 'strengths'. Very dwarfing root-stocks produce very compact and slow-growing trees. These are only commonly available for apples, but occasionally for cherries, too. Trees need stakes to support them all their lives and cannot stand competition from weeds. Grow them permanently in a 1.5m(5ft) circle of bare soil. Moderately dwarfing rootstocks are for apples. Use these to grow trees trained as cordons and for containers. They need support. Grow them in a circle of bare soil for the first five to ten years. Average dwarfing rootstocks – for apples, pears, cherries and plums – make a tree about two-thirds normal size. These produce compact trees for small gardens, and for fans and espaliers. Trees grown on dwarfing rootstocks begin to fruit when much younger and smaller than usual, but produce full-sized fruit.

How grafting is carried out

Grafting involves removing a short length of one-year-old shoot (called a scion) from the plant that you want to propagate and tying it onto the root system (rootstock) of another one. The rootstock passes sap and nutrients into the scion, which soon breaks into life and eventually grows into the new plant.

***Right:** This is the point at which the scion was grafted onto the rootstock. It is called the union.*

1 The two cuts and tongues match well. The scion should line up with one side of the rootstock, so that the bark on each member is touching.

2 The scion will remain in place, held together by the tongues. If the two pieces of bark do not correspond exactly, remove a sliver of bark.

1 Buy traps from garden centers or by mail order from organic suppliers. Do not assemble the flat kit until you are ready to use it.

2 The prescored plastic housing opens out into a tent that concentrates the scent of the lure, preventing it from being dissipated on the breeze. It also shelters the capsule holding the scent from the rain.

3 Press down the tent onto a hard surface so the base is flat. You need a level floor at least temporarily while inserting the lure and sticky trap. Even if it does not entirely retain its shape, it will be rigid enough.

A CODLING MOTH TRAP

Maggots are the biggest single pest problem affecting home-grown apples and plums, because they render the fruit inedible. At one time, the only effective control was to spray with pesticides every few weeks, but now there is an ingenious form of biological control—pheromone traps. Each trap consists of a sticky fly-paper trap contained in a weatherproof cover and a pheromone lure that mimics the scent of a female moth in the breeding season. Visiting males are attracted by the scent and are then held fast by the sticky paper. Being glued to the spot, they are unable to fertilize the females, who cannot lay eggs in the fruit, which remains maggot- and pesticide-free. You need a different pheromone for apple and plum codling moth, so use one of each if you grow both types of fruit. Hang up the traps at exactly the right time, so that you start luring male moths as soon as they appear. Late spring/early summer is ideal. If you leave it too late, many females will have been fertilized and have started to lay eggs. Conversely, in a cold spring, the appearance of the male moths will be delayed and traps hung up too soon may lose some of their effectiveness by the time the males arrive. Leave the traps in the trees until late summer. (Keep them afterward, as you can buy pheromone refills to use the following year.) One trap is enough to protect five trees. But if you live in an area with a large number of fruit trees, it is worth persuading your neighbors to use traps too, or the sheer force of numbers will be more than your own single trap can cope with.

4 Handling it by the corners, open out the card containing the glue. Do this in a covered place, free of dust or fluff, which would prevent flies adhering to it.

5 Stick the lure in the center of the paper. Male moths should pass over the maximum sticky paper in reaching it, to stand the greatest chance of getting stuck.

6 Gently press the top of the plastic tent down against a hard surface to make the base as flat as possible. Take the sticky card and carefully slide it glue-side uppermost along the floor or the tent. It should fit fairly tightly.

7 Fold up the two ends of the tent, inserting the flaps through the slots in the sides. The trap is much more rigid now, so there is no risk of the base popping up and gluing itself to the sides.

8 Hook the metal wire through the two pairs of holes in the roof and hang the trap in a convenient tree. If you have a group of trees, locate the trap in the most centrally placed one.

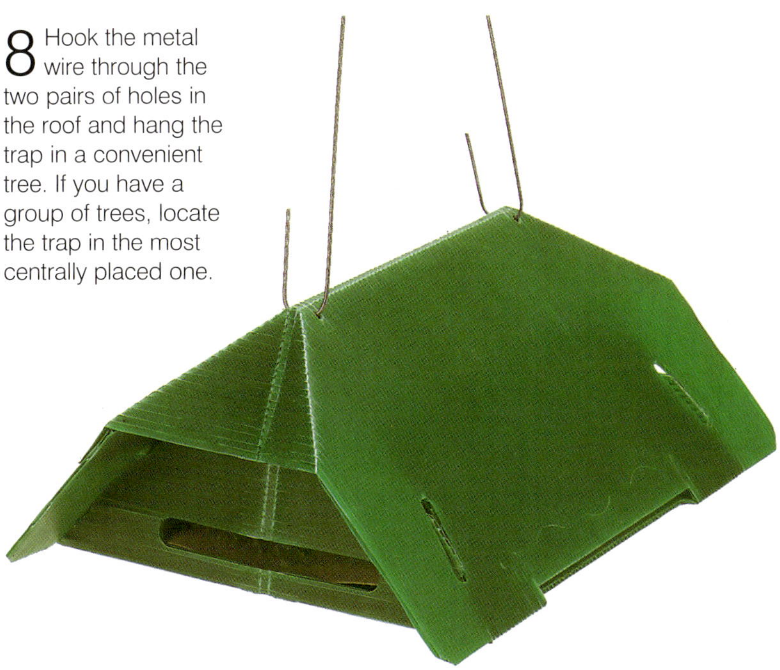

Codling moth damage

Codling moth maggots often bore through the center of the apple. When windfalls start to come off in autumn, it is usually the affected apples that fall off first. Perfect apples tend to stay on the tree until you pick them.

A messy hole on the surface of the fruit signifies codling moth caterpillar attack.

Below: *Cut open a damaged apple and the core area will be black and revolting. You may find the offending pink maggot of the codling moth. Damage is visible from early summer onward.*

Below: *This trap has more than earned its cost, with a good catch of male moths. The pheromone bait will need renewing after about five weeks if the trap is still attracting moths.*

STANDARD GOOSEBERRIES

Gooseberries are one of the most useful soft fruit bushes for a small garden. Though prickly, the plants are relatively easy to accommodate as they do not have to be grown as bushes. Instead, choose 90-120cm(3-4ft)-tall standard trees, which are pretty enough to plant in a flower border. Standards are particularly space saving in a small garden as they do not cast much shade, which means you can grow flowers right underneath them if you like. Ready-trained standard gooseberries are available, but cost more than bushes. However, they are easy to train for yourself, starting from cuttings, which root easily. Follow the same procedure as for training a standard fuchsia until the head has been formed. As long as the plants are well fed and watered while the fruits are swelling, productivity does not drop when they are grown in this way. A single plant is enough to provide a worthwhile crop of fruit, which is easier to pick than from bushes, as you do not need to bend down. If you only have room for one gooseberry in your garden, choose a dessert variety as you can eat the fruit fresh and cook it. Thin the unripe fruit in early summer when they are the size of a large pea and use them for pies. Remove up to half the total crop in this way. Then leave the rest to swell to full size and ripen fully on the plant. Pick them in midsummer to eat raw as a dessert fruit. (Protect ripening gooseberries from birds.) For convenience and to encourage fewer but larger fruit, prune bushes and standards in winter. Thin out congested stems and shorten all the current year's shoots to about 60cm (24in) from their base. With standards, also remove any shoots growing from the trunk or base of the plant.

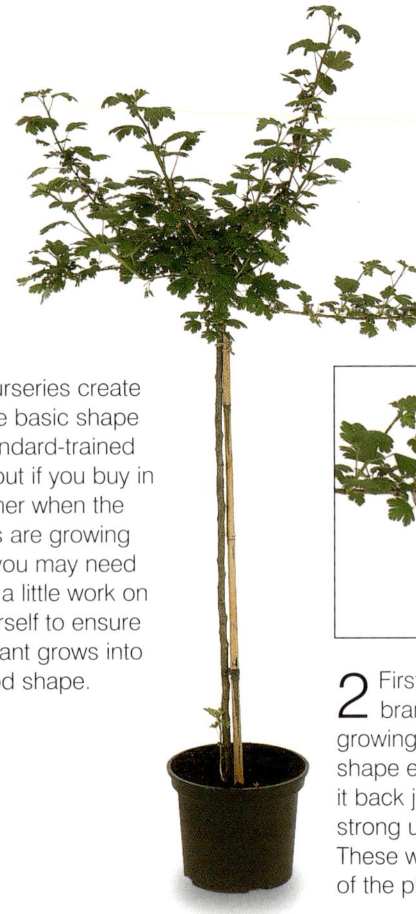

1 Nurseries create the basic shape of standard-trained fruit, but if you buy in summer when the plants are growing fast, you may need to do a little work on it yourself to ensure the plant grows into a good shape.

2 First, shorten the very long branch. If left, this would keep growing outwards, making the shape even more unbalanced. Cut it back just beyond a couple of strong upward-facing sideshoots. These will help to make the head of the plant bushier.

3 Shorten the other long shoots slightly. By removing the tips, these stems will each produce several sideshoots that will improve the shape and increase the potential cropping area in the following year. However, do not expect much fruit in the first year.

4 Always use sharp secateurs to make a clean, slightly sloping cut just above a leaf joint. Take care not to cut so close to the leaf joint that you risk damaging the bud in the angle between the leaf and the stem. This is where you want a shoot to grow from.

5 After pruning the head, check the stem and all around the base for unwanted shoots. These are not suckers, since a standard gooseberry grows on its own roots instead of being grafted, but if not removed, they try to turn the standard back into a normal bush.

6 Use the same planting technique as for a cordon apple tree. Prepare the soil, dig a large planting hole and sit the plant in it after removing its pot. Do not plant too deeply; the top of the rootball should be about level with the surface of the surrounding soil.

7 Hammer in a stake alongside the rootball. It should be about 45cm(18in) taller than the stem of the plant. A standard gooseberry will need staking for most of its life, and being top-heavy, needs supporting very firmly to prevent the stem breaking. Knock the stake in so the top is just below the lowest branch.

8 Fix the trunk firmly to the stake with proper tree ties, placing the rubber buffer between the trunk and the stem so that the bark does not get rubbed off in windy weather. This creates an open wound that would allow infection to enter. Place a second tie about halfway up the stem for extra security.

9 Complete the planting by shovelling a mix of topsoil and organic matter back around the roots to fill the planting hole. Firm it down gently, leaving a 'moat' around the plant. When you fill the moat with water, It goes straight to the roots and cannot run away.

Right: Green culinary gooseberries are ready for picking in midsummer when they are about 2.5cm (1in) long. Pruned bushes produce fewer but larger fruit.

U-cordons for gooseberries

Cordon-trained plants are the easiest to pick, as the plants consist of short sideshoots growing evenly spaced out along two main upright stems. Before planting a young bush, remove any shoots that are closer than 13cm(5in) to the roots, plus any buds among the roots.

1 After planting, prune the bush by removing any weak shoots, cutting back misplaced ones and shortening the rest by roughly half their length.

2 For a U-cordon, prune back to two strong shoots growing out opposite each other. Bend the shoots down carefully and tie them as horizontally as possible.

Right: *Planting gooseberries as single or double stem cordons is an excellent way of growing them where space is limited. They also make a good subject for creating a useful and attractive barrier between sections of the garden.*

Left: *'Lancashire Lad' is a large-berried, coarsely bristled but popular dessert variety. It ripens in early to midseason and has a good flavour. Green dessert gooseberries develop an amber tinge when ripe.*

PLANTING BLUEBERRIES

Although fruit trees and bushes normally grow best when they are planted in the garden soil, there are sometimes good reasons for wanting to grow them in pots. In a small garden, for instance, the only available space may be on a path or patio where there is no soil, so pots are the only practical way to grow them. And in a shady garden, the patio is often the only place that gets enough sun to grow fruit. Another common reason is that the garden soil is not suitable. Blueberries, for instance, must grow in acid soil, and will not grow or fruit well elsewhere. They dislike even the tiniest amount of lime. In pots, it is perfectly easy to suit them whatever your garden soil is like, just by planting them in ericaceous potting mixture. Blueberry plants are bushy shrubs that grow very well in containers, and are so attractive and productive that they are among the best choices for fruiting containers. The plants have clusters of large, white, bell-shaped flowers in early summer, followed by the distinctive fruit, which start out green and slowly ripen to blue-black. In autumn the leaves turn attractive tints of red and orange. The best time to plant a blueberry in a pot is in spring. Keep it well watered and feed regularly with liquid tomato feed. Protect the berries from birds. In winter, prevent the potting mixture from freezing by standing the pot in a greenhouse or sinking it to the rim in a garden bed. Report blueberries into fresh ericaceous mixture every two to three years in early spring, and topdress each spring when you do not repot them.

Planting a blueberry in a pot

1 High bush blueberries are ericaceous shrubs with pretty flowers in late spring, good autumn leaf color, and crops of tasty fruit that turn blue-black when ripe.

2 Choose a large tub and part-fill it with ericaceous potting mixture; do not add anything else. Site the tub in a sunny spot that is reasonably well sheltered.

3 Lift the plant out of its pot. Gently tease out a few of the biggest roots from the mass if it looks potbound. Sit the plant vertically in the middle of the tub.

4 Fill any gap between the rootball and the sides of the tub with more ericaceous mix and bring the level up to within 1in(2.5cm) of the rim of the tub.

5 Water the plant well. If your tap water is limey, save up rainwater or use water that has been boiled several times and cooled, since this precipitates out the chalk. Or else use a water filter.

Protecting your fruit bush from birds

Cover the crop early to keep it safe. Do not wait until the first fruits start to ripen; by then it is too late.

1 Protect the developing berries from birds while they are still green. Push four canes in round the sides of the tub, and unwind a roll of bird-netting loosely all round the plant.

2 Loosely gather up the edge of the netting immediately above the top of the plant and tie it to make the top of a temporary "minaret"-shaped fruit cage.

3 Secure the netting around the base of the pot with string to stop birds getting in underneath. Keep the netting quite loose and baggy and away from the fruit.

4 Close the side of the netting with pegs for easy access. Pick fruit every day or two once the first few fruit ripen. Do not leave them until they become too soft.

Unusual fruit

Where space is short, it can be a good idea to forget about growing conventional fruit and cultivate one or two more unusual kinds, specially if they are decorative enough to grow in a border, or produce fruit that is not widely available. Grow ericaceous species in large tubs of lime-free potting mix if your garden soil is unsuitable.

Above: *Cranberries are low evergreen plants with small pink flowers in early summer followed by red fruits. The plants need very acid and boggy soil, so grow in tubs with acidifying liquid feed.*

Below: *Worcesterberries look like small black gooseberries. An unusual and decorative novelty rather than seriously productive. Prune and grow as gooseberry.*

Left: *Japanese wineberry is a stunning ornamental that resembles a blackberry, with good foliage and masses of dense, fox-red bristles all over the stems. The fruit are wine-flavored and can be eaten raw, but the plants are not hugely productive.*

Right: *Blueberry needs a rich lime-free soil, but not as much acid as cranberry. Grow two plants of different varieties to get better pollination and, hence, larger crops. It does well in tubs.*

Planting and tying in

1 A young peach tree straight from the garden centre. When planting, use the rootball to judge the size of hole you need to dig.

2 Once firmly planted, the tree should be very slightly deeper than it was in its original pot, so that new roots form from the stock.

3 Cut back the tree to leave two suitable shoots to form the first rays of the fan. This allows you to start training from the right basis.

4 Cut back these shoots to two-thirds of their length. Prune to a bud on the upper surface to direct new growth upwards.

5 Tie two primary training canes to permanent wires, 23-30cm (9-12in) apart. Use plastic string or wire and bend in any sharp ends.

6 Tie the shoots to the canes with soft string. This avoids strangling the growing shoots, which can happen with plastic.

A FAN-TRAINED PEACH

As peaches and nectarines are natives of the Mediterranean, they can seldom be grown as free-standing trees in the open garden in cooler, temperate countries. There, they need the protection of a warm and sunny wall or fence to give of their best. Fan-trained trees are undoubtedly the most successful in this situation and training against a wall is always better than a fence because the brickwork holds a lot more heat. This is released at night and will frequently raise the temperature around the tree sufficiently to keep away a light frost. Fan-trained trees are better than espaliers, because peach branches are not always long-lived and may die back from time to time. If this happens on an espalier, it can take several years for a replacement to grow, develop and fruit, whereas with a fan, the 'spokes' are simply closed up to fill the gap and replacements are being trained outwards the whole time. When training a fan shape tree, carry out the work as well as you can, because what is done in the early years has a great influence on the tree's future.

Peaches and nectarines flower early in spring and you will normally need to hand pollinate them because few pollinating insects have emerged from hibernation when the blossom is out. On a warm sunny day, when the flowers are open, take an artist's soft paintbrush or a piece of absorbent cotton and draw it over the open flower. This collects pollen from the anthers and transfers some to the receptive stigma. Given relatively warm weather, fertilisation will soon follow and a fruit will develop. If there is a good set of fruit you will probably need to thin the fruitlets to ensure that fruit size does not suffer.

7 The peach tree is about to send out new shoots from the two that were trained in. Protect the tender growths from frost.

The fruiting stage

Peaches only fruit on the shoots that grew the previous year. Shoots growing from the base of a fruiting shoot will become fruiting shoots in the coming year. In early autumn, cut back nearly all those shoots that carried fruit to one or two new shoots that will have formed at the base.

1 Only leave those shoots that are to grow on and fill up gaps in the fan or replace existing and older shoots. The shoot being taken out here is growing straight out from the branch and can never be bent round and tied in properly.

2 Add more training canes as needed and check older ties for tightness. The righthand side of the tree is still dominant but leave it a bit longer. At the end of summer, remove the greater part of the dominant branch.

3 In the following spring, the result of the pruning and training is clear to see. The tree is carrying a good show of blossom and all is looking well for the first proper crop of peaches.

Hand pollination

Peaches flower before the pollinating insects are about. So before you count your fruitlets, you will need to pollinate the flowers by hand.

Right: *On a sunny day, gently wipe a soft paintbrush across the face of each flower so that pollen is transferred from the male anthers to the stigma.*

Left: *If the flowers are pollinated and fertilisation took place, and the summer was a good one, the result will be a crop of tasty peaches. This is a peach shoot in early summer after the first thinning of the fruitlets.*

Below: *The reward for attentive management; a crop of delicious peaches in the making.*

Pinching out

Right: *Early in the growing season, remove shoots about 2.5cm(1in) long, or shorter, embryonic shoots that are clearly growing in the wrong places. These will only have to be cut out later after the tree has wasted energy on them.*

GROWING STRAWBERRIES

Strawberries make excellent subjects for hanging baskets, windowboxes, growing bags, tubs and troughs. High-rise containers, such as strawberry pots with planting pockets in the sides, are a particularly good space-saving way of growing them in small gardens. Unlike many edible crops, strawberry plants are neat and compact, and also highly decorative with their apple-blossom-like flowers in spring followed by cascading green strawblets. They associate well with tubs of flowers, or can be added to a herb garden or potager-style vegetable garden to give height to a ground-level display. When grown in pots, ripening strawberries are far more easily protected from birds. Drape containers with netting or crop protection fleece from the time the first green fruits appear. Prevent slugs and snails spoiling the fruit by smearing crop protection jelly around the base of containers to prevent them climbing up. A strawberry container can be started any time in autumn or spring. 'Loose' strawberry runners are available in autumn and should be planted straight away so that the roots do not dry out. If you have access to a strawberry bed, you could also dig up spare runners from established plants in autumn to replant in containers. Small potgrown plants are also sold in spring right up until the time plants carry green fruit, however, the earlier in spring you plant them the better.

1 Make a support to stabilise the tower of pots by screwing a length of wooden pole to a flat base and sit the biggest pot over it.

2 Part-fill the pot with any good-quality potting mix. Leave a deep depression in the middle where the second pot will rest.

3 Put six strawberry plants around the edge of the pot, spreading the roots out as much as possible and then firming lightly.

4 Set the second pot in place. This should be sufficiently smaller to allow room for the first tier of plants to develop freely.

5 Firm and level the pot and part-fill with mix, mostly around the edges, leaving a depression in the centre for the smallest pot.

6 Plant four strawberry plants around the edge, but not directly above those in the lower pot, so the fruits hang down evenly.

7 Fit the smallest pot in place, taking care to keep the tower upright to prevent toppling once the plants are heavy with fruit.

8 Put two plants in the top and fill to the brim with mix. Fill any gaps between the lower plants with mix to prevent plants drying out.

9 Water each tier well. Moisture will drain down from the top pot, so after the initial watering, it will need more than the others.

10 Pour gravel into the saucer for extra stability and to hide the base plate. To move the tower, lift and steady using the 'handle'. Feed weekly with half-strength liquid tomato fertiliser.

Right: As the fruits reach full size, protect them from birds with a net supported on a frame. Tuck the netting loosely around the plant and hold it down with bricks. Pick the fruit daily. By early summer, the plants will have filled the container with fruit cascading down over the 'tiers'.

Planting strawberries in the ground

Strawberries are probably the most popular and easily grown fruit, and you can include some plants even in the smallest garden. Strawberry varieties are either of the summer-fruiting or perpetual-fruiting type. Summer-fruiting are the most popular and you can advance them under cloches or even in an unheated greenhouse. For later crops, use one of the perpetual varieties.Reduce the risk of infection from botrytis by putting down plenty of clean straw or proprietary matting between the rows so that the fruitlets are not splashed with rain or mud.

1 Buy strong, bare-rooted plants in late summer or early autumn. If you already grow strawberries in the garden save about 12 of their best runners to transplant then. Or buy young plants in small pots available from nurseries in spring.

2 It is important to plant strawberry plants deeply, so that the lower leaves rest on the surface of the soil. You should not be able to see the top of the roots. If you can, dig them out and replant them in a slightly deeper hole.

3 Place hoops over the green fruit to support netting. If the net rests on the fruit, birds will peck at it through the holes. Secure the edges with bricks.

Giant-flowered exhibition-quality begonias put on a dazzling display in this greenhouse.

PART TWELVE

THE SMALL GREENHOUSE

A greenhouse is the ultimate accessory for the hobby gardener, and even in the tiniest area there is room for one of the more compact models. It allows you to raise your own plants, grow tender exotics, create lush displays or grow warmth-loving edibles.

ESSENTIAL EQUIPMENT

The right equipment helps to make any greenhouse quicker and easier to look after. The basic essentials are staging or shelves to accommodate small plants in pots, and automatic ventilator openers that push the windows open on sunny days to control the temperature. A heater is also essential if you intend growing frost-tender plants through the winter. Electric fan heaters are the most commonly used; choose special greenhouse heaters, which are equipped with a built-in thermostat that can be set to maintain the required temperature in winter. However, when conservatories or lean-to greenhouses are built against the wall of the house, especially where there are connecting doors, the structure traps much of the heat escaping from the house and this is often enough to keep it frost-free without extra heating. If extra temperature control is needed in summer, install blinds either inside or outside the glass, and put an air circulator fan in the roof. You can also use an electric heater set to cold as an air circulator fan. A tap in or near the structure is useful, since watering is vital. For greater convenience, install a hose reel alongside the tap so that the hosepipe can be left connected but coiled away after use. A humidity meter and thermometer are handy, and a maximum/minimum thermometer 'stores' the extremes so you can tell if your heating and ventilation systems are cutting in correctly.

Below: Fit each roof ventilator with an automatic opener. This helps to prevent overheating on sunny days and saves you having to open and close the vents by hand.

Left: Louvred ventilators can be fitted low into the end or side walls of the greenhouse. They increase ventilation by allowing cool air to flow in as hot air goes out through the roof vents.

Left: Louvred ventilators are usually opened by hand on warm summer mornings and closed at night. However, special automatic openers can also be fitted to this type of ventilator.

Left: In autumn, replace shading with bubble wrap to eliminate draughts and reduce heating costs. Open vents on fine days to prevent condensation.

Below: Apply shading paint or dilute white emulsion to the outside of the greenhouse in early summer. Wash it off in autumn to give plants light in winter.

Above: Shading cools the greenhouse and protects plants from the sun. Fix shading fabric inside the roof and on the sunniest wall, with clips that fit into glazing bars.

Above: Electric fan heaters are the best way of heating a greenhouse in winter. Choose a model where the fan can be left running cold in summer for extra ventilation.

Below: Use a humidity meter to check growing conditions. In summer, plants enjoy above 70% humidity; in winter, keep it very low to discourage fungal disease.

Thermometers

A max/min thermometer lets you read the current temperature and monitor the highest and lowest temperature since the device was last set. Reset it morning or night every day.

Below: *Digital versions of max/min thermometers convert to Celsius/Fahrenheit readings at the slide of a switch.*

Above: *In traditional max/min thermometers, both ends of the mercury should read the same, giving the current temperature. To reset, press a central button.*

Adjusting a dial-type max/min thermometer

Left: *The black hand shows the current temperature, the blue one the minimum and the red hand the maximum. Once set, any changes will be obvious next time you come to check the instrument.*

Left: *First, turn the control knob to the right. This makes the stop on the dial push the blue hand. Move it so it lies directly underneath the black hand.*

Left: *Rotate the knob to the left so that the stop pushes the red hand under the black one. All three hands now show the current temperature.*

Using pebbles

Below: To increase humidity around a plant, place small pebbles into a large saucer. Add water, taking care that the level does not rise above the pebbles. The plant should not sit directly in water for long periods.

Right: Use expanded clay granules in sub-irrigation benches. They soak up large amounts of water. Spread out a 1.25cm(0.5in) layer over the watering trays.

Below: Stand pots firmly onto the bed and keep the granules damp. The mixture in the pots must be damp to start with or plants will not be able to take up water.

FEEDING AND WATERING

The secret of successful feeding and watering is to match the rate of both to the plant's growth rate. You cannot simply give plants the same amount of feed and water every week all year round; the rates should vary throughout the year, since plants themselves grow faster or slower and so have different requirements. In winter, some plants are dormant and need virtually no water. Others keep their leaves, but need a definite winter rest, with a low temperature, just enough water to prevent them shrivelling up and no feed at all. Most plants need lighter watering and feeding in winter, as they are growing more slowly. Even tropical evergreens kept at room temperature need a little less than usual, as light levels are lower and they are growing more slowly.

In spring, light levels and warmth increase naturally, so plants start to grow faster and need watering and feeding more often. By the time they have made quite a bit of new growth and are growing quickly, the rate needs increasing again. And in summer, particularly when they are in flower or fruit, plants need most feed and water. As flowers finish and the fruit is picked, decrease the amount of food and water gradually, and continue doing so for all plants as summer comes to an end and outdoor temperatures and light levels fall. Never stop watering suddenly; always cut down gradually, even with plants that become dormant.

Drip feed watering bags

Above: This self-watering system uses a bag that feeds a short run of drip line. Each pot has an adjustable nozzle.

Left: The bag holds enough water for several days, even in summer. Top it up as necessary. Liquid feed can be added to it.

Using a capillary matting water system

Capillary matting is a synthetic fabric capable of absorbing many times its own weight of water. Plants standing on it water themselves by drawing up all the moisture they need by capillary action. Thoroughly dampen the matting and water the plants well before standing them on it.

Right: Cut the matting to fit inside the watering trays, with the fluffy side facing upwards and the firm underside in contact with the tray. Smooth and press it into the corners.

Left: To water plants quickly, simply wet the front of the capillary matting, as water will move within the material. Use enough water to damp the matting well. Any surplus moisture will drain away through gaps in the watering trays.

Below: Cover the top of solid staging with capillary matting that runs down into guttering fixed along the edge of the staging. Fill this with water and the plants will virtually take care of themselves.

Feeding plants

When plants are watered by capillary matting or drip irrigation, it is easy to overlook feeding. In these cases, slow-release fertilisers added to the potting mixture before planting in spring are useful and effective.

Right: *Push slow-release feed tablets down into the potting mixture. They do not dissolve, so replace them every few months.*

Above: *If you prefer, you can still use liquid feed when watering automatically, but dilute and apply it to the pots, not via the capillary matting or watering system.*

Right: *Plants that are short of feed look pale. To replace missing nutrients quickly, spray plants with weak foliar feed. Liquid seaweed extract supplies trace elements.*

Above: Keep capillary matting damp using perforated tubing or irrigation fitted with small sprinkler nozzles connected to a hosepipe. Run the hose for five minutes or so every morning or evening, to water large numbers of pots.

1 A regulator reduces the pressure of your mains water supply to a constant low level. Screw this directly onto a threaded tap or attach an adaptor that plugs into a hose connector.

2 Attach a length of tubing to the outflow pipe of the pressure regulator. In this system, the supply tubing is 13mm(0.5in) in diameter.

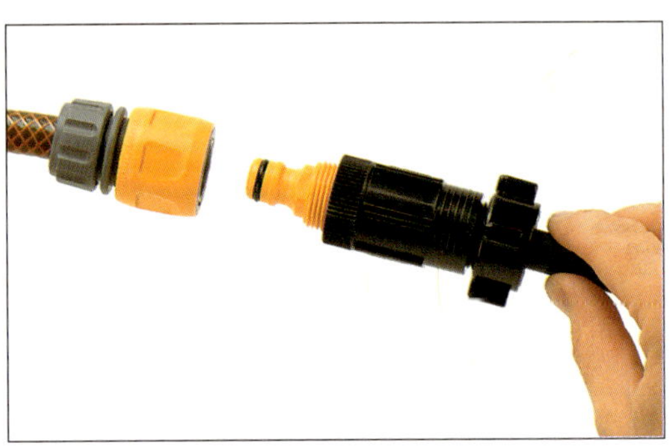

3 If you want to run your watering system from a standard hosepipe, first fit a hose end connector and plug in the pressure regulator. Do not turn on the water until you have assembled the entire system.

MICRO-IRRIGATION

The most efficient way to take care of watering if you cannot do the job daily by hand is to install an irrigation system. For plants in containers, the best strategy is to give each pot an individual watering nozzle connected by small-bore tubing to a normal hosepipe. This is much more efficient than using a sprinkler. To water, simply connect the hose to an outdoor tap and switch on. It is a good idea to have one nozzle hanging in an empty glass jar to monitor the amount of water being applied, so you know when to switch off. Although this is much quicker than watering each plant individually, you still have to turn the tap on and off – and it is easy to forget, resulting in a flooded garden. You can add a timing device, or 'water computer', that fits onto the tap and set it to turn the water on for a period each day and then switch it off. This is ideal when you are away for the weekend, or if you work long hours. The cost of a timing device is not great compared to the cost of the rest of the installation, and the extra expense is justified. You need not ask neighbours to take care of plants for you, nor is it obvious to potential intruders that you are away from home, because the system stays in place through the spring, summer and autumn. Since the pipes may deteriorate if frozen, especially with water still inside them, it is a good idea to remove irrigation systems in winter unless the pipework is intended for year-round use and is buried under the soil or a surface mulch. Check and flush out irrigation systems regularly, as the nozzles can clog up; you may not discover this until too late, when a plant dries up and dies.

4 You can control the flow of water to various parts of your system by fitting these taps. Simply cut the supply tube and push the ends over the flanges on the tap.

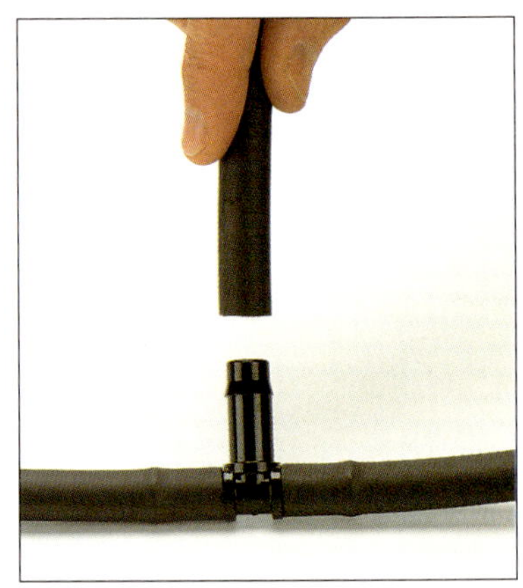

5 To create a 'branch' line in the supply tubing system, fit a T-connector as shown here. Use elbow connectors to turn corners and straight ones to make joins.

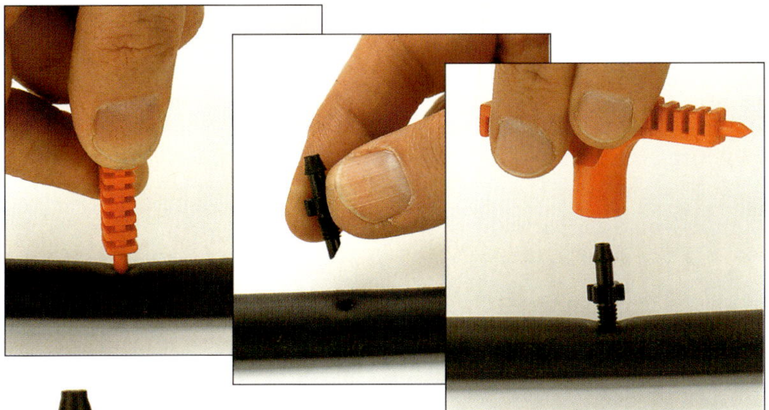

6 To connect lengths of smaller diameter tubing to the system, punch a hole in the supply tube with the plastic tool, insert a narrow tube adaptor and screw it in with the socket part of the tool. Fully screwed in, the adaptor creates a watertight seal with the supply tube.

7 Push the end of the narrow tube – in this system 4mm(0.17in) in diameter – onto the adaptor in the supply tube. For the system to work efficiently, make sure these 'micro' tubes are no longer than 1m(39in).

8 Once you have set up your system, flush water through it and then close off the supply tubes with these end sleeves. They are simple to fit and remove.

9 Push the supply tube through, fold it over and pull it back to trap the folded end in the sleeve to make a watertight seal. To remove the tube, simply reverse the steps.

10 You can plug various nozzles into the micro tube. The flow from this dripper can be adjusted by rotating the cap. Used inverted, it is ideal for hanging baskets.

Water computers

The simplest models switch off the water after a preset time. Others can be set to turn water on and off at different times and for various lengths of time. If you plan to use one to take care of watering when you are away from home, set it up well in advance to ensure that it is set up and operational. If you rely on it for day-to-day watering, check periodically for blocked nozzles or damaged pipes in the system.

11 This fixed-output dripper is a good way of providing slow and steady irrigation for containers and growing bags. Support the micro tube on a plastic stake to allow the drips to fall where they are needed.

Deadheading

Deadheading is specially worthwhile for plants with a potentially long flowering season, as it stops them setting seed and instead encourages a new crop of flower buds to form. Deadheading also helps reduce fungal disease by removing dead plant tissues that spores can live on.

1 Check greenhouse plants regularly and remove dead flower heads as soon as the blooms go over. Pick off the flowers complete with their stems.

2 Remove dead leaves, another potential source of fungal disease. They often occur naturally at the base of plants and do not indicate that there is a problem.

ROUTINE TASKS

The secret of growing plants successfully is to keep up with routine chores. They need not take long; some people enjoy doing 'little and often', while others prefer to allocate a particular time for their tasks. Feeding and watering, pest and disease control and monitoring ventilation are vital all year round, although the need for each varies with the rate of plant growth. As a general rule, water in the morning during dull weather and in winter to avoid leaving the air humid at night, which encourages fungal disease. During hot spells, water in the evening so that plants can take up water slowly overnight before strong sun causes it to evaporate. Other jobs are more seasonal. At the start of the growing season, divide any plants that need it, and repot or topdress others. This is also the time to pot up rooted cuttings or pot on young plants propagated at the end of the previous year. Soon after, they will need 'stopping' to encourage bushy growth. Do this by pinching out the growing tip of the young plants with the nails of your thumb and forefinger. As the season progresses, tie climbing plants to supports or train them around climbing frames. At the end of the season, clean the greenhouse thoroughly. Take all the plants outside, except those that are too big or heavy to move. Clean the glass inside and out, and wash off any remaining painted-on shading to allow as much winter light as possible to reach your plants. Take up capillary matting from the staging, wash and dry it and store it in clean bags in a shed for the following year. Throw away any that is no longer usable. Wash down the staging and flooring; use a fumigant smoke, candle or wash to kill pest and disease organisms if it is practical to do so. When the fumes have cleared, replace the plants.

Left: A potting bench gets most use in spring; it should be at a convenient height for working, with everything you need, such as pots and potting mixes, close at hand. Later in the season the bench can be used as normal staging.

Repotting potbound plants

1 A plant needs repotting when its roots form a tight ball inside the old pot. Roots may grow out through the drainage holes in the bottom. Knock it out of the old pot.

2 Sit the plant in the centre of a pot one size bigger, with the top of the rootball about 1.25cm (0.5in) below the rim. Fill in the gap with fresh potting mixture.

3 Gently firm down the new mix; this makes sure that it goes right down to the bottom of the new pot without leaving air pockets that roots cannot occupy, and which will cause the mix to dry out quickly.

Pinching out

Right: Nipping out the very tips of shoots encourages bushiness. Usually, newly potted cuttings of plants such as fuchsias and pelargoniums need stopping a second time, when the sideshoots resulting from the first 'stop' are about 5cm(2in) long.

Good hygiene

At the end of the season, give the greenhouse a thorough clean, so that there is nothing left to cause pest or disease problems during the winter. It is also usually the most convenient time to do the work. Start by emptying the structure completely.

1 Brush out the channels in glazing bars, where red spider mite and other pests often hibernate, ready to start an epidemic as soon as the weather warms up in spring.

2 Wash the glass inside and out. Use a sponge and warm water with a few drops of liquid detergent to remove paint-on greenhouse shading and any algae and dirt. In winter, light levels are low and plants need all they can get.

3 Remove capillary matting and wash and rinse it in garden disinfectant. In winter, plants need to dry out between waterings, so occasional hand-watering is best.

4 Wash watering trays, rinse with clean water and garden disinfectant, and leave to dry. Clean up plants and wipe pots before returning them to the tray.

A HEATED PROPAGATOR

The main advantage of a heated propagator is that it provides the right conditions for germinating seeds and striking cuttings – the two most widely used methods of plant propagation. It also avoids the need to create these conditions in a whole greenhouse or even indoors, if you have no greenhouse. And if only the propagator needs to be heated, you can save on energy costs. You can buy a propagator or make your own. If you build one yourself, make it a suitable shape and size to fit a certain number of standard seed trays. In the simple propagator featured here, heating is provided by an undersoil electrical cable that heats the planting medium, as well as the air in the propagator. Once you are able to create a favourable environment, it follows that plants can be propagated outside the normal season. Seeds can be sown in early spring or even late winter, so that plants are ready for planting out earlier. Once the propagator is set up and running, it can be used either for housing pots of seeds or cuttings, or cuttings can be rooted straight into the potting mixture in the propagator. A propagator is not without its responsibilities. The first one is temperature control. A thermostat will operate the heating cable, but a very high temperature can build up in a propagator that is standing in sunshine with the top on. Shade the propagator from strong sun by laying fine 'fleece' over the top, or rotate the ventilators in the lid of a commercial propagator to open them. Watering is another priority. It is vital that you water a propagator frequently during sunny weather, be it in summer or winter.

1 Having decided the size of the propagator, cut the wood accordingly. A base cut from a sheet of coarse-grade particle-board makes a strong foundation.

2 Using a mitre saw, cut the sides of the propagator absolutely square so that they butt together accurately. The result will be a firmer and neater job.

3 Once all the pieces have been cut accurately, drill pilot holes and screw the four sides together. Brass or alloy screws are best as they resist rust and corrosion.

4 With the sides assembled, screw the base into place using rustproof screws. For added strength, apply a wood glue in the joints. Plane off any overlaps.

5 Paint the inside and outside surfaces with a 'plant-friendly' wood preservative, such as this green horticultural stain. Without protection the wood will soon rot.

6 When the preservative is dry, add a 2.5cm(1in)-deep layer of sand. The heating cable will lie on this. Level and firm down the sand so that the cable will lie flat.

7 Snake the soil-warming cable back and forth across the sand base. You can buy purpose-made cable complete with a thermostat and fitting instructions.

8 Drill a hole in the side of the propagator and push through the thermostat rod. Suspend the rod above the cables, so that it crosses but does not touch them.

9 Be sure to install the rod correctly, otherwise you may get false readings that will either switch off the current too soon or leave it on too long. Cover the rod with sand.

Leaf cuttings are fairly long-lived, but in a propagator they root more quickly.

You can root strawberry plantlets while they are quite small.

You can use the space between the pots and trays to root cuttings in the potting mix in the base of the propagator.These are lavender cuttings.

Small seeds need warmth and moisture to germinate quickly and grow into strong seedlings.

10 Place the propagator close to a power point and in a position with good light but out of strong sunlight.

Temperature control

The thermostat rod detects the temperature of the sand and switches the electricity off or on to maintain a particular heat level. To adjust the temperature, turn the knob on the control box to the right setting. A reading of 15-16°C (about 60°F) will be fine for most purposes.

Making the lid

1 Make the lid from a sheet of twin-walled, translucent plastic. Start by cutting out a square at each corner of the sheet. It is light and easy to work with.

2 Score along the edges and fold up the sides to make a box shape about 20cm(8in) deep, ideal for normal use.

3 Join the edges with 'green-house tape', which is thicker, wider and stickier than regular tape and contains a UV inhibitor.

4 Make the lid slightly smaller than the base. Translucent plastic provides some shade; the double skin acts as an insulator to retain warmth.

SOWING SEEDS

Propagating your own plants is a particularly satisfying achievement, and a greenhouse can act as a plant nursery, producing young plants for use all round the garden and in useful quantities that can save you money. Without any special facilities, the greenhouse can be used for propagating plants that simply need the constant care and controlled conditions of a greenhouse environment. These include summer cuttings (of fuchsias, pelargoniums and other half-hardy perennials, and many easily rooted outdoor shrubs) and seeds that are sown in summer, such as hardy perennials and biennials, including winter and spring bedding plants. Seeds of houseplants and conservatory plants can also be sown in summer to take advantage of the natural heat in the greenhouse. However, bedding plants, tomato and cucumber plants, etc., need an early start, coupled with steady high temperatures. To raise these successfully, you will need a thermostatically controlled, electrically heated propagator. Begin in early spring after cleaning the propagator thoroughly. Put fresh, damp silver sand in the base and switch on the heat several days before sowing to bring the propagator up to temperature. Without a propagator, the best plan would be to buy seedlings of these plants (available in garden centres as 'plugs' ready for pricking out) a month or so after the normal sowing time, in mid- to late spring, and grow them in a moderately heated greenhouse.

Sowing tiny seeds

1 Wash out a small seed tray and fill it loosely with seed mix from a fresh bag. Level and firm it down lightly with a presser that fits the seed tray. These are coleus seeds.

2 Tip the seeds into your hand and, taking a pinch at a time, sprinkle them thinly all over the surface of the mix. To make it easier, you could mix the seed with dry sand before sowing.

3 Cover the seed with a thin layer of vermiculite (no more than one granule deep). It prevents drying out, but because of its colour, it will not prevent light reaching the seeds.

4 By sowing thinly, you can leave the seedlings to develop into small plantlets and then pot them up. This cuts out the pricking out stage, when very tiny seedlings are difficult to handle.

5 Pot up the strongest and healthiest seedlings, with a mixture of leaf colours and patterns. Pot into 9cm(3.5in) pots filled with good-quality potting mix.

Sowing medium-sized seeds

1 Sow larger seeds directly onto the surface of the flattened mix. Sprinkle them from a reasonable height for an even spread.

2 Gently release seed mix from your hand through a sieve. This distributes the mixture evenly, ensuring uniform germination.

3 Firm the mix in gently to ensure that the seeds and mix are in close contact and the mix does not dry out too fast.

4 After sowing, lower the pot into a container of water and remove it when the surface darkens, showing it is damp.

5 Put the pot into a propagator. This one, though unheated, will maintain higher humidity and a more even temperature than a room or greenhouse, so the seeds will germinate quickly and evenly.

Planting out plugs

Plug plants are sold growing singly in tiny cell pots or you can buy small seedlings ready for pricking out. Buying plug plants saves you the trouble and expense of sowing and raising your own seeds.

1 Some plants are sold in their own little propagator, with pink water-retaining gel that keeps the seedlings moist. Pot them up soon after you bring them home and harden them off gradually.

2 Push out each seedling from below with a dibber. If they have been kept well watered, the rootballs will come out easily and not fall apart when you handle them.

3 Fill up 7.5cm(3in) plastic pots with potting mix and make a hole about the same size as the plug. Drop in the plug and firm it very gently with your fingertips.

TAKING CUTTINGS

By propagating new plants from cuttings you can duplicate plants that you or your friends already have. It is a valuable way of keeping tender garden plants during the winter, as rooted cuttings take up far less space in a heated greenhouse than large mature plants. Cuttings also provide a good way of growing your own replacements for plants that naturally become leggy or woody and unproductive as they get older. Pelargoniums, fuchsias and many other greenhouse perennials benefit from being replaced with new young plants every year or two for this reason and any 'spares' make welcome gifts to take to gardening friends who, with luck, will reciprocate. Growing new plants from cuttings gives you a new plant in flower much faster than growing the same plant from seed. And it is the only way to propagate named varieties that you want to keep true to type. Saving seeds of these only results in mongrels that do not usually have the same characteristics as the parents. The most commonly used type of cuttings are stem cuttings, taken from the tip of a young shoot. These can be taken in spring as soon as new growth reaches 10cm(4in) long, and this method is often used to propagate dahlias or tuberous begonias forced into growth early to produce shoots for cuttings. But stem cuttings are often taken in late summer, especially when the aim is to overwinter tender perennials economically. However, some kinds of plants do not have much – or indeed any – stem; in these cases, take leaf cuttings. This is the way to propagate begonia rex, African violets and streptocarpus.

Taking soft cuttings

Take cuttings in late summer when the shoots are still soft but beginning to ripen from the base.

1 Take a cutting 7.5-10cm(3-4in) long from just below a leaf joint. Shorter cuttings root quicker, but also die quicker. Longer ones need more time to root.

2 Once you have removed a shoot, it is important to cut away certain parts to make it into a cutting, otherwise rooting will be delayed.

3 Aim to put five or six suitably sized cuttings into a 13cm(5in) half-pot, with one in the centre. Firm the cuttings in gently.

4 Water in the cuttings and keep them in a cool, shady place. Pelargoniums may not need any more water for several weeks if kept in shaded conditions.

5 The lower level of staging in a greenhouse is an ideal place to put the cuttings. If you put them on top, cover them with a single thickness of newspaper for shade until they root.

Leaf cuttings

1 To take a leaf cutting, remove the whole leaf from the stem without any bud. Snap off fully mature but still completely green, healthy leaves as cuttings.

2 Retain as many leaves as you will need. Remove the base cleanly with a sharp knife. This eliminates any torn and dead tissue that might become infected.

3 Push each leaf about 2.5cm (1in) into the mix, so that the base stays dark and moist and the leaf remains upright. Firm the mix down gently with your fingers.

4 Water the tray well with a fine-rosed watering can. Stand it in a sunny spot to encourage quick rooting. Make sure that the potting mix does not dry out at any time.

5 Stand the tray in a sunny spot. The leaf produces roots and after a few weeks, a small plant, or cluster of plants, develops amongst the roots and it is from these that the new plant develops.

Carnation pipings

Carnation cuttings, known as pipings, are pulled from the end of a shoot so that a small section of stem is removed from inside the leaf joint. Take the piping from a shoot with no flower bud at the top, so that the cutting can root without having to compete with the flower for sap.

1 Take the piping from an old section of plant. One good way is to pull it off and trim back the top if the break is in the wrong place.

2 Root the pipings in cells about 5cm(2in) deep. Carnations and pinks root in about the same time. Being in cells they will separate easily.

3 Pot the cuttings up singly or plant them out in the garden depending on the season and whether they are hardy pinks or border carnations.

4 Pot the rooted cuttings into 7.5cm(3in) pots, using a peat, or peat-substitute potting or multipurpose mix. Potting mix is best because it is made specifically for potting up.

Right: Create a tiered display in a greenhouse with a narrow shelf above the staging; use this to grow naturally cascading plants, such as trailing tuberous begonias.

Below: Use the main staging for bushy, upright plants or climbers trained round wire hoops, with trailing plants along the front. This saves space and looks decorative.

DISPLAYING PLANTS

Display techniques are a good way of making the most of under-cover growing space. The same basic collection of plants can be rearranged regularly to make different displays throughout the season. A collection of many small pots is also easier to see when raised up on staging. Choose shade-loving plants for the lower tier of two-storey staging. In a conservatory, choose staging that gets progressively narrower towards the top; it acts as a natural 'theatre' and ensures that all the plants receive enough light. Alternatively, use flat staging and raise up individual plants by standing them on upturned flowerpots. (Remember that these plants will dry out faster then those on the staging.) Plant very small or 'theme' plants, such as cacti, in bowls with driftwood or pebbles. Large striking plants are best potted up to make specimens; stand them in a decorative pot against a suitable background. Some types are suitable for training as standards, which take up less room and often look more ornamental. A large collection of conservatory shrubs look good when grouped together and planted in a soil border as a feature. Display climbers by training them over topiary frames, round large hoops, up obelisks or moss-filled wire netting pillars, or over a wall on trellis.

Creating height in a display

1 Upright plants with naturally dangling flowers, such as this fuchsia, lend themselves to being 'lifted', so that they stand out amongst shorter plants.

2 To disguise the upturned pot, stand another plant in front of it. Use tiered staging, shelving and hanging baskets to create a varied display on several levels.

Right: Two-tier staging with capillary matting on the top tier. Plants that need shade and extra humidity are growing on expanded clay granules below. Water plants once a day, using a slow-running hosepipe to damp down the contents of the tray

Below: Seasonal flowering plants, such as cineraria and calceolaria, are available in autumn. They are ideal for a cool greenhouse and being annuals, can be thrown away after flowering.

Training passion flower around a hoop

1 To train climbers such as this passion flower around a framework, unravel tangled stems and insert the frame into the pot.

2 Secure stems to the frame with plant ties or wire clips. Clips reopen easily, so you can add extra stems as you work.

3 As the plant grows, fix new stems into place until the framework is thickly covered with foliage. As the pot fills up with roots (around midsummer) the plant will begin to flower. This variety produces fabulous pink blooms.

POPULAR PLANTS

Popular greenhouse plants that are colourful, easily grown and forgiving of mistakes, form the basis of most starter collections. They include well-known species, such as tuberous begonias, gloxinia, coleus, fuchsias and the various types of pelargoniums. Plants are inexpensive and widely available at nurseries and garden centres. However they are easily raised from seed, cuttings or corms at home. They are the perfect way to build up experience at both running a greenhouse and cultivating and propagating a broad range of plants. With a good basic plant collection growing happily, it is then safe to broaden your horizons and begin adding choicer and more difficult plants. In this way, you can gradually vary your plant displays and experience an occasional challenge without risking too many potentially expensive failures. Since most beginners start with an unheated greenhouse, popular plants are a wise choice, as they do not cost much to replace if they cannot be kept during the winter. However, while the collection is small, it is usually possible to find room for a few pots of fuchsia and pelargonium cuttings on a windowsill indoors until spring. Tuberous begonia, gloxinia and other greenhouse bulbs are also easily kept over winter as they are completely dormant then, and can be stored as dry corms in a paper bag in a cool room indoors. Coleus and similar plants raised annually from seed can be bought as small plug plants in late spring and put straight into the greenhouse.

Right: Gloxinia *(Sinningia speciosa)* foliage forms a flattish rosette over the pot, with a cluster of large colourful bell flowers in the centre; plants keep flowering till late summer. Remove dead heads.

Below: Coleus enjoy high temperatures with high humidity and dappled shade. The secret of success is to nip out the tiny lavender flower buds that appear in the tips of the shoots in summer, to keep the leaves large and colourful.

Above: For spectacular results with large-flowered tuberous begonias, remove the pair of small single female flowers on either side of the large double male flower.

Left: *Pelargonium graveolens* is grown for its delicately cut, citrus-scented foliage. The scented-leaved pelargoniums need similar conditions to the zonal and regal pelargoniums but, unlike them, they have small uninteresting flowers.

Right: Regal and zonal pelargoniums grow to about the same size, in contrast to the miniature pelargoniums (left). The miniatures are becoming very collectable plants.

Below: African violets are compact plants with a symmetrical shape, and available in a range of types, colours and flower shapes. Grow them in a shady spot on a dish of damp pebbles.

Growing fuchsias

Fuchsias are easy to grow and flower continuously throughout summer and early autumn. Different varieties have either bushy, upright or trailing habits, which make them suitable for pots, as standards and for hanging baskets. The ones with particularly large flowers, such as 'Texas Longhorn' and the 'Californian Dreamer' series, are much better grown permanently under glass as their large blooms soon deteriorate when exposed to the weather. The 'Californian Dreamer' series also need warm conditions to flower well. Species fuchsias look quite different from the hybrids but require the same cultivation. Give them much larger pots and more feed and water. Large species need some support.

Above: *'Mary' is a spectacular triphylla hybrid whose long tubular scarlet flowers contrast nicely with the long-oval, dark purplish-tinged foliage. It is quite an old variety.*

Right: *'Space Shuttle', a hybrid of a species fuchsia, has unusual flowers in striking colours. Pinch out cuttings several times to encourage a bushy habit.*

Right: *Fuchsia arborescens is one of the species fuchsias, with large clusters of delicately scented flowers that resemble lilac. It can make a good bushy pot plant if pinched back as a cutting. Like all species fuchsias, plants tend to grow large, woody and straggly in time.*

EXOTIC PLANTS

Many people use their greenhouse to grow a group of plants they are specially interested in, so rather than planning for colour and year-round interest, they concentrate on the welfare of their plants – perhaps orchids, bromeliads or cacti. Some enthusiasts make no effort to display a plant collection, relying on grouping plants according to their cultural needs. But in a small garden, the greenhouse forms part of the outdoor floral display so it has to look good. A specialist collection needs slightly different display techniques, as a greenhouse full of cacti or orchids lacks the very varied plant shapes and forms of a mixture of popular plants. This is where props come in. Pot-grown cacti can be plunged to their rims in deep, gravel-filled trays decorated with quartz chunks and smooth pebbles, instead of shown on conventional flat-topped staging. Not only does this add atmosphere, it also makes the plants easier to grow, as their roots remain cool in an otherwise hot sunny greenhouse. Orchids suit gnarled tropical driftwood and dangling spanish moss. The same growing conditions and props also suit bromeliads, so you could mix them together for extra variety. And because all the plants in a specialist collection tend to be much the same in character, use varied shapes when creating eye-catching plant associations; for example, contrast a group of tall columnar cacti with low, domed or hairy kinds. Landscape orchids with houseplants such as selaginella and fittonia that like the same conditions. And space plants out well, so that you can appreciate each one; do not hide them by packing them in too closely.

Right: Train *Mandevilla rosea* up a wire in the greenhouse. Provide warm humid conditions and a rich potting mix for all mandevillas.

Left: When displaying orchids, provide staging with a moisture stage underneath. This purpose-built slatted staging allows the moisture from a water-soaked gravel bed to rise around the plants.

Above: A rack intended for kitchen utensils makes a good 'chandelier' for displaying naturally lax plants, especially where space is short. Plants are easy to lift down to water if you cannot reach.

Left: Passionflowers have a constant succession of large spectacular flowers throughout the summer. This striking *Passiflora* x *caeruleoracemosa* is suitable for an unheated house.

Planting up cacti

1 Almost fill a shallow terracotta bowl with cactus mix and plant a variety of cactus shapes. Add pieces of driftwood and tuck more plants in between. Folded paper is useful for planting species with hooked spines.

2 When the bowl is filled with plants, topdress the surface with fine gravel. The easiest and safest way to work the gravel between the plants is to pour it slowly and carefully from a fold of paper.

GREENHOUSE EDIBLES

A well-stocked greenhouse is like a walk-in larder filled with fresh seasonal fruit and healthy salad ingredients. Given good planning, you can have small quantities of different crops virtually all year round. An unheated greenhouse will supply you with fresh figs and greenhouse grapes in late summer, but do not plant them in the border and train them the traditional way, over the walls; this way, a single plant would occupy most of a small greenhouse on its own. Instead, grow them in pots, to keep them naturally compact, and train the fig as a bush or standard. Grow a grape vine on one main stem with horizontal side shoots trained out across the back wall of the greenhouse, or as a standard. You will get about six bunches of fruit per plant. In spring, plant early potatoes and courgettes in pots, allowing them to be moved outdoors after the last frost when you need the space for the next batch of summer crops once more. If you are not using all the space in the border for tomatoes, etc., in late spring, you could make early sowings of climbing French beans, baby beets, spinach to grow to maturity in the greenhouse, giving you fresh vegetables many weeks earlier than from plants grown outdoors. Although growing your own will probably not save you a great deal of money, the produce can be grown without chemicals and always tastes far better when fresh picked, as well as being very convenient if you live a long way from shops.

Strawberries in the greenhouse

Bring potted strawberry plants into the greenhouse in late winter, after they have experienced a cold spell outdoors. Put in very good light; feed and water sparingly until flower buds appear. Gradually increase watering and begin regular liquid feeding with half-strength tomato feed, as strawberries need plenty of potash. Hand-pollinate the flowers when they are fully open, using a fine artist's paintbrush. Feed and water generously while the fruit swells and ripens, and cover ventilators with netting to keep the crop safe from birds.

A standard grape vine

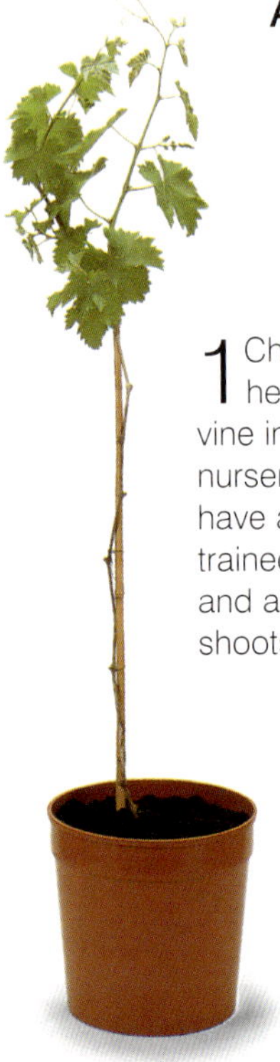

1 Choose a healthy young vine in a pot from a nursery. It should have a single stem trained up a cane and as few side shoots as possible.

2 Nip out the growing tip of the plant by gripping it firmly between thumb and forefinger. Water and feed regularly. Use a high-potash liquid tomato feed.

3 Remove the lower side shoots from the main stem, but leave the top four or five side shoots and nip out the growing tip of each. This will encourage branching.

Below: In temperate climates, you can use your greenhouse to grow dessert grapes that need warmth and a long growing season to mature and ripen properly.

Growing figs

1 Standard trained figs are very fruitful in the greenhouse. Start with a good straight upright plant with a single stem, as here.

2 Use your fingertips to nip out the very end of the growing tip. This encourages branching from the top of the plant.

3 After finger pruning, rub soil onto the cut to stop 'bleeding' that could weaken the plant. (Do not do major pruning now.)

4 Stop the side shoots when they reach about 7.5-10cm(3-4in). This encourages further branching and the development of a well-formed head.

5 The fruits appear as little green swellings. They will take several months to reach full size. Pick them when they change colour and feel soft.

Vegetables

Use the soil border to grow summer crops of tomatoes, cucumbers, peppers and aubergines, or perhaps cantaloupe melons or hot chilli peppers. They can be followed in autumn by winter salads such as lettuce, corn salad and overwintering spring onions.

Left: *Cucumbers in growing bags dry out quickly, so water them daily to keep the potting mixture evenly moist. (This avoids black patches at the blossom end of the fruit later on). Feed them often.*

Below: *Aubergines and peppers do well in pots of soil-based mixture. Support the bushy plants with short canes, and feed and water them as for tomatoes. Pick the fruit as soon as they are large enough to use.*

CITRUS FRUIT

Citrus are amongst the most rewarding fruit, as you get quite a good crop from relatively small trees, they look decorative all year round and the flowers are delightfully scented. One of the curious features of these plants is that they can have both flowers and fruit at all stages of development on the same plant at the same time. To be certain of getting a crop, choose named varieties that are grafted onto special rootstocks by the nursery. Do not use plants grown from seed, as they may not fruit for many years. You can find citrus plants trained as bushes or standard trees. The latter are best for a small greenhouse, because when they are inside for the winter you can stand other overwintering plants right under them.

In summer, it is best to stand citrus plants outside in the open air. Water them frequently and feed regularly with a high-nitrogen feed. Bring them inside in autumn, when the nights start to get cool, and reduce feeding and watering. In a free-draining mix kept barely moist, all kinds can be maintained at 5°C(40°F) since they are just 'ticking over'. Hardier types, such as Meyer's lemon, mandarin orange and kumquat, are not a problem if kept frost-free, but others are easier to maintain if kept warmer. Avoid widely fluctuating temperatures in both summer and winter, since this is a common cause of plants shedding leaves. They may also drop blossom and even immature fruit.

Above: *Citrus aurantium* 'Bouquet de Fleur' has very heavily scented double flowers. For this reason, the plant resembles gardenia, but is much easier to grow.

Left: *Citrus aurantium* 'Bouquet de Fleur' is one of the group of bitter oranges with very aromatic fruit, grown to produce essential oil of Neroli, used in eau de cologne.

Right: A standard kumquat makes a decorative evergreen tree for a conservatory heated enough to keep frost at bay. The fruit can be candied or used for decoration.

Refreshing the soil

1 For growing citrus plants, use a potting mix made up of about 20% perlite and 80% free-draining soil-based mix, with slow-release fertiliser added (see the maker's advice for the correct rate).

2 Citrus plants grown in containers do not need to be repotted every year, as they grow best when the pot is just about full of roots. Instead, topdress in spring; first, scrape away the top surface of the mix to a depth of about 2.5cm(1in).

3 If the exposed potting mix looks compacted, loosen up the next layer with the points of a dinner fork, taking care not to break any roots. Then replace with fresh potting mix to just below the rim of the pot. This will keep the plant growing well.

Above: Left unchecked, citrus plants make untidy bushy shrubs, but they can be pruned as short standards with a single trunk. The top can be trimmed to form a tidy dome shape.

Citrus plants from the sunroom

Other varieties

Left: Citrus limon *'Garey's Eureka', (formerly called 'Four Seasons' lemon) is a very popular variety for commercial crops because of its heavy crops and long season.*

Right: *The pink flower buds of 'Garey's Eureka' lemon are an attractive feature of the plant. They open into fragrant white flowers. Good for greenhouses.*

Right: *Tahiti lime (Citrus latifolia 'Tahiti'). A compact variety with large sweet seedless fruit; it is the best variety for home growing. A regular heavy crop of fruit that ripens reliably is assured.*

Above: *Variegated calamondin orange is a particularly good all-year-round plant, with good foliage, strongly perfumed flowers and a profusion of small fruit.*

Right: *The calamondin orange (Citrus mitis) produces many 2.5cm(1in)-diameter bitter oranges that remain on the plant for a long time, even when ripe.*

PESTS AND DISEASES

Under glass, good growing conditions not only favour plant growth, but also provide the ideal environment for pests and diseases. Insect pests such as greenfly can breed all year round in these protected surroundings, and if fungal diseases appear, their spores multiply rapidly in the warm humid air. Even regular spraying is not a guaranteed solution, since plants are often grown so close together that the leaves are not evenly covered, leaving some organisms untouched. In addition, some pests need specific pesticides to control them, and nowadays it is not unusual to find that some pests also develop resistance to certain products. The best way to keep pests and diseases at bay is to examine your plants regularly and to tackle problems as soon as they appear. Pick off mildewed leaves or blooms, and remove dead flower heads and damaged leaves before they can act as a source of infection. Use non-chemical controls, such as yellow sticky traps. A more long-term solution is to use biological control. Encourage wild beneficial insects, such as hoverflies and lacewings, into your greenhouse by not using chemicals and ensuring that ventilators are left open in suitable weather. Spiders, black beetles and centipedes are also beneficial.

Biological control for whitefly

Left: Whitefly resemble tiny white moths that congregate on the backs of young leaves and only fly if the plants are disturbed. The young whitefly are 'scales' stuck tight under leaves and these rarely respond well to chemical sprays, so biological control is the best way of dealing with them effectively.

Right: The biological control for whitefly is a tiny parasitic wasp, *Encarsia formosa*, which lays its eggs inside whitefly scales. Wasp larvae feed on the developing whitefly and the scales turn black. *Encarsia* is supplied as cards of whitefly scales containing wasp eggs. Hang these on the plants.

Aphids (greenfly)

Left: Large numbers of aphids will attack buds, flowers and young growths, turning them yellow and, in severe cases, causing die back and deformation.

Below: Black aphids, or blackfly, occur on buds and flowers, often on the underside of sepals and petals. Remove them by hand or use suitable insecticides.

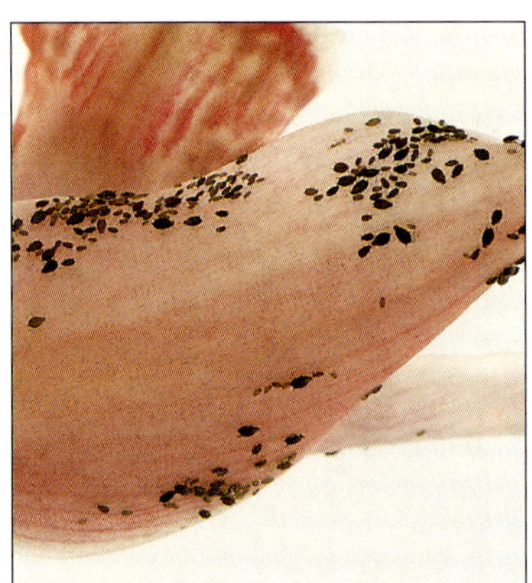

Left: The biological control for aphids is aphidoletes, a gall midge that lays its eggs near aphids. The small orange larvae that emerge feed on the aphids. Midge pupae are delivered in small tubs. Empty the contents onto damp paper covered by pots close to affected plants.

Right: Aphids parasitised by aphidoletes turn into brown 'shells'. The mummified bodies hatch out into the next generation of gall midges to keep up the good work.

Red spider mite

Left: With a lens you can see the small red spider mites on the underside of a leaf. They pierce leaves and suck out the cell contents, causing discoloration.

Right: The biological control for red spider mite is an even tinier predatory mite called *Phytoseiulus persimilis*. Open and hang the pots on the affected plants so emerging mites are close to their 'food'.

Scale insects

Right: Scale insects are like tiny limpets that cling to the leaves of many kinds of greenhouse and conservatory plants. Their hard covering makes them difficult to control.

Left: Control scale insects by using systemic insecticides, but the insects remain attached to the plant even after they are dead. Remove them individually with cotton buds as shown here.

Mealy bug

Right: Mealy bugs – small, grey, crawling insects covered with a white mealy powder and waxy threads – weaken plants by sucking sap. They can occur on all parts of the plant, but usually where flower stems join the main stem. Treat plants with systemic insecticide and remove dead insects after a few days with a cotton bud.

Traps and sprays

Sticky traps are a good method of non-chemical control for flying insects early in the year, but by midsummer they will also trap the beneficial insects that appear then, so take them down.

***Above:** Hang sticky traps above plants to catch flying pests. They are attracted by the colour of the yellow traps and then held fast. Use them just above the tops of the plants. Disturb the foliage to make whitefly swarm up.*

***Below:** Spray with fungicide to control fungal diseases under glass. Do not apply chemical sprays if you use biological control insects. Do not spray in bright sun or onto open flowers.*

Treating mildew

1 One of the most widely seen diseases under glass in late summer and autumn is powdery mildew, a mould that affects cucumbers, as here, and melons. It can also attack pot plants and tomatoes. Spray with a systemic fungicide.

2 Some products are sold ready-mixed in trigger operated containers that form their own spray gun. These are particularly convenient as no mixing is needed and you do not have to buy a separate sprayer.

Herbs, vegetables and flowers put on a stunning show.

INDEX

Page numbers in **bold** indicate major text references and main features. Page numbers in *italics* indicate annotations and captions to photographs. Other text entries are shown in normal type.

A

B

D

A note about plant names

The joy of gardening is burdened with a bewildering variety of plant names. Common names are often only relevant in a particular area of the world, whereas scientific (or Latin) names should form a universal language that successfully straddles the worlds of botany and horticulture. Unfortunately, plants commonly available in the gardening hobby are occasionally renamed by well-meaning botanists. Invariably, a plant you have come to know under one name seems to have acquired a new one that is nothing like the original. In this book, we have tried to reflect the latest scientific plant names, but each book can only present a snapshot of the current situation. If you are new to gardening, you may find this confusing, but you will soon learn to recognise the plants and enjoy them for the colour and beauty they bring to your garden – whatever they are currently called.

Picture credits

The majority of the photographs featured in this book have been taken by Neil Sutherland and are © Quadrillion Publishing Ltd. The publishers wish to thank the following photographers for providing additional photographs, credited here by page number and position on the page, i.e. (B)Bottom, (T)Top, (C)Centre, (BL)Bottom left, etc.

Peter Blackburne-Maze: 295(TL), 299(TC,TR), 303(TR,CR)
Ruth Chivers: 93(BR), 149(TR, Designer Delaney Cochran & Castillo, Leichtag Family Healing Garden, California)
Eric Crichton: 21(BL), 22(B), 29(BR), 36, 39(TL,TR), 70(TR), 75(TR), 79(BR), 81(TR,BR), 98(TR), 100(TR,CR,B), 101(TC,BL), 104(T,CR), 105(TL), 111(TL), 114(TR,BL,BR), 115(TL), 123(TL), 135(TL), 137(TR), 144(TL), 148(BR), 156, 187(TR,BR), 198(TR), 199(CR), 200(TR), 206(BL), 209(TR), 216, 218(BR), 219(B), 223(CR,BR), 236, 259(TR), 265(CL), 295(TR), 301(CR)
The Garden Picture Library: 22(TR, Bob Challinor), 30(Marianne Majerus), 333(TL,Mayer/Le Scanff)
John Glover: Half-title page, 21(TL), 26(T,B), 79(TR), 85(BR), 87(BR), 88(BL), 89(BL), 95(BR), 105(BL), 107(BL), 110(T,BL), 113(BR), 135(BL), 137(TL), 143(BR), 153(TR), 158(T,BR), 159(BL), 169(BC), 185(BL), 198(BR), 214(BR), 238(B), 239(BL,BR), 241(BR), 264(TR,TL), 294(BL), 336
Paul Goff: 38(BL)
Sunniva Harte: Copyright page, 21(TR, Designer Paul Thompson), 38(BR, Designer Paul Thompson), 71(TL), 205(BR), 213(BCL)
International Flower Bulb Centre: 189(BR)
Andrew Lawson: 28(B), 243(TL)
S & O Mathews: 12, 34, 68, 70(BL), 75(BL), 78, 80(B), 82(TR), 88(TR), 94(BL), 97, 104(BL), 111(CL), 113(BL,TR), 115(BL), 122(T,BL), 147(BL), 159(TL,CL), 198(BL), 199(TC), 208(TR,BR), 209(TL,BL), 215(CR), 238(CR), 255(CR), 262, 308, 325(BL)
Clive Nichols Garden Pictures: 28(T, Designer Deborah Lewis), 29(TR, Designer Keeyla Meadows), 32(Lambeth Horticultural Society), 38(TR, Beth Chatto Garden, Essex), 74(B, Netherfield Herb Garden), 79(TL, Designer Myles Challis), 99(BL, Designers Louise Hampden/Clive & Jane Nichols), 103(BL, Designer Jane Fearnley-Whitingstall), 122(BR, Designer Myles Challis), 132(Designer Jill Billington), 134(TR,B, Designers Clive & Jane Nichols), 141(BR, Designer Jean Bishop), 155(TL, Designer Fiona Lawrenson), 193(TL, Designer Jane Nichols), 203(TL, Vale End, Surrey), 207(TR, Mrs Glaisher, Kent), 218(T, Designer Deborah Lewis), 219(T, Designers Andrew & Karla Newell), 239(TL, Monk Sherbourne College), 280(TL, Designer Jane Nichols)
Geoffrey Rogers: Intro page, 70(BR), 85(TR), 87(TR), 89(TR), 90(B), 93(TL), 109(CLT,C), 243(BC), 295(BR). © Quadrillion: 52, 55, 56, 57, 268(TL,C,BC,BR), 269(TL,TC,TR,CL,BC,R)

Acknowledgments

The publishers would like to thank the following people and organisations for their help during the preparation of this book:

Abbott's Packaging Ltd. Horsham, West Sussex; Agralan Ltd., Swindon, Wiltshire; M. H. Berlyn Co. Ltd.; Blackmoor Nurseries, Liss, Hampshire; Blooms of Bressingham, Diss, Norfolk; Brogdale Horticultural Trust, Faversham, Kent; Bridgemere Garden World, Nantwich, Cheshire; Bulldog Tools supplied by Polyhedron Holdings, Sheffield, Yorkshire; The Citrus Centre, Pulborough, West Sussex; The English Garden Collection, Abingdon, Oxfordshire; Forest Fencing Ltd., Stanford Bridge, Worcestershire; Garboldisham Garden Centre, Norfolk; Hadlow College, Kent; Hall Place Gardens and Nursery, Bexley, Kent; The Hillier Plant Centre, Braishfield, Hampshire; Holly Gate Cactus Nursery, Ashington, West Sussex; Hozelock Ltd., Haddenham, Buckinghamshire; Iden Croft Herbs, Stapelehurst, Kent; W. E. Th. Ingwersen Ltd., East Grinstead, West Sussex; Merriments, Hurst Green, East Sussex; Millbrook Garden Centre, Gravesend, Kent; Murrells Nursery, Pulborough, West Sussex; Natures Natural Products Ltd., Long Melford, Suffolk; Old Barn Nurseries, Horsham, West Sussex; Polhill Garden Centre, Sevenoaks, Kent; Pots and Pithoi, Turners Hill, West Sussex; Scotsdales Garden Centre, Cambridge; Shore Hall Garden Designs, Braintree, Essex; Somerset Levels Basket and Craft Centre Ltd., Burrowbridge, Somerset; Town and Country Turf, Kingsfold, Horsham, West Sussex; B. & A. Whelan, Sheerness, Kent; Heather Gorringe at Wiggly Wigglers, Lower Blakemere, Hertfordshire.

The publishers would like to thank the following gardeners for allowing their gardens to be featured in this book:

S. Atterton, Sir Robert and Lady Clark, Chris and Pat Cornwell, Jean and Steve Jackman, Mr and Mrs Jackson, Bernadette and John Thompson.